Thanksgiving & Turkey Collectibles

Then and Now

John Wesley Thomas
and Sandra Lynn Thomas

4880 Lower Valley Road, Atglen, PA 19310 USA

Wild Turkey.
Male.

Published by Schiffer Publishing Ltd.
4880 Lower Valley Road
Atglen, PA 19310
Phone: (610) 593-1777; Fax: (610) 593-2002
E-mail: Info@schifferbooks.com

For the largest selection of fine reference books on this and related
subjects, please visit our web site at **www.schifferbooks.com**
We are always looking for people to write books on new and related
subjects. If you have an idea for a book please contact us at the above
address.

This book may be purchased from the publisher.
Include $3.95 for shipping.
Please try your bookstore first.
You may write for a free catalog.

In Europe, Schiffer books are distributed by
Bushwood Books
6 Marksbury Ave.
Kew Gardens
Surrey TW9 4JF England
Phone: 44 (0) 20 8392-8585; Fax: 44 (0) 20 8392-9876
E-mail: info@bushwoodbooks.co.uk
Free postage in the U.K., Europe; air mail at cost.

CONTENTS

INTRODUCTION

Thanksgiving, the most celebrated of all truly American holidays, is represented by a plethora of outstanding antiques and collectibles made from a wide array of materials. Ask any number of persons what Thanksgiving means to them and you will get many different answers depending upon their upbringing, circumstances, and even geographic location. If one were to draw a commonality among the responses, the defining attribute would be a gathering of an extended family and friends sharing a magnificently prepared meal reflective of regional tastes. For over 380 years since the First Thanksgiving, we, as Americans, have had a noble tradition of expressing thanks to a supreme being for all the bountiful gifts that have been bestowed upon us.

The authors of this book also have excellent reasons to value the spirit of Thanksgiving. For John, three Thanksgivings were spent away from home while on military duty as an Army Air Defense Artillery Officer in Germany during the "cold war." In 1963, his and most other Americans' Thanksgiving was indelibly marred by the tragic assassination of President John F. Kennedy. His next two Thanksgivings were, thankfully, uneventful. John's first Thanksgiving back in the States was among his best. A long term split in his family was rectified with his returning from the service as family members reconvened in the spirit of Thanksgiving togetherness. For Sandy, Thanksgiving is an important time to gather with family members now ranging in age from 87 years to 18 months and living apart in California and Texas, but together in spirit, and to give thanks as her family continues to grow in number.

Our current Thanksgiving is traditionally spent with family and friends, discussing the relative merits of different types of stuffing, participating in Turkey Trot road races, and, yes, watching the Macy's Parade as well as professional football games on television.

The collectibles that appear in the thirteen chapters awaiting you represent what we believe to be the largest collection in the United States devoted to Thanksgiving. It was formed over a ten-year period with significant assistance from on-line auction sites such as eBay. In the early 1990s, we had a rather sizable accumulation of Halloween memorabilia, but so did others, and those awesome collections have been definitively highlighted in at least five books. Sometimes inspiration comes from unsuspecting places. In our case, two articles that appeared in *Country Living*, the November 1994 issue, really gave impetus to defining our Thanksgiving collectibles interest. One article, "Talking Turkey in Maryland," portrayed a wide range of "decorative turkey collectibles capturing a uniquely American country spirit." The second article, "A Gobble, Gobble Here" was devoted to one person's collection of thirty-five German-made papier mâché candy containers in all sizes. Based on these and other articles, we were "hooked," so to speak, and our collection grew exponentially over the succeeding years.

As a source, an on-line auction site such as eBay is invaluable if one wants to collect memorabilia from many parts of our country. Given the original location of the First Thanksgiving, there appears to be decidedly more turkey-related material available east of the Mississippi River. To amass such a collection it would be physically impossible for a West Coast person to actively seek out such material from the East Coast unless one was willing to absolutely dedicate oneself to an effort spanning two or more decades. We relied upon three eBay categories to seek out Thanksgiving/Turkey memorabilia…**Turkey** (which includes the country), **Thanksgiving**, and **Wild Turkey**. As the holiday season approaches these categories tend to double or triple in size as sellers attempt to dispose of items that are in their inventories.

Most every book on collectibles issues a caveat on pricing, viz. that the values cited should not be taken as an absolute estimate of true value. Therefore, the values within this book were determined from countless hours of research and "real-time" input from on-line auction sites. Generally speaking, the values shown in annual versions of the many "antique and collectibles price guides" are, in the authors' opinion, not of great use and, at the worst, are on the high side. We realize that there are collectors and dealers that are "experts" on virtually every item in each of our chapters. Many of our collectibles have entire books devoted to that particular object. Also, we did not want to publish solely a "picture book." Instead it was our goal to bring true value to the reader so that anyone using this book will have a full understanding of the related background of most of the items shown, which comprehensively cover the range of Thanksgiving collectibles. It is our hope that this book in some way enhances your joy of future Thanksgivings and that a turkey or two might find its way into your Thanksgiving decorations or collection.

Chapter 1
THANKSGIVING, A HISTORICAL PERSPECTIVE

Thanksgiving is the quintessential American holiday. America's most famous short story writer, "O. Henry," wrote, "Thanksgiving Day…is the one day that is purely American." Taken at face value, Thanksgiving is a word of action. For if it were not for the courageous actions, fortitude, and the religious piety of our Pilgrim Fathers, America today would be a very different place. It is true that if the Plymouth Colony had not been established by a mixed group of religious dissidents and land seekers at that moment in history, then certainly within the next five to ten years, other English groups, perhaps with only gross economic intentions, would have assumed their place to the great regret of many generations to follow.

With over 380 years of historic background, Thanksgiving is America's national institution combining disparate elements of the harvest festival, civil and religious observances, and national patriotism. The long road to religious freedom in the New World was anything but easy, but the Pilgrims' Progress was a most thankful journey!

Postcard, embossed, publisher unknown. Uncle Sam is featured as he holds the reins of the turkey, "The National Bird of the Day." $5-10.

Timeline of Historic Events: 1000 A.D. to Present

Events Leading To "New World" Discoveries

1000-1020 A.D.: Leif Ericsson, a Viking captain, founded Vinland, the first European colony in North America, located in Labrador, Canada..

1492: Christopher Columbus (1491-1506), leading the *Santa Maria*, *Pinta*, and *Nina* after 70 days at sea, reached the Bahamas and the "New World" on October 12, and Hispaniola (Haiti/Dominican Republic) on December 25.

1497: John Cabot (Giovanni Caboto) in the ship *Matthew*, after 79 days at sea, discovered Newfoundland and the Great Banks

teeming with codfish. In 1522, the first seasonal fishing colony was established at Cape Breton.

1512: Juan Ponce de León, on April 2, was the first explorer to set foot in the present United States in Florida, which he named Pascua Florida (Easter Sunday).

1513: Vasco Nunez de Balboa was the first European to see the eastern part of the Pacific Ocean after crossing the Isthmus of Panama.

1519-22: Ferdinand Magellan was the first explorer to attempt to sail around the Earth. Although he was killed, one of his ships was successful.

1519-21: Hermán Cortez invaded and overthrew the Aztec Empire in Mexico.

1524: Giovanni Verranzano explored the Northeast coast of North America from the Carolinas to Maine, including the Hudson River, while searching for a Northwest passage to Asia.

1534, 1535, 1541: Jacques Cartier led three expeditions to Canada (which he named), searching for the Northwest Passage. He was unsuccessful in his attempt to start a settlement in Quebec but explored the St. Lawrence River.

1539-41: Hernando de Soto, looking for the legendary "Seven Cities of Gold," went on to discover the Mississippi River.

1540-42: Francisco Vasquez de Coronado led an expedition through Arizona, Texas, and Kansas looking for the "Seven Cities of Gold." In 1541, a "thanksgiving" ceremony was held during his trek.

1564: The French founded Fort Caroline on the Florida (Atlantic) coast, the first European colony on the mainland.

1565: Pedro Menendez de Avilés went to Florida and captured Fort Caroline from the French, then established the Spanish colony of St. Augustine forty miles south. A Mass of "thanksgiving" was held.

1577-80: Sir Francis Drake explored the California coast as part of the second major expedition to circumnavigate the Earth.

1598, 1601: Juan de Onate, in leading an expedition from Mexico, crossed the Rio Grande River, celebrated a ceremony of "thanksgiving," took possession of New Mexico for Spain, and established a settlement at San Juan. In 1601, Onate led an expedition across present Oklahoma to Kansas in a futile search for Quivira, the legendary city of silver.

1603-08: Samuel de Champlain, after many years of exploration, founded Quebec in present-day Canada in 1608.

In summary, the late fifteenth century and the sixteenth century comprised a remarkable period in world history with so many explorers and conquistadors from sea-faring countries embarking on perilous expeditions to seek out legendary treasures and land to claim for

their rulers. It was truly the Age of Exploration. In 1588, when the English defeated the Spanish Armada of King Philip II, they were also in the initial stages of their first colonization efforts in the present United States.

Initial English Colonization Efforts In America

1584-85: Captain Ralph Lane, under sponsorship by Sir Walter Raleigh, established the first English colony in America at Roanoke Island, part of the Outer Banks of North Carolina. The land was called "Virginia" in honor of Elizabeth, the Virgin Queen. Due to indigenous Indian problems, all the settlers went back to England.

1587: Captain John White tried to reestablish the colony at Pamlico Sound, Roanoke Island, with 107 settlers. On August 18, Virginia Dare was the first child born in the colonies. White returned to England for supplies.

1590: Captain White returned after three years, interrupted by the maritime wars with Spain, to find the settlement abandoned. Not a single survivor was ever found – one of the greatest unsolved mysteries of early America.

1606-07: On December 19, 1606, 104 "gentlemen – adventurers – settlers" sailed on the *Susan Constant*, *Godspeed*, and *Discovery* from London to Chesapeake Bay, Virginia, arriving on April 26, 1607. They finally anchored in the waters of the James River on May 13, 1607. On land, these settlers established Jamestown, the first permanent English settlement in North America. Within the first year, due to famine and pestilence, only 38 of the original 104 settlers were still alive in the New World.

1606-1610: Two joint-stock companies, the Virginia and Plymouth Companies, were chartered by the English crown to divide the colony and develop Virginia, which, at the time, encompassed much of North America. With the aid of Pocahontas, Captain John Smith helped avert the colony from starvation. Six hundred new settlers arrived at Jamestown.

1614: The first effective method of curing tobacco was developed. Tobacco was exported to England and, by 1619, the resultant profits established permanent security and affluence for the colony. In 1622, an Indian massacre claimed the lives of 347 settlers, almost wiping out the Jamestown settlement in one day.

1619: The first known African slaves (20) were sold by Dutch traders to Virginia tobacco planters as a source of cheap labor.

The British colonization efforts with respect to the Southern seaboard (Atlantic states) were precipitated by new restrictions on the use of arable land in England. This resulted in the spread of unemployment and vagrancy among tenant farmers. Colonization was stimulated by the notion that this non-producing excess population base could be attracted by the promise of free land in which a valuable cash crop would be developed. Then this crop would be sent back to England, thus insuring that the mother country would not have to rely solely upon their rival and hostile trading partners for future goods. In time, tobacco, rice, and cotton provided the ultimate return relative to the costs of setting up and supplying their New World colonies.

The colonization of the Northern part of this colony was stimulated by the same assumed economic benefits and rewards. However, the majority of these colonists were headed by men of deep religious convictions who were unwilling to accept the reigning Church of England's equivocal compromise between Roman Catholicism and fundamental Protestantism. Religious fervor took precedence over economic gain. These discontented people, against whom there was much discrimination, were called "**Puritans**" because they wanted to "purify" the Church of England (Anglicans) in three ways: (1) to simplify the existing ritual; (2) to rely on the written word of the Bible only; and (3) to strictly observe the Sabbath. These Puritans were split into several sects, but each hoped to remain within the Church of England in order to achieve their purifying reforms. However, the most radical group of all the Puritans was known as the "**Separatist Puritans**." The "Separatists," commonly known as "**Pilgrims**" (a term meaning traveler or wanderer that only came into popular usage in the 1840s in reference to the original settlers to Plymouth) formed the advance guard of the great Puritan exodus from the mother country, England, to the rugged unwelcoming shores of New England.

Diecuts. L to R: John Alden, 16"H; Priscilla, 15.25"H. Cardboard, multicolor. Dennison Manufacturing, No. 15F. c.1960s. $20-25 set.

Plymouth Colony From Founding to Assimilation

1602: Captain Bartholomew Gosnold sailed into Buzzards Bay, one of the waters surrounding Martha's Vineyard. However, the small island that he visited and claimed for England was not inviting to the would-be-colonists, who returned to England with Gosnold.

1607-08: George Popham, with a small party of speculators who hoped to form a trade network, undertook colonization of a coastal cape of Maine called Ft. St. George. However, the savage winter and the death of Popham convinced the settlers that the area was inhospitable, and they returned to England in 1608.

1615: Captain John Smith, from the Jamestown colony, along with a company of sixteen men, explored a section of the New England coast in and around Cape Cod Bay; it was he, not the Pilgrims, who gave the name "Plymouth" to the eventual final landing place of the latter.

1607-08: Of all the classes of Puritan "Nonconformists," the Pilgrim "Separatists," as the most openly radical religious group, were among the first to be persecuted by King James I. They were forced to flee from Scrooby, England (their center of religious activity) to Amsterdam, Holland and then a year later, to Leyden. There the Pilgrim exiles lived and worked for eleven years as lower class tradespeople.

1618: Despite freedom of religious expression in Holland, a small minority of the Pilgrim exiles still chose to emigrate to America (it was in 1684 that Cotton Mather, a Puritan religious leader, coined the term "Americans" in reference to the colonists). There were four reasons why the Separatist Pilgrims were willing to sacrifice their livelihood and brave the unknown in the area of the American seacoast set aside for the Virginia Chartered Companies of London and Plymouth: (1) On foreign soil they found it extremely hard to maintain a reasonable standard of living; (2) They were afraid that their children would grow up embracing the Dutch language and customs, which were liberal by Pilgrim standards; (3) A return to England was not warranted due to the continuing religious persecution; and (4) If Spain were to reconquer Holland, the terrors of the Inquisition could threaten their safety. Therefore, in 1618, a small splinter group of Separatists, having made the decision to emigrate again, set about to obtain a "patent" or license to colonize when events necessitate, as well as to raise the needed capital.

1618-20: After a series of successful negotiations with the Virginia Company of London, who had jurisdiction over the land ranging from present day North Carolina to New Jersey, the Separatists secured "venture" capital from a wealthy merchant, Thomas Weston, and purchased a small ocean-going vessel called the *Speedwell*. The first group of emigrants left on this boat from the Dutch port of Delfthaven, approximately fourteen miles from Leyden, embarking for the southern English port of Southampton on August 2, 1620.[1]

When the Pilgrims arrived at Southampton, they were joined by additional non-Pilgrim immigrants recruited by Weston to include some "merchant-adventurers." A second ship, the *Mayflower*, was chartered for this journey. In terms of weight and carrying ability, the *Mayflower* was three times the size of the *Speedwell*. While accounts vary, the Mayflower was listed as 180 "tuns" burden (a measure of the amount of barrels it could hold), 104 feet long with a beam of 26 feet and a draft of 13 feet. Originally, the *Mayflower* was used to transport wine from France to England.

Postcard. "Model of the Mayflower. Pilgrim Hall, Plymouth, Mass." Pub. By Smith News Store, Plymouth, Mass. #70452. The ship was designed and built by Mr. R.C. Anderson, of Southampton, England. It is the best model of the *Mayflower* and is acknowledged to be one of the finest ship models in the country. $10-12.

Brochure, front and reverse. *Of Plimoth Plantation,* The Living Folk Museum of 17th Century Plymouth. Foldout. 17.5"L x 11.5"W. Two-sided. 1976. $5.

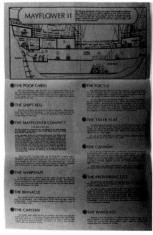

Postcard. "The Departure of the Pilgrims from Delft Haven, 1620." American Art Post Card Co, Boston, Mass., publisher. Original painting hangs in Pilgrim Hall, Plymouth, Massachusetts, a gift of ex-governor Alexander H. Rice of Mass. It is of great value, and at an exhibition in England won first prize of a thousand guineas. Artist: Charles Lucy, 1847. $10-12.

On August 15, 1620, the *Mayflower* and *Speedwell* left Southampton. However, after two attempts to sail, the *Speedwell* proved to be unseaworthy, and she and eighteen of her passengers and cargo were sent back to London. Finally, after one month of critical delays, the *Mayflower* set sail across the North Atlantic for the New World and the Virginia colony on September 16, 1620. The original passenger list, listing 102 persons of all ages, did not include the Master and Owner of the ship, Captain Christopher Jones and at least 25 crewmembers. These soon-to-be famous 102 passengers were divided as follows: Adult Colonists (59); Sailors hired for one year (2); Servants (presumed minors) (9); Girls (11); and Boys (21). Likewise, the passenger list was also divided between the **"Saints"** (41-55), who were the Pilgrim religious dissenters, and the **"Strangers"** (51-61), who, while they were Church of England members, sought economic opportunity rather than religious salvation. These Strangers included "goodmen" (ordinary settlers), hired male hands, and indentured male servants.

Postcard. "Embarkation of the Pilgrims." Pub. By Smith's News Store, Plymouth, Mass. Original painting hangs in Pilgrim Hall. Plymouth, Mass., Artist: Robert Walker Weir, 1843. $10-12.

The ocean passage was not without its serious problems. During a period of several Mid-Atlantic autumn storms and crosswinds, the *Mayflower* was "shrewdly shaken," the main transverse beam cracked in 'tween decks (main hold and the main deck), causing leakage from the upper cabins into the Pilgrims' quarters below. Of the 102 passengers that embarked from England, there was one death among the servants and one birth, a boy named "Oceanus" Hopkins. The ocean crossing took 66 days, which included a suspicious change in the ship's course to the north by which landfall was initially sighted at the tip of Cape Cod. When the *Mayflower* anchored off

Postcard. "Landing of the Pilgrims." Copyrighted and published by A.S. Burbank, Plymouth, Mass. Series 8747. Original painting hangs in Pilgrim Hall. Plymouth, Mass. 13' x 16'. Artist: Henry Sargent. $12-15.

what is now Provincetown on the Cape Cod peninsula, the Pilgrims were able to leave their travel-worn boat for a time and walk ashore on November 21, 1620, the date of their first landing in the New World.

Whether the *Mayflower's* change of course was the result of a covert agreement between the ship's Captain and the Pilgrims, or simply the result of poor navigation, the "Strangers" among them were very angered. The ramifications were that the whole group had no right to be where they had landed and, therefore, did not fall under the direct governance of the crown. Because of the fear of mutiny among the "Strangers," the "Saints" drew up an agreement called a "compact" and assembled the adult males, numbering 41 in all. They met in the *Mayflower's* cabin, where each adult male was persuaded to sign this compact by which they agreed to form themselves into "a civil body Politick" and promised "all due Submission and Obedience" to its "just and equal laws." The **Mayflower Compact**, a remarkable document for its time, was the first example of the new American tradition of government resting upon the equal consent of the governed. With the creation of their own commonwealth at hand, the Pilgrims (both "Saints" and "Strangers") then elected Deacon John Carver as the first freely chosen colonial governor.

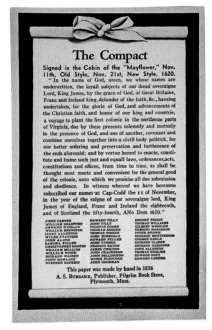

Postcard picturing "The Compact" which was signed in the Cabin of the the "Mayflower," November 21, 1620, Series 67127, Smith News Store, Plymouth, Mass. $10-12.

Postcard. "The Signing of the Compact in the Cabin of the Mayflower." Original painting hangs in Pilgrim Hall Museum, Plymouth, Mass. Artist; Edward Percy Moran. c.1900. $10-12.

The *Mayflower* carried the prefabricated parts of a shallop, or coastal longboat, which measured about 33 feet long, 9 feet in breadth, and a draft of 3 feet. The shallop needed to be restored as it was needed to explore the shallow coastal waters for favorable landing sites. From the day of the Pilgrims' first landing, Captain Myles Standish, the military leader of the colony, undertook three on-shore expeditions called "Discoveries" to search for a suitable place to establish a settlement. On both the November 25 and December 8 scouting trips, Standish and his men found a large quantity of seed corn and ears buried in the heaped mounds of an Indian burial ground. This corn probably saved the colonists from starvation. At this time, too, there was born to William White and his wife, a son, named Peregrine. He was the first white child born in New England.

The third "Discovery" was famous because it was responsible for bringing about the initial landing at Plymouth. On December 17 and 18, while encamped at Wellfleet Harbor, the Pilgrim explorers were attacked by a band of thirty to fifty Indians without sustaining any losses. They boarded their shallop and made for a more protective area in the midst of a snowstorm. On Monday, December 21, when the cold spell broke, the Pilgrims landed at Plymouth Harbor, although it was not recorded that the landing party actually stepped from their boat onto a large granite boulder, now called **Plymouth Rock**. While the importance of the "Rock" in history is wholly symbolic, it has been preserved for posterity. Each December 21 has now been observed as Forefathers' Day.

After an absence of one week, Myles Standish returned to the *Mayflower*, anchored at Provincetown harbor, with the good news that a permanent site for the new settlement had been found. With all due haste, the *Mayflower* sailed for the new harbor and made a successful passage on December 26. She remained anchored in Plymouth Bay until all the

Postcard of the original oil painting of the "Mayflower" in Plymouth Harbor, by William Halsall, 1882, which may be seen in Pilgrim Hall Museum in Plymouth, Massachusetts. Published by Bromley and Co., Inc., Wolfeboro, New Hampshire. $2-5.

Pilgrims were established on shore, a stay of four months, and then set sail for England on April 15, 1621.

Three postcards, H.W.V. Litho. Co., Series 800. These come from two similar sets of six postcards, one set recognized by the golden horseshoe and border of stars, and the second set by the gold border. All twelve postcards use the same embossed images of the Pilgrims and turkeys. $8-10 each.

Postcards. Top: "Plymouth Rock Portico." Photo by Brad Ashton. Scenic Art Oakland, Ca. $5. Bottom: "Plymouth Rock, Plymouth, Mass." Pub. Smith's Inc., Plymouth, Mass. $10-12.

The ninety-six days, from September 16 when the *Mayflower* made its third and last departure from Southampton to the actual landing of the Pilgrims at the Plymouth site on December 26, were among the most important and eventful periods in the history of America.

1621: On Saturday, January 2, the Pilgrims shuttled back and forth between the mother ship and the shore in their efforts to construct the first of many simple but adequate housing structures of hand-squared logs. While the *Mayflower* was cold, damp, and unheated, it did provide a certain measure of security against the miseries of rain, snow, and high winds. Unfortunately, exposure to this wintry weather, the lack of protection against infectious diseases caused by cramped on-board living conditions, and the virtual lack of proper food that was the immediate cause of scurvy, seriously undermined the strength of the Pilgrims.

By mid-March, fully one-half of the original 102 colonists had perished from a combination of exposure to the elements and malnutrition. Despite the documented tragedies and hardships, somehow the Pilgrims persevered in building their new settlement. The remaining families, widows, and single men were divided into nineteen family groups. Each of the families was given a plot of land, and each family was responsible for building their own home. The village street (now called Leyden Street) was laid out extending from the waterfront up to the top of Fort Hill (now called Burial Hill), where a temporary platform was erected, housing six cannons for the settlement's defense. Myles Standish was chosen Captain of this nascent military organization.

Print. "View of Fort Hill," showing the Pilgrim's first defensive stockade. 7" x 5". Artist: Not known. c. 1950s. $10-12.

Postcard, embossed. San Gabriel Publishing, Series 131, Copyright 1910 A. Von Beust, artist. A fall border of wheat, corn, and pumpkins decorates the scene of a Pilgrim family standing on shore as the boat sails away. $10-15.

Postcards. Top: "Town Square, 1st Church Burial Hill, Plymouth, Mass." Town Square is practically a continuation and widening out of Leyden Street. The original Town House, the Court House, and The Church of the First Parish (the first place of worship to have a bell), erected in 1637 or 1638, dominate the Square. Burial Hill, located above Town Square, was consecrated from the earliest year of the Colony as a place of sepulture. Bottom: View of Leyden Street, Plymouth, Mass. Both cards were published by A.C. Bosselman & Co., New York. Both were addressed to Miss Esther A. Burbank, Centre Carver, Mass. $10-15 each.

While the deaths of so many colonists was a definite hindrance to the infrastructure of the colony, amazingly, the leadership of the Pilgrim Fathers remained intact over the first six months. The important leaders of the Plymouth colony were: First Governor John Carver (DOD April 1621); Second Governor William Bradford (DOD 1657); Third Governor Edward Winslow (DOD 1655); Elder William Brewster (DOD 1643); Captain Myles Standish (DOD 1657); Elder Isaac Allerton; and John Alden, a cooper (barrel maker) by trade, who was best known for his marriage to Priscilla Mullins, a teenaged girl who had lost all of her family. It is a tribute to the endurance and fortitude of these singular leaders that they maintained their concentration and energy in spite of the fact that Bradford, Winslow, Allerton, and Standish all tragically lost their wives within the first year.

Postcard. "Priscilla and John Alden." Pub. By Smith News Store, Plymouth, Mass. #71565. $10-12.

On March 26, 1621, a providential visit occurred. The first recorded friendly encounter between the settlers and Native Americans in the Plymouth colony came about when Samoset, a lesser sachem (sub-chief) from the Abenaki tribe entered the village alone, exclaiming "Welcome, Englishmen." He had learned English from some fishermen whom he had met while they were resting on the New England coast of Maine. From Samoset the Pilgrims learned that the Patuxet Indians from the Plymouth area had been decimated in the plague of 1614. Shortly after, on April 1, Samoset returned with Tisquantum (Squanto), another English-speaking Indian, who had prior relationships (good and bad) with the English and who had inadvertently been forced to Europe as a slave. Nonetheless, he became a devoted friend of the Pilgrims and their chief negotiator and agent in dealings with the local Native Americans.

As it was the beginning of planting time, Squanto showed the Pilgrims (who did not have agricultural backgrounds) how to best work and fertilize the soil to achieve an optimum crop of corn, the major staple for both groups. Squanto was also instrumental in arranging a meeting between Massasoit, the Grand Sagamore of the seven or more villages that comprised the Wampanoag Nation, and the Pilgrims. The Wampanoag (the name means "People of the East") inhabited the southeastern portion of present-day Massachusetts including Cape Cod, the offshore islands, and an eastern strip of Rhode Island. After the

Pilgrims held a great ceremony honoring Massasoit as well as hosting a complimentary feast, Governor Carver and Massasoit entered into a treaty of peace as well as a mutual security pact. This pact between two independent governments remained inviolate throughout the lives of both Massasoit and the Pilgrim Fathers who sanctioned it.

Postcard. "Statue of Massasoit. Protector of the Pilgrims. Plymouth, Mass." The famous chief is looking far out to sea, as if already catching a glimpse of the approaching *Mayflower*. Artist: Cyrus Dallin. Gift of the Improved Order of Red Men. $10-12.

It was in 1675 that the truce was first broken by the son of Massasoit. Metacom (called satirically King Philip by the English), the Wampanoag sachem, secretly held parlays with other related tribes who were also fearful of being pushed out of their traditional lands. He and his allies initiated a fierce uprising against a number of New England settlements, causing over one thousand white settlers' deaths and tremendous property damage. Metacom was eventually killed in 1676, and the danger to the English settlers was over.

The rest of 1621 passed uneventfully, leading to a successful first harvest in the Autumn.

The First Thanksgiving – 1621

Due to timely Native American intervention, both the Jamestown and Plymouth colonies survived their first years. But it also took a strong measure of discipline, determination, and perseverance by the settlers to meet these challenges head on. After the Pilgrims suffered through thirteen months of untold hardships, a celebration of thanksgiving was prescribed for their survival.

There have been libraries full of books written about the actual events of the First Thanksgiving. While speculations and assumptions abound, there are very few facts including the date of this three-day event. For the Pilgrims, it was a well-deserved chance to unwind, but not particularly noteworthy when still faced with the raw realities of everyday life. Learned scholars specializing in that period of American history opine that the three-day cel-

ebration was held between September 21 and November 9, depending on whether the harvest of corn, barley, and peas came early or late in the season.

Postcards, embossed. Unnumbered, copyrighted 1907 Fred C. Lounsbury, known for the illustrated stanzas of children's poems. The poems honor the Pilgrims. Top: "And now when in late November, our Thanksgiving feast is spread, 'tis the same time-honored custom of those Pilgrims long since dead." Bottom: "On New England's rugged headlands, now where peaceful Plymouth lies, there they built their rough log cabins neath the cold forbidding skies." $8-10 each.

Assorted books and pamphlets on Thanksgiving (annotated in Bibliography). c.1960s-1980s. $5-50.

Assorted books and pamphlets on Thanksgiving and Plymouth (annotated in Bibliography). c.1897-1990s. $5-100.

There are only two surviving written references to the First Thanksgiving. The first was written by Governor William Bradford in his history of the colony titled *Of Plimoth Plantation 1620-1647* (in modern English).

"They began now to gather in the small harvest they had, and to fix up their houses and dwellings against winter being all well recovered in health and strength and had all things in good plenty. For as some were thus employed in affairs abroad, others were exercised in fishing, about cod and bass and other fish, of which they took good store, of which every family had their portion. All the summer there was no want; and now began to come in store of fowl, as winter approached, of which this place did abound when they came first (but afterward decreased by degrees). And besides waterfowl there was great store of wild turkeys, of which, they took many, besides venison, etc. Besides they had about a peck a meal a week to a person, or now since harvest, Indian corn to that proportion. Which made many afterwards write so largely of their plenty here to their friends in England, which were not feigned but true reports."

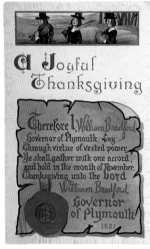

Postcard. Thanksgiving Series Number 956. 1910 A.S. Meeker, New York. Features the Proclamation by Governor William Bradford. The card is decorated by a top border picturing three Pilgrims, one carrying the turkey, one a rifle, and the last a pumpkin. $7-10.

The second reference was a letter dated December 11, 1621, written by Elder Edward Winslow to a friend in England and reprinted in *Mourt's Relation* (in modern English).

"Our harvest being gotten in, our Governor sent four men on fowling, that so we might after a more special manner rejoice together, after we had gathered the fruit of our labours. They four in one day killed as much fowl as, with a little help beside, served the Company almost a week. At which time, amongst other recreations, we exercised our arms, many of the Indians coming amongst us, and amongst the rest their greatest king, Massasoit with some 90 men, whom for three days we entertained and feasted.

And they went out and killed five deer which they brought to the plantation and bestowed on our Governor and upon the Captain and others."

Postcard. "The First Thanksgiving." Original painting hangs in Pilgrim Hall, Museum of Pilgrim Treasures, Plymouth, Mass. Artist; Jennie Brownscombe. $10-12.

Regardless of the dearth of information surrounding the events of the First Thanksgiving, we can be certain that it was more of a harvest festival than a religious Thanksgiving Day. Perhaps if the Indians did not make an appearance, this festival, probably a shortened version, would have had more religious symbolism. But due to the Pilgrims' consideration for their Indian friends, the festival was enjoyed in a more secular atmosphere culminating a period of intense stress and labor.

Postcards, embossed. L to R: Series 130, artist Frances Brundage; Series 642, copyright J. Herman 1912. Both postcards illustrate the relationship between the Pilgrims and the Indians. The two postcards are brightly colored and enhanced with red borders. $10-15 each.

Postcard, copyright 1906 P. Sander, N.Y., Series 502. Three Pilgrims in their finest dress make their way to the Thanksgiving celebration. $5-10.

As with many things, the legend of the event takes on a life disproportionate to actuality. If one is interested in gathering information on the First Thanksgiving, a trip to Plymouth, Massachusetts is a must. The city itself has over twenty historical points of interest re-lating to the Pilgrims. Three miles south of town is the Plimoth Plantation, an open-air living history museum. The main exhibits are a re-creation of a 1627 Pilgrim village, a Wampanoag Indian summer campsite, and, in town, the *Mayflower II*, a meticulously constructed-to-period-specifications of a square-rigged vessel replica. The *Mayflower II* was built in Devonshire and sailed from Plymouth, England to Plymouth, Massachusetts in 54 days, arriving on June 13, 1957. The extremely informative website of the Plimoth Plantation is www.plimoth.org.

Postcard souvenir folder, front. "A Souvenir Folder of Plymouth, Mass. Landing Place of the Pilgrims, 1620." A presentation of the many historic sites in Plymouth. Published by Smith's News Service. $25-30.

Postcard of the *Mayflower II*, a full size replica of the ship that carried the first permanent European settlers to the American shores in 1620. Photo by Werner J. Bertsch. $2-5.

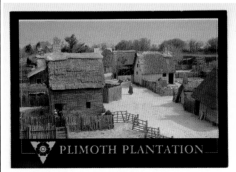

Postcard of Plimoth Plantation, the replica of Plymouth Colony on a hill overlooking Plymouth Harbor. $2-5.

Postcard souvenir folder, back. "Plymouth Rock under Portico and Plymouth Rock House. Plymouth, Mass." $10-12.

Postcard. "Pilgrim Progress," Plymouth, Massachusetts. A re-enactment of the Pilgrim colony leaving a church service in the Fort-Meeting House of the Pilgrims. This structure was reproduced by Plimoth Plantation in 1953. Color photo by The Dicksons. $10-12.

Right:
Plymouth memorabilia. Felt pennant. "Plymouth, Mass, Plymouth Rock" 11.5"L x 4.75"W. c.1940s. $18-20; Diecut Pilgrims' Hat. 6.75"L. "Pilgrim, Plymouth, America's Home Town," on brim "Thanksgiving Day 1949." $3-5.

Back in town, the Pilgrim Society, originating in 1820, was responsible for the construction of the Pilgrim Hall Museum (late 1820s), housing the finest collection of Pilgrim possessions anywhere. In the Great Hall of the Museum hang four large-scale stylized paintings illustrating the significant events concerning the Pilgrim exodus and arrival in America. These and other "heroic" paintings have been responsible for the "romanticization" and preservation of the spirit and image of Thanksgiving and of the Pilgrims themselves.

Postcard. "Interior, Pilgrim Hall, Plymouth, Mass." Postcard shows original oil paintings and Pilgrim artifacts. Pilgrim Hall was erected by the Pilgrim Society in 1824 as a monumental hall to the memory of the Pilgrims. The main hall is 46' x 39' with walls 22' high. $10-12.

Postcards. L to R, Top: Souvenir folder of Plymouth consisting of twenty views of historical Plymouth. Pub. By Smith's Inc. Plymouth, Mass. c.1940s. $20-25; "Massasoit Statue and Plymouth Harbor from Coles Hill. Plymouth. Mass." Coles Hill is the little grassed bluff, with stone steps facing the Rock, a parkway commanding a magnificent view. Here were buried nearly half the *Mayflower* passengers in the first winter. American Art Post Card Co., Boston, Mass.; Middle: "The First Fort – A Replica at Plimoth Plantation, Plymouth, Mass." Pub. By Smith's Inc., Plymouth, Mass.; Aerial view of Plymouth, taken over Plymouth Harbor; Bottom: "Town Square, 1st Church Burial Hill, Plymouth"; Leyden Street, Plymouth, Mass. $10-12 each.

In order to perpetuate the significance of the founding of Plymouth, the town hosted a Tercentenary Celebration which opened on Forefathers' Day, December, 1920. A set of three U.S. postage stamps was issued for the occasion (see Chapter 8). In the summer of the following year, the town sponsored a Plymouth Tercentenary Pageant, "Commemorating the Tercentenary (300 years) of the Landing of the Pilgrims on Plymouth Rock – December 21, 1620." This outdoor pageant involved over 1200 actors/actresses dressed in period costumes and was given on twelve separate days in July and August, 1921.

Travel/picture guides to Plymouth (annotated in Bibliography). c.1920-1998. $5-30.

Booklets. L to R: Official Illustrated Book. *"Plymouth Tercentenary, with A Brief History of the Life and Struggles of the Pilgrim Fathers."* Commercial Publishing, New Bedford, Massachusetts. Softback, 64 pages includes Pageant Program, 1921. $100+; Official Pageant Program. "The Pilgrim Spirit." Softback, 32 pages. Lists all 1300 people involved in the production. $20-25.

1622-1700: In the years to follow, the Pilgrims would be exposed to more failed harvests, frustration, and tragedy. But that did not stop the religious dissidents or the economic well-being seekers from coming to the Plymouth colony. By 1630, five more ships had arrived bearing new colonists and supplies. Plymouth, because of its increasingly rich agricultural heritage, prospered by selling food products to the fast developing settlements to the north. But after the 1640s Puritan migration to the Boston area slowed considerably due to an improving religious climate in England. By the late 1650s, the original leadership of the Pilgrims had died off. As the Plymouth colony lacked the true essentials for growth, being poorly located for the fishing and fur trade industries, it became increasingly dependent upon the more powerful Massachusetts Bay Colony, of which Boston was the center. Finally, in 1691, New England's first permanent settlement was taken over and merged into the virtual sovereign commonwealth of the larger Bay Colony with its own brand of uncompromising Puritanism.

Postcard. "Pilgrims Going to Church." This painting, of which the original belongs to the New York Historical Society, shows the citizens of Plymouth walking to one of their Sabbath services. They met from eight to twelve o'clock in the morning, and then met again in the afternoon. It was painted in the nineteenth century by George H. Boughton. $10-12.

Important Thanksgiving Proclamations and Events

1775: On April 19, British troops, trying to capture rebel stores of arms at Lexington and Concord, were attacked by Colonial Minutemen. November 23 was observed as Thanksgiving Day by the American Continental Army besieging Boston, as well as by the citizens of Massachusetts.

1776: July 4, Continental Congress adopted the **Declaration of Independence.**

1777: After 3-1/2 months of fighting, British General John Burgoyne surrendered his troops to the Continental Army under General Benedict Arnold at Saratoga on October 17. This major victory was the turning point in the War of Independence. The Continental Congress declared December 18 a "day of solemn Thanksgiving and praise" for this "signal success." **Thanksgiving Day 1777 was the first such celebration ever proclaimed by a national authority for all thirteen colonies**.

1781: On October 19, the British army surrendered at Yorktown, Virginia. This final defeat ended any British hopes of overturning the American Revolution. The Continental Congress authorized a Thanksgiving Day for December 13, 1781, and continued to set aside one Thursday every autumn as a day of grateful prayer up to and including 1784.

1789: On April 6, the United States Senate convened to count the ballots cast by members of the Electoral College for the first President of the United States. George Washington, former Commander-in-Chief of the American forces during the Revolutionary War, was unanimously elected. **The first Thanksgiving proclamation by a President of the United States was issued by George Washington, making November 26 a national holiday in gratitude for the enactment of the Constitution**.

Print. "Thanksgiving In the Olden Time." Artist: Stanley M. Arthur. *Harper's Weekly*, New York. December 2, 1899. 11"L x 16"W. Vignette: "Bellman Reading the Governor's Proclamation In A New England Town." Cover. $15-20.

1790-1861: Throughout these years, Thanksgiving, interpreted as a day of reflection and/or feasting, was randomly proclaimed as a holiday by Presidents and Governors according to their whims. Given the swirling political currents of this young nation, the states that made up the union were split over many issues, the most important of which was slavery. There was a need, therefore, to solidify the country as one nation under a unifying heroic legend. Already there were celebrations of uniquely American national holidays such as Washington's Birthday and the Fourth of July. The Landing of the Pilgrims or Forefathers emblematized the genesis of our nation's birth and, it was in this light, that the holiday was slowly adopted by non-New England states. In this vein, there began a "grass-roots" campaign in the 1830s and 1840s, without the distinction of centralized leadership, to proclaim Thanksgiving a national holiday. The idea of a "national" event got its start in 1833 when the U.S. Government, in an effort to strengthen its centralized powers, took control of all new territories instead of the individual states that had been claiming the land. During these times, states were free to observe Thanksgiving but there were two problems: (1) proclamations were erratic on a year-to-year ba-

sis, and (2) when the dates were chosen, they were not usually consistent on a year-to-year basis. However untidy these random state observances may have seemed, help was on the way in the personage of Sarah Josepha Hale. By 1841, Mrs. Hale, already a very successful writer for women's magazines, became editor of *Godey's Lady's Book*. In the two decades to follow, *Godey's* became the most widely distributed periodical of any kind in the United States. In 1846, Sarah Hale began her campaign to make the last Thursday in November a national holiday. As the editor of the nation's most read tabloid, Mrs. Hale used her powerful position as a "bully pulpit" to strenuously promote this idea. In addition to her widely read editorials, she embarked on an unremitting letter writing campaign to every state and territorial governor urging them to be consistent in proclaiming the last Thursday in November as Thanksgiving Day. For her uncompromising efforts, Mrs. Hale well-deserved the sobriquet of the "Mother of Modern Thanksgiving." However, more important matters were afoot. Eleven pro-slavery states seceded from the Union and formed their own Confederacy. The American Civil War began April 12, 1861 over the issue of states' rights for self-determination, the main concern being slavery.

1863: After two years of fierce fighting, a turning point evolved. At the Battle of Gettysburg July 1-3, 1863, the Union forces, in the largest battle to be fought in the Civil War, halted General Robert E. Lee's advance; the South seldom went on the offensive after that. The resounding Union victory led President Abraham Lincoln to declare August 6, 1863 "to be observed as a day of national thanksgiving, praise, and prayer… and to lead the whole nation…back to the perfect enjoyment of union and fraternal peace."

Mrs. Hale was not yet finished. She wrote another letter to President Lincoln imploring him to have the "day of our annual Thanksgiving made a national and fixed Union Festival…" The points she made were: (1) annual Presidential proclamation; (2) fixed uniform date; and (3) legal enactment of Thanksgiving, as a national holiday. **Lincoln** was moved by these clearly defined points, and on October 3, he **proclaimed a nationwide Thanksgiving Day for the last Thursday of November 1863** "… as a day of thanksgiving and praise to our beneficent Father who dwelleth in the heavens." This "Thankful Journey" from the Pilgrims' first celebration of the harvest in 1621 to President Lincoln's Proclamation of 1863 took 242 years to realize.

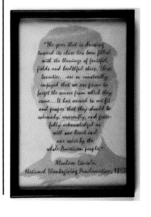

Framed Thanksgiving Proclamation. President Abraham Lincoln – 1863. Gold script superimposed over a full head photo. c. mid-1970s. $25-30.

Original Newspaper. *New York Tribune*, New York. Front page, banner. Full paper, Monday, October 5, 1863. $50+.

Print. "Thanksgiving Day, November 26, 1863." Artist: Thomas Nast. *Harpers Weekly*, New York, December 5, 1863. 16"L x 22"W. Hand-tinted. Main vignette: "The Union Altar," plus five more patriotic vignettes. $175+.

General Robert E. Lee surrendered his forces on April 9, 1865 at Appomattox Court House, Virginia. Just days later, on April 14, 1865, John Wilkes Booth assassinated President Lincoln at Ford Theatre, Washington, D.C. The Thanksgiving Proclamation for 1865 was delivered by President Andrew Johnson.

Prints. L to R: "Not To Be Deceived." Artist: unknown. *Frank Leslie's Illustrated*, New York, November 29, 1884. 10.5"L x 15.5"W. Veteran Gobbler (contemptuously): "That Talk About 'Countless Blessings' is All Nonsense – The President Means Turkey Every Time!" Also: Thanksgiving Proclamation" by President Chester A. Arthur. $25-30; "Thanksgiving Day 1887." Artist: unknown. *Frank Leslie's Illustrated*, New York, November 26, 1887. 11"L x 15.5"W. Vignette: Uncle Sam riding on overflowing cornucopia drawn by tethered Tom Turkeys. An allegorical figure of Anarchy is handcuffed. $35-40.

Page 4, Column 2 of the *New York Tribune*, Monday, October 5, 1863: "The National Thanksgiving Day," "A Proclamation by The President of the United States of America."

While every seated President since Lincoln has proclaimed Thanksgiving as a national holiday, members of Congress introduced bills to fix the date permanently. **On December 26, 1941, Public Law 379 established the fourth Thursday in November as the official date of the national holiday of Thanksgiving.**

1863 to Present: The celebration of a national day of Thanksgiving has continued as an unbroken tradition, becoming one of the most widespread, distinctive, and beloved of American observances. Is the celebration of the Thanksgiving holiday proper in the context of today's continuing emphasis on multiculturalism? This was the question posed in an interesting cover article by *Time* magazine, dated July 8, 1991, titled "Who Are We?" The author, Paul Gray, opined "American kids are getting a new – and divisive – view of Thomas Jefferson, **Thanksgiving**, and the Fourth of July." He offers the view that a growing emphasis on the nation's "multicultural" heritage glorifies racial and ethnic pride at the ex-

Print. "National Thanksgiving, December 7, 1865." Artist: Thomas Nast. *Harper's Weekly*, New York, December 9, 1865. 22"L x 16"W. Main vignette; "We Thank Thee O God Our Heavenly Father," plus six more patriotic vignettes. Also: "A Proclamation" by President Andrew Johnson. $150+.

pense of social cohesion brought about by shared ideals and values. With respect to Thanksgiving, the traditional view is that the bounteous harvest after the Pilgrim colonists' first harsh winter in New England was celebrated as a symbol of the harmony between the newcomers and the local Native Americans. The multiculturalists, mainly those with academic backgrounds, criticize that concept as an idealization of the destructive effects of colonial culture upon a variety of nonwhite peoples.

When your authors visited Plymouth at Thanksgiving some years ago to do research for this book, we observed Native Americans and their supporters gathered on Leyden Street for the activities relating to the "National Day of Mourning." This observance first began in 1970 as a non-violent way to offer a dissenting viewpoint by Native Americans that traditional concepts of Thanksgiving were distorted. Native Americans believe that celebrating Thanksgiving will only be valid when it is recognized that later colonists were responsible for the theft of Indian lands and the destruction of their traditional way of life. According to the sponsors, the United American Indians of New England, Native Americans are "mourning over ancestors and the genocide of our peoples and the theft of our lands."

Regardless of the diverse viewpoints on this inflamed subject, however merited they may be, it is very important that one undertakes some research by reading various informative books on the subject. It is especially important for children to obtain as much knowledge as possible so that they can form an independent opinion without being influenced by people with a political or social action agenda. There are many books written for children on the reasons for the celebration of Thanksgiving.

Today, we Americans have much to be thankful for. The huge influx of people that continue to enter our country seeking economic opportunities and the ability to live in freedom is a continuous affirmation of American values and the ideals on which this nation was founded.

Assorted children's books on *Thanksgiving* (annotated in Bibliography). c.1950s-1980s. $10-35.

Assorted children's books on *Thanksgiving* (annotated in Bibliography). c.1980s-1990s. $10-35.

Assorted children's books on *Thanksgiving* (annotated in Bibliography). c.1930s-1950s, $5-125.

The Youth's Companion. November 18, 1886. "Thanksgiving Number 1886." Artist: Russell & Richardson. 11.5"L x 16.5"W. Perry Mason & Co., Publishers, Boston, Massachusetts. Page 469. Illustrated Poem "Our First Thanksgiving Day." Lizbeth B. Comins. Twelve stanzas...Stanza #1: "*Children, do you know the story of the first Thanksgiving Day, founded by our Pilgrim Fathers in that time so far away?...*" $35-40.

John Martin's Book The Child's Magazine, **November 1932. Cover artist: Harold W. Griffin. 9" x 12". John Martin's House, Concord, New Hampshire. 52 pages of varied contents for the child ages 4 to 12. $12-15.**

Thanksgiving Day 2004-2010

For your enjoyment and future planning, Thanksgiving will fall on the following Thursdays of each year:

2004	November 25
2005	November 23
2006	November 22
2007	November 28
2008	November 27
2009	November 25
2010	November 24

Postcard, embossed, publisher unknown. A young woman presents the Thanksgiving turkey. The calendar month of November borders the scene. $5-10.

Thanksgiving Trivia

Here are some Turkey "words":

Turkey: Republic in Western Asia and South East Europe, 301,381 sq. miles, population 50,664,458.

Turkey: (pl – eys)
(1) **Species of birds** in the family *Meleagrididae*; the North American common turkey (*Meleagris gallopavo*) is large and mainly domesticated; the Central American turkey (*M. ocellata*) or the Ocellated turkey, is so called due to its markings with eyelike spots of color. Anatomically, the male ocellated turkey differs from its North American counterpart by its lack of a beard or chest tuff.
(2) **Slang** (a) a theatrical production of failure, a flop; (b) a stupid, foolish, naïve or inept person, a loser; (c) "talk turkey," colloq. Talk frankly and straight forwardly; get down

to business; means business; (d) three successive strikes in bowling.
(3) **Turkey cock**, c.1578, a strutting pompous, conceited or self-important person.
(4) **Turkey red**, c.1769: (a) brilliant durable scarlet pigment obtained naturally from the root of the madder or alizoarin (red coloring matter of the madder root); (b) a cotton cloth dyed with this as used in quilts.

Quilt, Hand-pieced. 12' x 15'. Cotton. "Boxed Diamond" pattern. Turkey-red on white needlework. Added pillow. Not signed. Provenance: Auction purchase, made by second generation member of General George A. Custer's (7th U.S. Cavalry) family c.1930s, $1200+.

Quilt. Close-up of pattern detail.

(5) **Turkey shoot**, c.1845: (a) a marksmanship contest usually at a festive gathering in which rifles or shotguns are fired at a moving target with a turkey offered as a prize; (b) something easily accomplished, a piece of "cake"; (c) an easy destruction of enemy troops, especially flying aircraft, viz., "The Marianas Turkey Shoot" June 19-20, 1944 where Japanese aircraft losses were 407 versus U.S. Naval aircraft losses of 39.
(6) **Turkey trot**: a ragtime couples' dance that is danced with the feet well apart and with a characteristic rise on the ball of the foot followed by a drop upon the heel.
(7) **Young turk**, c.1900-1905: a usually young dynamic person eager for, or advocating change within an organization; aggressive or impatient; zealous.
(8) **Cold turkey**: refers to the idea that heroin addicts who quit suddenly get so pale and covered with goose bumps that their skin looks like that of an uncooked turkey.

(9) **Turkish (adj):** Turkish bath, Turkish coffee, Turkish crescent, Turkish delight, Turkish knot, Turkish rug, Turkish tobacco, Turkish towel

We hope you enjoy testing your knowledge of the celebration of Thanksgiving with this holiday crossword puzzle. © 2004 Vocabulary University®.

Across

4 – one of the bands of Puritans who journeyed
6 – seasoned bread or fillings inside poultry
8 – act of watching attentively
9 – internal organs of a fowl
11 – a horn stuffed with foods, berries, *etc.*
15 – synonym for corn; pale yellow
16 – group of people who form in a new land
17 – name of ship that sailed to the New World (1620)

Down

1 – a sauce for salads etc.
2 – special activities that commemorate
3 – valued praise, favor or benefit
5 – unusually abundant meal
7 – distinct cry of the male turkey
10 – term also meaning Native American
12 – small, sour and dark red berry
13 – season when crops are collected
14 – one of oldest towns in southeast Massachusetts
18 – American harvest holiday in late November

[1]The dates given in this chapter are "New-style," based on the shift from the Julian to Gregorian calendars decreed by the papal bull (official document of the Pope) in 1582. Calendar changes in the 1600s required ten full days to be dropped, viz.: July 22 becomes August 2.

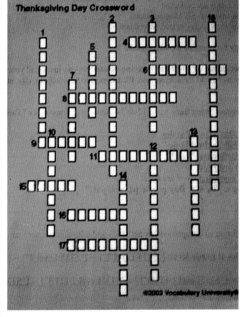

Crossword Puzzle. Thanksgiving Day Crossword. 18 clues © 2004 Vocabulary University®. No value.

Chapter 2
AMERICA'S PREMIER BIRD – THE WILD TURKEY

The Wild Turkey vs. The Bald Eagle

In the early days of our nation, there was much controversy over the selection of a bird that would best represent the strength of a fledging America. On June 20, 1782, the bald eagle was made the national symbol of the United States over the strenuous objections of Benjamin Franklin, who favored the wild turkey. In a letter written to his daughter on January 26, 1784, Franklin casts doubt on the propriety of using the eagle as a fitting symbol.

> *"For my own part I wish the bald eagle had not been chosen the representative of our country. He is a bird of bad moral character. He does not get his living honestly....For the truth, the turkey is, in comparison, a much more respectable bird, and withal a true original native of America..."*

Nevertheless, the bald eagle, selected as our national emblem, has appeared on all official seals of the United States, as well as on most coinage, paper money (beginning in 1861), and on many U. S. stamps.

Postcard publishers saw and depicted the selection of birds somewhat differently. The common theme on postcards and magazine covers often conveyed a similar idea.

Likewise, the Austin, Nichols Distilling Company, Lawrenceburg, Kentucky, in promoting *Wild Turkey*, its premium brand of bourbon, made turkey-shaped ceramic bottles over a period of eighteen years. In 1984, the company introduced the *Wild Turkey With Eagle* decanter in both regular and miniature sizes.

"Thanksgiving." **Artist: Emmett Watson.** *Colliers,* **November 28, 1931. In a patriotic color illustration the Thanksgiving Tom Turkey presents a dominant visage over the bald eagle (at least for a day)! $40-50.**

Wild Turkey Series 3, No. 4 with Eagle, 1984, miniature MIB. $50-70.

"Turkey and Eagle." Porcelain, 4.5" x 4.5". Made in Taiwan.

Contributions of John James Audubon

The quintessential depiction of an American Wild Turkey was originally part of a series of 435 life-size, full-color drawings by John James Audubon (1785-1851). Audubon was probably, along with John Muir, one of the greatest American naturalists. While his specialty was ornithology (the scientific study of birds), Audubon was the epitome of a natural history artist. From about 1808 until 1826, Audubon embarked on a series of travels throughout the eastern United States which resulted in a portfolio of more than two hundred full-size bird paintings and drawings. Obviously, in order to survive (he went bankrupt and ended up in debtors' prison due to a series of business failures), Audubon had to realize value from his efforts. He traveled to London, England where the printing technology and coloration of drawings was the greatest and where his "great works" were appreciated by willing and generous subscribers. This resulted in the publication of Audubon's *Birds of America* by Robert Havell, Jr., in four vol-

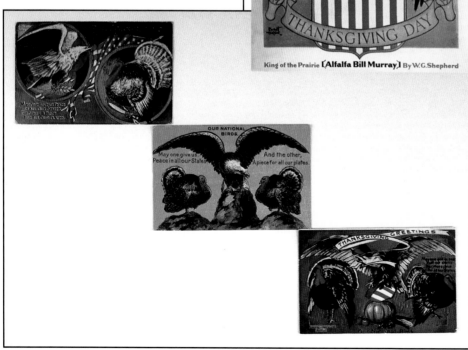

"Our National Birds," postmarked (L to R) Boston, Mass. Nov. 24, 1909; Buffalo, New York, Nov. 23, 1909; Columbus, Ohio, Nov. 19, 1908. $5-10 each.

umes released over a twelve-year period from 1826 to 1838. Each set contained 1,065 life-size prints of 489 different species of birds, on 435 separate plates, reproduced on a double elephant folio paper measuring 29-1/2 inches in width x 39-1/2 inches in height. It is estimated that between 171 to 176 complete sets were produced at a full-subscriber price from $870 to $1000 per set depending upon binding. All pictures were first painted in watercolor by Audubon between 1808 and 1838. These watercolors were turned into prints by the method of aquatint engraving on copper plates. Each print then had to be colored by hand (the bird(s) and their natural environment) in from two to six different colors and tints. It is estimated that no more than 125 complete sets have survived today. In a highly interesting article in *The Magazine Antiques*, October 2003, pages 103-113, titled "Cutting Up Audubon for Science and Art," the author, Robert McCracken Peck, discusses the status of the remaining 125 copies. This is important given, as we will soon see, the steady escalation in prices realized by the recent sales of separate copies of this double folio.

On November 26, 1826, the proof of Plate I, the *Great American Cock Male* (Wild Turkey) was completed. The original picture was painted by Audubon at Beech Woods Plantation, West Feliciana Parish, in central Louisiana in 1825 and modeled after a composition of several Tom Turkeys which the artist shot. This particular plate is the most famous of all the prints and usually commands the highest price, either at auction or from reputable fine art print dealers. There are several examples to cite: (1) Sotheby's (London) held a rare prints auction in 1987 with many of the Havell Edition bird prints for sale. The featured print was the Wild Turkey with a pre-sale estimate of $25,000; (2) Christie's (New York) auction in September 1987 sold the entire 435 print Havell folio sheet by sheet. The Wild Turkey (Plate 1) sold for $22,000 including 10% Buyer's Premium; (3) Sotheby's (New York) auction in June 1989 sold the Wild Turkey (Plate 1) for $13,000 excluding the 10% Buyer's Premium; and (4) Sotheby's (New York) auction of H. Bradley Martin's magnificent library of Audubon's books and manuscripts sold an entire Havell double elephant folio edition of 435 hand-colored etched plates in "exceptionally fine condition" for $3.6 million net. And, in London, in 1999, another single set sold for $8.3 million, a 2.3 times increase in only ten years. In today's market the same Plate I (depending on condition) would sell in the range of $95,000 to $125,000, and the companion Wild Turkey Hen, Plate VI, would sell from $50,000 to $65,000.

Auction Catalogues. L to R: Christie's (New York) John James Audubon. *The Birds of America*. Sale No. 6436, September 14/15, 1987. (Property of The Buffalo Society of Natural Sciences.) Sotheby's (New York) John James Audubon. *The Birds of America*. Sale No. 5889, June 23/24/1989. (Property of George Peabody Library of The John Hopkins University). $20-25 each.

Sotheby's Auction Catalogue showing "Wild Turkey – Male (Plate 1). $15,000-20,000 estimate for actual print.

Portrait of John James Audubon after Henry Inman (1801-1846) American School. Original portrait painted c.1831-1833. From Christie's (New York) Auction Catalog *John James Audubon and His Circle*. Sale No. 7756, October 29, 1993. $5000-7,000 estimate for actual portrait.

Sotheby's (New York) *The Library of H. Bradley Martin, John James Audubon, Magnificent Books and Manuscripts.* Auction catalogue. Sale No. 5870, June 6, 1989. $15-18.

Portrait of John James Audubon by John Woodhouse Audubon (son). c.1830s. From Sotheby's Martin Library Catalog.

After the Havell Edition, Audubon turned his attention to producing a smaller version of his work (one-eighth the size of a double elephant folio) to appeal to a wider range of subscribers. This was called *The First Royal Octavo Edition*, and was first published in Philadelphia by John T. Bower from 1839 to 1844. This seven-volume edition consisted of 500 hand-colored lithographs, 435 from the Havell Edition and the additional 65 based on new bird discoveries. It is estimated that 1,200 sets of the first Octavo edition (size 9.75" x 6.38") were produced and sold to at least 1,050 subscribers at a total price of from $100 to $120 depending on binding. To better understand Audubon, his background, and the forces that compelled him to create great works of naturalistic ornithological art, three books among many are quite informative. Details can be found in the bibliography.

Sotheby's (London) Print Auction Catalogue. Sale April, 1987. $17-20.

Right:
Books: L to R: *Audubon's America*. $70-100; *Audubon: Great National Work (The Royal Octavo Edition)*. $35-40; *Audubon's Birds of America (Popular Edition)*. $25-30.

Partly because the moderate pricing of the Royal Octavo edition of *Birds of America* was in reach of the majority of literate Americans, the book continued to enjoy great popularity through a succession of nine reprints ending in 1889. In 1890, a partial rendering of the Octavo edition was published when the state of Pennsylvania used ninety-nine chromolithographic copies of Audubon prints in B.H. Warren's *Report on the Birds of Pennsylvania*. When the book came out, a debate was sparked on whether chromolithographic prints were in fact superior to the hand-colored originals in terms of richness versus brilliant color. The subtlety of the colors of Audubon's original prints with regards to the bird(s), foliage, and flowers had a distinction of its own that latter day chromos would find hard to duplicate.

"Wild Turkey" Male, Plate #74, 11" x 14", from *Birds of Pennsylvania*, published by E.K. Meyers of Harrisburg, PA, 1890. $75-100.

Due to the reemergence of the popularity of naturalist artists like Audubon during the environment movement of the 1970s and beyond, there have been two complete facsimile editions produced of the entire *Birds of America* on double elephant folio paper. The first was produced by the Johnson Reprint Corporation (New York) and Theatrum Orbis Terrarum (Amsterdam) in the 1971 to 1973 time frame. This edition of only 250 produced sets sold for $6,960 in 1973. The second complete facsimile edition was produced by Abbeville Press in 1985. The four, leatherbound editions sold for $15,000. However, thirty of the most popular of the original 500 bird(s) prints were reproduced in a book titled *The Audubon Folio - 30 Great Bird Paintings*. Naturally, the Wild Turkey Gobbler was included in all its splendor. A Chicago-based fine arts firm in conjunction with the Chicago Field

Museum is utilizing their original folio by offering Audubon's *Fifty Best*©. This is a facsimile edition of fifty, full-sized, double elephant folio prints of the first Audubon edition of *Birds of America*. There are only 150 numbered sets, one-half are being sold complete for $37,500 each, while the individual sheets of the other 75 sets are being sold separately. The Wild Turkey print is selling for $2,800 and the Hen for $2,500.

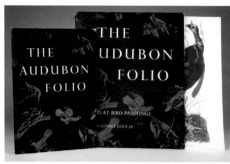

Folio, Book and Print "The Audubon Folio": Text by George Dock, Jr., (C)1964, Harry N. Abrams, Inc. New York, 14" x 17". $50.

The Wild Turkey – Close To Extinction?

Regretfully, in the 150 years since Audubon's death at least four North American birds have become extinct. They are the (1) Passenger Pigeon; (2) Carolina Parrot (parakeet); (3) Great Auk; and (4) Labrador Duck. Several others such as the (1)Whooping Crane; (2) California Condor; and (3) Ivory-billed Woodpecker are on the verge of extinction. Even though birds in general have great "powers of adaption," many species have been decimated beyond natural recovery due to the rapid acceleration of the tempo of east to west urbanization. Due to the relentless surge of human populations moving ever westward across the American continent from the time of the Civil War to the end of World War I, much habitat important to the survival of many wild animal species was destroyed. This movement enabled civilization to exploit the natural ecosystem and destroy the natural habitats by unrestrained lumbering of the forests and the drainage of marshes which nature provided. Added to this, a large list of birds suffered predatory onslaughts from intensely destructive methods such as market gunning, night shooting, fire, lighting (not lightning), netting, and trapping. During these times virtually no bird was afforded any legal protection, and hunting season existed almost all year around with no bag limits whatsoever. What the market and sport shooting did not accomplish was carried out by the poor and needy, who looked upon trash birds and their eggs as a source of protein. Lastly, the fashion mores of the time further depleted many species solely for their showy plumes and feathers. In the mid-twentieth century, ecologists warned about and were successful in banning many pesticides such as DDT, which was highly interruptive of the birds' gestation cycles.

Audubon's name has become indelibly associated with the formation of the country's

first bird preservation organization, the Audubon Society (www.audubon.org). Today, this society has expanded its mission to include the development of major new environmental protection policies and laws coordinated through 500 chapters nationwide.

The American Wild Turkey also suffered grievously due to the relentless exploitation by hunters for the domestic food markets, the elimination of much of their original woodlands habitat, as well as specific turkey-related diseases and parasites, all of which contributed to the rapid decline of the original turkey population. Due to their importance as a major source of protein in the food supply chain, wild turkeys were hunted almost to extinction, except for pockets where extreme terrain conditions protected them. It has been estimated that at the time of Christopher Columbus's discovery of America, approximately 40 million wild turkeys existed throughout the North American continent including Mexico. By the Great Depression, some 450 years later, wild turkeys had virtually disappeared from 18 of the 39 states that were part of their historical range. At its low point, the turkey population was estimated at 30,000, while occupying only 12% to 15% of its former range in the United States.

However, help was on its way! In 1937, the Federal Aid in Wildlife Restoration Act was enacted at the request of hunters and sportsmen. This Act imposed an excise tax on hunting equipment with the proceeds earmarked for wildlife conservation projects such as the purchase and protection of wildlife habitats. This was the start of a nationwide wildlife restoration program with federal financial assistance resulting in the initiation of a better wildlife conservation philosophy. Two important relief measures were imposed: (1) hunting regulations and game laws were enacted and enforced, and (2) trap-transplant-restocking programs were undertaken with much vigor. By the late 1950s, wild turkey restoration was well advanced to the point where the turkey had reoccupied most of the states from which it had formerly been extirpated, and was well established in areas beyond its original range. Now, some 57 years later, wild turkey populations occur in 49 of the 50 U.S. states (Alaska excluded), and it is estimated by the National Wild Turkey Federation that 6.4 million turkeys presently exist in the wild.

"Autumn Trio" color lithograph. Artist: Mark Anderson, signed and numbered print #378/400. Image size 19.75" x 14.75". Late 1990s. $50-75 (unframed).

Wild Turkey Classification

There are five subspecies of the wild turkey in the temperate region of North America and, together with all the varieties of domestic turkeys, they comprise a single highly variable species, *Meleagris gallopavo.* In the western United States there are three wild turkey subspecies: Merriam's Wild Turkey (*Meleagris gallopavo merriami*), Gould's (*Mg mexicana*) and Rio Grande (*Mg intermedia*). The western subspecies have whiter body feather markings and shorter legs than wild turkeys in the eastern United States.

In several respects, the western species does resemble the domestic bronze turkey and is, in fact, genetically closer in relationship to domestic turkeys than to its eastern subspecies counterparts. In the eastern United States, there are two wild turkey subspecies: Eastern (*Mg silvestris*) and Florida (*Mg osceola*). The eastern wild turkey is the most widely distributed, abundant, and the largest of the five distinct subspecies. It and the Florida turkey are also somewhat darker in appearance than their western cousins.

"Wild Turkey (Meleagris gallopavo)" color print. Artist: J. Lockhart. Autumn scene. 15" x 12". $25-30.

"Wild Turkey (Meleagris gallopavo)" color print. Artist: J. Lockhart. Winter scene. 15" x 12". $25-30.

Physical Characteristics of the Wild Turkey

The American Wild Turkey is the largest species of game-birds on the continent. The mature Tom (gobbler) stands four feet high with a wingspan up to six feet and weighs from twenty to thirty pounds on average depending upon the sub-species. The head and neck color of the adult gobbler is characterized by a patriotic combination of red (*caruncles,* i.e., fleshy protuberances), white (crown) and blue (bare skin of the neck). The *snood* is the limp, finger-like hanging appendage between the bill and the forehead while the *dewlap* is the pinkish flap of skin that hangs directly from under the throat. The word *wattle* is usually used as a combination term to include both the snood and the dewlap. Other distinguishing gobbler characteristics include a plumage of an iridescent metallic sheen, a bristly "beard" growing from the breast of over 10 inches in length and sharp leg spurs exceeding 1.5 inches. By comparison, mature hens are smaller in size by nearly one-half, possess none of the distinctive secondary sexual characteristics on the neck, and also lack beards and spurs. The hen's overall body color lacks the tom's metallic iridescent sheen. Typically, hens are brownish in color with light-edged body feathers when seen in good light. Nearly two months after mating, the Hen begins to lay her brown-speckled eggs, typically in a *clutche* consisting of eight to thirteen eggs which require about twenty-five days of continuous incubation. The hatchlings are called *poults* and weigh about two ounces at birth. As male poults grow in size they become yearling gobblers or *jakes* within six months of birth. Approximately one year later they exhibit all the characteristics of adult gobblers and join larger adult gobbler flocks.

"Wild Turkey" chromolithograph from *"Nests and Eggs of the Birds of the United States"*, illustrated by Thomas G. Gentry, published by J. A. Wagenseller of Philadelphia, Pennsylvania. 13" x 16". 1882. $90-100.

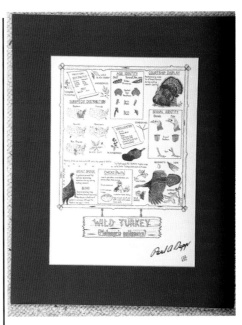

"Wild Turkey (Meleagris gallopavo)" brown and white lithograph. Artist: Paul A. Depp, signed and numbered #138/200. 11.5" x 16.75". $30-40.

At this adult stage, the gobbler is ready to attract a suitable Hen for mating purposes. For this the Tom Turkey displays mating plumage as well as other physical and vocal characteristics to gain the attention of a potential mate.

"Wild Turkey" color print No. 170. Artist: Ray Harm, signed. 20" x 24". Published by The Frame House Gallery, Inc. 1970. $50-75.

Wild turkeys are highly adaptable birds but need three elements: (1) fresh water; (2) trees at least fifteen to twenty feet in height in which to roost; and (3) differing seasonal habitats where they can feed, breed, and rest. What constitutes a good habitat depends upon the sub-species of the turkey. It is not uncommon for an adequate home range to be from one thousand to five thousand acres, given the magnitude of the three elements. The outstanding survival characteristic of the wild turkey is its highly developed sense of acute vision and hearing. The turkey's keen eyesight (a monocular 300-degree arc) allows him to ascertain movement, contrast, detail, and color almost instantaneously and very accurately. Therefore, the turkey's nervous temperament or "wildness" keeps him always on edge and ever alert for danger from every sort of predator. However, his weak spot is his poor nocturnal vision, which makes him vulnerable to night feeding predators. To avoid these problems, turkeys optimize their defenses by flocking together (safety in numbers!) and by roosting in tall trees which provide nighttime safety. If the wild turkey is caught out in the open, it can either fly for short distances up to 55 mph or run up to 22 mph to escape danger. This speed is necessary for, in many regions, the number one predator of turkeys is the free ranging feral dog.

While the information is somewhat dated, an interesting article titled "Fowls of Forest and Stream Tamed by Man" appeared in the March 1930 issue of *The National Geographic Magazine*. This article discussed the many attributes of wild and domestic turkeys (as well as other fowl), highlighted by beautiful paintings from life by Hashime Murayama.

L to R: "A Band of Turkeys, Turkey Farm, Near Sacramento, Cal," published by G. Knapp, Milwaukee, Wis., #3270, postmarked Sacramento, Ca., October 3, 1903, $5-7; "A Turkey Farm, Grandview, Wash," photo card, c.1920s, $5-10; "Turkeys Imperial Valley, California," published by Western Publishing, Los Angeles, Cal, c.1920s, $3-5.

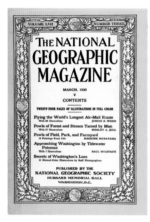

"The National Geographic Magazine." March 1930 issue. Cover. $25+.

Plate X. "Bronze Turkeys."

Plate XI. "White Holland Turkeys."

Domestic Production and Consumption

While the emphasis in this chapter has been on the American Wild Turkey, some mention should be made regarding the domestic turkey industry. Turkey production in the United States has more than tripled since 1970, reaching a high point in 1996 with approximately 303 million turkeys raised. In 2003, United States growers have raised 269.2 million turkeys from over 6,000 farms, generating some $2.7 billion in farm income. The top five turkey producing states for 2003 were (1) North Carolina (45.9 million); (2) Minnesota (45.5 million); (3) Missouri (27.5 million); (4) Arkansas (24.0 million); and (5) Virginia (23.0 million). The leading domestic turkey processor (1.21 billion pounds live weight) is Cargill, followed closely by Jennie O Turkey Store and Butterball Turkey Company. Mexico is by far the largest export market for U.S. turkey meat, accounting for 186 thousand pounds. Turkey production has made extraordinary advances over the past seventy-five years in terms of improvements in genetics, feed, disease control, and management practices. In the West, especially in California where turkeys were raised on the range as opposed to full or partial confinement as in the East, domestic turkeys suffered nutritional deficiencies due to the lack of "green feed." Now turkeys, regardless of growing conditions, are fed a balanced diet of corn and soybean meal mixed with a supplement of vitamins and minerals. Hens, which typically are sold as whole dressed birds, take fourteen weeks and weigh thirteen pounds at maturity before slaughter.

"A Flock of Turkeys," divided back, postally unused, published by Edw. H. Mitchell, San Francisco, Ca. #3267, c.1920s, $5-10.

During the last three decades, the consumption of turkey meat has evolved from a single-product, holiday-oriented main meal dish into a year-around diversified product line for all daily meals. Today, only 30% of turkey consumed is during the holiday period. In 2002, U.S. consumption of turkey was 17.75 pounds per person, an increase of 256% since 1970, when consumption was only 8 pounds per person. Likewise, turkey meat is the fourth protein source for American consumers behind chicken (80.5 pounds per capita), beef (67.6 pounds), and pork (51.5 pounds). Turkey consumption can still make great strides as chicken consumption still exceeds that of turkey by a factor of 4.5 to 1.

For further information concerning not only the wild turkey but also the domestic turkey industries, contact the National Wild Turkey Federation, Edgefield, South Carolina (www.nwtf.org or 1-800-THE-NWTF) or the National Turkey Federation, Washington D.C. (www.turkeyfed.org or 1-202-898-0100).

Books: L to R: *Turkey Management*, Marsden and Martin, 1939. $35-50; *The Book of the Wild Turkey*, Lovett E. Williams, Jr., 1981. $25-35; *The Wild Turkey and Its Management*, Oliver H. Hewitt, Ed., 1967. $150-175; *The American Wild Turkey*, Henry E. Davis, 1949. $225-250; *All About Turkeys*, Jim Arnosky, 1998. $17-20; **Pamphlets:** *The Purina Turkey Book, The Larro Turkey Book, Growing Turkeys* (Cornell Extension Bulletin #717), and *The Turkey Breeding Flock* (Cornell Extension Bulletin #912), each $5-7.

Chapter 3
THE THANKSGIVING TABLE

Wherever the earliest explorers to America first set foot, be it the areas now known as Texas, Florida, Maine, or Virginia, a simple Thanksgiving service was held in gratitude for their safe trip and arrival. However, none of these first visits resulted in any settlements of lasting duration. But with the Pilgrims, perseverance and a fortuitous set of circumstances were instrumental in keeping this colony at a subsistence level necessary for survival and eventual growth. Therefore, it was in October of 1621, one year after the Pilgrims' landing at Plymouth, that Governor Bradford felt confident to proclaim a day of thanksgiving to God based on the successful harvest of their first crops. According to one of the only firsthand accounts of the post-harvest celebration, Edward Winslow, one of the Pilgrim Fathers, wrote:

"Our harvest being gotten in, our Governour sent foure men fowling, so that we might after a more special manner rejoice together, after we had gathered the fruit of our labours; they foure in one day killed as much fowle, as with a little helpe beside, served the Company almost a weeke…"

Certainly this early Thanksgiving celebration included a prayer service under the watchful eye of an armed Pilgrim.

Illustrations. 10.5" x 16". L to R: *Harpers Weekly*, New York, December 2, 1882, "At the Church Door – A Puritan Thanksgiving." Artist: W. H. Low; *Harper's Bazar*, New York, December 15, 1887. "The First Thanksgiving, New Plymouth, 1621." Artist: W. L. Sheppard. $25-30 each.

This proclamation, which culminated in a three-day feast and celebration, had four purposes: (1) to thank the Lord for His goodness for insuring the survival of the colony through its very difficult first year; (2) to celebrate the bountiful harvest that would reasonably guarantee future continuance of the colony; (3) to thank the Indians for their unestimable assistance in helping the colonists to avoid starvation; and (4) to establish a lasting unity between the Wampanoag Indians and the English settlers.

The Pilgrims' three-day festival is credited by most scholars as the beginning of what we Americans have come to know and enjoy as "Thanksgiving." The first so-called "feast" had to feed 146 people relying solely upon the available resources at hand. Suffice to say, this first "banquet" consisted of *Fowle, Deere, Fishe,* corn, squash, pumpkins, and whatever other wild fruits and greens could be added. To the participants, especially the settlers who lacked most types of food stuffs, this was an epicurean event.

For nearly fifty years, this treaty held fast, with each group relying upon the other in a "give-and-take" relationship.

Photogravure. "The First Thanksgiving At Plymouth – 1621." Artist: J.L.G. Ferris. *After they had gathered their first harvest in America in 1621, the Pilgrim Fathers set aside a time for Thanksgiving and rejoicing. Their Indian friends visited them and for three days, they all feasted upon hasty pudding, clam chowder, wild fowl, and venison. $10.*

Poster. 14" x 17" *Dispatch Photo News Service*, New York, November 20, 1940. "Dress Rehearsal For a Turkey Dinner." Rehearsal for a realistic re-enactment of the First Thanksgiving Day, with all the trimmings, was held at Plymouth Mass., scene of the first New England settlement. $20-25.

Humorous Illustration. 8.5" x 11". *Life*. New York, no date. "The Original Thanksgiving Day in Old Plymouth." Artist: Harrison Cady. When development runs amok. $15-20.

Humorous sketch. 10.5" x 15" *Collier's The National Weekly*, New York, November 21, 1908. "Priscilla and the Pumpkin or An Indian Meal." Artist: R.F. Thomson. A Thanksgiving Episode of Colonial Days. $25-30.

Eventually this peace, born of mutual support and trust, eroded and, by 1675, a full-scale war had erupted between the descendants of both the Pilgrims and the Indians. By the time this war came to an end, eleven years later, the Pilgrims and many other successor groups of colonists had firmly established a foothold in New England.

Over the next 175 years, the observance of Thanksgiving became more frequent among individual states with the various Governors issuing proclamations to that effect.

As the exploration of America pushed our frontiers ever westward, there was a certain mindset among these settlers for keeping certain traditions intact so as to retain some of their past happy experiences. In 1846, Horace Greeley, an important editor and political leader of that day, touched upon these sentimental emotions by calling out to these "new" pilgrims…"Come home to Thanksgiving! Dear children, come home! From the Northland and the South, from West and the East, Where'er ye are resting, where'er ye roam, Come back to this sacred and annual feast."

Currier & Ives, important lithographers of that era (1857-1907), keenly tapped those nostalgic memories by issuing one of their most memorable prints entitled "Home to Thanksgiving." As we shall soon see, this scene has been reproduced on many Thanksgiving platters and plates. The following excerpt of the famous 6-stanza poem by Lydia Maria Child offers her view of "Thanksgiving Day":

"Over the river and through the wood,
To grandfather's house we'll go;
The horse knows the way
To carry the sleigh
Through the white and drifted snow…
Over the river and through the wood
Now grandmother's cap I spy!
Hurrah for the fun!
Is the pudding done?
Hurrah for the pumpkin pie!"

Some years later, in the depths of the American Civil War on October 3, 1863, President Abraham Lincoln, in an effort to promote a spirit of national unity, declared Thanksgiving day a national holiday. Now "official" feasting became a national pastime.

Important illustrated magazines of the 1860s, 1870s, and 1880s, such as *Harper's Weekly*, portrayed Thanksgiving in many ways – humorously, such as "turkey vs. man," or sentimentally, evoking fond memories of the past.

Illustrations. 10.5" x 15". L to R: *Harper's Bazar*, New York. December 15, 1877. "Preparing For Thanksgiving." Top: "Carving the Turkey." Bottom: "Estimating the Pumpkin." Artist: Abbey. $15-20; *Harper's Weekly*, New York, December 7, 1878. "A Dream, Before and After Thanksgiving Dinner." Artist: Thomas Nast. Hand colored. $40-50.

Harper's Weekly, New York. November 26, 1881. 11" x 16". "Who Said Anything About Thanksgiving Dinner?" Artist: Thomas Nast. $35-40.

Illustrations. 10.5" x 15.5". L to R: *Harper's Weekly*, New York, November 9, 1881. "Thirty-two Pounds, Massa"; *Harper's Weekly*, New York, November 26, 1881. "Done Brown, Sho's Yo'Bo'n!" Artist (both) J.W. Alexander. $35-40 each.

Print, reproduction. *Carrier's Ives*, New York City (1835-1907), "Home To Thanksgiving." **Original c.1857-1887. $20-25.**

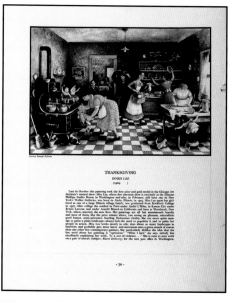

"Thanksgiving" Artist: Doris Enrick Lee (1904-1983). The original lithograph was painted in 1963 and portrays a lively farmhouse kitchen scene. This painting won first prize at the Chicago Art Institute's annual show. Most of Doris Lee's artwork had a naturalistic, semi-caricature look. $10-15 (art book print).

Harper's Weekly, New York, December 9, 1871. 15.25" x 10.75". "Thanksgiving At a New England Farmhouse." Artist: F.A. Chapman. $30-35.

While there was a huge market for illustrated journals and magazines, human to human intervention was lacking, especially when disparate families were separated by many miles and telephone and telegraph communications were not well established. But with the advent of the colorfully lithographed "penny" postcards in 1901, people were now able to share the symbolism of Thanksgiving in all of its many guises. These cards could be both sentimental in their appeal or amusing, showing the plight of the frantic turkey escaping the axe.

Postcards. L to R: A young cook with angel wings sharpens his knife as he is ready to serve the turkey in a scene decorated with pink carnations and candles, Embossed, Series 113B; Two cooks are presenting the Thanksgiving dinner, "May your Thanksgiving This year, Be full of good cheer," Embossed, Series 7017; Two children dressed in their bright red coats bring a pie to share with their family, printed Fairman Co., New York. $10-15 each.

Leslie's Weekly, New York, November, 1901. 10.75" x 16". "The Story of the Man Who Always Got the Wishbone and of the Wise Old Turkey Who Thought He Knew What. A Thanksgiving Threnody." Artist: Albert Levering. $25-30.

Six postcards depicting various Thanksgiving dinners as they are enjoyed by all. L to R, Top: Embossed, Series 566, notations in German on back side; A black family looks forward to their turkey, Embossed, Series 226; A message written, "Dear Cousin, Wish this was our picture having dinner together, don't you?", Series 716.
Bottom: A gold border decorated with fruits and flowers enhances the scene of the children dressed in their finery for Thanksgiving, Embossed, Series 2096, Gottschalk, Dreyfuss & Davis, publisher, Drawing ©1909 B. Hoffman; Artist H.B. Griggs poses the thought, "The First Thanksgiving Dinner-Party!" (a Pilgrim and Indian?), Leubrie & Elkus publisher, Embossed, Series 2263; Copyrighted 1907 by Fred Lounsbury with a poem, "And the children…should bless God for those brave Pilgrims and their first Thanksgiving Day." $10-15 each.

Subsequent chapters will delve more deeply into the use of illustrations and post-cards to commemorate this national holiday. The purpose of this chapter is to focus on the Thanksgiving table – the accessories and accoutrements that make eating a fine Thanksgiving dinner a pleasure, not only for the stomach but also for the eyes.

The following pages offer a comprehensive overview of platters, plates, and virtually every other tableware item that celebrates the turkey and its image in some appealing way. Cookbooks and menus round out this extensive chapter.

Thanksgiving Dinner, Anthony Dias Blue and Kathrn K. Blue. Harper Collins: New York. 208 pages. 1990. $20.

Platters

Match a large platter with a turkey motif, and you have the penultimate "King Tom" of Thanksgiving collectibles, the **Turkey platter**. In the American kitchens of the 1700s and 1800s, one would find all manner of wooden pieces, called *treen* (defined as "made of tree") used for preparing, serving, and storing food. **Wooden ware** was virtually the only kitchenware that was available to be used by most poor and rural folk as well as settlers on their westward migration. The wooden platters of that era were called trenchers (the term "trencher" is a derivative of the French verb, *trenchier*, meaning "to carve meat") and were used to serve large portions of meat or fowl. As both sides of the trencher platter were sometimes used for both serving and eating food, this woodenware was not decorated or painted.

In the Eastern seaboard regions of the United States, the "landed gentry" and others of wealth usually relied on imported **ceramic platters** and associated **plateware** from England for dining purposes. This was the norm until a fledgling pottery industry in America got its start in Ohio in the early 1870s. Before and after World War I, both British and American potteries vied for the honor of placing their products in the kitchens and dining rooms of the American consumer. There were several important distinctions between the two protagonists. English exports, until the end of the eighteenth century, were made for those wealthy enough to afford hand-painted decorative wares. Then a technological design change took place that revolutionized the industry. The **transfer printing process** made its debut in Caughley, Shropshire, England in the mid-1700s. Thomas Turner, a potter, developed a method for using tissue paper to "transfer" concise and detailed designs from inked hand-engraved copper plates to white-and-cream-bodied earthenware. As the technique improved over the next thirty years, it allowed entire sets of matching dinner plates (to the platter) and various other tableware pieces to be mass-produced and sold at prices very affordable to America's growing middle class. A tremendous export market developed, as Americans were eager for both illustrations of historical events of national interest as well as scenes of American towns, sites, and landscapes. While cobalt blue was the only color used by manufacturers for decades, eventually English potters began to master other colors, including shades of brown, red, mulberry, purple, and green.

Meanwhile, the indigenous American potters, while not competing directly with their English brethren, concentrated on producing mid-range tableware and sanitary goods for the expanding consumer market. American consumers typically sought out relatively inexpensive but good *decal* decorated (viz. printed transfers) white earthenware (called semi-porcelain or semi-vitreous) dinner platters and sets. This competition lasted until the advent of World War II. After the war was over, new and cheaper competition from abroad came mainly from Japan as well as other parts of Asia and Italy. Also, inexpensive materials such as hard plastics made serious inroads into the earthenware markets. In the ensuing forty years, most American potteries closed their doors, unable to compete against the onslaught of foreign goods.

As American consumers seem ready to once again embrace traditional turkey motifs on their platters, a brown transferware reproduction turkey platter is being sold by Williams-Sonoma, the San Francisco-based purveyor of gourmet kitchen products (www.williams-sonoma.com). Produced by Josiah Wedgwood & Sons, this large oval glazed transferware platter, 19.5" x 15.25", sells for $98 and has been a seasonal best seller since it was first introduced in 2001.

As defined, a turkey platter is a large serving plate, usually at least 16 inches in length. While the purely decorative turkey-motif enhances the value of the platter, the roast turkey itself becomes the center of focus at the critical moment of serving, when the platter design elements are hidden.

Platter materials include porcelain, ceramic, stoneware, glass, and metal. Since the various generic forms of ceramics can be both mystifying and intimidating to the collector, we have included a glossary of common terms at the end of this chapter.[1]

From the traditional to the new, the following images of turkey platters show the diversity and depth of this dinner table icon gathered from many countries.

American Platters

The East Liverpool area of Ohio has spawned many important American potteries beginning in the early 1870s. The abundance of local raw materials (viz. clay, coal, natural gas, and water) coupled with good transportation links provided the wherewithal for the start up of many successful firms. The *Homer Laughlin China Company*, founded by the brothers Homer and Shakespeare Laughlin in 1874, has been among the largest and most successful of all domestic potteries. Today, Homer Laughlin is one of the world's largest producers of institutional and retail tableware including *Fiesta*, the company's most famous pattern. As we will observe, Homer Laughlin made Thanksgiving platters of different shapes based on many of their popular dinnerware lines. Most of Homer Laughlin's decorative ware lines utilized decals (viz. printed transfers) as colorful design elements. On their turkey platters, Homer Laughlin used the same Tom Turkey decal (facing left) with a full fanned tail as part of a rural farmyard scene. Depending on the size of the platter, the decal was sized to fit. It is not known who designed this decal. Germany was the source of many decals or, possibly, Homer Laughlin's own art director, Don Schreckengost, has been suggested as the originator of the turkey decal. More likely, it was designed by a nameless artist who was employed by one of the many decalcomania firms serving the regional potteries. Since platters and plates made by other American manufacturers have employed the same decal or a close variant, the actual genesis of same remains a mystery.

Platter. 15"L x 13"W; Homer Laughlin. *Eggshell Cavalier* (style and shape). Lightweight oval, white base with 1.5" skytone turquoise blue rim edged in gold. Tom Turkey decal. Mark: "Eggshell Cavalier by Homer Laughlin USA C56N5" (made March 1956 at Plant No. 4-Newell, WV). $60-65.

Platter/Plate. L to R: 15.5"L x 12"W; Homer Laughlin. *Eggshell Nautilus* (style and shape). Lightweight oval. White base with 1.5" rim decorated with gold floral filigree. Tom Turkey decal. Mark: "Eggshell Nautilus USA H51N5" (made August 1951 at Plant No. 4 – Newell, WV). $60-65; Plate 9"D; Homer Laughlin (no marks), white base with 1.5" octagonal scalloped rim decorated with gold floral filigree. Tom Turkey decal. This common blank was outsourced in many cases to decorating firms to have decals applied before final glazing. c.1950s. $15-20.

Platter, 14"L x 12"W. Edwin M. Knowles China Co. (office – East Liverpool, Ohio; factory – Newell, West Virginia). Semi-vitreous oval shape. Ivory base, Tom Turkey decal with expanded scene. Marks: encased "K" with printed Knowles below; encircled "r." "USA 52-4"; signature "M. Moore". c.1950s. Knowles was founded in 1900 and closed in 1962. $40-45.

Backstamp showing "HL" cipher, company name, pattern style and shape, dates of manufacturing, and location.

Platter, 13.5"L x 11"W; Homer Laughlin, "Bountiful Harvest." Scene shows Pilgrims and Indians gathering food. Oval shape. Rose-pink, transfer printing. c.1955. $55-60.

Platter 15"L x 11"W; Embassy-USA. Vitrified china oval shape. White base with 1.5" medium green rim, outlined in gold trim both inner and outer. Tom Turkey decal. Marks: "Embassy-USA." c.1960s, $35-40.

Platter, 15.25"L x 12.5"W; Homer Laughlin, *Rhythm* (unmarked). Slim coupe style. Harlequin yellow, Tom Turkey decal. *Rhythm* was introduced in 1955 (based on the coupe shape) by designer Don Schreckengost. c.1955. $55-60.

Backstamp. "Bountiful Harvest." Rose-pink.

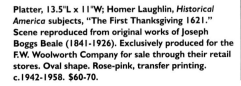

Backstamp. *Historical America.* Rose-pink.

Platter, 13.5"L x 11"W; Homer Laughlin, *Historical America* subjects, "The First Thanksgiving 1621." Scene reproduced from original works of Joseph Boggs Beale (1841-1926). Exclusively produced for the F.W. Woolworth Company for sale through their retail stores. Oval shape. Rose-pink, transfer printing. c.1942-1958. $60-70.

Platter, 13.75"L x 10.5"W; D.E. Mc Nicol Pottery Co., East Liverpool, Ohio. Semi-vitreous oval shape with handle extensions. White base with 1.75" deep scalloped rim in green luster and gold filigree inner trim. Expansive Tom Turkey decal. Marks: "D.E. Mc Nicol, East Liverpool, O." c.1915-1929. Mc Nicol was founded in 1892 and closed in 1954. $40-45.

Platter, 13.5"L x 10"W; Taylor, Smith & Taylor Company, Chester, West Virginia. Semi-porcelain oval coupe style. White base with 1.5" light green rim with gold floral filigree design. Tom Turkey decal. Marks: "Taylor-Smith-Taylor USA, Versatile, oven-proof 7-58-4." John Gilkes designed the *Versatile* shape, c. early 1950s-mid 1960s. T-S-T, founded in 1899, was sold to Anchor Hocking Glass Company in 1972. Production ceased in 1981. $35-40.

Platter/Plates. L to R: Candy dish 8"D; Statton (signed). White base, ornate scalloped rim with handle cut outs. Gold trim and burnishings. Tom Turkey decal (reversed image). c.1950s, $15-20; Cake Platter, 13.25"L x 12.25"W; No marks. White base with circular gold trim and handle extensions. Tom Turkey decal. c.1950s, $25-30; Plate, 9"D; *Painter's Palette*, cursive S on a palette image, "warranted 22K" – gold stamp. White base with 1.5" octagonal scalloped rim decorated with gold floral filigree. Tom Turkey decal. Sabin Industries, Inc., McKeesport, Pennsylvania (1946-1979) were primarily dinnerware decorators. c.1950s, $20-25.

Platters, Advertising Proprietary Premiums. L to R: 13.5"L x 10"W; Taylor, Smith & Taylor *Versatile* shape (unmarked). Sky blue, Tom Turkey decal. "Heard Furniture Co., 101 W. Grand Ave., Marshall, Texas." c. early 1950s–mid 1960s; 13.5"L x 11"W; Taylor *Shadow* shape so marked. White base with 1.5" granite gray rim decorated in a low-relief floral design. Tom Turkey decal. "Compliments of Bewley Furniture Company, Shreveport, Louisiana." c. mid 1960s. $25-30 each.

Stock decal. *Tom Turkey* image. This is one of several variants of the Tom Turkey decals with a full fanned tail. Although this image may have originated in Germany, it was a stock item at one of the decalcomania firms operating in the Ohio/West Virginia region. c.1950s to 1960s. $5.

Platter/Plate. L to R: 13"L x 12.5"W; No marks. White base with a 1.5" scalloped rim trimmed in gold. Handle extension. Tom Turkey decal. c.1950s, $25-30; Plate. 10"D; Homer Laughlin. *Rhythm*. White base with gold trim on rim. Tom Turkey decal. Marks: "Rhythm by Homer Laughlin USA ® J55N5" (Made October 1955 at Plant No. 4 – Newell, WV). $20-25.

Platters, L to R: 13.5"L x 10"W; No marks. Oval shape, white base with 1.25" light green rim, gold floral filigree design. Tom Turkey (right facing) with pine tree branch decal. c.1950s, $30-35; 13.75"L x 10.5"W; *Triomphe* ® USA Flintridge China Co. Oval shape, white base, dark green border with platinum rim trim. Tom Turkey (right facing) decal. Mark: "Triomphe ® USA. The founders of Flintridge China Co., Pasadena, California (1945-1970) developed a thinner and more durable form of china. In 1970, the firm was sold to Gorham, a division of Textron, Inc. c.1958. $30-35; 13.5"L x 11"W; Taylor, Smith & Taylor Company. Semi-porcelain oval coupe style, *Cathay* Taylorstone. White base with 1.5" rim decorated in blue and green pastels "modern" stylized design. Tom Turkey decal (right facing). Advertising premium: "Compliments of Teague Furniture Co., Lenoir, North Carolina." c. mid-1960s. $25-30.

In 1917, in the small eastern foothills town of Erwin, Tennessee, an inconspicuous little pottery was established by a railroad to promote industrial development for its shipping business. *Clinchfield Pottery* got its start by producing commercial semi-vitreous china tableware pieces decorated with stock decal applied patterns. In 1920, as a result of raising public money from a stock issue, the official name was changed to *Southern Potteries, Inc.* The renown trademark *Blue Ridge* first appeared about 1932 to better identify the company's output with its famous location. By the late 1930s, underglaze hand-painted decoration replaced most decals. The first designs were simple accent strokes but evolved into more complex patterns, based on, to a great extent, floral art work. When World War II halted the flow of imported chinaware to America, Southern Potteries took advantage of this and rushed to serve the expanding domestic market. The pottery became the largest producer of hand-painted china by the early 1950s, utilizing over 4,100 patterns on thirteen different pottery shapes in its annual production of 24 million pieces while employing over one thousand workers, one-half of whom were decorators and artists. Of these, some of the very best artists, numbering under ten, hand-painted and signed a very limited number of special designs on platters and other pieces. These pieces, typically done during and right after the war years, are extremely rare and, when available, command exceedingly high prices in the four-figure range among devoted collectors. Unfortunately, in the mid-1950s the same fate fell upon Southern Potteries as it had on most other domestic ceramics producers – a combination of cheap Japanese imports, escalating labor and materials costs, and new materials technologies such as Melmac forced the closure of the firm by 1957.

While the end came fast, the *Blue Ridge* line – under its distinctive circular logo stamp – has continued to attract collectors who are drawn to its uniquely American form of colorful hand-painted decoration.

Platter/Plate. L to R: 17.25"L x 13"W; Southern Potteries, Inc. *Blue Ridge* china, Clinchfield shape, hand-painted under glaze. "Thanksgiving Turkey." White base with four 2-leaf petals and stems on border. Rim edged in burlap green. Strutting Tom Turkey (facing right). No marks. c.1940s to 1957. $325+; Plate 10.25"D; Southern Potteries, Inc. *Blue Ridge* china, Skyline shape, hand-painted underglaze. "Thanksgiving Turkey." Marks: "Blue Ridge Southern Potteries 13L." c.1950s. $85+.

Platter, artist signed. 17.25"L x 13"W; Southern Potteries, Inc. *Blue Ridge* china, Clinchfield shape. Artist: Mildred L. Broyles. "Wild Turkey." White base with dark green and brown concentric border decoration. Woodland Tom Turkey at rest eyeing a choice bug. Marks: "Blue Ridge China Hand-painted. Underglaze Southern Potteries, Inc.," five line script backstamp. Artist signature in lower right periphery of scene detail. c. mid 1940s to mid 1950s. $2000+.

Platter/Plate. L to R: 17.25"L x 13"W; Southern Potteries, Inc. *Blue Ridge* china, Clinchfield shape (wide flat borders), hand-painted underglaze. "Turkey with Acorns." White base with alternating oak leaves and acorns on border. Rim edged in burlap brown. Tom Turkey (facing right) between haystacks. No marks. c.1940s to 1957. This Thanksgiving pattern is also found on the newer Skyline shape (1950 – no borders). Because of additional decoration elements, this pattern is more highly valued than the other Thanksgiving pattern. $400+; Plate 10.25"D; Southern Potteries, Inc., *Blue Ridge* china, Skyline shape, hand-painted underglaze. "Turkey with Acorns." Marks: "Blue Ridge Southern Potteries 14J." c.1950s. $100+.

Close-up of Mildred Broyles' signature on the artist-signed platter.

Platter. 19.25"L x 15.5"W; No manufacturer mark. White oval base, Oval shape, 2" scalloped rim edged in dark green, with multicolor fruits decoration. Multicolor hand-painted Tom Turkey. Mark: No marks. c.1970s. $30-35.

Platter. 19.25"L x 14.5"W; No manufacturer mark. Oval deep dish with undecorated 2" rim. White base, large hand-painted multicolor Tom Turkey. Indistinct marks, 1991? c.1990s. $30-35.

Platter, artist signed. 17.25"L x 13"W; Southern Potteries, Inc. *Blue Ridge* china, Clinchfield shape. Artist: Louise Gwinn. "Turkey Gobbler." White base with concentric yellow and brown border decoration. Tom Turkey is in a dark foreground woodland scene. Marks: "Blue Ridge China Hand Painted Underglaze Southern Potteries, Inc.," five line script backstamp. Artist signature is below the right set of wings on the periphery of the scene detail. c. mid 1940s to 1957. $1,750+.

Close-up of Louise Gwinn's signature on the artist signed platter.

Homer Laughlin and Southern Potteries occupied a very large space in the domestic production of decal and hand-painted dinner and tableware ceramics over much of the twentieth century. While these potteries were leaders in their field, there were many other potteries from California and elsewhere, which also established a niche in this very competitive arena. Whether the materials were ceramics or other mediums, holiday turkey platters were big sellers and were valued as family heirlooms and keepsakes. Many old platters exist in excellent shape today due to the care given and the fact that the platters were only used on a very random basis over the years.

Platter with box. 18.25"L x 14.5"W; Gladding McBean Company. Oval shape with a slight scalloped edge trimmed in brown. White base, large embossed hand-painted multicolor Tom Turkey with a 2.25" border decorated with multicolor produce items. Mark: Impressed "Made in California USA." Box: R 40 Turkey Platter-A Nasco Product." Gladding McBean (1875-1984), Glendale, California was not only the largest manufacturer of clay products in the USA but also made highly decorative dinnerware under the Franciscan name. In 1979, the firm was sold to Wedgwood, and production was moved to England in 1984 where it is still active today. c.1935-1940. $40-50.

Platters. L to R: 15.25"L x 11.5"W; Crown Potteries. Oval deep dish with scalloped rim trimmed in gold. White base, internal rim with a concentric thin gold stripe; Three Tom Turkey and Hen decals (facing right) of probable German origin. Marks: backstamp, light greenish blue of "crown" symbol and "C.P.Co." Crown Pottery(s) Company (1891-1955), Evansville, IN., made semi-porcelain and white granite dinner sets. c.1950s. $45-50; 12.5"L x 10.5"W; No marks. Oval serving platter/plate. Cream base, scalloped rim with crazing and some heat discoloration. Tom Turkey and Hen decal (facing right). Possibly an unmarked piece from Crown Potteries. c.1920s to 1930s. $15-20.

Platter. 19.75"L x 15.25"W; No manufacturer mark. Oval, deep dish with a 12-sided slightly scalloped rim. White base, large hand-painted multicolor Tom Turkey with a 3" border decorated with multicolor produce items. Mark: Small, flat "crown" symbol and "Made in Calif USA." c.1960s. $30-35.

Platter. 19.5"L x 14.25"W; No manufacturer mark. Oval deep dish with a heavy "clam shell" scalloped edge. Tan base shading to dark brown at the edges. Large embossed Tom Turkey. Mark: "CALIF USA PTK-1." c.1950s. $45-50.

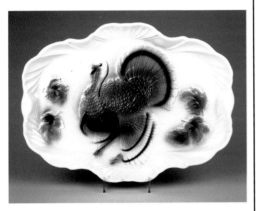

Platter. 18.5"L x 13.5"W; Lane & Company, Van Nuys, California. Rectangle shape with top and bottom extensions. White base, large embossed brown, tan, and green Tom Turkey, embossed oak leaves and border décor. Marks: "CALIF USA T-40." Lane & Company (1956-1967) was not a pottery manufacturer but a jobber/distributor. c.1959. $30-35.

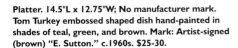

Platter. 14.5"L x 12.75"W; No manufacturer mark. Tom Turkey embossed shaped dish hand-painted in shades of teal, green, and brown. Mark: Artist-signed (brown) "E. Sutton." c.1960s. $25-30.

Platter. 16.5"L x 11.25"W; Nelson McCoy Pottery Company (1910-1990), Roseville, Ohio. Oval shallow coupe style with embossed relief of Tom Turkey and background features. Brown glaze. Mark: Stylized indented mold "McCoy 9370 USA oven proof." Part of *Cook and Serve* line. c.1950s to 1970s. $25-30.

Platter/Plate. 18.5"L x 13.75"W; Delano Studios, Setanket, Long Island, New York (1950s-1970s). Oval shape with a 2.25" rim. White base decorated with hand-colored Tom Turkey in flight. Border has four hand-colored designs: Tom Turkey, Tom Turkey with Hen and two leafy stems. Marks: stylized company mark "Decorated by (in ribbon banner) Delano Studios Setanket, L.I.N.Y." and "Hand-Colored." c.1960s. $30-35; Plate. 10.75"D; White base, hand-colored as above, 1.75" border rim trimmed in gold with an inner concentric gold stripe. Mark: "Decorated by Delano Studios Setanket L.I.N.Y. Dennis Ruleston." c.1960s. $20-25.

Platter. 15.5"L x 11"W; Pipestone, Freeland, Maryland. Oval shape having a dark gray concentric rim stripe encircling a 0.5" maroon checkerboard border trim. White base with a maroon stylized Tom Turkey design. Mark: Modernized buffalo mark "Buffalo 9508B" Backstamp: "Ancient Mimbréno-Indian Designs Replica from Santa Fe ATSF Dining Car Service." The original plate was made by Syracuse China and books for $300+ when available. The Tom Turkey design faces right. c.1990s. $90-100.

Plate/Platter. 12.5"D; Hadley Pottery Company, Louisville, Kentucky. Vitrified stoneware made from native clays. Light gray base with an underglaze stylized decoration of a whimsical Tom Turkey outlined in blue with added rust and green coloration. Rim borders outlined in blue with words "Happy Thanksgiving." Mark: M.A. Hadley Pottery signature. $25-30; Platter. 13.5"L x 9"W; Oval coupe style, vitrified stoneware. Light gray base with rim trimmed in blue. Underglaze design of whimsical Tom Turkey outlined in blue with added peach and green coloration. Mark: M.A. Hadley signature. The Hadley Pottery Company was founded in 1940 by M.A. (Mary Alice) Hadley, a Kentucky based artist. While Hadley died at 54 in 1965, the pottery continued to make dinnerware and other numerous ornamental pieces. Of the sixteen patterns currently in production, 95% of them are M.A. Hadley originals based on her freehand folkloric style. c.1990s. $60-75.

Platter. 21"L x 15"W; Brookpark. Oval deep dish with a 2.25" rim border decorated with a multicolor oak leaf garland. White base, large decaled multicolor Tom Turkey with a colorful Pilgrim background scene. *Melmac*, a melamine plastic product. Mark: Impressed "Brookpark 1521." c.1960s. $15-20.

Platters. L to R: 21"L x 15"W; Brookpark. 20.75"L x 14.5"W; Apollo Ware. Oval deep dish with a 2.25" rim decorated with a gold, brown and rust floral garland. White base, large decaled dark brown Tom Turkey with a farm barnyard background scene. *Melmac* plastic. Mark: Impressed "Apollo Ware Melmac by (script) Alexander Barna." c.1960s. $15-20.

Platter. 22.5"L x 16.25"W; Wendell August Forge, Grove City, Pennsylvania (1923 to present). Oval deep dish, 2.75" rim border with two handle cutouts. Hammered aluminum, large embossed Tom Turkey in strong relief. Mark: Indent stamp (in circle) "Hand Made Wendell August Forge ArtIron." c.1990s. $100-115.

Platter. 15.5"L x 11.75"W; Anchor Hocking Glass, Lancaster, Ohio (1905-present), a division of Newell Rubbermaid Company. Oval shape white milk glass rim border with embossed relief fruit decoration, rim trimmed in peach luster. Tom Turkey in high embossed relief. Mark: "Anchor Hocking 2390 Oven Proof Made in USA." c.1960s. $30-35.

Platter. 13.25"D; L.E. Smith Glass Company (1907-present). Circular clear glass serving dish with rim border decorated with an oak leaf garland in relief surrounding a Tom Turkey in relief. Unpainted. Catalog No. 1397/1. No marks. Current, $15-20.

English Platters

Up until the mid-eighteenth century, most wealthy Europeans had two choices for fine dinnerware: (1) earthenware covered with a thick, opaque glaze, or (2) expensive export ware from the Orient, mainly consisting of blue-and-white porcelain. Since the Chinese were loath to impart their formula for making fine porcelain and, therefore, possibly damaging their export market, European chemists got hard to work to discover a very acceptable alternative. Both the Austrians and the French discovered ways to produce a fine, hard white non-porous ceramic which was very close to a true porcelain. Meanwhile, as the British were experimenting in their search for porcelain, they discovered a "soft paste" or imitation porcelain in the early 1740s, which was quite satisfactory as an alternative. Soon after, the search led to the discovery of **bone china**, a material that was white, translucent, and had hardness properties ranging between soft and hard paste porcelain. The first factories to capitalize upon this technology were located in Chelsea, Worchester, and finally Staffordshire, England.

It was in the Staffordshire area, rich in raw materials, and having a variety of excellent transportation options, that the English tableware industry flourished. By the close of the eighteenth century, there were over 130 separate potteries both large and small. At first, decorations on ceramics were hand-painted followed by a glaze. In 1753, another technological change occurred – the invention of **transfer printing**, which allowed any pattern that could be engraved onto copper plates to be transferred to ceramics and mass-produced in great quantities.

Another English creation, **Flow Blue**, became a signature element in the tableware service lines of many potters. Flow Blue china was introduced in the early 1830s in order to emulate the attractive haziness of competitive Chinese export wares. Flow Blue is the name given generally to ironstone china (a hard, white non-translucent ware) that has a blue underglaze transfer-printed design that bled or "flowed" in the kiln, producing a hazy or cloudy blue image. The "flow" was created purposefully by the addition of ammonia salts during the firing process, which produced a flowing together of both the blue underglaze and transparent overglaze elements. Flow Blue china today is highly collectible as long as the images are not totally obscured and the blue is represented as dark, heavy flow.

With the advent of discovery of bone china and creamware along with the invention of transfer printing, the British ceramic industry grew enormously. By the 1850s, the Staffordshire Pottery district evolved into a major center of British ceramics production, represented by at least ten "pottery towns" including well-known names such as Burslem, Coleridge, Etruria, Longport, Stoke-on-Trent, and Tunstall. Two hundred years later the British china and earthenware industry, through its many mergers, acquisitions, and absorption of factories, is a strong force in the global production of ceramics. Three major "families" or groups comprise the bulk of British production today: (1) (Waterford) – Wedgwood Group, (2) Royal Worcester Spode Ltd., and (3) Royal Doulton Tableware Ltd. Potteries that were originally part of the now-defunct Ridgeway, Mason, and Coalport firms are now productive members of either the Wedgwood Group or Royal Doulton. Several of the many fine British potteries that exported tableware to the United States over the last 150 years produced among other patterns beautiful and traditional appearing transfer printed historic "views" of American patriotic scenes, as well as images of the Tom Turkey and Hen made exclusively for holiday use. The export market to America, which began in earnest after the Treaty of Ghent was signed in 1814 ending the War of 1812 between Great Britain and the United States, grew to enormous levels. In America, the prevailing view was that "good" dinnerware was of English or even French porcelain manufacter and that everyday dishes were cheaper domestic imitations of same.

Wedgwood Group

In 1759, Josiah Wedgwood (1730-1795) established a pottery at Burslem, Staffordshire.

This highly respected company had a complete line of ceramics, which included black basalts, bone china, creamware, jasper, luster, pearlware, and redware. Starting in the mid-1960s into the mid-1980s, Wedgwood had acquired at least ten pottery and porcelain firms such as William Adams & Sons, Coalport, Susie Cooper, Johnson Brothers, and Mason's Ironstone. In 1986, the Wedgwood Group accepted an offer from Waterford Glass of Ireland to combine operations, and in 1989, the Waterford-Wedgwood Group was created. Today, the Wedgwood Group of thirty existing and successor companies is one of the largest fine china and earthenware producers in the world.

One of the Wedgwood Group's most prolific producers of transfer printed turkey images was Johnson Bros (Brothers). Founded in 1883 in Hanley (now Stoke-on-Trent), Staffordshire by the three Johnson brothers, Alfred, Frederick, and Henry, the firm was distinguished by its production of an inexpensive, highly durable, underglaze printed whiteware termed "semi-porcelain." It is this quality ironstone tableware, both white and decorated, which has been, and still is, the mainstay of Johnson Bros' business. Of its decorative lines, the very popular export pattern, *Historic America*, was introduced in the 1930s. The various manifestations of Wild Turkey that Johnson Bros produced for the North American export market through their "Holiday" series were produced from the early 1950s to the mid-1970s. During that period, exports made up over 70% of the total sales of the firm. In 1968, Wedgwood acquired Johnson Bros, and in the early 1980s it became an active member of the Wedgwood Group.

Serving Dishes, assortment. Johnson Bros. Holiday/Wild Life Series, *His Majesty* pattern. L to R, Top: Dinner Plate 10.5"D, Square Salad Plate 7.5" square. Bottom: Cup & Saucer Set 5.5"D x 3.5"D cup, Oval Bowl 9"L x 7"W, Gravy Boat 8", and Underplate 7.75"L x 5.5"W. All hand colored in a brown woodland background. Mark: Brown backstamp, "His Majesty Johnson Bros England." c.1955-1975. $15-60 each.

Platter backstamp, Wild Turkeys.

Platter. 20.25"L x 15.5"W; Johnson Bros. Holiday/Wild Life Series, *Wild Turkeys* pattern. Cream 8-sided rectangle base, 2.75" highly decorated rim in a brown fruit and floral bouquet style. Hand colored two Wild Turkeys in flight over a woodland scene. Mark: Brown backstamp, "Wild Turkeys A Genuine Hand Engraving," encased in a shield "Windsor Ware Johnson Bros England." Reg. US. Pat. Off. All Decoration Under The Glaze Permanent & Acid Resisting Colors." Pieces marked with Windsor Ware, the trademark of a special range of patterns shipped to the Fisher Bruce Company of Philadelphia, an importer/wholesaler who dealt with patterns made exclusively for them. c.1951-1974. $325+.

Dinner Plates. Johnson Bros. Holiday/Wild Life Series. L to R: Plate 10.5"D; *Wild Turkeys* pattern. White slightly scalloped base, 1.75" highly decorated rim in a brown fruit and floral bouquet style. Hand colored single Wild Turkey in flight over a woodland scene. Mark: "Wild Turkeys Windsor Ware Johnson Bros. Pat N. 2167472/pend." c.1951-1974. $40-45; Plate 10.5"D; *Wild Turkeys Native American* pattern. White slightly scalloped base, 2" highly decorated rim in an alternating brown florals and standing turkeys pattern. Hand colored single standing Tom Turkey against a woodland scene. Mark: "Wild Turkeys Native American Windsor Ware Made in England Johnson Bros." c.1951-1974. $40-45.

Platter. 20.5"L x 16"W; Johnson Bros, Hanley, Staffordshire, England (Wedgwood Group). Holiday/ Wild Life Series, *His Majesty* pattern. Cream 8-sided rectangle base, 2.25" decorated rim in a multicolor produce and floral style. Hand colored Tom Turkey in a brown woodland background. Mark: Brown backstamp, "His Majesty Made in England by Johnson Bros." "A Genuine Hand Engraving All Decoration Under The Glaze Detergent & Acid Resisting Colour Pat Pend." This is the same platter pattern without the hand coloring that is sold as a reproduction by Williams-Sonoma. c.1955-1975. $200+.

Platter backstamp, *His Majesty*.

Platter. 20.25"L x 15.75"W; Johnson Bros. Holiday/Wild Life series, *Woodland Wild Turkeys* pattern. Cream 8-sided rectangle base, 2.75" highly decorated rim in an olive green woodland birds, cameos, and floral bouquet style. Hand colored four wild turkeys (one with full fanned tail) in a woodland scene. Mark: Olive green backstamp "Woodland Wild Turkeys Windsor Ware Made in England by Johnson Bros." "A Genuine Hand Engraving All Decoration Under The Glaze Permanent & Acid Resisting Colours Pat © 474050." c.1951-1974. $325+.

Platter. 20.5"L x 16.25"W; Johnson Bros Holiday/Wild Life Series, *Barnyard King* pattern. Cream 8-sided rectangle base, 2" decorated rim (rope edge) in a brown continuous flying ducks and squirrels cameos style. Hand colored Tom Turkey in a barnyard scene. Mark: Brown backstamp. "Barnyard King Made in England A Genuine Hand Engraving Johnson Bros England." "All Decoration Under the Glaze Permanent & Acid Resisting Color Pat. No.: 164113," c.1950-1970. $250+.

Platter. 19.75"L x 15.5"W; Johnson Bros Historic America Series, *Home For Thanksgiving* pattern. Cream oval base, 2" decorated rim in a brown oak leaves and acorn garland. Multicolor on brown scene: "Welcome Home Greeting." Mark: "Historic America Home For Thanksgiving Johnson Bros England." Patent No: 111255 Reg. U.S. Pat. Off. Made in England." There were approximately fifteen American scenes on various dinnerware pieces. c.1930s-1974. $250+.

Platter backstamp, *Woodland Wild Turkeys.*

Platter backstamp, *Barnyard King.*

Platter backstamp, *Historic America Home For Thanksgiving.*

Many other members of the Wedgwood Group also produced transfer printed ware for export encompassing historic scenes and images of turkeys.

Platter/Plate. Johnson Bros. Holiday/Wild Life Series, *Wild Turkeys Native American* pattern. L to R: Platter 17.25"L x 14.25"W; Cream 8-sided rectangle base, 1.75" highly decorated rim in a brown woodland birds, cameos, and floral bouquet style. Hand colored Wild Tom Turkey and Hen in a woodland scene. Mark: Brown backstamp, "Wild Turkeys Native American Windsor Ware. Made in England by Johnson Bros." "A Genuine Hand Engraving All Decoration Under The Glaze Permanent & Acid Resisting Colours. Pat. Pend." It has been suggested but not yet documented that this particular pattern was used exclusively as a rewards premium for the top salespersons for the firm of Austin-Nichols, the producer of *Wild Turkey Bourbon.* c.1951-1974, $325+; Plate 10.5"D; *Wild Turkeys Native American* pattern. Mark: Same as platter. c.1951-1974. $40-45.

Platter backstamp, *Wild Turkey Native American.*

Platter. 20.75"L x 16.5"W; Wedgwood & Co., Ltd., Tunstall, Staffordshire, England. White 12-sided rectangle base, 2.5" decorated rim in a cocoa brown floral bouquet. Transfer-printed brown color Tom Turkey in a meadow scene. Mark: "Wedgwood & Co., England Reg. Trademark No: 547269 Made in England." Wedgwood & Co., founded in 1860, was renamed Enoch Wedgwood Ltd, in 1965. Taken over by the Wedgwood Group in 1980 and renamed Unicorn Pottery. Design registered in 1909. Manufactured July 1955. $150-175.

Platter/Plate. Wedgwood & Co., Ltd., Tunstall, Staffordshire, England. Platter 17"L x 13.25"W; White oval deep dish base, 2.25" recessed rim decorated in dark *Flow Blue* floral bouquet. *Flow Blue* Tom Turkey on grassy foreground pattern. Mark: Blue decal "Imperial Porcelain 'Clytie' (pattern), Wedgwood & Co., England." Mark in use c.1906+, manufactured 1932. $900+; Plate 9"D; White round scalloped dish, 2" rim decorated in dark *Flow Blue* floral bouquet set off by raised filigree trim. *Flow Blue* Tom Turkey. Mark: Blue stamp "Royal Semi-Porcelain 'Clytie' (pattern), Wedgwood, C.L., England." c.1909-1959. $100+.

Platter. 19"L x 15"W; William Adams & Sons, Tunstall, Staffordshire, England. White oval deep dish base, 2" rim decorated in a continuous heavily embossed leaf and branch design. Colored lithographed printed scene based on N. Currier's engraving of "Home to Thanksgiving." The Johnson Bros platter dealing with the same subject added a Turkey to the scene. Mark: Black decal "Home to Thanksgiving; a cartouche emblem, Made in England Adams Est. 1657 England." William Adams & Sons was founded in 1769. In the twentieth century, the firm was known for its printed patterns of historical subjects. In 1960, Adams joined the Wedgwood Group and is still active today. c.1914-1955. $175-200.

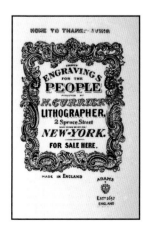

Platter backstamp, *Home to Thanksgiving*, Adams, Made in England.

Platter. 19"L x 15"W; A.J. Wilkinson Ltd., Burslem, Staffordshire, England. Cream oval base, 2.25" rim decorated with brown floral bouquets outlined by a scalloped rope border. Multicolor Tom Turkey with a haystack and thorny branch. Mark: Brown backstamp "Royal Staffordshire Dinnerware by Clarice Cliff Made in England." Clarice Cliff (1899-1972) was one of England's most successful interpreters of British Art Deco. She produced and painted a wide variety of extremely colorful designs from abstract geometric patterns to stylized landscapes and floral motifs. Clarice joined A.J. Wilkerson in 1916 and worked for Newport Pottery after its acquisition by Wilkerson in 1920. Her extraordinary modern tableware reached its peak of popularity in the 1930s. She retired in 1965. A. J. Wilkerson was taken over by W. R. Midwinter in 1964, which then became part of the Wedgwood Group in 1970. c. early 1950s to mid-1960s. $250+.

Platter backstamp. Royal Staffordshire. Clarice Cliff.

Royal Worcester Spode Ltd.

In 1751, the Worcester Porcelain Company acquired the necessary pottery operations to produce utilitarian wares, especially tea and dessert sets. Due to their emphasis on quality, Worcester was one of the great innovators of English porcelain. In the nineteenth century, a series of partnerships and mergers brought further technical improvements and stylistic advances that enabled the Worcester Royal Porcelain Company (as it was then known) to produce extravagant ornamental pieces, Limoge-style enameled porcelains, and avant-garde Japanese and Persian porcelains. The company was also considered to be among the very best in terms of decal decoration, the use of jeweled porcelain, and the soft tints of its colored porcelain that emulated the gilded colors of Art Nouveau glass.

In the twentieth century, some changes were made in order to reduce Worcester's traditional dependence on high-quality decorative ware and painted and gilded porcelains. The main change was the hiring of skilled artists to model and produce a series of naturalistically painted ceramic sculptures, such as animal, flower, bird, and historical military models and themes. In the 1950s and 1960s, Worcester began an expansion program which included the acquisition of several Staffordshire branded potteries such as W.T. Copeland and Palisay Pottery Ltd. The biggest merger came in 1978, when Spode was acquired to form Royal Worcester Spode. Spode was founded in 1770 by Josiah Spode, who pioneered the development of bone china. Over the years, Spode became a major manufacturer of transfer-printed blue-and-white tableware and domestic pottery. Spode has an enormous library where 70,000 tableware patterns are archived. Royal Worchester Spode is comprised today of thirteen potteries or successor companies and most of the combined firms' porcelain is still hand-decorated.

Platter. 17.25"L x 13.5"W; W. T. Copeland & Sons, Ltd., Stoke-on-Trent, Staffordshire, England. White 8-sided deep dish base, 2" rim decorated with a blue floral bouquet outlined by a 0.5" white rope border. Tom Turkey printed in blue (facing right) on a meadow background. Mark: Blue backstamp "W.T. Copeland & Sons Stoke-on-Trent England-incised 18Es-impressed Spode In Pl." W.T. Copeland & Sons, founded in the early nineteenth century, bought Spode in 1833 after which the Spode name largely disappeared. The combined firm's fine reputation for underglaze blue printed ware continued until the merger with Royal Worcester in 1978. c.1918. $425.

Platter. 19"L x 14.5"W; W.T. Copeland & Sons, Ltd. Stoke-on-Trent, Staffordshire, England. White 8-sided deep dish base, 2" rim decorated with a blue floral bouquet outlined by a 0.5" rope border. Tom Turkey printed in blue (facing left) on a meadow background. Mark: Blue backstamp – stacked rectangle shape "Copeland," "Spode," "England." Indent mark: "Copeland Spode Imperial." c.1920. $425+.

Royal Doulton Tableware Ltd.

In 1815, John Doulton founded this firm by purchasing a small London-based pottery. Throughout the rest of the nineteenth century Doulton (which became Royal Doulton in 1902) produced large quantities of domestic and industrial stoneware, architectural and garden ware, and art pottery. Through an acquired pottery in Burslem, Staffordshire, Royal Doulton became a major producer of tableware and popular domestic ware in both earthenware and bone china. In the twentieth century, the company catered to the collectible market by introducing the famous Series wares including images and shapes based on the Dickens figures. Another early series was Bunnykins, a huge range of rabbit designs created in 1934, which has proven continuously popular for seventy years. Royal Doulton's character and Toby jugs and lady figurines have been collected since the 1930s. After World War II, Royal Doulton sold its interests in stoneware drainpipe and sanitary ware production. In the 1960s, through a series of mergers that incorporated famous potteries such as Minton, Royal Crown Derby, and Ridgways, Royal Doulton established itself as one of the world's largest manufacturers of fine bone china, emphasizing more traditional patterns that have popularity in the bridal markets. The company operates through thirty-one entities or successor companies, all of whom strive to maintain a balance between the demands of the table ware market and the needs of the collectors market.

While the "Big Three" of English tableware production over the years expanded by acquisition and merger, several notable independents have prospered. These include *Wood & Sons, Burslem, Staffordshire* (1865-present), and *British Anchor Pottery Co., Langston, Staffordshire* (1884-1982) who exported a wide range of tableware and commemoratives under the *Rowland Marsellus* importer's mark to the United States until 1937.

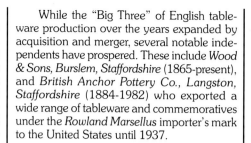

Above: Platter. 21.25"L x 17.25"W; Woods & Son(s), Ltd., Burslem, Staffordshire, England. White oval base, 2" rim decorated in a brown floral bouquet. Brown transfer-printed design of a Hen with a Tom Turkey in a rural background Mark: Brown backstamp showing man holding sign "Wood's Burslem England." Circled "Enoch 1784, Ralph 1750." Woods & Sons, founded in 1865, was known for good-class dinnerware, tea, toilet, and fancies. Grew by acquisition and had a long collaboration with the famous designer, Susie Cooper. The company is still active today selling high standard contemporary style tableware. 1931. $175-200.

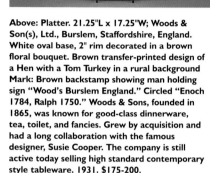

Platter backstamp, Wood's Burslem England.

Platter. 21"L x 17"W; Doulton & Company, Burslem, Staffordshire, England. White oval base, 3" rim decorated in an intricate printed blue cartouche and filigree design. Large *Flow Blue* Tom Turkey. Mark: Blue decal – standing lion on crown symbol "Royal Doulton England" encircling four interconnected Ds. Circle "Burslem Doulton England." Numerals 19, 47. After 1968, became Royal Doulton Tableware, Ltd. c.1947. $800+.

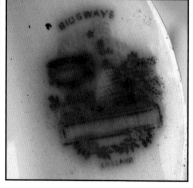

Platter. 17"L x 14"W. Ridgways. White oval base, 2.25" scalloped rim decorated in a blue floral bouquet. Large *Flow Blue* Tom Turkey facing right. Background – Tom Turkey, Hen, and Farmhouse. Mark: Impressed stacked numerals 2/09. Flow Blue Ridgways, Hanley, Staffordshire, England, printed urn and beehive mark, c.1891-1920. The Ridgway name has been associated with the manufacturer of British pottery since the beginning of the nineteenth century. Of the many firms with the name Ridgway over the years, *Ridgways* was founded in 1879 from several predecessor companies. Today, Ridgways is a subsidiary of the Royal Doulton Tablewares, Ltd. $600+.

Platter. 21.25"L x 17.25"W; Woods & Son(s), Ltd., Burslem, Staffordshire, England. White oval base, 2" rim decorated in a blue floral (hand-colored) bouquet. Blue transfer-printed design of a Hen with a Tom Turkey in a rural background with certain scene elements hand-colored. Mark: Blue backstamp showing man holding a sign "Wood's Burslem England." Circled "Enoch 1784, Ralph 1750. 1931. $350+.

Platter. 20"L x 14.5"W; Attributed to a Staffordshire pottery such as Mason's or Spode. White 8-sided scalloped deep body, 2.25" rim edged in rose-pink. Rim is decorated with floral bouquets. Tom Turkey (facing right) rose-pink transfer-printed in a meadow scene. Mark: None. c.1890-1940. $200-225.

Platter/Plate. Barker Bros Ltd., Longton, Staffordshire, England. Platter 20"L x 16"W; White oval base, 2.5" rim decorated with hand-colored fruits and floral bouquet. Tom Turkey printed in brown (facing left) on a brown landscape with clouds. Mark: Backstamp, cartouche shape "Made in England by Barker Bros Ltd For Weil Ceramics & Glass Inc." Barker Bros, founded in 1876, was a manufacturer of advertising ware and a full range of "medium class" domestic goods including ironstone tableware. Barker closed in 1981. c.1950s. $100-150; Plate 11"D; White round base, 2" rim decorated with hand-colored fruits and floral bouquet. Tom Turkey printed in brown on a brown landscape. Mark: Backstamp "Royal Tudor Ware Barker Bros Ltd. England." c.1950s. $40-50.

Platter. 16.75"L x 13"W; British Anchor Pottery Co., Longton, Staffordshire, England. White 8-sided rectangle base, 2.25" rim decorated with blue transfer-printed vignettes of eight historic Plymouth and Pilgrim scenes. Blue transfer scene of Plymouth in 1622 with sites of interest noted. Mark: Blue backstamp - encased circle mark "A.S. Burbank Plymouth Mass," "Copyrighted 1908 by A.S. Burbank," enclosed diamond mark "R & M" Staffordshire, England." A.S. Burbank was a famous Plymouth, Massachusetts-based book, stationery, and art store proprietor. His store was called the Pilgrim Bookstore. The Rowland & Marsellus Company (1893-1937) was an American import firm who commissioned various Staffordshire potteries, such as British Anchor, to supply them with transfer-printed historic scenes ware. c.1908. $750+.

Platter/Plate. The Rowland & Marsellus Company, Staffordshire, England. Platter 19.5"L x 15.75"W; White oval base, 2.5" rim edged in brown. Rim is heavily decorated with ten hand-colored (yellows and browns) vignettes of Tom Turkeys and floral bouquets. Tom Turkey (facing left) hand-colored transfer-printed in a meadow scene. Mark: Brown backstamp - encased diamond mark " R & M," below "Staffordshire England." c.1893-1914, $175-200; Plate 10.25"D; White round base, 2" rim edged in brown. Rim is heavily decorated with six hand-colored vignettes, as on the platter. Tom Turkey (facing right) hand-colored transfer-printed. Mark: Brown backstamp "R & M Co. Staffordshire England." c.1893-1914. $40-50.

Platter backstamp, views of Plymouth 1622.

Platter. 19.25"L x 15.5"W; The Rowland & Marsellus Company, Staffordshire, England. White oval base, 2.5" rim edged in purple. Rim is heavily decorated with ten purple vignettes of Tom Turkeys and floral bouquets. Tom Turkey (facing left) purple transfer-printed in a meadow scene. Mark: Purple backstamp – encased diamond mark "R & M," below "Staffordshire England." c.1893-1914. $175-200.

Japanese, Italian, and Miscellaneous Platters

With the culmination of World War II, the United States government developed an "official" agenda of quickly reestablishing some sense of normalcy to the defeated Japanese nation. One such plan was to help the Japanese restore their non-wartime manufacturing capacity, including their porcelain and ceramics industries. This plan was a success as many pre-war ceramic name factories got their "second wind" and successfully began exporting wares to the United States and elsewhere. With regard to Thanksgiving platters, Japan relied on "tried and true" traditional scenes based on transfer printed designs. Like Homer Laughlin's ubiquitous Tom Turkey decal, the Japanese used a traditional front facing Tom Turkey decoration with either a fence or a "crooked tree branch" as a scene enhancement. By the early 1970s, most American ceramics manufacturers had been driven out of business, primarily by the onslaught of low cost imports from Japan and other Pacific rim countries. Therefore, at the lower end of the ceramics market, the Japanese made great inroads. At the higher end, the English continued to maintain their product and quality superiority by establishing large production and marketing families through mergers.

The Italians also exported much tableware in the 1970s and 1980s, sensing and, therefore, rushing to fill a void in the market that was searching for a "different look." Unlike the Japanese, the Italians exported bright decorative hand-painted ware with much similarity to California-style tableware of the same period. The Chinese were also active selling a distinctive form of colorful enamelware to the mass market.

Platter/Plate. Maruta, Japan. Platter 20"L x 14.5"W; Cream oval base, 2.5" rim decorated with brown flowering stems and rose colored flowers. Tom Turkey (facing right) transfer-printed in brown on a hand-colored background. Mark: Brown backstamp, script "Maruta Ware Japan." Maruta was among the main pottery and ceramics firms to initiate production after World War II. Their ware is considered of medium to high quality. c.1950-1960s, $125-150; Plate 10.5"D; Cream round base, 2" rim decorated with brown floral bouquets and three Tom Turkey cameos. Tom Turkey brown hand-colored transfer print. Mark: Brown backstamp, script "Maruta Ware Japan." c.1950s-1960s. $18-23.

Platter. 19"L x 14.5"W; George Zoltan, Lefton Company, Chicago, Illinois. White oval base, 2" scalloped rim with multicolor pastels of fruits and vegetables. Multicolor pastels Tom Turkey (facing right). Mark: Label – "Lefton China Hand Painted 05758." Incised "Japan." The Lefton Company was founded by George Lefton in 1940, who acted as an export agent to bring Japanese porcelain to America through his company. In 1946, Lefton began to import good quality Japanese porcelain, much of which was his own designs. The company is still active today. c. mid-1950-1960s. $30-35.

Platter. 19"L x 14.5"W; Japan. Creamy-tan oval base, 2" rim in brown shadings decorated with polychrome fruits and vegetables. Tom Turkey with full fanned tail (facing forward) hand-colored transfer print in brown and yellow shades with a fenced background. Mark: Brown backstamp, a Tom Turkey symbol "King Tom An American Tradition Hand Decorated Under Glaze Genuine Ironstone." c.1960s-1970s. $60-85.

Platter backstamp, "King Tom An American Tradition."

Platter/Plate backstamp, "Maruta Ware Japan."

Platters. L to R: Japan. 18"L x 13.75"W; White oval base, 1.75" slightly scalloped blue rim decorated with a multicolor fruit garland. Tom Turkey (facing left) transfer-printed in blue with green and rose accents standing in a rose garden. Mark: No marks. c.1960s. $40-45; 18"L x 13.75"W; Cream oval base, 1.75" slightly scalloped brown rim decorated with a multicolor fruit garland. Tom Turkey (facing left) transfer-printed in brown with green, blue, and rose accents, standing in a rose garden. Mark: No marks. c.1960s. $30-35.

Platter. 18.5"L x 14"W; Japan. White oval base, 2.25" slightly scalloped rim in charcoal shadings decorated with polychrome fruits and vegetables. Tom Turkey with full fanned tail (facing forward) hand-colored transfer print in rose and yellow shades with fenced background. Mark: Backstamp, triangle symbol "NSP," "Ironstone Hand Decorated." c.1960s-1970s. $50-75.

Platters. L to R: 18.5"L x 14.5"W; Japan. White rounded rectangle deep dish base, 1.75" rim decorated in brown fruit and floral bouquets. Tom Turkey with full fanned tail (facing forward) hand-colored transfer print in dark blue and yellow shades with a "crooked tree branch" background. Mark: Brown decal – encircled lion symbol with floral décor. Gold label – "A.A. Importing Co. St. Louis Mo. Made in Japan." c.1960s-1970s. $50-55; 16.5"L x 12"W; White oval base, 1.75" rim decorated in cobalt blue fruit and floral bouquets. Tom Turkey with full fanned tail (facing forward) hand-colored transfer print in blue shades and green with a "crooked tree branch" background. Mark; Blue decal – encircled lion symbol with floral décor. "Made in Japan." c.1960-1970s. $50-55.

Platter. 18"L x 13.75"W; Century Serveware, Japan. White earthenware platter of which the entire design is a Tom Turkey. "Mayflower" Brand. Mark: Embossed – "Mayflower...Century...Japan." c.1980s. $40-50 with box.

Platter/Plate. Japan. Platter 18.5"L x 14"W; Plate 10"D; White hand-colored fruits and vegetables. Tom Turkey dark charcoal hand-colored transfer print. Mark: Backstamp "Hand Painted Japan." c.1960s-1970s. $15-20.

Platter backstamp with label.

Platter. 17.75"L x 14"W; Signature Housewares, Inc, Westlake Village, California. White oval base, 2" slightly scalloped rim embossed with fruit and floral bouquets. Embossed Tom Turkey. Mark: embossed – signature Housewares, Style No. 54. Red and gold label "Made in Japan." c.1990s. $30-35 with box.

Platter. 18.5"L x 13.75"W; Japan. Cream oval base, 2.25" slightly scalloped brown rim with hand-colored fruit and floral bouquet. Tom Turkey (facing front) transfer-printed in brown with blue, green, yellow, and rose accents. Mark: Back embossed "Japan," paper label "M-230-2901-10." Box mark: "Imported – Hand Colored Traditional Early American Holiday Platter Japan." c.1960s. $40-45 with box.

Platter/Plate. L to R: Italy. 18.25"L x 14.5"W; White deep dish oval base, 2.25" scalloped rim decorated with wheat stalks. Multicolor hand-painted Tom Turkey, no back or foreground accents. Mark: Backstamp "Made in Italy." c.1970s. $25-30; Plate. 10"D; White round, 1.75" slightly scalloped rim highly decorated with multicolor fruits and vegetables. Multicolor Tom Turkey. Mark: "Made in Italy." c.1970s. $10-12.

Platter. 18"L x 14.5"W; Italy. White oval base coupe style with a scalloped rim decorated with pastel colored fruits and nuts. Tom Turkey hand colored in black and yellow shadings. Mark: Backstamp "Made in Italy 327." c.1960s. $30-35.

Platter. 20.25"L x 15.75"W; Italy. White oval base, 2.25" scalloped rim edged in brown. Embossed rim decoration. Multicolor hand-painted Tom Turkey. Mark: "Hand painted 2842 Italy." c.1960s. $35-40.

Platter. 18.25"L x 14.5"W; Oval shape with slightly scalloped edge trimmed in dark brown. White base, large hand-painted multicolor Tom Turkey with 2" border decorated with multicolor produce and florals. Mark: "Made in Italy." c.1960s. $30-35.

Platter. 20.5"L x 15.5"W; Villeroy & Boch, Dresden, Germany. White oval base, 2.75" slightly scalloped rim highly decorated with cobalt blue floral garland. Hen and Tom Turkey transfer-printed in cobalt blue standing on a meadow scene. Mark: Blue backstamp, eagle and banner symbol "Villeroy & Boch, Dresden, V.N. 2217. Made In Germany; incised encased stacked C,EM,00." Villeroy & Boch, founded in 1748 and still very active today, is a Mettlach, Germany based ceramics manufacturer and supplier of lifestyle products for the home. The firm opened a Dresden factory in 1856 but was nationalized by the Communists after World War II. c.1874-1945. $750+.

Platter. 19.75"L x 15.25"W; Italy. White oval base, 2.5" scalloped rim edged in medium green, decorated with green 3-leaf stems. Multicolor hand-painted Tom Turkey in black, yellow, and rose shadings. Mark: Backstamp "Italy." c.1970s. $45-50.

Platter. 20.5"L x 16.5"W; Italy. White 8-sided base, recessed rim edged in light green. Rim decorated with multicolor fruits. Multicolor hand-painted Tom Turkey in black, grayish blue, yellow, and rose shadings. Mark: Backstamp "Italy." c.1960s. $40-45.

Platter. 19.25"L x 15.5 W; Italy. White oval base, 3.25" scalloped rim decorated with multicolor fruits and vegetables. Large black hand-painted Tom Turkey with yellow and rose accents. Mark: Backstamp "Made Italy 203." c.1970s. $40-45.

Platters/Plate. Hong Kong. Platter 18"L x 14"W; White oval enamel metalware (tole) base, 2.5" rim decorated with a colorful hand-painted medley of fruits and vegetables. Multicolor hand-painted Tom Turkey with yellow and green as the predominate palette. Mark: Backstamp "Made in Hong Kong E-1363." c. late 1940s-mid 1960s. $20-25; Plate 10.25"D; White round enamelware base, 1.75" rim decorated as the platter. Multicolor hand-painted Tom Turkey of which a vivid green and yellow predominates. Mark: No marks. c. late 1940s-mid 1960s. $5-8; Platter 17.75"L x 13.25"W; White oval enamel metalware (tole) base, 2.25" rim decorated with a colorfully hand-painted medley of fruits and vegetables. Multicolor hand-painted Tom Turkey with blue and brown as the predominant palette. Mark: No marks. c. late 1940s-mid 1960s. $22-27. All of this type of enamelware was made in the British colony of Hong Kong and then shipped to the West Coast, where the brightly decorative pieces were more appreciated than in the Midwest or East Coast. Most pieces were unmarked but those that were almost always had the "E-1363" mark. Values reflect unchipped pieces as enamelware is subject to such defects.

Platter. Hong Kong. Showing differences in painting style and palette. $20-25.

Platter. 17.5"L x 13.5"W; Weiss Ceramics, Brazil. White oval base, 2" rim edged in pea green, inner rim encircled by a pea green ridged border. The hand-painted rim is decorated with pastel colored vegetables. Multicolor hand-painted Tom Turkey in pastels. Mark: Brown backstamp "Weiss Turkey Platter, Dishwasher Safe, Made and Hand Painted in Brazil." c.1956-1976. $25-30.

Platter. 19.5"L x 15"W; Mexico. Bright pewter ware. Hand crafted, heavily embossed Tom Turkey image. Mark: Blue and silver label "Hecho in Mexico." c.1960s. $75-90.

Plates

The same materials, processes, and forms of decoration that were used to make attractive turkey platters can also be assumed in the production of plateware. However, size is another matter. Earlier, we defined *platters*, in terms of size, of having a length of at least 16 inches, although, as we have seen, some are smaller than the minimum. In the realm of *plateware*, there are at least twelve different types of plates that can be used for the dinner table. They range in size from Service Plates having a maximum diameter of 14 inches (also called chargers or buffet plates) to Fruit Saucers having a minimum diameter of 5 inches. Most plateware used strictly for decorative purposes follows the diameters of a Dinner Plate (10 to 11 inches) or a Luncheon Plate (9 to 9.5 inches).

Platters were made primarily to serve large portions of meat, fowl, or fish. Because of their utilitarian nature, platters were not heavily decorated. Plates, on the other hand, were the perfect medium in terms of surface size to accept a decorative format. Therefore, plates can be separated into two categories: (1) utilitarian items but still attractively decorated, and (2) non-utilitarian novelty giftware items. This latter category is termed *collector plates*. The history of "limited edition" collector plates can be traced back to 1895 when the concept of producing porcelain plates in limited quantities first began. Harald Bing, director of the Danish porcelain-manufacturing firm, Bing & Grøndahl, produced a decorative plate as a Christmas commemorative. This blue plate with white accent swishes featured a design of the Copenhagen skyline in winter. It was named "Behind the Frozen Window," dated 1895, and sold for 2 Kroner ($0.50). Only 400 plates were made before the mold was broken. This first true collector plate is now priced in the $6,000 range. The series begun by Bing & Grøndahl in 1895 continues today; a new plate has been issued for each of more than one hundred Christmases that have come and gone since.

The contemporary or present-day collector plate market was inaugurated by Wedgwood in 1969 when the firm introduced its first in an annual series of Christmas plates. This first plate was blue with a white sculptured likeness of Windsor Castle. The introductory price was $25 and today its value is approximately $75, down considerably from a high point of $240 reached in the 1990s. After this successful introduction, the stage was set for the opening salvo in the limited-edition plate boom that rocked America. The Franklin Mint of Franklin Center, Pennsylvania (founded in 1964), along with dozens of other companies, soon began to produce collector plates starting in 1970. Franklin Mint was especially known for its etched sterling silver plates, the first of which was designed by Norman Rockwell. This plate also had a Christmas theme, "Bringing Home the Tree," the size of issue stating to be 18,321 and selling for, then, a very high price of $100. Today that value is stated to be $300. Needless to say, success bred imitation, and the number of manufacturers issuing plates along with the types and subject matter of plates offered in the market multiplied at an exponential rate. Many manufacturers hyped their plates as long-term potential investments. This "story" rang true to many "collectors-investors" because during the 1970s and into the early 1980s, inflation was rampant and it was thought that "hard assets" would retain and even increase in their value. Eventually, the supply of plates greatly exceeded the demand and the "secondary market" for such plates and related collectibles declined to the point where there was no virtually no activity. Plate prices dropped 50 to 75% from their highs, and the speculative bubble burst much like the stock market of the late 1990s. However, with the growth of on-line auction sites, a renaissance could be beginning for a select group of truly limited-edition, well-made plates from experienced manufacturers. Today, while collector plates are gain-ing some renewed interest, contemporary figurines, ornaments, and artist-signed lithographs occupy a much larger market share. What was a $10 billion market for "collectibles" in 1998 declined to $6.5 billion by 2001. Certainly, the effects of 9/11 and the recessionary economy contributed to this collapse. Franklin Mint took note of this by announcing in November 2003 that they were exiting the "collectibles" market except for some specific areas as part of a business restructuring program. A 40-year reign came to an abrupt end.

The plates that are shown here, like their counterpart platters, all have Thanksgiving or the Turkey as their theme. These plates are either decorative utilitarian or collectible limited-edition.

Postcard. "Eat hearty let the day be your excuse. Thanksgiving Greeting." Publisher Nash, Series 28, postmarked Afton, Iowa, November 13, 1913.

Postcard. "May This Bird Call You to a Joyous Feast. Thanksgiving Greeting." Publisher Nash, Series 28.

American Plates

Except for some of the older utilitarian plates dating prior to World War II, the large majority here are "limited-edition" collector plates.

Plate. 8"D; Franklin Mint, Pennsylvania. Solid sterling silver (92.5% silver). Individually etched and serially numbered. "The First Thanksgiving." Stevan Dohanos artist and illustrator. The First Annual Franklin Mint Thanksgiving Plate – 1972. Issue price $125. No. issued: 10,142. Serial No. 5008. Plate issued with Certificate of Authenticity and velvet lined designer box with a library slipcase. Weight 5.86 troy ounces = $49.15 worth of silver based on 1972's average silver price. Melt value end of 2003 = $32.50. $40-45.

Plate. 8"D; Franklin Mint. Solid sterling silver. Individually etched and serially numbered. "American Wild Turkey." Stevan Dohanos artist and illustrator. The Second Annual Franklin Mint Thanksgiving Plate – 1973. Issue price $125. No. issued: 3,547. Serial No. 563. Weight 5.82 troy ounces = $13.78 worth of silver (1973's silver price). Melt value = $32.15. $40-45.

Plate. 8"D; Franklin Mint. Solid sterling silver. Individually etched and serially numbered. "Thanksgiving Prayer." Stevan Dohanos artist and illustrator. The Third Annual Franklin Mint Thanksgiving Plate – 1974. Issue price $150. No. issued: 5,150. Serial No. 563. Weight 5.78 troy ounces = $25.20 worth of silver (1974's silver price). Melt value = $31.90. $40-45.

Plate. 8"D; Franklin Mint. Solid sterling silver. Individually etched and serially numbered. "Family Thanksgiving." Stevan Dohanos artist and illustrator. The Fourth Annual Franklin Mint Thanksgiving Plate – 1975. Issue price $175. No. issued: 3,025. Serial No. 186. Weight 5.75 troy ounces = $23.50 worth of silver (1975's silver price). Melt value $31.75. $45-50.

Plate. 8"D; Franklin Mint. Solid sterling silver. Individually etched and serially numbered. "Home From The Hunt." Stevan Dohanos artist and illustrator. The Fifth Annual Franklin Mint Thanksgiving Plate – 1976. Issue price $175. No. issued: 3,474. Serial No. 5614. Weight 5.75 troy ounces = $23.15 worth of silver (1976's silver price). Melt value = $31.75. This was the last in the limited-edition Thanksgiving Series by Dohanos. At the peak of silver prices reached in 1980 ($49.45 high, $20.98 average), the melt value of these plates averaged $110. The price decline of the melt value over the past twenty or more years is approximately 71%, the same exact price decline from the original issue price that these plates may be worth today. $45-50.

Plate. 8"D; Franklin Mint. Close-up view of etched scene – 1976.

Plates. L to R: 8.5"D; Sterling China Company, East Liverpool, Ohio. Off-white ceramic base with slightly scalloped rim. Decaled Tom Turkey and Hen. c.1920s. $15-18; 10.25"D; Limoges China Company, East Liverpool, Ohio (name changed to American Limoges China Co, 1900-1955). White semi-vitreous base with a 1.75" slightly scalloped rim in cobalt blue, trimmed in gold with gold floral design. c.1910-1930. $45-50; 9.25"D; Harker Pottery Company, East Liverpool, Ohio (1890-1972). Pastel luster semi-vitreous base trimmed in gold. Decaled Tom Turkeys (2). Mark: bow & arrow symbol "Semi-porcelain." c.1890+. $20-25.

Plate. 9.25"D; Buffalo Pottery Company, Buffalo, New York (1901-present). Light green base shading to dark green at the rim. Scalloped rim edged in gold. Tom Turkey on shoreline painted image under glaze. Mark: back – green mark with Buffalo symbol. "Semi-vitreous Buffalo Pottery 1907 No. 1319." c.1907-1946. $150+.

Plates. L to R: 10"D; Wheeling Pottery Company. Wheeling, West Virginia (1879-1910). *La Belle China. Flow Blue* 2" scalloped rim with a gold embossed design. There are six gold floral bouquets that drape down from the rim towards the well. On the rim there are twelve dotted raised enamel flowers interspersed amongst the scroll. Decaled Tom Turkey. Mark: backstamp in green "WP La Belle China." c.1893+. $200+; 10"D; Wheeling Pottery Company. *La Belle China.* Same rim design. Decaled Hen Turkey. Same mark.c.1893. $200+.

Plate. 8.25"D; Pickard China, Chicago, Illinois (1893-present). White ceramic base. Hand transfer print of wild turkeys in brush, 1.25" rim hand-decorated with a gold band and concentric gold stripe on the inner rim. Mark: back – gold stamp, banner and lion symbol "Pickard China Made in U.S.A. Hand Decorated." c.1938-present. $50-55.

Plate. 10"D; Denham Pottery. Close-up view of turkey rim design.

Plate. 10"D; Denham Pottery, Dedham, Massachusetts (1896-1943). Grayish-white intentional crackled glaze, 1.5" cobalt blue rim, hand-painted continuous pattern of ten Tom Turkeys. Inner cobalt blue concentric lines on rim margin. Mark: back – blue rectangle stamp "Denham Pottery," with sitting rabbit design. Denham was well-known for their unique crackle design. The pottery used many animal design images, but the rabbit was the most common. c.1929-1943. $375+.

Plate 11.25"D; Pennsbury Pottery, Morrisville, Pennsylvania (1951-1971). Light tan shading to brownish tan at the rim. Brown 0.5" rim band, followed by a green inner stripe. Brown floral scroll decoration. Hand-painted Amish couple carrying food tray offset by a flowering tree and a rose heart. Mark: back- Pennsbury Pottery 1232-D." c.1950s. $75-80.

Plate. 10.25"D; Atlas China, New York, N.Y. White ceramic base, 5.25" diameter multicolor painted transfer of a painting by Anna Mary Robertson "Grandma" Moses (1860-1961). "*Catching the Thanksgiving Turkey*," c. early 1940s. Mark: back-printed - A poem: "Anna Mary Robertson Moses" Atlas China, New York, N.Y. © Grandma Moses Properties, Inc. Limited First Edition." c.1970s. $100+.

Plate. 13.5"D; Unknown maker. Powder blue coupe style. Hand-painted multicolor Tom Turkey against backdrop of vine covered trees. Mark: back in brown "A. Harring '51." $40-50.

Plate. 9.5"D; American Commemoratives. White ceramic base, 1.25" rim, embossed, decorated with autumn produce. Multicolor transfer print. "*The Pilgrims' First Thanksgiving, Plymouth, Mass 1623.*" Mark: back - American Commemoratives – Limited Edition series 1001-1006 J.H. Sargent Made In U.S.A." c. mid-to-late 1970s. $10-15.

Advertisement. General Mills. 10" x 13.5". "The 90 Thanksgivings of Grandma Moses." Based on her painting, "Catching the Thanksgiving Turkey." Ad, November 1950. $15-18.

Plates. L to R: 8.5"D; *Antique Trader*. The Babka Publishing Company, Dubuque, Iowa. Cobalt blue shadings on a white base. "*Pilgrims Thanksgiving 1971.*" Designed by E.A. Babka. Limited Edition of 1,500. Issue price $10.95. Mark: back "Original Design – Limited Edition Collector Plate – E.A. Babka – The Babka Publishing Co. Dubuque, Iowa." $10-15 MIB; 8.5"D; "*The First Thanksgiving – Thanksgiving 1972.*" Limited Edition of 1,000. Issue price $10.95. Mark: back – "Original Design – Limited Edition Collector Plate – E.A. Babka – The Antique Trader Weekly – Dubuque, Iowa." $10-15 MIB.

Right:
Plate. 7"D; Frankoma Potteries, Sapulpa, Oklahoma (1933-present). Prairie green glaze. Impressed Wild Turkey. Wildlife Series 1978 issue "*Wild Turkey*" Edition of 1,000. Mark: back – embossed circle "Meleagris Gallopavo A symbol of Wildlife Restoration and Conservation. Oklahoma Wildlife Federation. The Wild Turkey." ©JF1978 Joniece Frank. John Frank initially established Frank Potteries, which was changed to Frankoma Potteries in 1938. The Frankoma name is a contraction of Frank and Oklahoma. The firm developed a distinctive style of unique glazes using rutile, a mineral containing titanium dioxide. The use of this mineral allows the fired clay to be exposed through the glaze. $65-70.

Above:
Plate. 8.5"D; The Edwin M. Knowles China Company, Newell, West Virginia. Collector Plates (1974-1997). Multicolor hand-painted on a coupe plate style. One of seven plates issued from 1978 to 1984 for the Americana Holidays series – "Thanksgiving"- 1979. Artist: Don Spaulding. Production run one year. Issue price $26. Mark: back – black printing "Plate Number 14230A. Second Series Limited Edition Closed in 1979. Bradex Number 84-41-2.2" $20-25 MIB.

Plate. 10"D; Iroquois China Company, Syracuse, New York. *Casual China* line. Nutmeg color. Artist hand-painted multicolor design over glaze of Tom Turkey in a forest scene. Mark: brown backstamp - script: "Iroquois Casual China by Russell Wright." Iroquois China was founded in 1905 and closed in 1969. c.1950s+. $25-30.

Plates. L to R: The Edwin M. Knowles China Company, Newell, West Virginia. Collector Plate #1. One of six plates issued from 1986 to 1987 for the Childhood Holidays series – *"Thanksgiving"*- 1986. Artist: Jessie Willcox Smith. Production 97 firing days. Issue price $19.50. Mark: back – black printing "Plate No. 582C. Second issue Limited Edition Closed in 1986. Bradex No. 84-K41-2.2." $12-15 MIB; Collector Plate #2. One of six plates issued from 1986 to 1987 for the Upland Birds of North America series – *"The Wild Turkey"*- 1987. Artist: Wayne Anderson. Production run 150 days. Issue price $27.50. Mark: back – black printing "Plate No. 1689A. Fourth issue Limited Edition Closed in 1987. Bradex No. 84-K41-20.4. Plate issued under the sponsorship of The Wildlife Society of Bethesda, Maryland." The Edwin M. Knowles China Co. terminated its operations in 1963. In 1974, a foreign manufacturer of collectibles purchased the rights to the Knowles name, but no production is done domestically. $18-20 MIB.

British Plates

The British manufacturers of serveware never really bothered to cater to the American market obsessed with the 1970s mindset of realizing positive investment returns from "limited edition" collector plates. This is interesting because it was Wedgwood, arguably the most respected ceramic manufacturer in England, who initiated the emergence of the collector plate market by issuing a line of annual commemorative plates commencing in 1969. In the ensuing thirty or more years, British plateware manufacturers found it much more profitable to sell tableware to a broad American market than to predict the uncertainty of changing tastes precipitated by fleeting fads. Flow blue and other traditionally designed plateware are generally what has been exported to America, and much of it has appreciated over the years unfettered by the collector plate stigma.

Plate. 8.5"D; Southern Living Gallery. Multicolor hand-painted on a porcelain coupe style. Rim edged in gold. Image of Tom, Hen and their five poults. One of twelve plates issued in 1983 for the Game Birds of the South series – *"Wild Turkey."* Artist: Antony Heritage. Production run 19,500. Issue price $39.95. Mark: back – brown stamp "Game Birds of the South by ©1982 Southern Living Gallery from original paintings by Antony John Heritage. This is plate number 11948 of an edition limited to Wild Turkey." $30-35 MIB.

Canapé Dish. 10"D; Maker unknown. Tan porcelain body divided into three food compartments. Rim and dividers heavily embossed with multicolor autumn produce. Center Tom Turkey is a toothpick holder. c.1970s. $25-30.

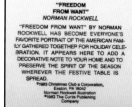

Back detail of "Freedom From Want" plate.

Buffet Plate. 10.5"D; Johnson Brothers, Hanley, Staffordshire, England (Wedgwood Group). Historic America Series, *Frozen Up-Thanksgiving*. Cream body with rim band in brown transfer pattern of oak leaf garland. Brown multicolor winter scene of an old mill, horse-drawn sleigh, and a Tom Turkey. Mark: brown backstamp – eagle and banner symbol "Thanksgiving Historic America Frozen Up." John Bros. England. Patent No. 111286. Reg. U.S. Pat. Off. Made in England. All Decoration Under the Glaze Permanent Acid Resisting Colors. c.1930s-1974. $55-60.

Right:
Plates. L to R: 6.38"D; R. H. Inc. (Made in Japan). White porcelain base, 1" rim edged in gold. Brown inner ring. Multicolor decal under glaze. Mark: "Thanksgiving" by Norman Rockwell – A Special Edition Collector's Plate Produced on Fine Porcelain." c. early 1980s. $10-12; 10"D; Christmas Club, Inc., Easton, Pennsylvania. Cream porcelain deep dish base, 1.25" light brown rim with a scroll decoration. Brown transfer-printed illustration, "Freedom From Want," by Norman Rockwell. In script, "The Warmest of Holiday Tradition." Mark: back – brown stamp "Freedom From Want Norman Rockwell...everyone's favorite portrait of the American family gathered together for holiday celebration..." ©1983 The Curtis Publishing Company. $15-20.

Plate. 10"D; The Rowland & Marsellus Company, Staffordshire, England. White base with slightly scalloped rim and recessed center. Cobalt blue transfer pattern of fruit and floral décor on rim band. Blue and white scene of *John Alden and Priscilla* in the forest. Mark: cobalt blue backstamp – diamond symbol – "R & M Co," banner "John Alden and Priscilla by Staffordshire England." c.1893-1914. $100+

Plate. 10"D; A.G. Richardson & Co., Ltd., Staffordshire, England. White base with 8-sided rim. Medium blue transfer pattern on rim band of four historical vignettes interwoven with a basket weave cartouche. Vignettes are (1) American Indian, (2) Pocahontas Saving Life of John Smith, (3) Mayflower in Plymouth Harbor, and (4) Return of the Mayflower. Blue and white scene of "*The First Thanksgiving in America.*" Mark: backstamp "Colonial Times by Crown Ducal England." c.1925-1939. $40-50.

Plate. 10.25"D; Attributed to The Rowland & Marsellus Company. White base with deep recessed center. Cobalt blue transfer pattern on rim band of six Pilgrim historical vignettes: (1) Old Fort Burial Hill, (2) Pilgrim Monument, (3) Pilgrim Hall, (4) Spinning Wheel, (5) Canopy over Plymouth Rock, and (6) Mayflower. Blue and white scene of *Plymouth Rock 1620*. Mark: blue backstamp – double circle "ASB," "A.S. Burbank Plymouth Mass." Copyrighted 1906 by A.S. Burbank Plymouth, Mass. c.1893-1914. $100+.

Plate. 10.25"D; A.G. Richardson & Co., Ltd., Tunstall & Ferrybridge, Staffordshire, England. White base with heavily scalloped rim. Mulberry transfer pattern on rim band of floral bouquets. Mulberry and white scene of "*The First Thanksgiving in America.*" Mark: backstamp "Colonial Times by Crown Ducal England." A.G. Richardson & Co., Ltd. was founded in 1915. The company's most widely used trademark was Crown Ducal. Enoch Wedgwood bought this firm in 1974, and, today it is part of the Waterford-Wedgwood Group. c.1925-1939. $40-50.

Below:
Plates. L to R: Jonroth, England. Plate #1: 9.75"D; White base, recessed dish with cobalt blue transfer print pattern on rim band of seven historical vignettes; (1) Pilgrim Hall, (2) Mayflower in Harbor, (3) Priscilla, (4) National Monument, (5) Plymouth Rock, (6) Portico over Plymouth Rock, and (7) John Alden. Blue and white scene of "*Landing of the Pilgrims.*" Mark: blue backstamp, crown atop circle "Jonroth England." "Old English Staffordshire Ware," "Imported for Rawling Distributing Co., Winchester, Mass." c.1930s. $35-40; Plate #2: 9.75"D; White base, recessed dish with cobalt blue transfer print pattern on rim band of floral bouquets. Blue and white scene of *Mayflower at Sea*. Mark: same as Plate #1. c.1930s. $35-40; Plate #3. 9.75"D; White base, recessed dish with cobalt blue transfer print pattern on rim band of floral bouquets. Blue and white scene of *John Alden and Priscilla* at her spinning wheel. Mark: blue backstamp "Why Don't You Speak for Yourself, John?" Longfellow quote. Same Jonroth mark as on earlier plates. c.1930s. $35-40.

Buffet Plate backstamp. *Frozen Up*, Johnson Bros.

Plate. 7.75"D; William Adams & Sons Ltd., Tunstall & Stoke, Staffordshire, England. White base with a rose-pink transfer pattern on rim band of floral bouquets. Scene, encircled by a solid rose-pink band, is a rose-pink transfer sketch of *John Alden and Priscilla* in a forest. Mark: rose-pink backstamp – banner: "John Alden and Priscilla." "Old English Staffordshire Ware." "Made in Staffordshire, England by the Adams Potteries Est in 1657 Imported for...Plymouth Rock Gift Shop Plymouth, Mass." William Adams & Sons was founded in 1769. From early in the twentieth century, the firm was known for a range of earthenware decorated with finely engraved scenes of historic subjects. In 1966, Adams joined the Wedgwood Group and is still active. c.1914-1940. $20-25.

Plate. 10.75"D; Crown Works, Burslem, Staffordshire, England. Cream base with a stylistic decoration of green and tan semi-circular leaves on the inner surface of the 2" rim band. Hand-painted Tom Turkey in brown shades with a smaller turkey in the background. Mark: gray backstamp – in script "Susie Cooper" Crown Works Burslem England, impressed 241,21. Susie Cooper (1902-1995) was one of the leading tableware designers of the twentieth century. She was known for her decorative modernism and stylized abstraction motifs. Her firm, Susie Cooper Pottery, was involved with a number of moves including Crown Works in 1931, Bursley Ltd. in 1933, Jason China in 1950, and R. H. & S.L. Plant in 1958. Wedgwood Group acquired Susie Cooper Ltd in 1966. c.1932-1964. $100-115.

Oval Plate. 11" x 10.25". Johnson Bros. Coupe styled base with a Pareek (off-white) background. Hand engraved transfer and hand-painted image. "Holiday" series – Gamebirds pattern. This pattern was manufactured in sets of six, each with a different bird (s) depicted: *Wild Turkey* (s). Mark: dark brown backstamp "Game Birds" "A genuine hand engraving all decorating under the glaze." Made in England by Johnson Brothers Wild Turkey Pat. Pend. Ironstone. c.1953-1976. $75-80.

Plate. 10"D; A. J. Wilkinson Ltd, Burslem, Staffordshire, England. White base with a purple transfer pattern of an oak leaf garland on a 1.75" rim band. Purple transfer print of a Tom Turkey. Mark: purple backstamp "Royal Staffordshire Dinnerware by Clarice Cliff Made in England." A.J. Wilkinson was taken over by W. R. Midwinter in 1964, which then became part of the Wedgwood Group in 1970. c. early 1950s-mid 1960s. $70-75.

Plate. 10"D; Burgess & Leigh Ltd, Burslem Staffordshire, England. Cream base with a 1.75" rim band on which there is a 0.25" wide circular green strip accented by four curlicues. Tom Turkey in shades of green and blue. Mark: backstamp "Burleigh Ware designed by Harold Bennett N.R.D. England." Burgess & Leigh, founded in 1862, is one of the few independent family-owned potteries left in Staffordshire and is still active today. The Burleigh Ware pattern mark has been in use since 1932. c.1950s+. $60-65.

Plate 10.25"D; William Adams & Sons Ltd., Tunstall & Stoke, Staffordshire, England. Cream base with a 1.75" rim band hand engraved and hand colored pattern of flowers and berries. Tom Turkey in brown shades standing in a bamboo thicket. Mark: back transfer – "Wild Turkey." "The Birds of America from original drawings by John James Audubon"; Standing rectangle symbol; "Printed from five engravings and coloured by hand." c.1920s-1950s. $150+.

Plate. 10.25"D; Josiah Wedgwood & Sons, Etruria, Staffordshire, England. White base with a 1.88" rim band transfer decorated with gold, red, and green floral bouquets. The outer rim is edged in green. The inner golden orange Greek key rim encircles a hand-painted Tom Turkey standing by a pond in the meadow. Mark: black backstamp "Formosa (pattern), Wedgwood Etruria England"; in red "All 390/12"; impressed "01/AKF." Josiah Wedgwood, founded in 1759, operated their pottery in Etruria from 1769 to 1940. In 1989, Wedgwood merged with Waterford LLC (Ireland) to form Waterford Wedgwood Group. April 1903 (due to date cipher AKF). $125-150.

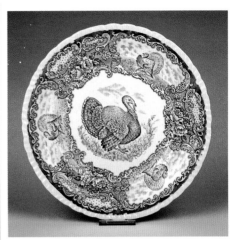

Plate. 10"D; Churchill China, Staffordshire, England. White base with 2" fluted rim band hand engraved and machine colored pattern of flowers and berries. Tom Turkey in gray and brown shades stands in a thicket of ferns. Banner reads "Meleagridiana." In the late 1990s Churchill Tableware introduced a series, "Wild Life," based on nineteenth century color print reproductions from the original copper engravings. Churchill acquired many of the plates when it was founded in 1984 after a merger of two potteries with successor firms dating back to the nineteenth century. Mark: black backstamp – seated lion symbol, "Wildlife Churchill Myott Factory archive illustrations. Adapted from original copper engravings." c.1995-2000. $15-20.

Plate. 10.5"D; The Boehm Studios, Malvern, England. White bone china base, rim edged in 14 carat gold. Original image of Tom Turkey and Hen drawn by Edwin Boehm. Multicolor image tan hand-crafted and decorated by Boehm artists in England. Plate titled "Wild Turkey," is No. 6 of the 8-plate collection Game Birds of North America series. Limited edition of 15,000 issued. Mark: back print "The Boehm Studios" Game Birds of North America Plate Collection by the Boehm Artists in the USA and England. Wild Turkey (no number or date)." Series issued in 1984. $75-85.

Plate. 10.25"D; Royal Crown, Staffordshire, England. White base with a "pie-crust" rim edge; 2" rim band in a highly decorated brown transfer pattern of three Tom Turkey vignettes. Brown and white Tom Turkey image Mark: Brown backstamp "Royal Crown Made in Great Britain." Royal Crown appears to be a jobber, a distributor or exporter much like Rowland & Marsellus. c.1910s-1930s. $50-55.

Plate. 10.75"D; Boehm Porcelain Studio, Malvern, Worcestershire, England. White bone china coupe shape with rim edged in 14 carat gold. Original pencil sketch of a Wild Turkey family was made by Edward Marshall Boehm in the 1950s. This plate, entitled "Wild Turkey," is one of eight in the Gamebirds of North America series. Each of the pencil sketches has been preserved by lithography. Mark: black backstamp – horsehead symbol stacked over a stylized crown "Boehm Fine Bone China"; in a banner "Game Bird series," "Wild Turkey Meleagris gallopavo Made in England." Boehm, founded in 1950 in Trenton, New Jersey, is still active today. In the mid-1970s, production was moved to England. c. late 1970s-1990s. $40-50.

Plate. 10"D; W. R. Midwinter Ltd., Burslem, Staffordshire, England. White base with a 1.25" rim band. Multicolor hand-painted Tom Turkey whose image bleeds into the outer rim. Mark: Backstamp "Turkey" W. R. Midwinter Ltd. Burslem England. Midwinter, founded in 1910, acquired A. J. Wilkinson's Newport Works in 1964. In 1968, the firm merged with J. & G. Meakin, but was taken over by the Wedgwood Group in 1970. c.1960s. $50-55.

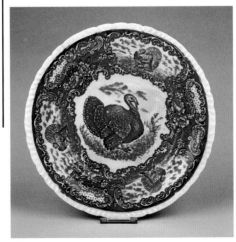

Plate. 10"D; The Rowland & Marsellus Company, Longton, Staffordshire, England. White base with a "pie-crust" rim edge; 2" rim band in a highly decorated cobalt blue transfer pattern of three Tom Turkey vignettes. Blue and white Tom Turkey image. This particular image was used by many British firms and is seen often. Mark: "R & M" Staffordshire England. c.1893-1900. $50-55.

Plate. 10.75"D; G. L. Ashworth & Brothers, Hanley, Staffordshire, England. White base with a scalloped rim known as the Vista pattern; 2" rim band in a highly decorated blue transfer pattern of flowering branches and leaves. Blue and white Tom Turkey image with a house in the background. Mark: Blue backstamp – crown symbol, "Mason's"; in banner "Patent Ironstone China," England "Guaranteed Permanent Acid Resisting Colours." G.L. Ashworth was founded in 1862 as an amalgamation of predecessor firms such as G. M & C. J. Mason. The firm was renamed Mason's Ironstone China Ltd. in 1968 and then became part of the Wedgwood Group in 1973. The traditional style printed Vista tableware is highly regarded and quite rare in some images. c.1970s-1980s. $250+.

Plate. 10.5"D; W. T. Copeland (Josiah Spode), Stoke, Staffordshire, England. White interior base, very slightly scalloped rim with 0.25" blue and white stylized "key" rim edge design; 1.25" medium blue and white transfer pattern of floral bouquets. Light blue transfer outline of a Tom Turkey beside a tree. Mark: Blue backstamp – standing rectangle symbol "Copeland, Spode, England," in script "Turkey No. 12." The Spode Game Bird Series plates were produced between 1920 (dated first use of the mark) and 1950. They were made as accent pieces to the Spode "Camilla" dinnerware pattern produced in a rosy-red and medium blue colors. It is possible that there were up to thirty-six different game plates produced. Spode was founded in 1770 but was purchased by W.T. Copeland in 1832. By 1970, only the Spode name was used for ceramics and the Copeland name eliminated from all references. Royal Worchester purchased Spode in 1978. c.1920-1950. $60-65.

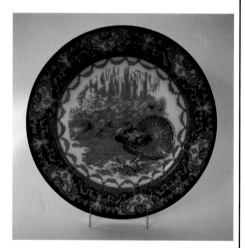

Plate. 10"D; Royal Doulton, Burslem, Staffordshire, England. White base with 1.5" rim transfer-printed *Flow Blue* pattern of cartouches. *Flow Blue* image of a Tom Turkey and seven hens in a forested scene. Watteau pattern. Mark: Blue backstamp – printed urn and banner mark with crescent symbol "Watteau Doulton Burslem England," impressed "dime" circle "Doulton Burslem England," impressed "6-02." Royal Doulton Tableware Ltd., founded in 1815, is very active today having over thirty successor companies that make up its creative and corporate base. c. 1902. $150+.

Plate. 10"D; Cauldon Potteries, Shelton, Staffordshire, England. White base with a scalloped 1.75" rim transfer-printed *Flow Blue* pattern of floral bouquets and curlicue banners. Flow Blue image of a Tom Turkey in brush. No pattern name. Mark: Blue backstamp "Cauldon England," impressed "Cauldon." Cauldon, founded in 1904, was acquired by Pountney & Co., in 1962. They became part of the Wedgwood Group in 1967. c.1905-1920. $150+.

Below:
Plates. 10"D; Woods & Son (s), Ltd., Burslem, Staffordshire, England. Showing four varieties of transfer-printed color combinations. L to R: Blue and white; Blue rim with multicolor accents and background (dark navy blue Turkey); rose-pink and white; and brown rim with multicolor accents and background (dark brown Turkey). Mark: Various colored backstamps showing man holding sign "Wood's Burslem England." circled "Enoch 1784, Ralph 1750." c.1930s. $75+ (single color); $125+ (multicolor).

Plates. 10"D; Cauldon Potteries. View of six plates. $900+.

Oval Child's Dish. 8"L x 6.25"W x 1.5"H; Staffordshire Potteries Ltd., Longton, Staffordshire, England. White ironstone body with the inner and outer rim margins edged in gold. Decoration: rim-gold encased letters "Baby's Plate"; Bowl bottoms – multicolor Tom Turkey/Two Hens decal; printed words "The Turkey's Noted For Conceit and He's Extremely Good to Eat." Mark: Backstamp – six-pointed star encased by a circle "Stoke-on-Trent Staffordshire England." "C Bros Trademark." Staffordshire Potteries was formed from an amalgamation of many early twentieth century potteries in 1950. During the 1950s to 1970s, the firm produced many mugs and nursery sets for children based on comic characters. Today, Staffordshire produces a wide range of tableware and advertising ware. c.1950s. $100+.

Miscellaneous Plates

As noted earlier, the manufacture of limited edition plates first began in Europe. Today, countries like Denmark and Germany still have well-respected firms that continue to produce attractive, holiday-oriented plates. For the most part, these plates do not have any utilitarian value unlike the older plates from England. Still, there are European manufacturers who design plates almost exclusively for the American markets and have a very secure following.

Plate. 7.5"D; Lund and Clausen, Copenhagen, Denmark. "Copenhagen Blue" and white lithography underglaze. Scene depicts a Tom Turkey with a Pilgrim couple next to a log house in the background. Titled "Thanksgiving 1973." Issue price $14. Production run one year. Mark: Blue backstamp – crown symbol, "L & C A/S Copenhagen Denmark." $15-20.

Plates. L to R: Bing & Grøndahl, Copenhagen, Denmark. Plate #1: 8.25"D; Multicolor lithography underglaze. Scene depicts a roast turkey with all the trimmings observed by a Colonial couple in the background. Titled "The Colonial Thanksgiving." Artist: Jack Woodson. From "The Thanksgiving Day Plate Collection." Production run limited to one year. 1988 Edition Plate No. 1/Number #219. Mark: Blue backstamp – three towers symbol "B & G Copenhagen Porcelain Bing & Grøndahl." $15-20; Plate #2. 8.25"D; Multicolor lithograph underglaze. Scene depicts Pilgrim couple bringing food. Titled "The Pilgrims Thanksgiving." Artist: Jack Woodson. From "The Thanksgiving Day Plate Collection." Production run limited to one year. 1987 Edition Plate No.1/Number #087. Mark: same as before. $15-20. Bing and Grøndahl was founded in 1853 and, in 1895, issued for Christmas the first ever limited edition plate. The firm is still active today.

Below:
Plates. L to R: Bareuther & Co., Waldsassen, Bavaria, Germany (1866-present). 7.75"D; Cobalt blue and white lithography underglaze. "Thanksgiving Series" 1971-1984. All plates were limited edition porcelain in an annual quantity of 2,500. The first two years of plates were issued without special boxes. Starting in 1973, a maroon and white box with a cellophane see-through and a brochure were issued. Plate #1 (1971) "First Thanksgiving"; Plate #2 (1972) "Harvest"; Plate #3 (1973) "Country Road in Autumn." "Mark: All plates titled "Thanksgiving" and date; all have blue backstamp of crown symbol – "100 Jahre" "Bareuther Waldsassen Bavaria Germany.". $10-12 each.

Plates. L to R: Bareuther & Co., Waldsassen, Bavaria, Germany. 7.75"D; Cobalt blue and white lithography underglaze. "Thanksgiving Series." Plate #4 (1974) "Old Mill Stream"; Plate #5 (1975) "Wild Deer in Forest"; Plate #6 (1976) "Thanksgiving on Farm." Mark: Same as before. $10-12 each MIB.

Vase and Bowl. Royal Bayreuth. Tettau, Bavaria, Germany. Royal Bayreuth specialized in fine lithographic paintings and aerographic sprayed decoration. Vase. 5.25"H x 3.25"D; Fine chinaware, footed bulbous base. Pattern "Boy and Turkeys" (rural scene). Mark: Backstamp dual lions symbol – "Royal Bayreuth-Bavaria." c.1885-1915, $275+; Bowl. 10.25"D; Six-sided bowl, rim has gilded accents with a "gold bead" decoration. Pattern "Boy and Turkeys" (rural pastoral scene). Mark: Same as before. Royal Bayreuth was founded in 1754 and is still active. Their fine porcelain and figural items are almost exclusively exported. c.1885-1915. $500+.

Plate. 10"D; Charles Ahrenfeldt, Limoges, France (1859-1969). White porcelain base, 2" rim edged in gold. Rim band multicolor stylized floral bouquets. Tom Turkey in shades of black, brown, and yellow on a greenish yellow field. Mark: Backstamp "C.A. Ahrenfeldt Limoges France." c.1891+. $45-50.

Figural Plate. 10"L x 10.38"W, slightly oval. White figural base of Tom Turkey outline. Hand-painted colors of rose, black, and green. Mark: Green circular backstamp "Made in Czechoslovakia." c.1918-1938. $75-85.

Tureen. 8.75"H x 12"L x 13"W; Multi-green shadings, heavily embossed glazed figural body of various vegetable designs. Mark: "© Sigma ® The Tastesetter. Made in Italy. MCMXXXIII" (label and impressed). c.1983. $150+.

Figural Divided Plate. 10"D; Maker not known – possibly Italian. Majolica 5-compartment canapé dish. Multicolor Tom Turkey design that encompasses the plate. Turkey head is a toothpick holder. Mark: None. c.1980s. $40-45.

Tureens, Covered Bowls, and Miscellaneous Ceramic Items

In addition to the expected platters and plates, the well-appointed Thanksgiving table will also have other complementary serveware pieces, both utilitarian as well as decorative in nature. The next important item would be a tureen. By definition, a **tureen** is a wide, deep, **covered bowl** made for the use of a ladle and, depending on the size, used for soups, gravies, or other sauce-type condiments. Most serveware items have a dual role – functional usage and decorative accessory to add charm and color to enhance a festive occasion. Luckily, the rounded shape of a turkey lends itself well to the constructions of tureens and bowls of all shapes and sizes. Figural glass items, as opposed to ceramic serveware pieces, are fully covered in Chapter 4.

Tureen. 8.75"H x 9.75"L x 13"W; Multicolor embossed glazed figural body. Dark rose and mint green ladle, 12"L. Mark: Backstamp – black "Japan." c.1980s. $60-65.

Divided Plate – side view showing depth.

Tureen. 12"H x 13.75"L x 9.75"W; Multicolor embossed glazed figural body. White ladle, 12"L. Mark: Backstamp – black "E" (encircled) Italy, 485." c. mid 1980s. $50-60.

Covered Bowl. 8"H x 8.75"L x 10.5"D; Multicolor embossed glazed figural lid. Gray and black glazed "basket" dish with handles. Mark: Backstamp – green shield symbol "Morikin Japan." c.1980s. $50-55.

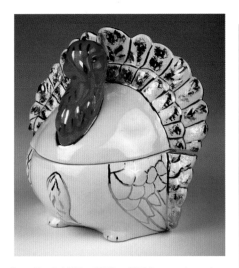

Gravy Bowl. 6.5"H x 4.75"L x 7"W; Ivory embossed figural glazed body. Bright red wattle with gold burnished and trim accents. Ivory glazed ladle with gold trim. Mark: Backstamp – gold script "Eva Woodcraft Georgetown Canada." c.1970s. $25-30.

Relish Bowls. L to R: 6.5"H x 7.5"L x 4.5"W; Multi-brown shadings. Embossed glazed figural Tom Turkey with cowboy hat. Ladle opening. Figural poult lid. Mark: back – impressed under glaze "ceramica garmon." c.1970s. $50-60; 6.5"H x 7.5"L x 4.5"W; Terra-cotta and tan shadings. Embossed glazed figural Tom Turkey with cowboy hat. Ladle opening. Figural poult lid. Mark: back-impressed under glaze "ceramica garmon." c.1970s. $50-60.

Gravy Bowl. 7"H x 5.5"L x 7.25"W; Yellow embossed glazed figural body. Dark red wattle, brown accent mark with blue shadings and trim. Ladle. Mark: Back – incised initials "KV"; on rim of lid – impressed "S L Clutters ©." c.1970s. $25-30.

Gravy Bowls. L to R: 6.5"H x 5.25"L x 3.75"W; Brownish-gold with black and green shadings, rose-pink wattle. Embossed glazed figural body. Ladle in burnish rose shades. Mark: Back "Made in Italy. c. 1980s. $25-30; 6.5"H x 6.5"L x 4.5"W; Multicolor embossed glazed figural body. Ladle opening. Mark: Back – gold and black foil sticker – winged horse symbol "Chase Japan." c.1970s. $25-30.

Gravy Bowls. L to R: 5.75"H x 6"L x 5"W; Multicolor embossed glazed figural body. White glazed ladle. Mark: No marks. Japan? c.1980s. $20-25; 5.75"H x 6"L x 5"W; Multi-color embossed glazed figural body. White glazed ladle (right side). Mark: Back – impressed "Brazil." c.1980s. $20-25.

Teapot/Gravy Dispensers with Handle. L to R: 7.25"H x 8.5"L x 7"W; Multi-black and gray shadings. Embossed glazed figural Tom Turkey with rump lid. Mark: "© Omnibus 1990 42 oz." c. early 1990s. $50-55; 5.25"H x 7.75"L x 5"W; Multicolor embossed glazed figural body. Mark: Back – impressed "© Otagiri," silver label "Japan." c. early 1990s. $45-50.

Candy/Nut Bowls. L to R: 6.75"H x 5.75"L x 6"W; Brownish tan and golden yellow tail. Embossed lightly glazed figural Tom Turkey. Hand-painted mold. Mark: Incised "LJ 1981." $20-25; 5.5"H x 4.75"L x 5"W; Gray shading airbrushed on white, bright red wattle, embossed lightly glazed figural Tom Turkey. Hand-painted mold. Marks: No marks. c. early 1980s. $20-25.

Hors d'oeuvre Server/Toothpick Holder. L to R: 6.25"H x 6.5"L 3.5"W; Dark brown tones, ivory wing accents, rose wattle. Dark green pick holder base. Glazed embossed figural body, Tom Turkey in stride. Mark: No marks – Wahpeton Pottery Company, North Dakota, "Rosemeade." c. early 1950s. $90-100; 6"H x 6"L x 5"W; Dark multicolor medium glazed embossed figural body, bright red wattle, twenty pick holes. Mark: Back – underglaze green circular wreath with flower petal "Japan." c. late 1970s. $50-55.

Relish Bowls/Serving Dishes. Bowl 5"H x 5.5"L x 4.6"W; Multicolor hand-painted glazed embossed figural body. Ladle. Mark: Not marked but is "Brad Keeler Artwares, Los Angeles, California." c. late 1940s to early1950s. $80-100 each; Tidbits Serving Dishes. 4.75"L x 3.75"W; Multicolor hand-painted embossed figural dish. Mark: Not marked but "Brad Keeler Artwares." c. late 1940 to early 1950s. $40-50 each.

Relish Bowls. L to R, Top: 5.75"H x 6"L x 5.5"W; Tan and light green shadings, light rose wattle. Glazed embossed figural body. Ladle opening. Mark: No marks. c. 1970s. $15-20; 5.25"H x 6.25"L x 4.75"W; Brown and green hand-painted glazed embossed figural mold. Ladle opening. Mark: Back – black script "Buddie 1959." $20-25; 5"H x 5"L x 3.6"W; Multicolor glazed embossed figural body. Ladle opening. Mark: No marks. c. 1970s. $20-25. Bottom: 5.25"H x 5"L x 5"W; Gray, rose, and teal pastels. Glazed embossed figural body. Ladle opening. Mark: No marks – Thomas Ceramics. c. early 1980s. $20-25; 4.5"H x 4.5"L x 3.5"W; Dark brown with cream tail accents, dark rose wattle. Glazed embossed figural body. Mark: No marks – Wahpeton Pottery Co., Wahpeton, N.D. "Rosemeade." c. late 1950s to 1960s. $150+; 4.5"H x 4"L x 3.75"W; Teal and orange matte color, embossed figural body. Ladle opening. Mark: Indistinct impressed mark on lid. c.1980s. $15-20.

Napkin Holders. L to R: 6"H x 6.13"L x 6.5"W; Green, rose, yellow and red glazed embossed figural body. Mark: Black backstamp "MCD Distributing, 1993." $20-25; 4.75"H x 4"L x 4.6"W; Mustard, brownish tan, grayish blue, and green with dark rose wattle, glazed embossed figural body. Mark: "C-7488" Napco. c. late 1970s. $30-35.

Wall Pocket with Utensils.7"H x 6"W; Multicolor glazed hand-painted embossed figural body with three hooks for serving utensils. 7"H hand-painted fork and two pastry servers. Mark: Bottom green stamp – shield symbol encased "Morikin Japan and wreath." Utensils mark: "Japan." c.1970s. $25-30.

Demitasse Set (6-piece). Erwin Pottery, Erwin, Tennessee. Pot and Lid: 6.25"H x 7.75"L x 4.5"W; Sugar and Lid: 3.25"H x 5"L x 3.75"D; Creamer: 2.38"H x 4.5"L x 3"D; Plate: 7"D; White body with green, brown, and black images hand-painted under glaze. Set is based on Southern Potteries Colonial shape. Cups and saucers would also be a part of this set. Mark: On body "N.P (Negatha Peterson); bottom black stamp "Erwin Pottery Hand Painted Erwin Tenn.", c.1960s. $200+.

Fitz and Floyd Collectibles

Fitz and Floyd, founded in 1960, is a Dallas, Texas (corporate offices in Lewisville, Texas) based designer of fine ceramics and decorative accessories. Much of their giftware is holiday-seasonal in nature and is sold through the better specialty, department stores, and mail-order catalogs. A Fitz and Floyd ceramic item is easily recognized by its colorful, scrupulously designed appearance and meticulous attention to detail. All of their crafted items are hand-painted, and many of these items have figural identities that occasionally segue into the whimsical. Production of hand-painted giftware and fine china is managed in various plants throughout Asia. Fitz and Floyd also produced ceramic items of lesser quality and detail under the Omnibus brand name. In 2000, in order to strengthen their product line, Fitz and Floyd acquired two U.S. based firms producing seasonal fragrances in many styles and uses as well as decorative accessories.

Covered Vegetable Bowl. 10.25"H x 8"L x 8"W; Fitz and Floyd. Whimsical standing Tom Turkey, with paint palette associated with forest animals and pumpkins. Multicolor glazed handcrafted china. Made in Taiwan. 1995. $140+.

Covered Vegetable Bowl, two views. 10.5"H x 11"L x 8.75"W; Fitz and Floyd. *Autumn Bounty*, seated Tom Turkey on a footed nest. Multicolor glazed handcrafted china. 1997. $130+.

Covered Vegetable Bowl. 9"H x 9.5"D; Holds 1.25 quarts. Fitz and Floyd *Thanksgiving Banquet*, seated Tom Turkey on a green bowl with corn stalks in heavy relief. Multicolor glazed handcrafted china. Made in Taiwan. 1993. $150+.

Teapot with leaf finial lid. 8"H x 8"L x 7"W; Holds 33 ounces. Fitz and Floyd. *Thanksgiving Banquet*, standing Tom Turkey with brown braided handle. Multicolor glazed handcrafted china. Made in Taiwan. 1993. $100+.

Side view of Fitz and Floyd teapot.

51

Pitcher. 10.5"H; 1.75 quart size. Fitz and Floyd. *Harvest Pitcher*, decorated with high relief corn stalks, fall vegetables, and grapes. Corn stalks ear handle. Multicolor glazed handcrafted china. Made in Taiwan. 1995. $75+.

Assortment. L to R: Serving dish (Cranberry Server) 10.5"L x 6.5"W; Fitz and Floyd. *Pilgrims Progress*. White oval dish decorated with Pilgrim and Turkey figures. Pastel colored glazed handcrafted china. Made in Taiwan. 1990. $20-25; Candleholders (pair). 8.5"H; *Pilgrims Progress*. Multicolored pastel handcrafted china. 1990. $200-225.

Pitchers. Fitz and Floyd. L to R: *Thanksgiving Banquet*. Standing Pilgrim Man with Musket. 9"H x 3.75"D; Holds 23 ounces; Standing Pilgrim Woman with Basket. 8.75"H x 3.75"D; Holds 18 ounces; Standing Indian with Robe. 9"H x 4"D; Holds 1 quart. Multicolor glazed handcrafted china. Made in Taiwan. 1993. $40-45 each.

Salt and Pepper Shakers

From the earliest times in recorded history when humans first sat down to share a meal, condiments and spices have been an integral part – whether to enhance or even to disguise the taste of the food. Therefore, condiment dispensers, better known as **salt & pepper shakers**, have a long and storied history and have attracted a very sizable base of collectors.

Salt and pepper shaker pairs produced before World War II, while made in bright and colorful glazes and/or decal-decorated, were utilitarian items made for a special purpose – all work and no show. After World War II, people's tastes began to change (no pun), prompting the production, usually from Japan, of colorful figural and whimsical ceramic salt and pepper shakers. Thanksgiving holiday designs consist, for the most part, of Tom and Hen Turkey pairs, while the balance is made up of Pilgrim sets, "nesters," and "nodders." The sixty or more shaker sets pictured here, except where noted, are all made of glazed ceramic materials, made in Japan (backstamp or labels), and date from the late 1940s to the late 1960s. While values depend on CARL, viz. condition, age, rarity, and location (of production), the values range from $10-20 per pair. Specifically, pairs in sizes from 2" to 3.5" should sell in the $10-12 range, sizes from 3.75" to 4.5" should sell in the $13-16 range, and sizes that exceed 4.5" should sell in the $17-20 range.

Assortment. L to R, Top: Serving Platter. 15.5"L x 11.5"W; Omnibus @ OCI (Fitz and Floyd). White oval base, 1.75" rim edged in brown and decorated with corn and flowering branches in high relief. Multicolor hand-painted Tom Turkey in relief on a cross-hatched background. Mark: "Omnibus @ OCI 1993 China." $50-55; Serving Plate. 8.25"D; Fitz and Floyd. Tom Turkey holding a pie. Multi-color glazed handcrafted china. Made in Taiwan. 1995. $30-35; Bottom: Candleholder (dual). 4.5"H x 6.25"D; Omnibus by Fitz and Floyd. Multicolor glazed handcrafted china. Made in China. 1996. $25-30; Candleholder (pair). Large 5"H, small 4"H; Fitz and Floyd. *Thanksgiving Banquet*. Multicolor glazed handcrafted china. Made in Turkey. 1993. $35-40.

Shakers. Japan. L to R, Top: 5"H, $17-20; Bottom: 3.5"H, $13-16.

Shakers. Japan. L to R, Top: 4"H, $13-16; Bottom: 3.3"H, $10-12.

Shakers. Japan. L to R, Top: 3.25"-3.75"H, $10-16; Middle: 2.5"-3.75"H, $10-16; Bottom: Japan (2) 3.75"H, $13-16; United States (2) 3.75"H, $13-16; Wahpeton Pottery Company, Wahpeton, North Dakota USA "Rosemeade, (2) green and silver label, $60-75.

Shakers. Japan. L to R, Top: 3.5"H, Napcoware. $10-12; Bottom: 3"-3.75"H, $10-16.

Shakers, Japan and USA. L to R, Top: 3.75"-4"H, $13-16; Middle: 2.5"-3.5"H, $10-12; Bottom: 2.5"-3.6"H, $13-16.

Shakers. Japan. All rows: 2"-3.75"H, $10-16.

Shakers. Japan, China and USA. L to R, Top: 2"-3.75"H, $10-16; Middle: 3.25"H, $10-12; Bottom: 2.5"-3.25"H, $10-12.

Shakers. Japan. L to R, Top: 4"-5.5"H, $13-20; Middle: 3.25"-3.5", $12-16; Bottom: 2.56"-3.5"H, $15-18.

Shakers. Kay Finch, Corona del Mar, California, USA. Tom Turkeys (pair) 3.5"H, matte brown, black stamp. c.1948-1955. $80-100 for the pair.

Shakers Sets. L to R: Décor Set, consisting of glass tray, 4.5"L x 1.5"W; Glass Shakers with red plastic tops, 1.75"H; Plastic Turkey, 2.5"H. Mark: Japan. c.1960s. $8-10; Glass Set, consisting of glass tray in the shape of a turkey tail, 3.75"L; Glass Shakers with metal tops, 1.5"H. Marks: No marks. c.1960s. $15-18.

Nodders Set. 2"H x 3"L x 2"W. Tom and Hen Turkey, 2.75"H. Front panel floral decoration. Mark: Red stamp – one-half garland symbol "Japan," impressed "Patent TT." c.1930s. $75+; Round Shakers. 2.5"H, scalloped tops. Hand-painted Tom Turkeys. Mark: Red and silver foil label "Lefton Reg. US Pat. Off Exclusives Japan," green stamp "2267N." c.1950s-1960s. $25-30.

Left and below:
Nester. Two parts. Nesters are those sets in which one shaker rests entirely upon the other shaker. Tom Turkey, 2.25"H. Nest (four eggs), 1"H. Hand-painted under glass. Sold as a gift – souvenir black, gold, and red foil label "Niagara Falls Canada." Mark: Black stamp "Germany," blue stamp – symbol "High Bee in a V," circular tan and blue paper label 1 50." Made by W. Goebel, Rodenthal, (W) Germany. c.1957. $30-35.

Shaker Sets. Pilgrims and related. Japan and USA. L to R, Top: 3.5"-4.25"H, $13-16; Middle: 3.5"-3.75"H, c. late 1990s, $10-12; Bottom: 2.75"-5"H, $10-20; Plymouth Rock, 3.25"L x 2.25"W. Mark: Blue and white label "Made in Japan. c.1990s, $10-12.

Shakers. Japan. L to R, Top: Cornucopia, 2"H; Roast Turkey on Platter, 3.5"L x 2"W x 2.25"H; Bottom: Turkey eggs (pair), 3"L x 2"H; Roast Turkey on Platter, 3.75"L x 2.25"W x 2.25"H, $15-18.

Pie Vents

"Sing a Song of Sixpence, a Pocket full of Rye, Four and Twenty Blackbirds baked in a Pie."

Exchange "pie birds" for "blackbirds" in the ditty above and the meaning of the use of pie birds becomes clear. In Victorian times, during the nineteenth century, the English **pie funnel**, as it is called in Britain, served a strictly utilitarian function. The purpose of the pie funnel is twofold: (1) it should support and lift the pastry crust above the filling during cooking, and (2) it should ventilate the pie so that the filling does not boil over in the oven. A pie funnel or **vent** is usually made of heat resistant glazed pottery, 3" to 5" in height, with arches at the base to allow steam to enter and vent. In the mid-1930s, a creative innovation took place and the simple round or square vent took on a new shape while still retaining its old role. After World War II, figural and novelty vents in an enormous selection of shapes came into the marketplace. The most popular sculpted shape was that of a bird with its head raised (and mouth open), hence the term **pie bird**. These bright and cheery designs are almost always handcrafted and hand-painted by individual ceramicists, and pie birds or vents from the English are considered highly desirable and very collectible. Most, if not all of these vents, will never see the insides of a baked pie!

Pie Birds. L to R: Cubboard Classics, Deer Trail, Colorado. Pilgrim Woman and Man, hand-painted, 4"H. Mark: C.C. 95. 75 sets made. $40-45 pair; Thanksgiving Turkeys (wearing a feather and a hat), hand-painted, 3.75"H. Mark: Happy Thanksgiving #1 of 125 sets made. C.C. 96. $35-40 pair.

Pie Birds. L to R, Top: Tom Turkey (yellow base), 3.75"H. Mark: "MB". c.1990s, $25-30; Bottom: Tom Turkey, 3.5"H. Sky-blue glaze. Marks: No marks. c.1990s. $35-40; Tom Turkey, 4.6"H. Chocolate brown glaze. Marks: No marks. c.1990s, $25-30; Tom Turkey, 3.6"H. Beige, brown, and black matte. Marks: "SR" Sammie Roberts, Fresno, California. c.2000. $30-35; Tom Turkey head, 4.75"H. Black, gray, white, and red matte. Marks: "F97." c. late 1990s. $30-35; Tom Turkey 4.75"H. Tan with black and brown splatters. Mark: No marks. c.1990s. $25-30.

Pie Birds. L to R: Pilgrim Boy, 5"H. Holding basket of produce. Marks: No marks. c.1990s. $30-35; Pilgrim Girl, 5"H. Clasping hands. Mark: No marks. c.1990s. $20-25; Pilgrim Woman, 4.5"H. Mark: "CH." c.1990s. $35-40.

Pie Funnels. L to R: Tom Turkey, 2.75"H. Brown, golden brown, and mustard glaze. Marks: "R. Bass." "Happy Thanksgiving #4/250." Rachel Bass, Bath, England, is the daughter of Stuart Bass. c.1999. $50+ MIB (The Celebrations Collection); Tom Turkey, 3.38"H. Dark brown, green, and gray glaze. Mark: "S. Bass." Stuart Bass, South Moulton, England. c.1999. $50+ MIB (The Celebrations Collection).

Chocolate and Ice Cream Moulds

The *cacao* bean, highly valued by the Aztecs, Incas, and Mayas of ancient Mexico, was used both as a medium of exchange and as the basis for a potent home brew. Mixed with hot water and a flavoring agent, the ground *cacao* was turned into a mildly stimulative drink called *chocolatl*. In the sixteenth century, Hernando Cortez, conqueror of Mexico, brought back to the Spanish court the methodology for converting the bitter *cacoa* bean into a sweetened chocolate drink. For the next three hundred years, chocolate was consumed only in liquid form until a series of manufacturing and chemical advancements produced an edible form of chocolate paste amenable to be formed into "cakes" or blocks.

In order to convert the unstable chocolate paste into a solid chocolate form, the structure of chocolate moulds required two basic elements: (1) a material that would assist in the heat exchange needed to cool the paste, and (2) a shiny non-adhering surface that would be both shock-resistant and affordable. Out of necessity, invention is bred! The steel-making industry of the early nineteenth century started to produce strong and malleable sheet metal that was tin-plated to prevent rusting, thereby allowing a hygienic surface. At the same time, a metal stamping machine was developed capable of mass-producing single-piece items with a hollow interior.

In 1832, therefore, skilled tinplate workers in France, imbued with emerging technical innovation, were the first to manufacture fancy tinplate hollow moulds for chocolate makers. These moulds were in the shapes of people, animals, or objects. Pewter metal was also in use, and the resulting moulds could be used for both ice cream or chocolate.

For the next thirty years, the French, especially, the Lé Tang firms, were the dominant mould makers. Then in the mid-to-late 1800s, three German firms became the major suppliers of moulds used in Europe and the United States. The largest and most famous of the German firms was Anton Reiche, founded in 1870 in Dresden. At its peak during the 1930s, the Reiche catalogue enumerated over 50,000 different moulds. When the company marked its moulds, it did so with a distinctive ANTON REICHE DRESDEN stamp placed between two small curving triangles, the top of each indicating the first and then the last digit of the year of manufacture e.g. 3————7. During World War II, in February, 1945, Dresden was almost totally destroyed during the Allied bombing raids and resultant firestorm. After the war, the firm rebuilt under the auspices of the Deutsche Demokratische Republik or DDR. Due to the vagaries of operating under such a controlled system, the firm of Anton Reiche went out of business in 1972.

NFFM: Hinged and clamped, with hinged bottom plate, back to back Turkeys. Anton Reiche, 6.5" x 9.5". $275-325.

NFFM: Hinged, clamped and banded, with hinged bottom plate, Tom Turkeys. Anton Reiche, 7.75" x 10.75". $300-350.

NFFM: Hinged, clamped and banded, with hinged bottom plate, Tom Turkeys. Anton Reiche, 5.5" x 11.25". $450-500.

NFFM: Hinged, clamped and banded, with hinged bottom plate, Tom Turkeys; showing three open moulds joined together.

In the United States, the two main manufacturers were Eppelsheimer & Co. and T.C. Weygandt. The Eppelsheimer brothers began production of chocolate moulds in New York City in 1880. In 1910, the firm was purchased, but the name Eppelsheimer & Co. was retained. Due to its quality reputation, the firm became the largest manufacturer of domestic moulds. Eppelsheimer marked its moulds with a distinctive spinning top design. In 1947, the firm was again purchased, this time by American Chocolate Mould Company (still in business). Due to the rising cost of quality tinplate and the increasing demand for cheaper plastic moulds, ACMC phased out its metal chocolate mould production, and the name Eppelsheimer faded into oblivion by 1974.

NFFM: Basic open two-piece mould, Tom Turkey, opening at bottom and removable tail (used for solid chocolate forms). Eppelsheimer, 9" x 8.5". $650-750.

The T.C. Weygandt Co. was originally Anton Reiche's United States agent, beginning in 1885. When World War II started in 1939, shipments from Germany ceased. In order to survive, T.C. Weygandt began to produce some of Anton Reiche's designs in New York City. After the war, T.C. Weygandt continued to produce metal moulds until 1969 when cost considerations dictated closure. Domestic moulds were stamped T.C. WEYGANDT CO. NEW YORK. Today, high-grade plastic moulds are predominant due to cost considerations but with some loss in detail.

The terms *moulds* and *molds* can be used interchangeably and are both correct in their usage. The authors prefer to use the British word variant *mould*, due to its European origin.

Chocolate moulds can be divided into two main classifications: (1) **Novelty Full Figure Moulds** (NFFM) and (2) **Flat Moulds**. The Novelty Full Figure moulds have at least two mirror image pieces and are three-dimensional in shape. Flats are one-piece moulds used to form half figures and simple geometric shapes.

L to R: NFFM: Basic open two-piece mould, Tom Turkey, opening at bottom, secured with flange clamp. T.C. Weygandt, postwar #16220, 4.75" x 4.5". $100-150. NFFM: Basic open two-piece mould, Tom Turkey, opening at bottom, secured with flange clamps. Jaburg Bros.- New York (due to fantail design and detail), 4.75" x 4". $100-150.

L to R, Back: NFFM: Basic open two-piece mould, Tom Turkey, opening at bottom, secured with two flange clamps, Eppelsheimer #274, 7.5" x 7.5". $450-550. NFFM: Basic open two-piece mould, Tom Turkey, opening at bottom, secured with two flange clamps. Eppelsheimer #8223, 6.75" x 6.25". $350-450. Front: NFFM: Basic open two-piece mould, Tom Turkey, opening at bottom, secured with two flange clamps. Eppelsheimer #7502, 6" x 5.5". $225-275. NFFM: Basic open two-piece mould, Tom Turkey, opening at bottom, secured with one flange clip. T.C. Weygandt #193, 6" x 5". $125-175.

Left:
Close-up of Eppelsheimer's spinning top trademarked design with catalogue style number 4922.

L to R: NFFM: Basic open three-piece mould, Tom Turkey, opening at bottom and removable tail with three flange clamps, 5.25" x 4.75". $125-175. NFFM: Basic open two-piece mould, Tom Turkey, opening at bottom, secured with three pins and one clamp with removable tail. T.C. Weygandt & Co., made in New York U.S.A Germany, #14230, 4" x 4". $100-150. NFFM: Hinged and clamped mould, Tom Turkey, with patented interlocking flange (U.S. Patent No. 1948146-1948). Eppelsheimer-1937 design, 4.75" x 4". $125-150. NFFM: Basic open two-piece mould, Tom Turkey, opening at bottom, secured with two flange clamps (one left off to show marking). Anton Reiche (T.C. Weygandt Made in Germany #16220), 5" x 4.25" (marked HH – personal mould with person's initials). $150-200.

Flat Mould (Bar Mould): A three-dimensional model of two differing sized turkeys in pot metal framed by Plaster of Paris. The matrix is the negative (female mould) of the stamp and is engraved hollow, 4" x 5". $30-50.

Flat Mould: Soldered and framed, Tom Turkeys. Eppelsheimer, 13.75" x 10". $150-200.

Reverse, signed – Pfeil & Holing New York City # 229, a confectionary firm with its own special order bar, circa early 1900s. The firm still is in business today as a seller of cake decorations.

Flat Mould: Lollipop or sucker mould with ring clamp, tinware, Tom Turkey, 3.5" square. Eppelsheimer, $40-60. In the mid-1950s, a box of one dozen chocolate Turkey Pops retailed for $0.59.

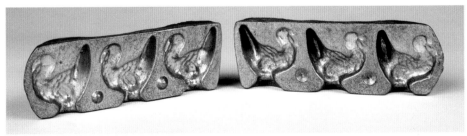

Ice Cream Mould: Basic open mould, three Turkeys, pewter, 2" x 6". $50-70.

L to R: Ice Cream Mould: Closed hinged mould, open configuration – facing away, pewter, 3.5" x 3.75". Eppelsheimer #650, $125-150. Closed hinged mould, closed configuration – facing together, pewter, 3.5" x 3.5", marked LP. $125-175.

L to R: Ice Cream Mould: Closed hinged mould, open configuration from bottom, pewter, 4.5" x 3". Eppelsheimer #429, $125-150; Closed hinged mould, closed configuration, pewter, 4.5" x 3". Eppelsheimer #429, $125-150.

Ice Cream Mould: Closed hinged mould, roasted turkey, pewter, 2.25" x 4.25". Eppelsheimer, $85-115.

"O' how dark it is
Here in the back of the shop.
People walk by me,
But never stop.
I sit here
With no choice, but to wait
For time and wear have sealed my fate.
I am, but an old tin can
That has a dirty label;
With not enough appeal
To grace a table…"

Condition notwithstanding, even "an old tin can" can usually find a home these days.

Coffee Tins/Go-With. L to R: A.J. Kasper Company, Chicago, Illinois and Kansas City, Missouri. *Turkey Brand Roasted Coffee,* 11"H x 5"D; 3 pounds capacity. Gun metal gray base, red graphics, charcoal gray Tom Turkey. c.1905-1915. $600+; *Turkey Brand Roasted Coffee.* 5.75"H x 4.25"D; 1 pound capacity. Same graphics. c.1905-1915. $450+; Go-With Watch Fob. A.J. Kasper Company. *Turkey Brand* Tom Turkey image on heavily patina pot metal.c.1905-1915. $300+. Rare.

Close-up of A.J. Kasper *Turkey Brand* watch fob.

Postcard advertising *Turkey Coffee.* The National Drink, A. J. Kasper Co. Illinois. "Uncle Sam Prefers Turkey Coffee." c.1907-1915. $22-25.

Food Tins and Related Kitchen and Farm Items

Tins, spice packages, cake pans, food spreaders and picks all bear at least an indirect relationship to the Thanksgiving dinner table in that these items act as conveyances for food storage and preparation. Several of the pieces portrayed are excellent graphic representations, which adds enormously to their collectibility. These tins and other items are integral links in the chain of memorializing the turkey image.

Antique tins have become highly sought-after collectibles since the 1970s. Such tins were used and reused many times as storage equipment, so it is virtually impossible to find mint or near mint tins today that have not been subject to dents, scratches, or even rust. Rare tins are scarce enough, however, that having a good to fair example is worth the effort of acquisition. We have included part of a poem written by Ernest L. Pettit, a well-known tin container collector in the 1970s, to summarize the thought:

Coffee Tin/Commercial Covers. L to R: J.B. Maltby, Inc., Corning, New York. *Red Turkey Brand Coffee,* 6"H x 4.25"D; 1 pound capacity. Slip lid. Cream and navy blue base, graphics and Tom Turkey image in red. c.1905-1915. $175+; Commercial Covers. Top: *Red Turkey Food Products,* J.B. Maltby, Inc. Wholesale Grocers. Corning. Jul 21-15 to Big Flats, New York. $40-50; Bottom: *Red Turkey Wheat Flour,* J.B. Maltby, Inc. Wholesale Grocery. Corning. Jun 20- 1912 to Big Flats, New York. $50-60.

Syrup Tin. J. Stromeyer Company, Philadelphia, Pennsylvania. *Turkey Brand Golden Table Syrup.* 5.25"H x 5"D; 4 pounds, 8 ounces. Red shield on dark blue base, small Tom Turkey insert. c.1920s. $100+.

Knife Food Spreaders/Picks. L to R: Spreaders. Boston Warehouse Trading Corporation, Norwood, Massachusetts. Set of four stainless steel knives, 4.75"L; Model No. 12-119. Images: Pilgrim Man, Pilgrim Woman, Indian, Turkey. Made in China. c.1995. $13-15; Turkey Picks. No marks. Set of six turkey food picks. 2.75"L; Green and red Tom Turkey holder. c.1990s. $8-10 MIB.

Very colorful graphic images of the Tom Turkey were not only lithographed on tin containers but also printed on a wide range of cloth materials. **Flour sacks** and **turkey mash sacks** (yes, domestic turkeys have to be fed) were also decorated with "eye-appealing" graphics. Given the extremes of conditions that domestic turkey growers had to endure prior to the 1970s, it is a wonder that any turkey feed sack survived, given the many "alternative" uses for which these empty sacks could be used.

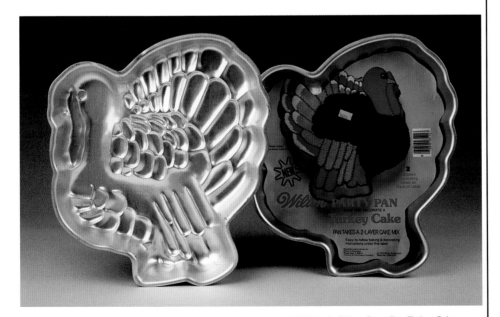

Spice Tins and Boxes. L to R: The William G. Bell Company. Boston, Massachusetts. *Bell's Poultry Seasoning.* Heavy paper box. 3.75"H x 2.5"L x 1.25"W; 1.5 ounces. Yellow base, red banners, Tom Turkey. A 10¢ box was sufficient to flavor the dressing for 100 pounds of meat or poultry. c. early 1900s. $10-15; *Bell's Seasoning* (a mixture of ground sage, marjoram, and spices). Heavy paper box, tin pouring spout. Same graphics. c.1930s. $10-13; E. R. Durkee & Company Elmhurst, Long Island, New York. *Durkee's Poultry Seasoning* (Mace) Lithographed tin. 4"H x 2.25"L x 1.25"W; 4 ounces. Green base, red and green graphics. Tom Turkey insert on black banner. c.1940s. $22-25; Rico Manufacturing Company, Nashville, Tennessee. *Regoes Rubbed Sage* (Imported Dalmatian). Lithographed tin. 4.25"H x 2.5"D; 2 ounces. Dark navy blue base, yellow and red banner, blue Tom Turkey insert. c.1950s. $15-18.

Flour Sack. Lehi Roller Mills Company, Inc., Lehi, Utah. *Turkey Brand* enriched bakers flour made from Hard Turkey Red wheat. Heavy cotton muslin, 24"L x 36"W; 100 lbs. net weight. Black, brown, and blue turkey graphic. c.1990s. $18-20.

Cake/Mold Pan. Wilton Enterprises. Woodridge, Illinois (Division of Pillsbury). *Wilton Party Pan Turkey Cake.* Bright tinware figural Tom Turkey shape with original insert. 13"L x 11.25"W x 1.75"Depth. Holds 2-layer cake mix. © 1979. Discontinued. $18-22.

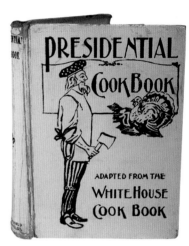

Mash Sack. Larrowe Milling Company (General Mills, Inc.), Detroit, Michigan. *Larro* turkey breeder mash (crushed meal). Heavy cotton muslin, 20"L x 37"W; 100 lbs. net weight. Red and blue graphics. c.1940s-1950s. $30-35.

Mash Sack. Ralston Purina, St. Louis, Missouri. *Turkey Startena* "checker-etts." Heavy cotton muslin, 21"L x 37"W; 100 lbs. net weight. Green graphics on red checkerboard. c.1950s. $15-18.

Cookbooks

Go into any well-stocked retail bookstore chain or large independent bookseller and one will find that a considerable amount of shelf space has been given over to **cookbooks** of all types. There is tremendous diversity in the offerings, which range from traditional books, viz., *Better Homes & Gardens New Cookbook* (fifty years old) to regional, viz., Cajun and Pacific Northwest seafood, and finally to ethnic. One can buy books from famous chefs, viz., Julia Childs, James Beard, and Jeremiah Tower; books by food critics like Craig Claiborne of the *New York Times*; or books promoting the cuisine of specialty restaurants under in-house celebrity chefs such as Wolfgang Puck. If the surfeit of cookbooks is not enough to indulge in, there are also books put out by cooking schools exposing their philosophies; books which sponsor charity or good works, viz., Junior League; books by specialty food retailers; books by food processors; books on "how-to" grill and barbeque; books on specific foods such as breads, broccoli, or bananas; books on specific tastes such as vegan or kosher; books on the national cuisines of our world's countries; diet books posing as cookbooks; and finally coffee table books that are more for show than tell. Many authors – namely Martha Stewart and her classic book, *Entertainment*, published in 1982 – tied many recipes together under a theme that provided the wherewithal for ways a host and hostess could cope with feeding sizable number of guests without resorting to catering.

Mash Sack. Hales & Hunter Company, Chicago, Illinois. *Red Comb* turkey mash. Heavy cotton muslin, 20"L x 37.5"W; 100 lbs. net weight. Red and blue graphics, brown turkey graphics. c.1940s-1950s. $35-40.

Regardless of the wide range of available guides, cookbooks were meant to be used and enjoyed. One of our books shown here, the *Presidential Cookbook*, is a treasure trove of recipes from the turn of the nineteenth century, with lengthy handwritten recipes by one or more of the original owners. This shows that a cookbook's unique function is as a reference for the kitchen, rather than taking its place on a dusty and forgotten shelf. The books shown are representative of many of the categories cited.

Cookbook, *Presidential Cook Book.* Adapted from the White House Cook Book. The Saalfield Publishing Company, Akron, Ohio, 1905: 410 pages. In the late 1890s, *The White House Cook Book* was the best selling and had the widest circulation of any cookbook to that date. *The Presidential Cook Book* was a condensed and less expensive version of the former, whose author was that era's world-famous chef, Hugo Ziemann. An excerpt from the book's Poultry section on Roast Turkey reads "the lower part of the leg (or drumstick, as it is called) being hard, tough, and stringy, is rarely ever helped to any one, but allowed to remain on the dish." The Poultry section also presented four recipes for preparing pigeons! $25-40 (well used).

Regional cookbook, *Let's Talk Turkey – Adventures and Recipes of the White Turkey Inn.* F. Meredith Dietz. The Dietz Press, Richmond, Virginia, 1948: 320 Pages. The White Turkey Inn, Danbury, Connecticut, first opened for business in 1905, was housed in a circa 1760 building. This book was written as both a history of the "Inn" and as a cookbook with recipes that made the "Inn" famous. One chapter, "Tale of the Turkey," discusses various attributes of domesticated turkeys including the "Inn's" namesake, the White Holland Turkey. Also disclosed is the "Inn's" famous and secret recipe for White Turkey Conserve. $20-25 with dust jacket.

Menu front, The White Turkeys Restaurant at the White Turkey Inn, Danbury, Connecticut. $10-15.

Luncheon menu, the White Turkey Inn, dated Wednesday, September 3, 1947. Sample entrée: "Plantation Turkey Royal with Mushroom Sauce, $1.65."

Cookbooks. L to R: *Wild Turkey Cookbook*. A.D. Livington. Stadspool Books, Mechanicsburg, Pennsylvania, 1995: 175 pages. Presents more than 199 ways to prepare the wild turkey. $15; *Totally Turkey Thanksgiving Cookbook*. Artex Housewares, Oakland, California, 1996: 70 pages. This small book suggests that the best tasting turkey is a free-range, organically raised one. $5; *Wild About Turkey*. The National Wild Turkey Federation. The Wimmer Companies, Inc., Memphis, Tennessee, 1996: 250 pages. Contains more than 300 recipes provided by members and supporters for grilling, baking, smoking, and barbequing both the wild and domestic turkey. The deep-fried whole turkey (a regional, but fast becoming a national favorite specialty) is discussed, along with special regional Thanksgiving menus. $20; *Chef Wolfe's New American Turkey Cookery*. Ken Wolfe and Olga Bier. Aris Books, Berkeley, California, 1984: 155 pages. This book is a primer or step-by-step master class complete with techniques and recipes on roasting a 22-pound turkey in just over two hours by first disassembling the whole turkey into its major sections. $15-18.

Cookbooks. L to R: *Thanksgiving Cookery*. James W. Baker with Elizabeth Brabb. The Brick Tower Press, New York, 1998: 92 pages. This book was issued under the Traditional Country Life Recipes Series. The first one-third of the book is devoted to Thanksgiving History in the United States; the rest is a compilation of recipes to produce the traditional Thanksgiving feast. $10; *Thanksgiving 101*. Rick Rodgers. Broadway Books, New York, 1998: 166 pages. The author owned a catering company that specialized in cooking regional American foods. Under the auspices of one of the country's largest poultry producers, he traveled throughout the United States teaching Thanksgiving cooking classes. This book is a collection of the very best Thanksgiving recipes gathered on his cooking and lecture tours. $15; *The Thanksgiving Cookbook*. Holly Garrison. Macmillan, New York, 1991: 340 pages. The author, a food writer and consultant, was the food editor of *Parents* magazine for several years. The book contains more than 340 recipes, from "tried and true" traditional ones to regional classics featuring the preparation of different types of fowl including the wild turkey. $15.

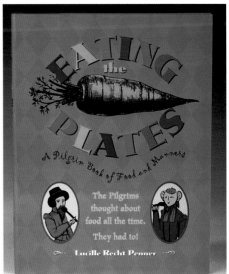

Cookbook, *Eating the Plates. A Pilgrim Book of Food and Manners*. Lucille Penner. Simon & Schuster Books, New York, 1991: 117 pages. Provides an account of what the Pilgrims ate and how they spent their days, including recipes to prepare a complete Pilgrim dinner. $16-20.

Menus

While the above section on cookbooks briefly discusses the diversity of same, these books are static indicators of specific time capsules of food history. The bridges that span these time elements, in order to bring life to various and sundry cooking styles, are **menus**. As historical documents, menus provide an ongoing perspective into the changing tastes of food and beverage consumers from the past. Since the end products of cookbooks are menus, both provide an equal amount of pleasurable interest for the collector of the expanding field of cooking-related ephemera.

Specialty food magazines, of which there are many, represent the last leg of this culinary stool. They offer emerging and sometimes provocative insights to the continual evolution of American cuisine. One of the most influential and longest-lived American culinary magazines was *American Cookery*, which was first published by the Boston Cooking School in 1896 and ceased publication by 1947. Pairing a complete collection of *American Cookery* with a complete run to date of *Gourmet Magazine* would provide an unequaled study of American eating habit spanning parts of three centuries.

Civilian Menus

Menus can be broken down into many segments, but we have categorized them into **civilian** and **military** groupings. Obviously, all of the menus depicted have Thanksgiving dinner as their central theme. Because of the holiday, the majority of menus shown are from restaurants associated with leading hotels.

Menu. *Seventh Avenue Hotel*, Pittsburgh, Pennsylvania. Obverse image depicts turkey in field with trees. $75+.

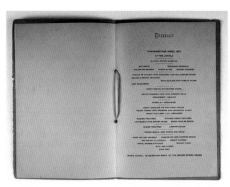

Menu. *Hotel Lincoln*. Thanksgiving menu dated 1907. "Roast Turkey with Dressing and Cranberry Sauce." $18-20.

Menu. *Seventh Avenue Hotel.* Thanksgiving menu dated 1910. "Roast Spring Turkey, Chestnut Stuffing, Cranberry Sauce." $18-20.

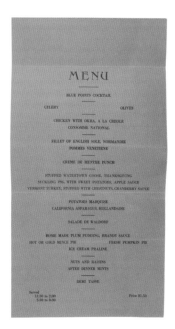

Postcard. Thanksgiving Menu Replica. Nash Series 47. Fairmont, Minnesota, November 11, 1915. $5-10.

Menu. *Hotel Ohio*, Youngstown, Ohio. Souvenir menu dated November 1916. Obverse is an image of "First American Thanksgiving 1621," based on a painting by Jennie Brownscombe. "Vermont Turkey Stuffed with Chestnuts. Cranberry Sauce $1.50." $18-20.

Right:
Postcard. "The Turkey's Dinner." MAB, Made in Germany. 1912. A humorous reversal on the main Thanksgiving dish. $12-15.

Menus. L to R, Top: *The Continental*, Philadelphia, Pennsylvania. 1892. "For we are too young to be eaten you see." "Spring Turkey/Stewed Terrapin." $75+; *Hotel Endicott*, New York. Thanksgiving menu dated and signed by ten guests, November 24, 1910. "Rhode Island Turkey, Stuffed with Chestnuts, Cranberry Sauce. $1.50 cover." $50-60; *Hotel Newton*, New York. Thanksgiving menu dated November 28, 1912. "Vermont Turkey, Chestnut Dressing, Cranberry Sauce. $40-50; *Hotel Ormond*, Thanksgiving Menu dated November 25, 1915. "Stuffed Young Turkey, Chestnut Dressing, Brown Gravy, Cranberry Sauce." $35-40. Bottom: *Hotel San Remo*, New York. Thanksgiving menu dated November 25, 1920. "Roast Stuffed Vermont Turkey, Cranberry Sauce." $20-25; *Hotel Sovereign*, Chicago, Illinois. Thanksgiving menu dated November 27, 1930. "Baked Young Turkey with Chestnut Stuffing, Cranberry Sauce. $2.00." $30-40; *The Franconia*. 1933. "Roast Maryland Turkey, Chestnut Stuffing and Homemade Cranberry Sauce $1.50." $20-25; *Beacon Café*, Boston, Massachusetts, 1925. "Roast Stuffed Vermont Turkey, Cranberry Sauce. $10-15.

Menus. L to R, Top: *The Penn Sheraton Hotel*, Philadelphia, Pennsylvania. Thanksgiving menu dated November 27, 1947. "Thanksgiving Tom Turkey, Chestnut Dressing, Giblet Gravy, Cranberry Sauce. $3.50"; *The Warwick*, Philadelphia. Thanksgiving menu dated November 25, 1948. "Roast Pan Fed Young Tom Turkey, Home Dressing, Fresh Cranberry Basket. $5.00"; *The Sheraton Hotel*, Philadelphia. Thanksgiving menu dated November 25, 1948. "Roast Vermont Turkey, Chestnut Dressing, Giblet Gravy, Cranberry Jelly. $3.50"; *Engineers Club*, Philadelphia. Thanksgiving menu dated November 25, 1948. "Roast Maryland Turkey, Chestnut Dressing, Cranberry Jelly. $2.50"; Bottom: *Engineers Club*, Philadelphia. Thanksgiving menu dated November 23, 1950. "Roast Maryland Turkey, Chestnut Dressing, Cranberry Jelly. $2.50"; *John Bartram Hotel*, Philadelphia. Thanksgiving menu dated November 25, 1948. "Roast Young Maryland Turkey, Giblet Sauce, Chestnut Dressing, Cranberry Jelly. $4.25"; *John Bartram Hotel*, Philadelphia. Thanksgiving menu dated November 23, 1950. "Roast Young Vermont Turkey, Giblet Sauce, Cranberry Jelly, Chestnut Stuffing. $4.50"; *John Bartram Hotel*, Philadelphia. Thanksgiving menu dated 1951. "Roast Young Vermont Turkey, Giblet Sauce, Cranberry Jelly, Chestnut Dressing." $4.50." $8-10 each.

Menus. L to R, Top: *Pioneer Hotel*, Tucson, Arizona. Thanksgiving menu dated November 30, 1939. "Roast Young Tom Turkey, Giblet Dressing, Cranberry Jelly. $1.50." $35-40; *Edgewater Beach Hotel*, Chicago, Illinois. Thanksgiving menu dated November 20, 1941. Twelve different main entrees including "Roast Vermont Turkey, Chestnut Dressing, Giblet Gravy, Cranberry Sauce. $2.25." $35-40; *The University Club*, Boston, Massachusetts. Thanksgiving menu dated November 26, 1942. "Roast Native Turkey, Chestnut Stuffing, Cranberry Sauce. $2.50." $20-25; *The Waldorf Astoria*, New York. Thanksgiving menu dated November 25, 1943. "Roast Turkey, Chestnut Stuffing, Cranberry Sauce. $5.00." $100+; Bottom: *The Read House*, Chattanooga, Tennessee. Thanksgiving menu dated November 29, 1945. "Roast Young Turkey, Sage Dressing, Giblet Gravy, Stewed Cranberries. $1.50." $10-15; *The Old Hingham House*, Hingham, Massachusetts. Thanksgiving menu dated November 22, 1945. "Roast Native Turkey, Sage Dressing, Giblet Gravy, Cranberry Sauce. $10-15; *Pioneer Hotel*, Tucson, Arizona. Thanksgiving menu dated November 28, 1946. "Roast Young Tom Turkey, Cornbread Dressing, Giblet Gravy, Cranberry Sauce. $2.50." $30-40; *The Warwick*, Philadelphia, Pennsylvania. Thanksgiving menu dated November 27, 1947. "Roast Stuffed Maple Crest Tom Turkey, Chestnut Dressing, Old Fashion Fresh Cranberry Sauce. $4.50." $8-10.

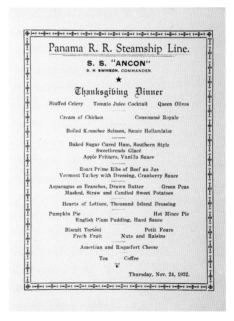

Menu. *S.S. Ancon* – Panama Railroad Steamship Line. Thanksgiving menu dated November 24, 1932. "Vermont Turkey with Dressing, Cranberry Sauce." $30-35.

Menu front. *R.M.S. Queen Mary.* A section of Doris Zinkeisen's main *Painting in the Verandah Grill.*

Billboard Sign, *Larison's Turkey Farm Inn.*

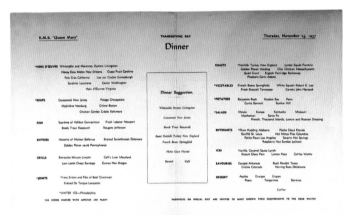

Menu. *R.M.S. Queen Mary* (Cunard White Star). Award White Star Thanksgiving menu dated November 25, 1937. "Roast Norfolk Turkey New England." Also included selections of Squab, Plover, Chicken, Quail, Partridge, Guinea Hen, and Pheasant. $40-50.

Of equal interest are menus and related ephemera from food restaurants that specialize in serving turkey meals and dishes, not just at Thanksgiving, but also *every* day of the year.

Postcard. View of *Larison's Turkey Farm Inn and Restaurant,* corners of Routes 206 & 24, Chester, New Jersey. Dexter Press, West Nyack, New York. c. early 1950s. This famous restaurant started in business serving "Famous Country Style Turkey Dinners," in 1945. The restaurant, which operated in a 200-year-old farmhouse, was combined with a real 70-acre farm, raising, among other farmyard animals, turkeys for the kitchen. On December 31, 2000, local newspaper headlines noted "Larison's Turkey Farm serves its last dinner." But, good news: the restaurant, under new management and ownership, reopened for business in early May 2002. The original home has been retained. "Larison's A Tradition For Generations." $8-10.

Postcard. Kimball's Green Ridge Turkey Farm, Route 3, Nashua, New Hampshire. Tichnor Bros., Inc. Boston, Mass. c. late 1930s, $5-8.

Postcard. Painted view of *Hart's Turkey Farm Restaurant*, Jct. Routes 3 & 104, Meredith, New Hampshire. Dexter Press, West Nyack, New York. This equally famous restaurant got its start in 1954 when the Hart Brothers decided to merchandise their farm-raised turkeys. Since that initial beginning, the restaurant has had many expansions and today it can seat over 500 people. One highlight, based on the assertions of the original owner, Russ Hart, is displayed throughout the restaurant's many dining rooms: the "world's largest turkey plate collection." The restaurant today is still owned and operated by two generations of the Hart family.

Memorabilia, *Willie Bird's Restaurant* and *Willie Bird Turkeys*, Santa Rosa California. The Benedetti family, who were long-time turkey breeders in Sonoma Country, California, started a "free-range," naturally fed turkey operation in 1963. Today, the $7 million business raises approximately 85,000 turkeys annually on four ranches, accounting for about 52,000 "Willie Birds" served on Thanksgiving tables. Prices begin at $2 per pound dressed and can command upwards of $100, depending on size, from specialty retail outlets such as Williams-Sonoma. The family restaurant has been serving various plates of turkey and homemade turkey sausage since 1980. Their web site is www.williebird.com. $3-5.

Memorabilia from *Hart's Turkey Farm Restaurant*. Brochures, placemat, matches. $3-5.

Left and below: Menu, *Hart's Turkey Farm Restaurant*. "Every Day is Thanksgiving Day." 44th Anniversary menu, 19.5"L x 22"W. Regular Turkey Plate, $11.75. 1998. $5-8.

Military Menus

It is said that "an Army travels on its stomach." We are sure that this applies to all units of our country's Armed Forces, whether on foreign or domestic duty. Regardless of location or circumstances, the Quartermasters of all units made sure that our service personnel received a hot Thanksgiving meal with all the trimmings.

Menus. Top: *United States Naval Academy*. Midshipmen's Mess. Annapolis, Maryland. Thanksgiving menu dated 1910. "Roast Turkey, Cranberry Sauce." $100+; Bottom: *Section Naval Base*, La Playa, California. Thanksgiving menu dated November 28, 1918. "Roast Young Imperial Valley Turkey with Walnut Dressing, Cranberry Sauce, Giblet Gravy. $45-50. L to R: *U.S.S. New Orleans CL-22*, Shanghai, China. Thanksgiving menu dated November 30, 1911. "Roast Turkey, Giblet Gravy, Chestnut Dressing, Cranberry Sauce." The Boxer Rebellion came to an end in 1900. $80-90; *American Expeditionary Forces 29th Blue and Gray Division*. Division Headquarters Troop. Thanksgiving menu dated November 28, 1918. World War I ended on November 11, 1918. "Broiled Rib Roast and Roast Milk Fed Pork," but no turkey. $80-90 (with placecards); *Company C, 6th Anti-aircraft Machine Gun Battalion*, Camp Wadsworth, Spartanburg, South Carolina. Thanksgiving menu dated November 28, 1918. "Roast Young Turkey with Dressing, Giblet Gravy, Cranberry Sauce. $25-30.

Menus. L to R, Top: *U.S.S. Camden AS-2* (Flagship), Control Force United States Fleet, New London, Connecticut, Thanksgiving menu dated 1925. Rear Admiral H. H. Christy, U.S.N. Commander. "Roast Turkey, Giblet Gravy, Oyster Dressing, Cranberry Jelly." $40-50; *U.S.S. Marblehead Cl-12* (late of Cuban waters), Navy Yard, Boston, Massachusetts. Thanksgiving menu dated November 25, 1926. "Roast Turkey with Apple Dressing, Giblet Gravy, Cranberry Sauce." $30-35; *U.S. Marine Barracks*, Mare Island (Vallejo), California. Thanksgiving menu dated November 29, 1928. "Roast Young Tom Turkey, Oyster dressing, Giblet Gravy, Cranberry Dressing." $20-25. Bottom: Submarine Squadron Four U.S. Submarine Base, Pearl Harbor, Territory of Hawaii. Thanksgiving menu dated November 24, 1932. "Roast Young Turkey, Chestnut Dressing, Giblet Gravy, Cranberry Sauce. $70-80; *U.S. Marine Corps Base*, San Diego, California. Thanksgiving menu dated 1929. "Roast Young Turkey, Oyster Dressing, Cranberry Sauce." $35-40; *Twenty-Seventh Company Quartermaster*, Shanghai, China. Thanksgiving menu dated 1931. "Roast Turkey, Sweet Dressing, Cranberry Sauce. $60-70.

Menus. L to R, Top: *U.S.S. Mississippi BB-41*, Navy Yard, Portsmouth, Virginia. Thanksgiving menu dated November 30, 1933. "Roast Young Turkey, Cranberry Sauce, Celery Dressing, Giblet Gravy." $50-55; *U.S.S. Lexington CV-2*, Long Beach, California. Commissioned in 1927, lost in action at the Battle of Coral Sea, May 1942. Thanksgiving menu dated November 25, 1937. "Roast Imperial Turkey, Oyster Dressing, Giblet Gravy, Cranberry Sauce." $100+; U.S. *Submarine Base*, Coco Sota, Canal Zone. Thanksgiving menu dated 1937. "Roast Young Tom Turkey, Sage Dressing, Cranberry Sauce, Giblet Gravy." $40-45; *Headquarters Company, 7th Infantry*, Vancouver, Washington. Thanksgiving menu dated 1939. "Roast Turkey, Cranberry Sauce, Giblet Gravy, Oyster Dressing." $25-30. Bottom: *U.S.S. California BB-44*, Long Beach California. Heavily damaged at Pearl Harbor, Hawaii, returned to duty 1944. Thanksgiving menu dated November 21, 1940. "Roast Tom Turkey, Cornbread Dressing, Giblet Gravy, Cranberry Sauce." $60-70; *U.S. Naval Training Station*, San Diego, California. Thanksgiving menu dated November 21, 1941. "Roast Tom Turkey, Giblet Gravy, Oyster Dressing, Cranberry Sauce." $30-35; *Hickam (Air) Field*, Pearl Harbor, Territory of Hawaii. Established in 1935 as Hawaii's principal Army airfield and bomber base. Bombed by the Japanese on December 7, 1941 resulting in 121 men killed. Thanksgiving menu dated November 27, 1941 (ten days to the Pearl Harbor attack). "Roast Tom Turkey stuffed with Chestnuts, Giblet Gravy." $100+.

Thanksgiving Booklets (Services and Menus). L to R: *Thanksgiving Day in England 1943*. 48-page booklet based on a photographic and descriptive record of Thanksgiving Day ceremonies as it was spent in nine British cities by American Forces as guests of the English. November 25, 1943. $50-60; *A Service For The Celebration of Thanksgiving Day for the American Forces in Great Britain*. November 22, 1945. Westminster Abby, London, England. $30-35; *American Thanksgiving Day Celebration*. Royal Albert Hall, London. November 22, 1945. $30-35.

Menu Front. U.S. Naval Air
Station, No. 28, Hawaii. November
1945. $40-50.

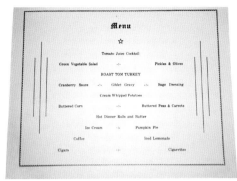

Menu, Thanksgiving Day. U.S. Naval Air Station.
November 22, 1945.

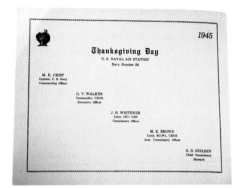

Menu. U.S. Naval Air Station, Commanding Officers.
November 1945.

303rd ASA Battalion (8th United States Army). The
Korean War (or Police Action) started on June 25,
1950 with an invasion of South Korea by North Korea.
Over three years later, an Armistice Agreement was
signed on July 27, 1953. Thanksgiving menu dated
1953. "Roast Young Tom Turkey, Sage Dressing, Giblet
Gravy, Cranberry Sauce." Menu was property of Sgt.
Anthony Maiona. $20-25.

Menus. L to R, Top: *U.S. Naval Barracks*, Harbor Island, Seattle, Washington. Thanksgiving menu dated 1945. "Roast Young Tom Turkey,
Giblet Gravy, Cranberry Sauce, Oyster Dressing." $25-30; *386th Infantry*, Honshu Japan. Thanksgiving menu dated November 22, 1945.
"Maryland Roast Turkey, Sage Dressing, Brown Giblet Gravy, Cranberry Sauce." $45-50; *Prisoner of War Camp, 386th SCU Camp, Claiborne,
Louisiana*. Thanksgiving menu dated November 22, 1945. "Roast Turkey, Giblet Gravy, Oyster Dressing, Cranberry Sauce." $40-45;
Headquarters, HQ Detachment & Co. C. 302 Medical Battalion, 77th Infantry Division, Sapporo, Japan. Thanksgiving menu dated November 29,
1945. "Roast Turkey, Giblet Gravy, Dressing, Cranberry Sauce." $50-60; *San Francisco Naval Shipyard*, San Francisco, California. Thanksgiv-
ing menu dated 1951. "Roast Young Tom Turkey, Sage Dressing, Giblet Gravy, Cranberry Sauce." $20-25. Bottom: *Headquarters U.S.
EUCOM*. Thanksgiving menu dated 1956. "Roast Tom Turkey, Dressing, Giblet Gravy, Cranberry Sauce." $25-30; *Vietnam* (generic menu).
Thanksgiving menu dated 1967, "Roast Turkey, Turkey Gravy, Cornbread Dressing, Cranberry Sauce." $30-35; *214th Combat Aviation
Battalion (Assault and Support Helicopters)*, Vietnam. Thanksgiving menu dated 1967. "Roast Turkey with Bread Dressing, Giblet Gravy,
Cranberry Sauce." $35-40; *Air 3rd Squadron, 11th Armored Cavalry Regiment (Phu Loi) Vietnam* (generic menu). Thanksgiving menu dated
1968. "Roast Turkey, Cornbread Dressing, Turkey Gravy, Cranberry Sauce." $30-35.

[1]This Glossary contains common terms used to describe the evolution of pottery production and its various end products. It is hoped that this summary of terminology will help with the understanding of various ceramic types. Some of these terms are used synonymously and overlap in descriptions.

(1) **Clay**: An insoluble, soft earthy material produced by the chemical weathering of feldspar (alumina and silica), the most abundant rock-making materials in our earth's mantle. There are several distinct clay materials, which can be segregated into *primary* and *secondary* clays: Primary clay, known as *kaolinite,* is derived from volcanic rock and is only found in a few deposits throughout the world. Kaolin is a hard, white, heat and water resistant clay with very few impurities. Secondary clay has been formed by mechanical weathering, which is a natural process of rock breaking due to the forces of nature. This decomposition is then deposited by wind and water as sediment. The resultant clay, depending upon the amount of mineral impurities in its structure, is fairly porous and is quite common.

(2) **Pottery**: A general term for hardened objects made from **clay** or clay mixtures which are subjected to heat in some form, rendering the pottery impervious to liquids to some degree.

(3) **Ceramic**: A clay-based material that can be fired in a kiln at temperatures high enough (>1800 degrees F) to form a stable hard material which, to varying degrees, retains the characteristics of impermeability and heat absorption. If the clay is subjected to even higher temperatures (>2350 degrees F), a point of vitrification is reached where the particles forming the ceramic melt and fuse together, producing a hard glass-like substance impervious to heat, liquids, or knife scratches. Prior to the glazing process, a mixture of water, sand, and powdered mineral substances are applied to the *biscuit* (low temperature fired molded greenware piece). When the piece is fired again at a higher temperature, the resultant liquid coating of glass (termed *glaze*), renders ceramics impermeable to liquid absorption. Depending upon the application method, the surface sheen can be either glossy or matte. There are four main types of glazes: (a) feldsparic used on porcelain, (b) lead used on bone china, (c) tin used on earthenware, and (d) salt used on stoneware.

(4) **Porcelain**: A hard, nonporous, vitrified translucent (glassy quality) ceramic made from a primary clay as kaolin and other mineral materials. The formula for making porcelain is termed *paste*, with a composition that is either *hard* or *soft*. Feldspar porcelain consists of 50% kaolin, 25% feldspar, 20% quartz, and 5% clay. Due to the high percentage of kaolin, this "hard paste" vitrifies at a high, or "hard," temperature. *Bone china*, consisting of 50% animal bone ash, 30% kaolin, and 20% feldspar, vitrifies at a lower, or "soft" temperature. However, bone china is not "soft-paste porcelain." Rather, soft-paste (artificial) porcelain is a composition of a range of material but does not contain kaolin. The term *china* now specifically refers to bone china but, in a very generic sense, refers to all clay-based dinnerware. However, *fine china* refers to non-bone china and is used synonymously with porcelain china, differing only as to the type of glaze used.

(5) **Earthenware**: A softer, slightly porous, relatively low-fired opaque ceramic with a clear glaze made from various types of secondary clays and other mineral materials. Earthenware consists of 35% quartz, 25% clay, 25% kaolin, and 15% feldspar. Depending on the particular mineral composition, earthenware can range from the very dense to brittle. The categories which make up earthenware, in descending order of density or hardness, are: 1) stoneware, (2) semi-porcelain, (3) ironstone, (4) creamware, and (5) majolica. *Stoneware* is a high temperature-fired, partially or fully vitrified ceramic body of great density and hardness varying in body color (due to mineral impurities) from brown to light bluish-gray. It is very chip-resistant and is usually finished, for aesthetic reasons, with a clear salt glaze. *Semi-porcelain* or *semi-vitrified porcelain* is a slightly porous glazed earthenware made primarily from *ball clay*, a fine-grained light colored material, that renders it less shiny and translucent than true porcelain. It is fired at high temperatures that semi-vitrifies the body and is covered with a lead glaze. *Ironstone* is also made with ball clay but is mixed with ground feldspar, a mineral called china stone, hence the name ironstone. It has a thick, opaque texture, vitrified into a hard non-porous ware glazed with a white tin material. *Creamware* is also made with ball clay and is usually mixed with kaolin to strengthen its composition. Creamware is fired at high temperatures making it a durable ceramic but not as strong as stoneware due to temperature differentials. When fired, the composite material becomes a light cream color associated with a slight yellowish tinge, hence the name. Creamware is covered with a transparent lead glaze. *Majolica* is the "softest" form of earthenware in that the clays used are less dense and, when fired, harden but do not vitrify in the kiln. Therefore, these wares are fairly brittle, prone to chipping, and porous, but can be molded into elaborate forms with thick, brightly colored lead and tin glazes.

Chapter 4
GLASS TURKEYS

No mention is made in any documented sources that when the Pilgrims first landed at Plymouth, Massachusetts, in December, 1620, they had in their meager possessions any utilitarian forms of glassware. However, it is almost certain that the Pilgrims brought with them a homegrown version of potash glass made in a coarse, heavy style in the natural shades of amber and green. While there were attempts by certain groups of American settlers in the seventeenth century to establish an indigenous glass industry, all met with failure, and the colonists were dependent on England for their supply of utilitarian glass objects such as drinking vessels, bottles, pitchers, and window pane glass. After the American Revolution, there were several serious attempts in the late eighteenth century to jumpstart the moribund glass industry, only to see those efforts fail from lack of government financial support. It was not until the nineteenth century that a series of protective tariffs, trade embargos, and events such as the War of 1812 (which eliminated British glass competition) were responsible for stimulating domestic glass production. In 1827, the first major innovation in glass making techniques in more than two thousand years was developed. An industrious American named Deming Jarves, founder of the Boston and Sandwich Glass Company, patented an "improvement" that mechanically pressed a blob of molten glass into an iron mold to create the shape of the desired design. The invention of machine pressed glass, smooth on the interior and elaborately patterned on the exterior, tripled glass production and enabled the glass industry to evolve from a mouth blown or mold-blown handicraft glass art to an industrialized, cost effective business. Now, for the first time, not only could glassware be mass-produced in different shapes and sizes, it was also possible to produce complex novelty and figural decorative items.

In the prosperous American households of the past 150 years, there has been an emphasis, especially with respect to days of special importance, on creating tablescapes of great beauty and elegance. Thus, in addition to displaying china and silver, the well-appointed Thanksgiving table shown brightly with many glass items either refracting or reflecting light from all sources. The popularity of pressed and patterned glass ranged from purely utilitarian glassware items that complemented place settings to the more decorative items that enhanced the entire table setting. This chapter will, therefore, attempt to cover one aspect of decorative or novelty pressed glass: the figural turkey, in several sizes according to its use.

A comprehensive search of available literature and Internet websites indicates that at least ten American glass companies have, over various times, produced pressed glass turkeys in four standard sizes. The sizes (in length) and their generic descriptions are as follows: 2" Turkey Salt; 5" Turkey on Nest (TON); 7" Jam Jar/Covered Dish; and 9" Jam Jar/Covered Dish. The sizes stated are approximate "rules-of-thumb" as the actual measurements among manufacturers will vary according to their respective mold sizes. In each case, the turkey, in addition to serving as a decorative item at the Thanksgiving table, also had an authentic function as a container of either condiments, candies, sauces, or soups.

Defunct Manufacturers of Glass Figural Turkeys

The following is a list of companies that have made a pressed glass turkey at one time or another. Many of these companies have either closed or merged and, subsequently, certain of their molds were sold to other companies who remain in production today.

Cambridge Glass Company, Cambridge, Ohio. The company was founded in 1901, closed in 1954, reopened briefly, and closed again in 1958. Cambridge, over the years, was among the most highly regarded makers of fine glass items (i.e., tableware, stemware, and tumblers) in the country. In 1930, the large 9" Turkey Covered Dish was first produced by Cambridge. The firm used the letter "C" enclosed in a triangle trademark after 1920. In November 1960, Imperial Glass Company of Bellaire, Ohio, acquired the Cambridge molds and equipment. There is an organization devoted to collectors and dealers called the National Cambridge Collectors, Inc. Their website is:
webmaster@cambridgeglass.org.

Challinor, Taylor & Company, Tarentum, Pennsylvania. David Challinor, in conjunction with a financial partner, David Taylor, assumed operations in 1885 at a site along the Allegheny River. For a six-year period, Challinor, Taylor was the acknowledged leader in the production of slag glass, for which a patent was obtained in 1886. The firm's slag or variegated glassware, termed "mosaic," was the "open mix" variety where typically separate pots of opal and amethyst colors were carefully mixed and heated to the proper consistency before molding. In 1891, Challinor, Taylor pioneered the production of animal-shaped covered dishes (CAD) in its "Farm Yard Asssortment" series. It was at this time that the firm created the first standing Turkey Covered Dish, which became the "poster Tom" for every subsequent "turkey jar/dish" produced to the present. The Challinor turkey was produced in clear crystal and in clear with vividly painted decoration. In that same year, the company, operating as the Standard Glass Works, became part of the United States Glass Company, a consortium of nineteen glass companies operating in Pennsylvania and other northeastern states. The U.S. Glass Company continued production of the turkey dish from the original Challinor mold until approximately 1900. It is possible that U.S. Glass also produced this item in milk glass. The last mention of the large standing turkey dish was an illustration of same in the company's 1898 catalog.

Degenhart Crystal Art Glass, Cambridge, Ohio. Two brothers, Charles and John Degenhart, worked for Cambridge Glass for nearly one-half century until John retired in 1946 and Charles died in 1953. During a good part of their employment with Cambridge, the brothers, on the side, enjoyed a well-regarded reputation as producers of quality paperweights and other pressed glass novelties. In 1947, John Degenhart founded Crystal Art Glass primarily to produce paperweights. In the ensuing seventeen years, until John's death in 1964, his factory produced over fifty styles of pressed novelty items. When John died, his widow, Elizabeth, against all odds, took over the operation and managed a very successful glass business until her death in 1978. Later that year, the factory was sold to Bernard Boyd, who, at the time, was Degenhart's chief glassmaker as well as the one responsible for creating over two hundred colors for which the firm was well known.

Degenhart's product line was very diverse and included paperweights, covered dishes, salts, toothpick holders, candy dishes, wine goblets, novelties, and whimsies. In 1961, the company introduced its 5" Turkey Covered Dish based on a c.1900 McKee Glass Company mold. This mold used a split ribbed base. It has been ascertained that in the late 1960s (probably 1967), these turkey dishes, as well as other selected Degenhart items, were hand stamped with a "D". Beginning in 1972, the first mold marks were incorporated inside the bottom of the base using the letter "D" enclosed by a heart outline. By 1977, most of the molds were marked.

A self-adhesive sticker featuring a gold heart outline with a gold script **D** was used in the 1970s. These stickers were used by customers to mark their unmarked Degenhart glass pieces. Therefore, stickers would most likely be found on items produced prior to 1970.

In the company's seventeen years of production, the covered turkey dish was produced in approximately fifty separate colors with rubina (a non-slag green color with dark brownish red shadings) being the most elusive to find.

Degenhart's heart enclosed D.

Degenhart Crystal Art Glass 5" Turkey Covered Dishes. L to R, Back Row: Light Amberina, c.1972. $65-85; Honey Amber, c.1972. $50-60. Middle Row: Dark Cobalt, c.1976. $55-65; Mint Green, c.1972. $60-70. Front Row: Light Gold, c.1972. $50-60; Vaseline, c.1975. $60-70.

Imperial Glass Company, Bellaire, Ohio. The company was founded in 1901 by an ex-riverboat captain named Edward Muhleman. Production was initiated in January 1904. Over the years, until 1950, Imperial marked its glass and tableware with four distinctive trademarks. In early 1951, the company's most familiar trademark, "I" super-imposed over "G", was introduced. In the 1960s, Imperial began re-issuing some of its old designs in Carnival Glass, including the 5" Turkey on Nest. The "IG" trademark was applied to most of the re-issues of old designs. Also in 1960, while the company bought the assets of Cambridge Glass, it did not re-introduce the famous large standing turkey mold of Cambridge. In 1984, after the owners could not resuscitate the company, Imperial closed and its assets were sold to Lancaster Colony and Consolidated International.

Degenhart's self-adhesive sticker.

Imperial Glass Company. 4.65"H, 5.5"L, 3.65"W with label and IG trademark. L to R: Milk Glass. $40-50; Peacock Carnival. $40-50.

John E. Kemple Glass Works, East Palestine, Ohio; Kenova, West Virginia. In 1945, John Kemple founded his glass factory based on "authentic reproductions" of previously purchased molds from defunct companies. In the early 1950s, John purchased a considerable number of molds from McKee Glass Company, which added to his total of over 1,100 molds that were eventually obtained from several firms. Up to the time that the East Palestine plant burned down in 1956, Kemple produced only white milk glass and blue milk glass items. At his newly built Kenova plant, he expanded his color repertoire to total fifteen, including an End of Day multi-color slag. After twenty-five

Degenhart Crystal Art Glass 5" Turkey Covered Dishes. Based on the "official" list of about fifty colors made at the Degenhart factory for covered animals (turkeys). Lid 4.75"L, 4.5"H, 3.5"W; Base (nest) 5.38"L, 4.25"W. L to R, Back Row: Grey Slag, c.1972. $70-100; Custard Slag (Light), c.1972. $75-85. Front Row: Caramel (Dark), c.1976. $85-90; Milk White, c.1972. $60-70.

years in business, the Glass Works folded when John died in 1970. His widow, Geraldine, then sold over eight hundred molds, including a 5" Turkey on Nest (split rib) to Wheaton Glass Company of Millville, New Jersey. The turkey dish is not known to have a mold mark, but is sometimes found with a yellow and gold foil sticker. Since 1979, all use of the Kemple molds was discontinued and they were placed in storage, where they remain today.

Kemple Glass Works 5" Turkey Covered Dish on Split Rib Base. Lid 4.75"L, 4.5"H, 3.5"W; Base (nest) 5.5"L, 4.25"W. Opaque Milk Glass, c.1950s. $100-125.

McKee Glass Company, Jeannette, Pennsylvania. In 1852, McKee & Brother's Glass Company opened a factory to produce pressed glass. Thirty-six years later, in 1888, the factory was relocated to Jeannette where many types of kitchen-wares were also made. In 1899, McKee joined the National Glass combine, but that association lasted only until 1903 when the Company again became independent and reorganized as the McKee Glass Company. In 1951, after ninety-nine years in business, the McKee factory was sold to and became a division of Thatcher Glass Manufacturing Co. Coincident with the sale, McKee sold over three hundred molds, including covered animal dishes (CAD) to the Kemple Glass Works. Included in those molds, of which twenty-one were separate animals and birds, was a 5" turkey dish with a split rib base with straight sides. Some of these dishes carried a mold mark of the McKee name spelled out in script. McKee's turkeys, typically, were made in white milk glass and rarely caramel. The signed covered animal dishes are quite rare.

L.G. Wright Glass Company, New Martinsville, West Virginia. The company was founded in 1937 by Lawrence Gale "Si" Wright to act exclusively as a middleman or broker, buying glass items from the major glass producers and reselling to glass retailers and antique dealers. From the early days, Si Wright not only accumulated some original old molds from defunct producers but also ordered new molds to be made for his own versions of popular historic patterns from the late nineteenth century. He then negotiated with the various glass manufacturers for the best price, given the color complexity and production run of the pattern. As L.G. Wright glass products were rarely marked, and given Si Wright's reticence to discuss any facet of his operations with outsiders, it is almost impossible to distinguish his glass from some of the older originals or be able to determine which glass manufacturer (of fifteen or more) actually was responsible for the production of said pattern.

Wright, over the years, produced two covered turkey dish molds: (1) the 9" Turkey Covered Candy Box (No. 70-17), sometimes called a Jam Jar, (based in all probability on a Czechoslovakian import of a 1925/1926 vintage with some changes); and (2) the 5" Animal (Turkey) Candy Box (No. 80-15). The nest portion of the 5" dish is a basket weave base with a scalloped, braided edge design. The turkey lid is either possibly a reproduction of a McKee original or based on a McKee-

inspired Wright design. In most cases, these turkey dishes were contracted out to be produced by either Fenton Art Glass Company or Westmoreland Glass Company. However, none of these items were marked. Going one step further, none of the two aforementioned companies ever produced a figural turkey under their own name.

In 1969, Si Wright passed away, but his wife, Verna Mae, carried on the family-owned distribution business until her death in 1990. In Wright's 1979 Supplemental Catalogue, four separate colors or combinations were indicated for the 9" turkey box: amethyst carnival, amethyst with milk glass head, white milk glass, and white milk glass with carnival head. After Verna Mae's death, another owner prevailed for nine more years until the operation was shuttered on May 31, 1999. From May 27 through May 31 of that year, an auction was held to liquidate the remaining finished goods stock of L.G. Wright and to sell 745 mold lots. At the auction, the third largest mold buyer was Mosser Glass of Cambridge, Ohio. Tom Mosser, the owner, purchased 124 molds, including the 9" large covered turkey mold for $10,000, the highest price paid for any mold at that auction and, to date, for any turkey mold.

L.G. Wright Glass Company Turkey Candy Box. Lid: 4.75"L, 4.25"H, 3.5"W. Base (nest): 5.25"L, 4.13"W. L to R, Back Row: Purple and White Slag. $60-70, Deep Amethyst. $30-40. Middle Row: Clear Light Blue, c.1987. $35-45, Royal Blue. $40-50. Front Row: Amethyst. $30-40, Amberina. $50-60.

L.G. Wright Glass Company. Detail of basket weave design for the base.

Needless to say, a great amount of controversy continues today regarding the correct identification of the 9" Turkey Jam Jar/Covered Box. Essentially, there were only four possible manufacturers of the largest turkey dish. There are presently two existing producers of a 9" and a 7" turkey dish, well marked, that will be covered later in this chapter. A very detailed and erudite explanation of the distinguishing characteristics of the turkey dishes from the four defunct manufacturers is covered extensively by noted milk glass expert and retired English professor Frank Chiarenza in two articles written for *Glass Collector's*

Digest (now out of business); they are found in the October/November 1994 and the February/March, 1999 issues. These *are must read* articles for all dealers and collectors who want to be knowledgeable and avoid identification misconceptions.

The main problem among dealers and those who sell on Internet-based auction sites is the attribution of any large turkey dish, be it 9" or 7", as a "Cambridge Turkey." While there may be an ulterior motive behind such attribution (in terms of a higher selling price), we believe it is out of naïveté as well as lack of precise knowledge of what distinguishes a "Cambridge Turkey" from the other covered dishes of a similar nature. Frank Chiarenza, in the February/March 1999 article, states the problem very accurately: "many dealers and collectors apparently just assume every standing turkey is a Cambridge product. The connection is so firmly fixed between the famous Cambridge name and its much admired turkey that for some people 'Cambridge' is practically a generic label that attaches to all glass turkeys."

Very briefly, one has a Cambridge Turkey if two important factors are present: (1) Feathers of the tail – perfectly smooth, except for a middle quill; and (2) Surface on the underside of the base – bumps with an irregular mushy surface overall. The Challinor/U.S. Glass, the Czechoslovakian import, and the L.G. Wright turkeys all have highly detailed feathering and, most importantly, have a waffle (crisscross), patterned base. The price of a true Cambridge turkey is, depending on the color, much higher than the other dishes. For instance, at an eBay auction held in 2001, a very rare Caprice Blue (Moonlight blue) turkey did not make the seller's reserve, topping out at $1,975. At the National Cambridge Collectors Convention auction, held in March 2002, a rare Gold Krystol Turkey and cover sold for $1,050. A more typical Cambridge turkey would sell for $500 or more to a knowledgeable buyer.

9" Turkey Jam Jar/Covered Dish. L. G. Wright: Cobalt, Crystal. $125-150 each.

9" Turkey Jam Jar/Covered Dish. Cambridge Glass: Amber. $500-600.

9" Turkey Jam Jar/Covered Dish. Czechoslovakian Import: Salmon Pink. $400-500.

9" Turkey Jam Jar/Covered Dishes (topsides of base and feather details). L to R: L.G. Wright (Cobalt): (a) waffle pattern does not extend out to rim, (b) feathering very apparent; Czechoslovakian Import (Pink): (a) waffle pattern does extend to the sides of the rim, (b) feathering very apparent; Cambridge Glass (Amber): (a) no waffle pattern, (b) no feathering except for middle quill.

9" Turkey Jam Jar/Covered Dishes (underside of base). L to R: L.G. Wright (Cobalt): waffle pattern is not carried through to the outer edges; Czechoslovakian Import (Pink): waffle pattern is carried through to the outer edges; Cambridge Glass (Amber): no waffle pattern but has a mushy, furrowed surface.

9" Turkey Jam Jar/Covered Dishes (rump details). L to R: L.G. Wright (Cobalt): pattern of leaves and foliage readily apparent; Czechoslovakian Import (Pink): pattern of leaves and foliage same as L.G. Wright but with more leaf shape and size; Cambridge Glass (Amber): sparse pattern of foliage with little leaf detail and design.

day, the third and fourth generations of the Boyd family tree, Bernard F. Boyd, his wife Sue, and their son John Bernard Boyd, are hard at work, not only maintaining the quality of their predecessors' output, but also injecting creativity in new color schemes for the years ahead.

Luckily for the collectors of Boyd's glass products, the family decided in 1978 to mark their items so that future collectors could ascertain when the original item was produced. As the trademark table below shows, every five years a subtle change was made to the Diamond B by the use of line bars to distinguish between five-year spans.

Boyd's Crystal Art Glass 5" Turkey Covered Dish. Lid 4.75"L, 4.4"H, 3.5"W; Base (nest) 5.38"L, 4.25"W. #1 Frosty Blue, 2/20/79 (Boyd's First TON). $85-100.

Active Manufacturers of Glass Figural Turkeys

At the present time, there are three glass manufacturers producing covered animal dishes in the turkey design format.

Boyd's Crystal Art Glass, Cambridge, Ohio. This firm was founded October 10, 1978, by Bernard C. Boyd and his son, Bernard F. Boyd. The elder Mr. Boyd purchased the assets of the Degenhart Glass Company as well as most of its molds from the estate of Elizabeth Degenhart in the year of her death. Formerly, Bernard C. Boyd was Degenhart's glassmaker, and he had accumulated more than sixty years in the profession. Ten years later, in 1988, Bernard C. Boyd passed away at age eighty, but not before passing on a legacy that included the use and, in some cases, the design of over two hundred molds plus the chemical formulas responsible for formulating more than three hundred separate colors. To-

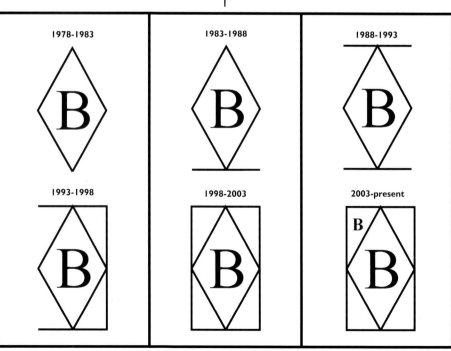

1978-1983	1983-1988	1988-1993
B	B	B
1993-1998	1998-2003	2003-present
B	B	B

Boyd's Crystal Art Glass 5" Turkey Covered Dishes. L to R (in order of production date and color): #3 Lemon Ice (opaque), 9/14/79; #10 Willow Blue, 8/14/80; #18 English Yew (opaque), 1/14/83. Trademark: Diamond B. Values range from $60-70 each.

Boyd's Crystal Art Glass 5" Turkey Covered Dish. #9 Candy Swirl, 6/23/80. Trademark: Diamond B. $60-70.

Boyd's Crystal Art Glass 5" Turkey Covered Dishes. L to R: #38 Thistlebloom, 12/17/87; #40 Rosewood, 5/19/88. Trademark: Diamond B with lower horizontal bar. Values range from $50-60 each.

Boyd's Crystal Art Glass 5" Turkey Covered Dishes. L to R: #50 Cobalt Carnival, 12/12/89; #57 Buckeye Satin, 8/21/91. Trademark: Diamond B with upper and lower horizontal bars. Values range from $40-50 each.

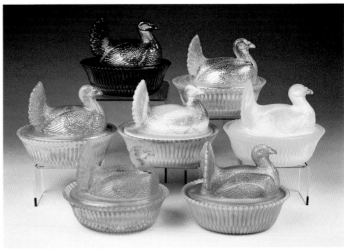

Boyd's Crystal Art Glass 5" Turkey Covered Dishes. L to R, Back Row: #67 Chocolate Carnival, 8/26/94; #70 Vaseline Carnival, 7/19/95. Middle Row: #69 Sunkiste Carnival, 2/10/95; #65 Vanilla Coral, 3/25/94; #75 Lemon Custard, 10/24/97. Front Row: #77 Tangy Lime, 9/11/98; #76 Alpine Blue, 3/6/98. Trademark: Diamond B with upper, lower horizontal bars and right vertical bar. Values range from $30-40 each.

Boyd's Crystal Art Glass 5" Turkey Covered Dishes. L to R, Back Row: #79 Peacock Blue, 8/13/99; #80 Dark Millennium Surprise, 4/5/00. Front Row: #78 Rosie Pink, 5/14/99; #80 Millennium Surprise, 4/5/00. Trademark: Diamond B with four enclosed bars. Values range from $25-30 each.

In the continuation of their marking scheme, Boyd has introduced a small **B** in the upper left hand corner of the boxed Diamond B trademark. In the year 2004, Boyd will begin to utilize this new mark when they begin production of new 2" and 5" Turkeys. On the *rare* occasion that Boyd needs to issue an item with a prior existing color, they mark it with a script *Boyds* molded in the base. To date, with respect to Turkey Covered Dishes, only the 2" Salt has been reissued in the cobalt and vaseline colors. Boyd's 5" Turkey mold was purchased from Degenhart, at which time Island Mould and Machine Company of Wheeling, West Virginia, altered the mold base for Boyd's trademark. The 2" Salt is formed from Degenhart's chick base, and the lid was made for Boyd's by Laurel Mould of Jeannette, Pennsylvania.

Boyd's Crystal Art Glass 2" Turkey Salt. Lid: 1.88"L, 1.5"W; Base (nest) 2.5"L, 2"W; 1.75" overall height. L to R, three variations: Avocado Clear, Avocado Satin, Avocado Hand Painted (introduced 9/14/99). $10-13 respectively.

A typical production run for the 5" Turkey ranges between fifty to one hundred dishes but can be much lower (in the teens) due to the complexity of the glass colors and resultant breakage or two hundred, which can be completed in one four-hour turn. Some of the finished product of both the 5" and 2" Turkeys receive a *satin* treatment in which the item is dipped in an acid bath for a matte finish. Further, the 2" Salt is sometimes selected (not the entire run) for *handpainting* in which an employee of Boyd's paints the tail feathers and some facial features, after which the Salt is refired in the kiln.

Boyd's Crystal Art Glass 2" Turkey Salt. Vaseline Hand Painted (introduced 4/25/94). Due to the current high cost of uranium dioxide, Boyd's has discontinued production of Vaseline glass for the time being. $15.

Retail pricing for the 5" Turkey is $22.00, but if it is made in carnival, red, or slag, it is priced at $24.00. Correspondingly, the 2" Salt is priced at $9.00, but any of the three different treatments raise the price to $10.00.

Boyd's Crystal Art Glass 2" Turkey Salt. L to R: Cobalt, Vanilla Coral, Vaseline, Milk Chocolate, Chocolate Carnival. All marked with a Diamond B enclosed on three sides, introduced between 1/11/94 and 8/12/94. Values range from $15-18 each.

Boyd's Crystal Art Glass 2" Turkey Salt. L to R: White Chocolate, Pale Orchid, Banana Cream, Banana Cream Carnival, Sunkiste, Sunkiste Carnival. All marked with Diamond B enclosed on three sides, introduced between 9/6/94 and 2/27/95. Values range from $14-17 each.

Boyd's Crystal Art Glass 2" Turkey Salt. L to R: Milk White, Royal Plum Carnival, Vaseline Carnival, Mint Julep, Bernard Boyd Black. All marked with a Diamond B enclosed on three sides, introduced between 3/16/95 and 10/15/95. Values range from $14-17 each.

Boyd's Crystal Art Glass 2" Turkey Salt. L to R: Crystal Carnival, Capri Blue, Mirage, Purple Frost, Purple Frost Carnival, Marshmallow. All marked with a Diamond B enclosed on three sides, introduced between 2/8/96 and 3/17/97. Values range from $14-17 each.

Boyd's Crystal Art Glass 2" Turkey Salt. L to R: Lemon Custard, Alpine Blue, Moss Green, Rosie Pink, Peacock Blue. First salt marked with a Diamond B enclosed on three sides, rest marked with a Diamond B fully enclosed, introduced between 10/30/97 and 6/21/99. Values range from $12-15 each.

Boyd's Crystal Art Glass 2" Turkey Salt. L to R: Harvest Gold, Aruba Slag, Jade, Purple Fizz. All marked with a Diamond B fully enclosed, introduced between 11/1/99 and 12/4/00. Values range from $12-15 each.

Boyd's Crystal Art Glass 2" Turkey Salt. Nightwatch Black Carnival Hand Painted 2/15/01. Marked with Diamond B fully enclosed. $13-16.

A complete list (year end 2003) of the colors and introduction dates of Boyd's 5" and 2" Turkey items is included here for reference. To give one an idea of the color diversity and popularity of certain of Boyd's items, the 2" chick salt has been produced in over 185 colors relative to the 45 colors produced for the 2" turkey salt. Boyd also has a very helpful website, especially for color identification: www.boydglass.com.

5" Boyd's Turkey

Color	Date
1. Frosty Blue	2-20-79
2. Redwood	4-16-79
3. Lemon Ice	9-14-79
4. Ice Blue	10-4-79
5. Ice Green	10-19-79

Color	Date
6. Heather	1-28-80
7. Chocolate	3-24-80
8. Persimmon	5-6-80
9. Candy Swirl	6-23-80
10. Willow Blue	8-14-80
11. Impatient	10-1-80
12. Delphinium	3-13-81
13. Cobalt Blue	10-30-81
14. Snow	2-5-82
15. Lavender	3-30-82
16. Crown Tuscan	9-10-82
17. Golden Delight	10-29-82
18. English Yew	1-14-83
19. Cornsilk	5-6-83
20. Sunburst	7-22-83
21. Violet Slate	12-16-83
22. Platinum Carnival	3-16-84
23. Heatherbloom	8-3-84
24. Mulberry Mist (only 14)	3-8-85
25. Touch of Pink (only 13)	3-29-85
26. Carmel	8-26-85
27. Custard	5-22-86
28. Heliotrope	6-12-86
29. Seafoam	8-8-86
30. Bamboo	8-15-86
31. Misty Vale	10-16-86
32. Kumquat	11-13-86
33. Confetti	2-6-87
34. Candyland (only 21)	7-8-87
35. Oxford Gray	9-2-87
36. Baby Blue	10-19-87
37. White Opal	11-11-87
38. Thistlebloom	12-17-87
39. Orange Calico	2-17-88
40. Rosewood	5-19-88
41. Pistachio	6-17-88
42. Ritz Blue	8-3-88
43. Cambridge Blue	9-7-88

Color	Date
44. Autumn Beige	9-16-88
45. Plum	10-12-88
46. Alexandrite	6-2-89
47. Enchantment	7-19-89
48. Shasta White	8-18-89
49. Grape Parfait Carnival	11-7-89
50. Cobalt Carnival	12-12-89
51. Sunglow Carnival	3-8-90
52. Orange Spice	5-15-90
53. Crown Tuscan Carnival	8-6-90
54. Spinnaker Blue	10-19-90
55. Patriot White	3-22-91
56. Vaseline	7-3-91
57. Buckeye	8-21-91
58. Classic Black	11-27-91
59. Classic Black Carnival (8)	11-27-91
60. Cardinal Red	3-30-92
61. Primrose	8-21-92
62. Cashmere Pink	12-23-92
63. Nile Green	2-22-93
64. Waterloo	5-7-93
65. Vanilla Coral	3-25-94
66. Milk Chocolate	7-19-94
67. Chocolate Carnival	8-26-94
68. Banana Cream	11-18-94
69. Sunkiste Carnival	2-10-95
70. Vaseline Carnival	7-19-95
71. Mint Julep Carnival	9-22-95
72. Capri Blue	5-24-96
73. Mirage	11-1-96
74. Marshmallow	3-18-97
75. Lemon Custard	10-24-97
76. Alpine Blue	3-6-98
77. Tangy Lime	9-11-98
78. Rosie Pink	5-14-99
79. Peacock Blue	8-13-99
80. Millennium Surprise	4-5-00
81. Aruba Slag	8-25-00

Mosser Glass Inc, Cambridge, Ohio. The firm was founded in 1959 by Thomas R. Mosser as the **Variety Glass Company**. Tom acquired his glassmaking skills from the time he was an employee of the Cambridge Glass Company until its closing in 1954. He was able to purchase some molds from Cambridge and those, along with ones made from his own designs, formed the nucleus of his own glass factory. Variety Glass's expertise then, as now, is in the contract production of glass lenses, industrial and pharma glass such as beakers and funnels. In 1971, Tom formed **Mosser Glass** to concentrate on art glass as opposed to the commercial side of the business. Over the past thirty or more years, he has either purchased from defunct companies or has made to order between five thousand and six thousand molds. Tom Mosser is now retired, but the two operations are still under family control with his son Tim as the manager. Mosser has manufactured three glass turkey items over the lifetime of the firm. In 1973, Tom introduced the 3" Figural Turkey Toothpick from a mold of his own design.

Mosser Glass Figural Turkey Toothpick Holder. 3"H, 3.75"L, 2.5"W at tail. Purple Carnival. $12.

Mosser Glass Figural Turkey Toothpick Holders. L to R, Back Row: Amethyst, Marigold Iridized, Purple Carnival, Teal Iridized. Middle Row: Cranberry Ice, Black Amethyst, Hunter Green, Jadeite (Martha Stewart). Front Row: Amberina, Cobalt Blue, Blue, Crystal. Values range from $11-13 each.

Color	Date
82. Ivory Blush	7-27-01
83. Cherry Red	10-16-01
84. Purple Valor	12/11/01
85. Salmon	8-2-02
86. Sky Blue	9-20-02
87. Pearly Pink	10-29-02
88. Honey Amber (only 40)	4-25-03
89. Blue Flame	7-28-03

2" Boyd's Turkey Salt

Color	Date
1. Cobalt	1-11-94
2. Vanilla Coral	3-15-94
3. Vaseline	4-25-94
4. Milk Chocolate	6-27-94
5. Chocolate Carnival	8-12-94
6. White Chocolate	9-6-94
7. Pale Orchid	10-10-94
8. Banana Cream	11-10-94
9. Banana Cream Carnival	12-1-94
10. Sunkiste	1-11-95
11. Sunkiste Carnival	2-27-95
12. Milk White	3-16-95
13. Royal Plum Carnival	4-10-95
14. Vaseline Carnival	6-26-95
15. Mint Julep	8-24-95
16. Mint Julep Carnival	9-25-95
17. Bernard Boyd Black	10-15-95
18. Crystal Carnival	2-8-96
19. Capri Blue	5-10-96
20. Mirage	10-2-96
21. Purple Frost	12-12-96
22. Purple Frost Carnival	1-15-97
23. Marshmallow	3-17-97
24. Lemon Custard	10-30-97
25. Alpine Blue	4-3-98

Color	Date
26. Moss Green	8-11-98
27. Rosie Pink	4-27-99
28. Peacock Blue	6-21-99
29. Avocado	9-14-99
30. Harvest Gold	11-1-99
31. Aruba Slag	8-17-00
32. Jade	9-12-00
33. Lemon Splash Carnival	10-4-00
34. Fantasia Blue	10-30-0
35. Purple Fizz	12-4-00
36. Nightwatch Black Carnival	2-15-01
37. Spring Beauty	4-13-01
38. Petal Pink Carnival	5-16-01
39. Ivory Blush	7-26-01
40. Cherry Red	10-18-01
41. Purple Valor	11-19-01
42. Cranberry	2-7-02
43. Blue Orchid	5-3-02
44. Dark Butternut	6-3-02
45. Salmon	8-19-02
46. Sky Blue	10-15-02
47. Pearly Pink	11-25-02
48. Columbia Green	2-10-03
49. Honeycomb	5-16-03
50. Blue Flame	9-4-03

While the company does not keep precise records as to when a specific color was used, they can, at least, document the colors used in recent years. To date, they are: apple green, amethyst, cobalt blue, crystal, hunter green, cranberry ice, marigold, purple carnival, and teal iridized. The first six colors have also undergone a satinized treatment as well. The going retail price for the toothpick holder is currently $11.00.

For Martha Stewart's "Martha by Mail" catalog operations, Mosser was hired to produce between 1,000 and 2,000 handmade figural turkey toothpicks in the jadeite color, starting in the year 2000. This special order necessitated a production run of approximately four "turns" (400 items per turn) of four hours duration for each turn. This same exact turkey toothpick has been distributed by L.G. Wright (in five colors) as item # 77-93 and Viking Glass, each with the respective firm's paper label.

In 1978, Tom also introduced a 2-1/2" standing Turkey Statue as a decorative item, but it was discontinued in 1994. At the L. G. Wright Glass Company auction in May 1999, Tom Mosser spent $10,000 to purchase the mold for the 9" Covered Turkey Box. Shortly thereafter, he attempted a production run in cobalt. Unfortunately, there was a problem with the mold and only a few pieces survived the initial run. After some time had elapsed, this valuable mold was reworked and today the 9" Covered Turkey has been successfully reintroduced. The initial colors are Marigold Carnival and an Iridized Crystal retailing for $65. The Covered Turkey Boxes are sold with the Mosser trademark (the letter **M** enclosed by the state of Ohio outline). Mosser also hosts an informative website at www.mosserglass.com.

Mosser Standing Turkey Figurine. 2.5"H, Cobalt Carnival. Marked with an M. **$15.**

L.E. Smith Glass Company, Mount Pleasant, Pennsylvania. The company was founded in 1907 by Lewis E. Smith, specifically to make glass containers for his line of mustard condiments. For the first two decades of business, Smith's early product line featured cooking articles and other utilitarian objects such as glass percolator tops, fruit jars, and juice reamers . In the mid-1920s and onward, the company made glass tableware in many of the common Depression era colors. By the end of that decade and into the 1930s, Smith became especially well known for its black glass. Like many small firms that needed expansion capital, L. E. Smith was purchased and owned by Libbey Glass of Toledo, Ohio, from 1975 to 1986. The firm was then sold to Carlow, a Pittsburgh area diversified consumer products firm. In 1995, American Glass Inc., a subsidiary of NBI Inc. of Longmont, Colorado, was the successful bidder for the operating assets of Smith. Today the company has a very balanced product line still operating out of the same original plant. L.E. Smith's two hundred employees are divided among several main product lines: (1) lighting goods, technical and industrial glassware, blocks and tiles; (2) glass tableware, kitchenware, and drinkware items; and (3) glass novelties and decorative objects. More than 700 items are part of the L.E. Smith glass line, produced from about 1,200 in-house molds.

With regard to Smith's considerable line of figural animal pieces, the company has made a 6" Two-piece Covered Turkey Candy Box/Covered Bowl from a mold of their own design dating from the late 1940s or early 1950s. The Smith turkey has alternately been identified by the company as a 7" covered Turkey Serving/Soup Bowl (on their retail shipping box) or a 6" covered Turkey Candy Box (by their website under Kitchenware). In both cases, it is designated as Item #207/1. Presumably the 7" measurement is from the base

to the top of the head, whereas the 6" measurement is from the base to the top of the tail. In any event, there should be no mistaking the L.E. Smith turkey dish from those of Challinor/U.S. Glass, the Czechoslovakian import, Cambridge, or the LG. Wright/Mosser items. The L. E. Smith dish is not only shorter in height by approximately 1" to 2", but the length of its base is also shorter by 2.25" or more. Also, the feathering is quite detailed. Lastly, the surface on the underside of its base is partially pebbled.

For an indeterminate period of time up to the mid-to-late 1990s, Smith marked their turkey dish with an **S** enclosing a very small **g** and **c**. Since late 1997, Smith has been marking the turkey dishes with a script or cursive **S**. The vast majority of covered turkey dishes sold today on the various Internet auction sites are those from L.E. Smith and are of recent vintage. The company has not found it necessary to keep precise records of all the colors produced over the years for the Covered Turkey Dish due, in part, to their many owners, as well as to the fact that Smith does not consider themselves as a "collectible" concern and, hence, such non-production records were not of paramount importance. However, authors Lee Garmon and Dick Spencer in their 1993 book, *Glass Animals of the Depression Era*, gave a partial listing of colors for the turkey dish used throughout the 1970s and early 1980s. This list, which has not been corroborated by Smith's management, can be helpful in the identification of some of the company's older turkey dishes. Garmon and Spencer's color list is as follows: 1973/74 (crystal, crystal lustre, gold, amber, amethyst, ruby carnival, green carnival, amberina); 1975/6 (amber); 1980 (crystal, amberina); 1981 (peach lustre) and 1982 (crystal, frosted crystal with special paint treatment).

L.E. Smith (no marks) 7" Covered Turkey Dish. (7"H to top of head, 5.75"H to top of tail, 6.75"L; Base (nest) 4.63"L x 4"W). 10 oz. capacity. L to R: Amberina, Peacock Blue. $50-70 each.

L.E. Smith (no marks) 7" Covered Turkey Dish. L to R: Pinkish Amber, Light Pink, Amber, Dark Amber. $40-55 each.

L.E. Smith (no marks) 7" Covered Turkey Dish. L to R: Cobalt Blue, Clear Green. $45-55 each.

Currently, the L. E. Smith Covered Turkey Dish enjoys wide popularity. The company now produces the item in crystal and amber for non-exclusive use. They package their turkey dishes in an attractive signature black box in use since 1998 for dating purposes. For Williams-Sonoma, a well-known specialty retailer of home furnishings and kitchenware in the United States, the company has made the Turkey Box only in clear sage green for the exclusive use of Williams-Sonoma's clientele. Likewise, Smith has also been under contract for several years to Martha Stewart, for her "Martha By Mail" catalog, to produce the turkey dish in three colors: opaque green glass, milk glass, and opaque caramel. These colors, to date, are exclusive to Martha Stewart. Due to the long production run for Martha Stewart items, one will find that these figural turkeys can be marked with one or the other of Smith's hallmarks.

L.E. Smith (no marks) 7" Covered Turkey Dish. L to R: Iridescent Crystal, Carnival, Amber Carnival. $35, $75, and $60 respectively.

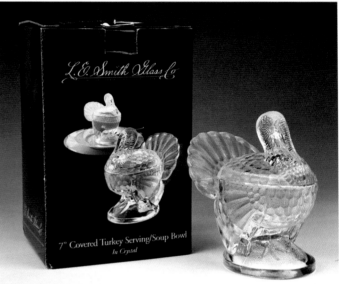

L.E. Smith 7" Covered Turkey Serving/Soup Bowl with Box: Crystal (Item #207/1) $25-30.

In 1982, the Levay Distributing Company (now Intaglio Designs Ltd. of Alton, Illinois) special ordered clear crystal as well as a frosted crystal turkey dish with hand-painted red head and snood. A clear crystal dish from Levay with flash red applied on the wings and tail also exists. Alternatively, several versions of a completely painted turkey dish in various colors have been documented. It is not known, in the case of the fully painted turkeys, whether these are the result of a one-of-a-kind special order or a do-it-yourself home project. This painted form is termed "All-Over Decorating" or "AOD" and can be considered a type of "Goofus" glass in that the manufacturer or distributor of these pressed glass crystal (clear) turkeys subsequently applied surface "cold paint" (not furnace fired), which can flake or chip off over time due to handling or environmental factors. Most of these painted turkeys date from the 1980s.

According to Lori Brodak, L.E. Smith's National Sales Manager, "the evolution of the covered turkey candy box from a highly collectible item of many colors to a more functional role as a Thanksgiving/Harvest table utilitarian bowl in traditional autumn and pastel colors is noteworthy." Once the turkey covered dish appeared on page 193 of Martha Stewart's first book, Entertaining (published in 1982), as well as more recently in the Martha By Mail and Williams-Sonoma on-line and off-line catalogs, it became looked upon as an individual serving container for soup or cranberry sauce. Its 10-ounce capacity makes it convenient to hold many edible items. The retail price of the turkey dish from both outlets is $25.00. Otherwise, the non-exclusive colors usually sell for more than $25.00 at many upscale, specialty retail stores across the country.

L.E. Smith (no marks) 7" Covered Turkey Dish. L to R: Crystal with Rose flashing on tail, wings, and snood. $35-$40; Handpainted (AOD) Dark Brown, Red Head, Green Base, and White detailing. 30-40; Crystal with handpainted red snood $28-33.

L.E. Smith (all marked) 7" Covered Turkey Dish. L to R: Milk Powder Blue (S mark), Opaque Green or Jadeite (S mark), Milk White (S mark), Caramel (S mark), Caramel (S mark) $40, $35, $60, $30, and $30 respectively.

Production of the turkey dishes is still done one piece at a time. A typical production run for one four-hour turn is about 800 complete units. On an annual basis, Smith produces "tens of thousands" of the turkey dish. L.E. Smith's website is www.lesmithglass.com.

Lastly, there is one foreign firm making a non-utilitarian decorative glass turkey. **Waterford Wedgwood PLC,** Kilgarry, Waterford, Republic of Ireland, was founded in 1783 by brothers George and William Penrose. The firm lasted sixty-eight years until prohibitive taxes forced its closing in 1851. After World War II, in 1947, Waterford was re-formed and, today, is one of the world's leading producers of heavy cut-glassware and other specialty decorative items, including a crystal Thanksgiving Turkey.

Through this chapter, the terms, "dish," "jar," "box," and "bowl" have been used interchangeably for the large (7" or more) turkey piece. There is no right or wrong nomenclature, but the word "dish" seems to convey the most modern terminology at present. It is also the hope of the authors that the information presented in this chapter will be instrumental in the correct identification of a wide range of turkey dish sizes and shapes.

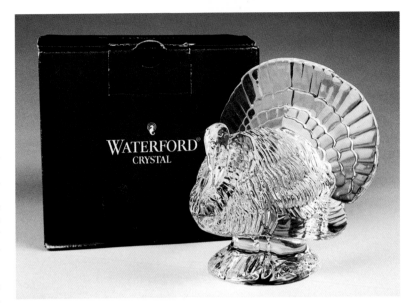

Waterford (Ireland) Crystal Thanksgiving Turkey with Box. 4.5"H, 4.5"W, 4"L. $100-110.

Miscellaneous Glass Figural Items

Shown are an assortment of miscellaneous glass items, both utilitarian and decorative in nature.

Mexican Crystal Vase with yellow and orange swirls, teal green shading. 9.25"H, 5.13"L, 5"W. $20-25.

Miscellaneous Glass Figural Items. L to R: Avon Iridized Peach Crystal Turkey Candleholder. Head 2.38"H, 3.13"L, 2.63"W. $8-$10; Mosser (marked M) Cobalt Satin Turkey. 3"H, 2.5"L, 2.5"W. $11-$13; Mosser (unmarked) Vaseline Indian Toothpick Holder. 2.63"H, 2"D. $13-15.

Avon Products (New York, NY) Men's After Shave Figural Wild Turkey Decanters with Box, 6 oz., c.1974-1976. Pressed dark amber glass with silver and red plastic head. Two varieties: Deep Woods and Wild Country. 7.75"H, 4.75"L, 2.5"W. $10-12 for MIB.

Chapter 5
CERAMIC/POTTERY TURKEYS

Articles made expressly for the Thanksgiving table over the ages are extensive and range from the very rare and costly to the mundane and cheap. These tabletop turkey utilitarian ware and decorations were comprehensively covered in Chapter 3. However, there have been many turkey image items produced generally for their decorative value, either as functional adjuncts to the Thanksgiving table or as purely ornamental pieces designed to enhance the spirit of the holiday. The objects covered in this chapter include those produced on a ceramic or pottery base. Included in this category are cookie jars, pitcher and wash bowl sets, and planters. Succeeding chapters will deal with candy containers and decorative accessories of all materials.

Cookie Jars

Cookie jars have been produced and collected in some form since the early twentieth century. Over these years, the subject matter changed from utilitarian jars to that of whimsical items with many shapes and bright glazes representing the finest of pop art. Andy Warhol (1928-1987), a very "famous" pop artist and New York based "bon vivant," collected cookie jars as a way of documenting the more colorful aspects of kitchen goods. After he passed away in 1987, a majority of his personal collectibles was auctioned at Sotheby's in April 1988. What took the auction spectators by surprise was that Warhol's collection of 139 vintage cookie jars were sold for an amazing amount of $247,830. The pre-auction estimate of each jar was approximately $25. After the notoriety of this newsworthy event made its way into the regular collecting channels, the cookie jar boomlet began in full force, precipitating the writing of many books on cookie jar manufacturers and valuations of their output. Cookie jars were meant to house the favorite cookies of the day and, as such, were subject to rim chips and crazing. Also, details of the jars usually were decorated with over-glaze hand-painted "cold" paints that were not durable and, therefore, susceptible to flaking and scratches.

American Bisque, **Nelson McCoy**, **Shawnee**, and **Treasure Craft** were among the largest domestic manufacturers of cookie jars. Of this group, **Nelson McCoy** (and its antecedents) was probably the most prodigious producer of vintage cookie jars. It is estimated that McCoy produced over three hundred different pattern-molds during its history.

There were actually three McCoy firms at one time or another located in the Roseville/Zanesville, Ohio region. This area had vast stoneware clay beds and other natural resources which attracted many potteries of all descriptions. The first two McCoy family firms, W. Nelson McCoy (1848) and J.W. McCoy (1892) generally produced domestic wares for

Magazine Ad. "Who Says The Old Cookie Jar Is Gone?" Uneeda Bakers (Nabisco), November 1934. 10" x 13". Brands included: John Alden Molasses Cookies, Priscilla Butter Cookies, and Miles Standish Chocolate Cookies. $5-8.

kitchen use. While the demise of the W. Nelson Pottery is lost to history, the J.W. McCoy Pottery, in 1911, became known as the Brush-McCoy Pottery Company, taking its name from its new General Manager, George Brush. After the McCoy name was dropped in 1925, the Brush Pottery Company continued producing some highly collectible cookie jars until its sale in 1971. The third firm, Nelson McCoy Sanitary Stoneware Company (Pottery), was formed in 1910 by J. W. McCoy and his son, Nelson, for the purpose of manufacturing utility and decorative wares. In 1925, the McCoy family sold their interest in the Brush-McCoy Pottery and, by 1926, expanded the existing pottery to produce earthenware specialties and artware. In 1967, in 1974, and again in 1988, the firm was sold but the valuable and well-known McCoy mark was always retained. In early 1990, the Nelson McCoy Pottery, after eighty years of longevity, terminated its operations due to financial considerations regarding foreign competition.

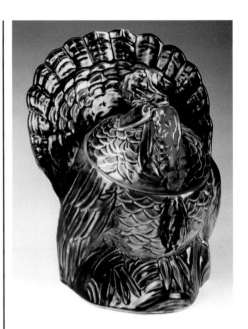

Tom Turkey Cookie Jar, 11.5"H x 8"W. Dark green and brown glazes, red cold paint on wattle. Factory mold No. 23. Stylized McCoy indented mark. Nelson McCoy Pottery, Roseville, Ohio. c.1945. $350+. This 1945 cookie jar also came in a seldom seen white glaze version that books for $400+.

Tom Turkey Cookie Jar, 9.25"H x 7.75"W. Brown glaze over an ivory base, yellow scarf tag with "Cookies" incised, red cold paint on wattle. Factory mold No. 176. Stylized McCoy indented mark with USA letters. Nelson McCoy Pottery, Roseville, Ohio. c.1959-1960. $250-275. This 1959-1960 version also came in several brown green glaze colorations. The shorter difference in height as well as the colorful head detail separates the cookie jar from the older, darker glazed version.

Side detail of the 1959-1960 cookie jar showing the more flared tail feathers.

Tom Turkey Cookie Jar, 9"H x 8.5"W. Medium brown glaze flaring to white on the feather tips, rose glaze wattle. Poult perched on the lid as a finial. No marks. Morton Pottery Company, Morton, Illinois. c.1950s. $70-80. The Morton Pottery Company was in operation from 1876 to 1976. They also made a similar turkey cookie jar in brown spongeware on a yellowish base.

Tom Turkey Cookie Jar, 8.5"H x 10.5"L x 8.25"W. Black, brown, gold, and white glazes. Oval bowl bottom. Marks B.B.K. Made in U.S.A. #193. c.1940s. $70-80. In 1941, Brad Keeler, a skilled clay modeler, started to produce specialized ceramic artware, including a naturalistic line of birds and fowls (numbering over fifty different designs) such as flamingos, swans, egrets, pheasants, ducks, and turkeys. Through the years until his untimely death in 1952, the Brad Keeler Artwares also produced an extensive array of quality household goods such as buffet serving dishes, ginger jars, planters, and smoking sets with ashtrays.

"Thanksgiving" Cookie Jar, 12.63"H x 6.75"W. "Mammy" style image, white glaze body and hand decorated in colors of brown, tan, green, and black with gold accents. The skirt design incorporates two Tom Turkeys, a haystack with pumpkins, and trailing stems with leaves. Signed Negatha P. Marked with a black stamp: Erwin Pottery, Hand Painted, Erwin, Tenn, and in script: By Original Blue Ridge Artist. c. early 1990s. $275-300. Negatha Peterson was one of the premier decorators for the now defunct Southern Potteries (1917-1957), Erwin, Tennessee. This firm produced the famous Blue Ridge Pottery line. Negatha joined Southern in 1941 and worked there until the dissolution of the firm. She began making her famous "Gold Tooth Mamy" (her spelling) cookie jars until her retirement in the mid 1990s. Negatha made only five or six cookie jar molds and no two jars are decorated exactly alike. Her jars are considered highly collectible.

Marking detail on bottom of cookie jar.

Tom Turkey Cookie Jar, 11.5" tail x 8" head x 9.25"W. Glazed dark brown, black, and green shadings, bright red wattle. Stands on footed base. No marks. Inscription: "Painted by Buddie 1959." Hobbyist bisque greenware mold, home decorated, c. late 1950s. $25+.

Tom Turkey Cookie Jar, 11.5" tail x 8" head x 9.25"W. Glazed white with black markings and red wattle. No marks. Stands on footed base. Inscription: black "A.N.T. 61." Hobbyist bisque greenware mold, home decorated, same as previous photo. c. late 1950s. $25+.

"Harvest Turkey" Cookie Jar, 15" tail x 12" head x 13"L x 9"W. Glazed colors: iridescent green sheen, black, brown, mustard, grayish blue head, dark red wattle on a green base. Hang tag. Marks – bottom: embossed eight-sided star, impressed "Radko." Christopher Radko's "Home for the Holidays" Collection. Made in China © 2002. $200 MIB.

"Harvest Turkey," side view facing left.

L to R: Tom Turkey Cookie Jar, 9.5" tail x 10" head x 8.75"W. Glazed dark brown shading with red, orange, and yellow accents. Atlantic © Mold. Hobbyist bisque greenware mold, home decorated. c.1970s. $25+. Tom Turkey Cookie Jar, 9.75" tail x 9.75" head x 7"W. Glazed dark brown shading with red, orange, and yellow accents. © Baron Molds 1975. Hobbyist bisque greenware mold, home decorated. c. late 1970s. $25+.

L to R: Tom Turkey, 9.25" tail x 9.75" head x 8.75"W. Glazed dark brown shading with red-orange accents, bright red wattle. Standing on green base, yellow crawed feet. Atlantic © Mold. Hobbyist bisque greenware mold, home decorated. c.1970s. $30+. Tom Turkey, 9.25" tail x 9.75" head x 8.75"W. Glazed dark greenish gray shading, dark teal head with bright red wattle. Standing on gray base, yellow clawed feet. Atlantic © Mold. Hobbyist bisque greenware mold, home decorated. c.1970s. Inscription: "Hand paint Patt Schade Nov. 1970." $30+.

Pitcher and Wash Bowl Sets

Pitcher and wash bowl sets with a turkey image were made by Mount Clemens Pottery Company, who, in 1967, purchased the assets of McCoy Pottery. While the Mount Clemens trademark (a boxed tankard with the initials MCP) was used on the pitcher, the wash bowl was incised with the encircled McCoy mark and the USA letters. The pitcher has a 1968 copyright, which means this set was made from 1968 to early 1974 when the Mount Clemens interest was sold to Lancaster Colony Corporation. Regardless of ownership changes, the firm was still known as the Nelson McCoy Pottery Company and utilized the stylized McCoy mark. It should be noted that many collectors do not realize the pitcher and wash bowl were sold as a set. In numerous instances the pitcher by itself has been offered for sale. Values are for the set only.

Ceramic and Pottery Planters

Ceramic and pottery planters, due to their wide array of shapes, colors, and glazes, are a specialized collecting entity unto themselves. There are three types of planters: (1) head types; (2) wall pockets; and (3) figural. Obviously, the turkey image fits into the third category. As so defined, planters and related pieces are rather small, shallow objects that one would normally use to "pot" live plants or flowers. The vast majority of these floral planters were made in Japan, although some early pottery objects were crafted in the United States and Europe. However, from the 1960s on, due to the simplicity of most planter molds, production was established in low wage cost countries such as Japan.

Many planters were unmarked while others are stamped "Made in Japan." Most of these also had foil or paper labels signifying the U.S importer/designer, such as "Enesco," "Inarco,"

L to R: Pitcher with Wash Basin/Bowl. Pitcher 9.5"H, Bowl 12"D x 3.25"H. Pitcher decoration: high relief embossed turkey on two sides. Bowl decoration: continuous half-circle "ruffle" design on rim. Pitcher marks: boxed tankard design and MCP (Mt. Clemens Pottery) 19©68USA. Bowl marks: 7516, encircled McCoy ©USA. Shown in three production glazes: dark olive green, cobalt blue, and egg shell white with brown flecks. On some pieces, this glaze tends toward a dark brown. Nelson McCoy Pottery Company (Mount Clemens Pottery Company). c.1972. $65-75 for the complete set, with cobalt blue being the rarest of the three primary glazes.

Marking detail of bowl and pitcher.

"Lefton," "Napco," and "Relpo." Over the past twenty years, production eventually shifted to Taiwan and China. As a way of dressing up the Thanksgiving table or its surrounding area, figural planters were often given as "thank-you" gifts. One note of caution: yesterday's jam jar or candy dish could be construed as today's planter absent the lid. Many functional dishes have had their lids broken or lost and, hence, the item now has become an open-mouth planter contrary to its original purpose.

L to R: Whimsical Planters. Comic Tom Turkey with Indian Girl. 6.25"H x 6.25"L. Golden yellow matte glaze, brown accents with red and black cold paint, 4" diameter circular planter. Silver foil label "Neal's Plant Exchange, California. U.S.A. Made in Taiwan R.O.C." c.1980s. $15-20. Comic Pilgrim Tom Turkey with Pilgrim Hat and Bowtie. 5.5"H x 4.25"W. Glazed brown, black, red, and white color. White glazed rectangular planter. 4"L x 2"W. Black stamp Relpo #C932 (Made in Japan). c.1980s. $10-15. Comic Pilgrim Tom Turkey with Musket and Pilgrim Hat, 6"H x 4.75"L. Brown matte glaze with painted blue head and red wattle, 3" diameter circular planter. Gold and black foil label "Inarco Japan." Black stamp E-5066. c.1980s. $20-25.

L to R: Tom Turkey Planter, 6"H x 7"L. Glaze of black, brown, gold with white accents, dark brownish red wattle. Medium green base. No marks. c.1980s. $10-15. Tom Turkey Planter, 6"H x 7"L. Glaze of black and brown with white accents, dark brownish red wattle. Medium green base. No marks. c.1980s. $10-15. Tom Turkey Planter, 6"H x 6"L. Matte glaze of black, dark brown and forest green with blue and rose accents. Green base. Paper label © Geerings Greenhouses, Inc. Made in China. c.1990s. $10-15. Tom Turkey Planter, 6"H x 7"L. Glaze of medium brown with black, green and red accents, bright red wattle. Dark brown base. Retail paper label "Woolworth." c.1990s $10-15.

L to R: Tom Turkey Planter, 7.38"H x 7"W. Glaze of brown and tan shades, rose-red wattle. No marks. Listed as No. 3335 "Turkey" in the 1939 Morton catalog of holiday novelties. Lids were made for these planters to be used as cookie jars (see page 82, top left). Morton Pottery Company, Morton, IL. c.1940s. $40-45. Tom Turkey Planter, 7.88"H x 6.25"W x 8.75"L. Glaze of dark rose brown with green accents, red wattle. Glazed and unglazed wedge bottom. Attributed to American Bisque Company, Williamston, WV. c.1970s. $25-30.

Right:
L to R: Tom Turkey Planter, 4.5"H x 4"L. Matte glaze of brown, tan, yellow, and black with blue accents. Pale rose wattle. Has opening for bud stem in wattle. (Napco) C-5994 (blue stamp). c.1980s. $10-15. Tom Turkey Planter, 5.75"H x 5"L. Matte glaze of brown, tan, light yellow, and black with blue and black accents. Pale rose wattle and black clawed feet. Markings include an impressed black N, 1920 and a gold and red foil label "Napcoware Import Japan." c.1980s. $15-20. Tom Turkey Planter, 7.25"H x 6.25"L. Matte glaze of golden brown, tan, and pale yellow with blue and black accents. Pale rose wattle. Markings include a blue stamp boxed Napcoware, C5991 and a silver foil label "National Potteries Co. Cleveland, O Made in Japan." c.1980s. $30-35. Tom Turkey Candleholders (2), 3.5"H x 3.5"L. Matte glaze of brown, tan, and yellow with blue and black accents. Pale rose wattle. Markings include a blue stamp boxed NAPCOWARE, C-5988 and a silver foil label "National Potteries Co. Cleveland, O Made in Japan." c.1980s. $20+ set.

L to R: Tom Turkey Planter, 6.25"H x 6.5"L. Matte glaze of ivory, brown, and tan with red and gold accents. Reddish gold wattle. Light green base. White glazed bottom. No marks. c.1970s. $15-20. Tom Turkey Planter, 6.25"H x 6.5"L. Matte glaze of ivory, tan, and brown with red and gold accents. Bright red wattle. Pale green base. White glazed bottom. No marks. c.1970s $15-20. Tom Turkey Planter, 6.5"H x 7.25"L. Glaze of black, brown, and yellow on white. Rose wattle. Brown base. White glazed and unglazed wedge bottom. No marks. Attributed to American Bisque Company, Williamston, W.V. c.1970s. $25-30. Tom Turkey Planter, 6"H x 5.75"L. Glaze of green shades and gold with black and blue accents. Red wattle. Light green base. White glazed bottom. No marks. c.1980s. $12-17.

L to R: Tom Turkey Planter, 6.5"H x 6"L. Glaze of brown, blue and black with white accents. Bluish green base. Bright red wattle. Glazed bottom. Markings include raised R (Rubens logo) encircled Japan, 6145, and gold and red foil label "Rubens Originals © Los Angeles Made in Japan." c.1980s. $20-25. Tom Turkey Planter, 6"H x 5"L. Glaze of brown and tan shades with blue accents. Dark green base. Rose wattle. Glazed bottom. Marked impressed 7478 (Napco?) c.1980s. $20-25. Tom Turkey Planter, 4.75"H x 4"L. Matte glaze of brown and tan shades with blue and black accents. Green base. Bright red wattle. Marked with an incised boxed "Relpo 5503" c.1980s. $15-20. Tom Turkey Planter, 4.75"H x 3 75"L. Glaze of gold with black accents. Bright red wattle. Marked with an incised boxed "Relpo" T851. c.1980s. $15-20. Tom Turkey Planter 6.5"H x 5.75"L. Matte glaze of brown and tan shades, pale yellow with blue and black accents. Pale green base. Bright red wattle. Markings include an incised boxed "Relpo 5293," and a gold and blue foil label "Relpo, Chicago, Ill. Made in Japan." c. 1980s. $20-25. Note: NAPCO and RELPO planters, without marks, are virtually indistinguishable except that Napco turkeys have an elongated, away-from-the-body wattle while Relpo turkeys have a flat painted wattle.

Tom Turkey Planter, 10"H x 7"L x 9.5"W. Matte colors of brownish beige. No painted decoration. Incised on left wing base "Kay Finch Calif. V." Kay Finch Ceramics, Corona del Mar, CA. c.1950s. $350+. Rare. Katherine (Kay) Finch (1903-1993) with her husband, Braden, started her ceramics studio in 1938 in Santa Ana, California, but moved her operation to Corona del Mar in 1939. The studio, well known for its art pottery, planters, and animal and bird figurines, ceased operations in 1963 after Braden's death. Finch's artware is very collectible.

L to R: Tom Turkey Planters. Each measures 4.75"H x 5"L. Glaze of various shade intensities of brown and tans with black accents. Red cold paint on wattle. Unglazed bottoms. No marks. Listed as No. 619 "Turkey" in the 1939 catalog of novelty planters. Morton Pottery Company, Morton, Illinois. c. 1940s. $17-20 each. According to knowledgeable sources, these turkeys were packed two dozen per carton and then sold to major chain retailers of that era for $1.92 per dozen.

L to R: Tom Turkey Planter, 7.25"H x 6.25"L x 6.75"W. Glaze colors of tanbark brown, charcoal, green, "pearlized" maroon with gold accents. Unglazed bottom. No marks. Kay Finch. c. late 1940s to 1950s. $125+. Rare. Tom Turkey, 4.75"H x 3"L x 5"W. Glaze colors of tanbark brown and dark maroon with gold accents. No marks. Kay Finch. c. late 1940s. $100+.

Right:
Tom Turkey Planter, 11.25"H x 10.5"W x 14.5"L. Leaf motif container. Bright red glaze with black and gray accents. Greenish gray wattle. Glazed bottom. Detailed and heavy construction. Marked Royal Haeger R 1961 U.S.A. c.1960s to 1970s. $100-125. The Haeger Pottery Company was established by Daniel H. Haeger in Dundee, Illinois in 1871 to manufacture bricks. By 1914, the firm was producing art pottery wares. In 1938, Royal Hickman was hired as the lead designer. He created the Royal Haeger line of premium artware based on Art Deco influences. The firm is still in operation, presently in Macomb, Illinois with a full line of figurines and other art pottery items.

Tom Turkey Planter, 6.5" tall x 11"L x 6.5"W. Exterior: Matte shadings of gray to brown. Highly decorated in the Art Deco style with glaze "jewels" and geometric shapes of navy blue, medium blue, rose, forest green, and mint green colors. Interior: glaze pearlescent luster. Markings: incised blue "Amphora," blue underglaze oval stamp "Amphora Made in Czechoslovakia," and blue incised mold number 1509. c.1918 to 1938. $800+. Very Rare. Amphora, Trnovany, Czechoslovakia. Prior to World War I, Amphora pottery (matte or low gloss glazes) was made in Turn-Teplitz, Austro-Hungary. After World War I, Bohemia, Moravia, and Austrian Silesia, through the Treaty of Versailles, were ceded to make up the newly created country of Czechoslovakia with Czech names superceding the German nomenclature. Amphora was designed to be artistic and beautiful as well as useful and functional.

"Tom Turkey Planter," Amphora, side view facing left.

Chapter 6
CANDY CONTAINERS

No "well-dressed" Thanksgiving table of the first half of the twentieth century was complete without the addition of novelties and favors for the dinner guests. Primarily, these novelties consisted of **candy containers** and **boxes** designed to hold sweets or nuts. As the majority of Thanksgiving novelties are in the figural form of Tom and Hen Turkeys, it should come as no surprise that this traditional icon is well represented in every shape and size of candy container. Much less represented in these tabletop decorations are other fowl, such as geese, ducks, roosters, hens, and even pheasants and pigeons.

Turkey containers were made from one of four types of materials: (1) papier mâché, (2) plaster of Paris (chalkware), (3) composition, or (4) pressed cardboard. The three main sources of containers were: (1) pre/post war Germany, (2) pre/post war Japan, and (3) America. Sizes of a turkey gobbler ranged from 1-1/2 inches to 13-1/2 inches high, while sizes of the turkey hen ranged from 2-1/4 inches to 10 inches high. A dressed roast turkey container ranged from 3 inches to 10 inches long. There also were many variants of construction, which included (1) the placement of the candy opening, such as the neck, rump, or base, and (2) placement and construction of the legs and talons in either heavy pot metal or wire legs and whether the turkey is standing alone or as part of the base.

Therefore, in order of importance for valuation purposes, one must consider (1) size, (2) condition, and (3) country of origin, including the date of production. Our private collection includes over one hundred turkey candy containers of all types purchased over the years from a wide variety of sources. As result of our investigation observed over a ten year period, we offer the following baseline valuation grid for the pricing of turkey gobbler containers. Please remember, this is a strictly subjective guide and its importance lies in the premium or discount given for certain varieties rather than the actual prices, which can change rapidly in response to ever-changing seasonal market conditions.

Turkey Container Valuation Grid
(German Manufacturer, 1895-1939)

Size (inches)*	Condition**		
	M/NM	EXC	VG
13.50	$1,100	$850	$800
11.75	950	675	525
10.75	725	500	375
9.00	500	375	275
7.50	300	200	145
6.75	200	150	110
5.50	125	80	55
4.75	100	75	50
4.50	80	55	38

Size (inches)*	Condition**		
	M/NM	EXC	VG
3.50	70	48	30
3.00	60	40	25
2.25	55	38	20
1.50	50	35	15

* Based on importer's catalog dimensions; sizes will vary by 1/4 inch.

Condition: **M – flawless; out-of-the-box condition; **M/NM** – virtually blemish free; some paint rubs; no crazing or paint flakes; bright polychrome paint; **EXC** – mild to moderate crazing; paint flaking and/or with some paint scratches or chips; **VG** – moderate crazing; paint flaking and mild paint loss; mild cracks and chips with very little loss of material; loose candy compartment closure or plug; dull polychrome colors.

(Do not purchase if the container is repaired or repainted, has severe cracks and scrapes, 1/4" loss or more of body material, two or more broken or lost leg talons, or loss of plug closure or cardboard slide.)

The Valuation Grid assumes that a Turkey Gobbler of varying sizes was "Made in 'Germany'" of papier mâché material, typically in the toy producing center of Thuringia, during the period 1895 to 1939. In order to adequately value turkey candy containers for certain variations such as areas of production, gender, type of material, and location of the candy closure, the following premiums and discounts (in percentage terms) should be applied to the Valuation Grid and adjusted accordingly.

Area of Production
US Zone Germany	(-10%)
Western Germany	(-15%)
Japan (prewar)	(-10%)
Occupied Japan	(-15%)
Japan (postwar)	(-20%)

Gender/Type
Hen	(+30%)
Roast Turkey	(+25%)

Material
Cardboard (pressed paper)	(-25%)

Candy Closure Location
Head/Rump	no change
Base of Body	(-15%)

Type of Legs
As part of a base	(-10%)

Mounted on Round Box   (+15%)

Nodders   (+20%)

Japanese material is accorded a discount due to its relatively cruder form of workmanship as evident in less distinctive molds and less authentic coloration.

Another problem in valuation concerns the pricing of "unmarked" containers. While the identification guide is far from flawless, most unmarked containers have differences in either the painting of the head/wattle and/or the tail feathers. Generally, the container is German if the head/wattle is painted in red/bluish pastels as opposed to the red/white norm for the Japanese version. Additionally, the container is German if the tail feathers are outlined in white; the Japanese version usually has no outlines. If the container is unmarked and cannot be readily identified, then let your pocketbook be your guide, preferably at some discount below market prices. Again, it must be stressed that, above all, **size** and **condition** are of paramount importance. These candy containers used to be quite expensive but, with the onset of online auctions, prices have seemingly softened and have leveled out. As of this writing, reproductions have not made their presence known. Contemporary American artists have crafted similar objects but these are well marked.

Tom Turkey Container, 10.75"H. Metal legs, rump opening, polychrome and metallic. Germany, c.1895-1939. Mint, $800.

Tom Turkey Container with original box and packing, 8"H. Base support, base opening, polychrome with mustard tail outlined in black and white. Mark: "Made in US Zone Germany." c.1945-1949. MIB, $500+.

Tom Turkey Containers (6), 10.75"H to 5"H. Showing a variety of metal legs and bases, polychrome. German, c.1895-1939. Various conditions and values.

Tom Turkey Containers (8), 6.25"H to 4.5"H. Showing a variety of metal legs and bases, polychrome. Marked Germany, Western Germany, and Japan. c.1895-1939. Various conditions and values.

Hen Turkey Containers (11) 5"H to 1.13"H. Showing a variety of metal legs and bases, including a Tom Turkey and two Hens on a circular box (2.88"H – Germany). Polychrome and white. Marked Western Germany; some unmarked. c.1950s. Various conditions and values.

A flock of Tom Turkey Containers (21), 5.75"H to 2.25"H. Showing a variety of metal legs and bases, polychrome, bronze, and tans. Various marks: Germany, Western Germany, Japan, Made in Occupied Japan, and Made in Japan. c.1895-1950s. Various conditions and values.

Roast Turkey Containers (2). L to R: Roast turkey, 3.63"L. Reddish-brown, bottom side flap closure, wooden feet. Germany. c.1895-1939. Excellent, $70. Roast turkey, 3.5"L. Brown, string tension bottom side closure. Unmarked (Germany?). c.1895-1939. Excellent, $60.

While Germany produced some very interesting **pressed/molded cardboard candy containers** prior to World War II, the USA became the postwar leader in this type of manufactured goods. Molded "pulp" and cardboard items began appearing soon after World War II. Virtually all the popular post-war Halloween JOLs and other lanterns were made by this process, and "pulp" items were produced for about twenty or more years until foreign competition began issuing plastic holiday novelties.

Tom Turkey Containers (2). L to R: Turkey Container, 14.25"H x 11.5"L. Wooden foot on cardboard. Half body opening. Airbrushed gray to tan shades with black and white accents; grayish blue head with red wattle. Molded cardboard construction. Marked: Germany. Excellent, $650+. Turkey Container, 7.5"H x 5.5"L. Wooden foot on cardboard. Half body opening. Airbrushed gray shades with black and white accents; medium blue head with red wattle. Molded cardboard construction. Marked: Germany. Very Good, $125+.

Left:
Tom Turkey Containers (2). L to R: Turkey container, 6.5"H x 3.63"L. No opening. Composition. Reproduction of original. Shadings of brown, beige, and tan with grayish black accents; green base. Marked: "HS" "Reproduction." Made by Kay Stamm, an artist in Pennsylvania, 2000. Mint, $60+. Turkey container, 6.75"H x 3.63"L. Molded pressed cardboard. Bottom flap opening. USA. c.1950s. Very Good, $75+.

Tom Turkey Containers (3). 7"H x 5.25"L. Base support with bottom plug opening. Molded pressed "egg-carton" type cardboard. L and R: Brownish orange shades, marked: T-3; Center: White base with airbrushed orange and green pastels, marked: T-4. ATCO (Animal Trap Company of America), Lititz, Pennsylvania (now owned by ECCO). In the very early twentieth century, ATCO invented mousetraps and also made other animal traps. After World War II, ATCO began making wooden duck decoys and papier mâché holiday candy containers. NMT (Near Mint) to VG. c. 1940s-1950s. $50-80 each depending on condition.

Tom Turkey Container, 9.5"H. Wrapped metal legs, rump opening, "antiqued" brown with dark brown accents and rose wattle. Molded paper composition. Item No. T0417. Bethany Lowe Designs, Osco, Illinois. Bethany Lowe was established in 1985 to handcraft vintage holiday collectibles. 2003. Mint, $50.

Another area of much interest is that of **"reissued" candy containers** made by German manufacturers from the original molds. One such famous mold-maker, Carl Schaller, founded his firm in 1894 and, until 1939, created many holiday molds (Easter, Halloween, Thanksgiving, and Christmas). These papier mâché novelties were exported to the USA and sold primarily through large retail chains such as F.W. Woolworth. After World War II, Ino Schaller, one of Carl's six sons, reopened the family business, initially making items from pressed cardboard. Currently, Dieter Schaller, the grandson of Ino, and his son Thomas produce papier mâché turkeys, rabbits, and other figures from the original prewar molds for sale through Christopher Radko, a USA based major importer of holiday ornaments from various European countries.

Lastly, **glass candy containers** comprise a major collecting area of interest, as most of these small items were American made, generally from Pennsylvania. Clear glass containers were mass-produced in a myriad of shapes and sizes that would appeal to children. Colorful candy pieces were then inserted to add eye appeal. To have any value, the container's original metal closure must be present.

Other variants of candy containers, such as plastic lollipop holders, were popular in the 1960s. And, at almost any retail candy store, one can buy a "real" chocolate turkey wrapped in foil and made from plastic candy molds.

Tom Turkey Container, 3.5"H x 2.38"W x 1.38" rectangle base. Clear pressed glass. Remnant of red paint on head. Original tin sliding closure, discolored. The Turkey "Gobbler" is identified as #790 in the 1986 edition of *The Complete American Glass Candy Containers Handbook* by Eikelburner and Agadjanian. American made (Pennsylvania?). c.1890-1930. Excellent, $150+.

Tom Turkey Containers (2). L to R: "Stuffed Turkey," 13.75"H x 10.5"W. Polychrome with metallic copper and black accents; teal glitter. Marked: (L) Ino Schaller Family 1996. Papier mâché, #35/600. (R) Ino Schaller Family 1996. Papier mâché, #26/600. German. Mint, $325+ each. Produced exclusively for Christopher Radko, New York, New York.

Tom Turkey Containers (4). L to R: "Stuffed Turkey," 13.75"H x 10.5"W. Mark: #26/600 (1996). Mint, $385+; "Tommy Turk," 4.25"H x 2.75"W, Mark: #3/600 (1997). Mint, $75+; "Tom Turk," 5.25"H x 4"W, Mark: #9/600 (1997). Mint, $90+; "Thomas Turk," 7"H x 5.25"W, Mark: #70/600 (1997). Mint, $110+. Ino Schaller Family. Papier mâché. German. All produced exclusively for Christopher Radko, New York, New York.

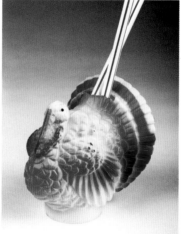

Tom Turkey Lollipop/Sucker Holder, 3.5"H x 3.13"L x 3.13"W. Shades of orange over white, red wattle. Plastic body. Narrow opening in front of tail feathers for holding lollipops. Original price 29¢. No marks. E. Rosen Co/Rosbro Plastics, Providence, Rhode Island. c.1950s, $35-50.

Tom Turkey Hollow Mold Milk Chocolate, "The Real Thing." 4"H. Multicolor foil wrapped. 3.5 oz. Distributed by See's Candy Shops, Inc., So. San Francisco, California. Edible value!

Chapter 7
THANKSGIVING DECORATIONS

Toward the end of the nineteenth century (1890s), the Thanksgiving holiday was firmly established among Americans as a day to give thanks for our many bounties as well as a secure union. In fact, it was in 1890 that the U.S. Government declared the "end of the frontier" after the last aborted Native Americans resistance was quelled at Wounded Knee, South Dakota. While there was and are many forms of Thanksgiving festivities, the preeminent social event is the traditional dinner shared alike with family and friends. And, as discussed at length in Chapter 3, what Thanksgiving dinner table would not be complete without a roast turkey and all the trimmings? Associated with this bountiful table were many functional, decorative turkey accouterments, such as glass, pottery, and papier mâché items. These decorations have been covered in prior chapters. However, just as important, there are many items that serve primarily as non-functional decorative items to add a particularly festive flavor to the Thanksgiving table. These decorations include paper displays, candles, figurines, centerpieces, and other ornamentations of varying natures.

Paper Decorations

The most important category of traditional Thanksgiving decorations is that of **paper decorations,** encompassing a wide range of items including tableware accessories, party magazines and booklets, banners, centerpieces, invitations, place markers, bridge tallies, crepe paper items, nut baskets and cups, and cardboard decorations. As the twentieth century progressed, each of the aforementioned items ebbed and flowed in popularity. Today, the Thanksgiving table shares few of these vintage decorations.

The leaders in the design and production of popular paper decorations were the **Dennison Manufacturing Company** of Framingham, Maine; **The Beistle Company** of Shippensburg, Pennsylvania; and the **CA Reed Company** of Williamsport, Pennsylvania. Of the three, only the Beistle Company, founded in 1900 in Pittsburgh, Pennsylvania, by M.L. Beistle, is still in operation today. Their current web page states that they are "the oldest and largest manufacturer of theme decorations and party goods." Beistle's on-line seasonal goods catalog for FALL/THANKSGIVING lists 111 products. Many of these products are detailed paper die-cuts of turkeys, Pil-

grims, and Indians, the same timeless designs that have been produced almost continuously (except during World War II) since the early 1920s. The Beistle Company, in 1910, was the first American firm to produce honeycombed tissue and incorporate that technology into new lines of paper decorations.

The Dennison Manufacturing Company was founded in 1844 by Andrew Dennison. While initially making jewelry boxes, the firm expanded into the production of tags, labels, and tissue paper. They, too, segued into the die-cut and party supplies lines after the turn of the twentieth century, being best known for their extensive line of Halloween products. Unlike Beistle, Dennison was unable to compete successfully against foreign competition in holiday decorations in spite of having other business lines such as printing and packaging equipment.

In 1990, Avery International Corporation of Pasadena, California, brought about a stra-

tegic merger of interests with Dennison. The resultant company today is Avery Dennison Corporation, a multi-billion dollar global leader in the production of pressure-sensitive adhesives and materials. Alas, no decorations are being produced by this firm today.

L to R: Decorative Thanksgiving Borders, crepe paper. 10'L x 6.5"W. Continuous image of Tom Turkey in farm setting on yellow background. Dennison Manufacturing, c.1950s, $40-45. Decorative Tablecloth, paper. 7'L x 4.5"W. Continuous image of multicolor Tom Turkey on yellow background. c.1950s. $45-50.

Cooperative Housekeeping Magazine, date unknown, c.1920s. "Marching Through the Thanksgiving Dinner from Place-Cards and Turkey Paper to Menu and Thanks." Advertisement to sell novelties and favors through the magazine. Full page. $5.

Tom Turkey, multicolor, two-sided cardboard with brown, orange, and yellow honeycomb fold-out body. 18"H x 13"L. Beistle Company. Made in U.S.A. c.1960s. $50-55.

Decorative Thanksgiving Banner, crepe paper. 9.8'L 20"W. Continuous image of large multicolor Tom Turkey in farm setting on yellow background. Dennison Manufacturing c. 1950s. $60-65.

L to R: Tom Turkey, multicolor two-sided cardboard with brown, yellow, and red honeycomb fold-out body. 15"H x 11"L. Amscan, Inc., Elmsford, New York. Made in Taiwan. c.1990s, $10-15. Tom Turkey, multicolor two-sided cardboard with dark brown, yellow, and red honeycomb fold-out body. 12"H x 9"L. Amscan, Inc, Elmsford, New York. Made in Taiwan. No. 28822. c.1990s. $8-13.

L to R: Tom Turkey, multicolor die-cut standup cardboard. 8"H x 13"L. Unmarked. c.1950s, $8-10. Tom Turkey, multicolor die-cut standup cardboard. 6.25"H x 8.5"L. Unmarked. c.1950s. $5-7.

L to R: Tom Turkey, multicolor two-sided cardboard with dark brown, brown, and orange honeycomb fold-out body. 13"H x 9.5"L. Beistle Company. Made in U.S.A. c.1950s, $40-45. Tom Turkey, multicolor two-sided cardboard with dark brown, orange, and yellow honeycomb fold-out body. 13"H x 9"L. Unmarked. c1990s. $15-18.

Tom Turkey, heavily embossed cardboard in light tan to sepia tones, easel back. 9.75"H x 10.25"L. Embossed "Germany." c.1910s. $75+.

L to R: Tom Turkey, multicolor two-sided cardboard with two honeycomb fold outs: yellow haystack, orange pumpkin. 11.5"H x 12"L. Beistle Company. c. 1950s, $60-65. Tom Turkey, multicolor two-sided cardboard with two orange honeycomb fold-outs. 9"H x 6.5"L. "Turkey Gobbler Centerpiece Made in U.S.A. Pat. No 1,593,647 No. 5814." Beistle Company. c.1940s. $50-55. Tom Turkey, multicolor two-sided cardboard with two orange honeycomb fold-outs. 8.5"H x 6.5"L. Beistle Company. Made In U.S.A. c.1950s. $40-45.

Thanksgiving multicolor, one-sided die-cut, standup or pin-up cardboard images (9). L to R: Tom Turkey, 9"H; Corn shuck, 7"H; Pilgrim couple, 7"H; Tom Turkey, 12.5"H; Tom Turkey, 6.75"H; Pilgrim couple, 8.5"H; and Indian Brave, 8.5"H. Dennison Manufacturing. c.1950s-1960s. $15-20 (Tom Turkey, 12.5"H); $8-10 each (all others).

Pilgrim couple multicolor, one-sided die-cut, standup or pin-up cardboard. 16"H. No. 15F, Dennison Manufacturing. c.1960s. $20-25 set.

Napkin square with four corner images encased by orange border. Tom Turkey with eight jacks; boy carving pumpkin; red schoolhouse; and picket fence with billowing clouds. 14" square crepe paper. Unmarked. c.1940s. $15-20.

Bridge Tallies. L to R: "Auction Bridge," two parts detailing points for various tricks. Litho cardboard. 5"H x 2"L. Made in U.S.A. by Gibson for U.S. Playing Card Co., c.1900s. $22-27 for set of eleven. Pilgrim couple, multicolor, two-sided die-cut cardboard. Silk blue and yellow tassels. No. 515T. 4"H x 2.25"W. Unmarked. Made in U.S.A. c.1930s. $55-60 for set of five.

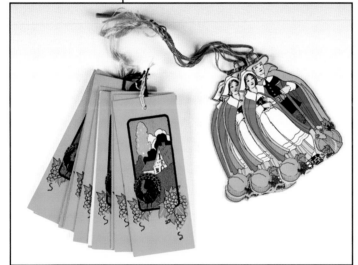

Nut Baskets (5), multicolor crepe paper body with twisted handle. Thanksgiving image scraps attached, 2"H x 2.75"D. Unmarked. c. late 1940s to early 1950s, $8-10 each. Nut Cup (1), red metal cup with die-cut metal turkey mounted on side. Cup 0.75"H x 2.5"D. Black stamp "Germany" c.1930s. $120+.

Thanksgiving images, Thanksgiving related candles represented turkeys, Pilgrim boys and girls, and Indian braves and squaws. The more contemporary and expensive candles of recent vintage are sometimes made of beeswax.

The premier company producing wax figural candles from the 1940s through the 1960s was the **Gurley (Novelty) Company** of Buffalo, New York. In 1926, Franklin Gurley bought W & F Manufacturing with the original intent to produce chocolate figural items from molds. However, manufacturing difficulties precluded this attempt and Gurley instead settled on candle manufacturing. Figural candles produced by Gurley have either one of two markings on a circular cardboard bottom: "Gurley Candle Co. Buffalo, N.Y. Made in U.S.A." or "Gurley Novelty Co. Buffalo, N.Y. Made in U.S.A." Later figural items, including hollow chocolates produced for retail greeting card chains, sometimes used the W & M Mfg. Co. mark. From the authors' observation of their collection of one hundred figural candles, the "Novelty" mark was used less frequently. But relating the price of respective candles (ranging from 15¢ to $1.19) to the company mark does not shed any information as to the precise dates of manufacture. It appears that Gurley produced the bulk of their figural candles during the late 1940s and 1950s. Lastly, it is also our observation that Indian figural candles are less frequently found. The complete Indian figures (both brave and squaw) should have their head feathers intact. These are fragile components and are prone to snap off.

Another vintage line of figural candles were made by **Socony-Vacuum Oil Company**, usually in boxed sets. What is not generally well known is that Socony-Vacuum contracted with Gurley in the late 1930s to produce a colored line of figural candles of their own design. Socony-Vacuum Oil became Mobil Oil in 1966 after some mergers.

Like many other novelty items of the mid-twentieth century, the use of figural candles as home decorations melted away. Gurley-style candles are relatively easy to find but condition (not used) and vibrant coloring are very important.

Candles

Ranking second in importance in traditional Thanksgiving decorations are **candles**. Now one would think that candles are a functional item…meant to be lit and enjoyed. However, Thanksgiving related candles were artistically molded and realistically painted. Early figural candles, made exclusively of paraffin wax, were sold in a variety of shapes and sizes. But given the narrow range of

"Thanksgiving Novelty Candles." Display boxed set of twelve assorted figural wax candles. L to R: John Alden, 3.38"H; Priscilla, 3"H; Tom Turkey, 3"H; Indian, 3.25"H; 15¢ each. Gurley Novelty Company, Buffalo, New York. No. 6254. c. late 1940s. $80-90 for set.

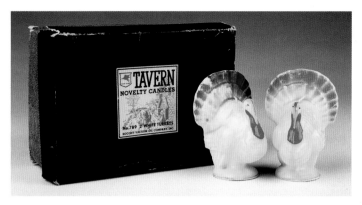

"Tavern Novelty Candles." Boxed set of two figural wax candles. Tom Turkeys (2), creamy white with orange accents, red wattle, 3.5"H. Socony-Vacuum Oil Co., Inc. No. 789 "2 White Turkeys." c. late 1940s. $20-25 for set.

Tom Turkeys Figural Wax Candles, flock of eighteen. Sizes range from 2.5"H to 6.75"H. Original prices range from 15¢ to 98¢ each. Gurley Candle (Novelty) Company, Buffalo, New York, c.1940s/1950s. $4-12 each depending on size.

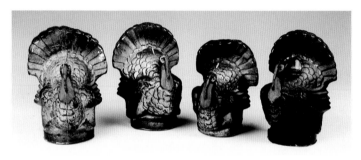

Tom Turkeys Figural Wax Candles (4). Sizes range from 4.25"H to 5.5"H. Original prices range from 25¢ to $1.19. Black, slate, brown, and purple metallic iridescence, red wattles. Gurley Candle Company, Buffalo, New York. c.1950s. $8-10 each.

Thanksgiving Figural Wax Candles (14), c.1950s. L to R, Back row: John Alden, 5.25"H, 35¢; Priscilla, 5"H, 29¢; Indian Girl, brown dress, arms folded, 5.5"H; Indian Girl, red dress, arms folded, 5.5"H; Indian Boy, red pants, arms crossed, 5.5"H. $12-18 each. Middle row: John Alden with Gun, 3.25"H, 15¢; Priscilla, royal blue dress, 3"H, 19¢. $5 each. Front row: John Alden with Gun, 3.25"H, 15¢; Priscilla, gray dress, 3"H, 19¢; Indian Chief, pale yellow pants, arms crossed, 3.25"H, 29¢; John Alden with Gun, brown suit, 3.25"H, 15¢; Priscilla, brown dress, 3"H, 15¢ (rare set); Pilgrim Boy and Girl, white, pale gray with orange accents, 3"H, boy, 2.5"H, girl. Socony-Vacuum Oil Company, Inc. (Tavern Novelty). $5-7 each, brown colorations. $10-12 each. Indian figurals command a premium if the feather wick is intact.

"Thanksgiving Candles. Dinner Table/Mantle Decorations." Boxed set of six figural wax candles. John Alden, 3.25"H; Priscilla, 3"H; 59¢ each (original). Gurley Novelty Company, Buffalo, 5, New York. Box lacks cellophane insert. c.1950s. $40-50 for set.

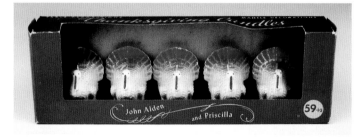

"Thanksgiving Candles. Dinner Table/Mantle Decorations." Boxed set of five figural wax candles. Tom Turkeys (5), white with brownish, red and olive green shadings; 2.38"H x 1.88"W. 59¢ each (original). Gurley Novelty Company, Buffalo, 5, New York. Box lacks cellophane insert. c.1950s. $40-50 for the set.

"Tavern Novelty Candle." Boxed set of four figural wax candles. Pilgrim couple (2), Boy, 3"H; Girl, 2.5"H. White, pale gray and orange accents. Box label misidentifies contents as "4 small pilgrim boys." Socony-Vacuum Oil Company, Inc., No. 787. c. late 1940s. $20-25 for set.

Tom Turkey Figural Wax Candle, 7"H x 6.63"W. Vivid multi-color. Fitz and Floyd, Made in Italy. c.1990s. $20-25.

Thanksgiving Figural Wax Candles (5). L to R: Tom Turkey, 4.38"H x 3"W, orange, 75¢ original price. "Norcross Heirloom" W & F Mfg. Co., Inc., Buffalo, N.Y. 14240 Made in USA, c.1960s. $10-12. Tom Turkey, 6"H x 4.25"W, matte colors of blue, green, browns, and yellow. USA. c.1970s, $8-10. Tom Turkey, 3.75"H x 3.75"L, white with red wattle. Tom Turkey, 3.75"H x 3.75"L, brownish-black with red wattle. Tom Turkey, 4"H x 3.75"L, brown, white accents with red wattle. Latter three candles, Georgetown Candle Company, Georgetown, Texas. c. late 1990s. $10-12 each.

Thanksgiving Figural Wax Candles (4). L and R: Indian Chief and Indian Squaw, 10"H. Middle: Tom Turkeys (2), 9.25"H. All artistically designed and expertly painted. Lorelie Candles, Gatlinburg, Tennessee. © 95P. $20-25 each set of two.

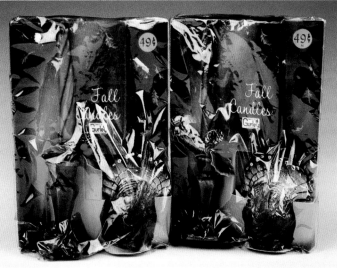

"Fall Candles," 6.25"H, Tom Turkey 2.5"H. Full cellophane package. 49¢ original price. Gurley Candle Company, Buffalo, New York 14240. c.1970s. $8-10 each package.

Left:
Thanksgiving Figural Wax Candles (2). Pilgrim Man, 7.75"H and Pilgrim Woman, 7.25"H. Dark to light shades of gray, hand-painted facial features and clothing. c. 1930s. Colonial Candle Company of Cape Cod, Inc., Hyannis, Massachusetts. $15-20 for pair.

Right:
"Tom Turkey Clear Taper Holders." Set of four, 2"H. Made in China. $16. "Tiny Tapers." Set of six. 10"H. Orange and light yellow colors. USA. $5. Both sold by Williams-Sonoma, San Francisco, California.

Decorative Items for the Home

From the 1920s to the 1960s, Thanksgiving decorations for the home centered on simple die-cut and crepe paper novelties as well as wax figural candles. Ready to take their place was a wide variety of both inexpensive and expensive **decorative objects** such as molded and sewn centerpiece items, figurines, turkey replicas crafted of various materials, hinged Limoge-style boxes, ornaments, light sets, and even rugs and doorstops.

Centerpieces can set the mood for the table décor and the resulting use of favored accessories. Thus, centerpieces range from true replicas of a Tom Turkey used in more formal settings to whimsical versions suggesting a relaxed spirit.

Tom Turkey Centerpiece, 10.25"H x 10"L x 10"W. Ceramic, white with painted red wattle and beard. No marks. c.1990s. $50+.

Tom Turkey Centerpiece, 15"H x 13.5"L x 11"W. Cast plaster, multi-colors of black, slate gray, dark brown tail feathers with yellow tips; green oval base, no marks, c. late 1990s. $100+.

Tom Turkey Decorative Centerpieces (2). L to R: 7"H x 5.38"L x 5.38"W. Glazed molded cardboard in colors of brown and rose. No marks. USA. c.1950s, $15-20; 8.5"H x 9.75"L x 9"W. Painted pressed recycled wood fibers with clay. White "distressed" crackle finish with painted red wattle. La Scala, Chico, California. c. late 1990s. $15-18.

Tom Turkey Centerpiece, 12.75"H x 10"L x 7.5"W. Cast plaster, multi-colors of black, bluish black, light blue wings, tan tail feathers with white tips; green oval base, Dallas Gift Show Import, c. late 1990s. $100+.

Tom Turkey Decorative Centerpieces (2). L to R: 12"H x 8.25"L x 12.5"W. Painted palm frond stems in brown, brownish red, tan, and red; painted wooden head. No marks. c.1990s. $12-15; 9"H x 9"L x 8"W. Brown wicker body; cutout tin head and tail. No marks. c.1990s. $12-15.

Tom Turkey Whimsical Centerpiece, 17"H x 6.63"L x 15"W. Painted wood in colors of black on beige, yellow feet, and red head. Hand-made raffia tie. Don Sharp, USA. c.1991. $50+.

Figurines occupy a very large space in the realm of decorative accessories. They also can vary widely in price due to whether they were individually produced by an artist as part of a numbered series or more common objects that one could buy at a retail outlet. The following is a good sample of turkey-image figurines. Many important European and American ceramic producers have done their part over the years to translate the raw material of ceramics into a viable collectible honoring the turkey.

L to R: Figural Pilgrim Woman holding food platter, 10"H. Painted resin, felt base. Figural Pilgrim Man holding roast turkey platter, 10.75"H. Painted resin, felt base. No marks. c.1990s. $25-30 for the set.

Figural Tom Turkey, "Large Turkey Banquet Ice Cream Mould." 8"H x 8"L x 4.5"W. Hand-cast and hand-painted "chalkware" from an Eppelsheimer, New York, antique ice cream mould. Catalog item No. 9567. Mould Number #34. Vaillancourt Folk Art, Sutton, Massachusetts. 1995. $200+. This firm was established in 1984, when the founders, Gary and Juli Vaillancourt, started the production of hand-cast, hand-painted chalkware figurines from antique chocolate moulds. Today Vaillancourt produces hand-made figurines for every major holiday, especially Christmas. Each figurine is cast in a mould from their collection of over 2,000 antique chocolate and ice cream moulds. The cast chalkware figurines are then hand-painted in artist's oils, antiqued and signed, numbered and dated. Their Christmas figurines alone are sold in more than 3,000 stores and catalogues nationwide. The firm's informative website is www.vaillancourtfolkart.com.

Tom Turkey Centerpiece, 13"H. Cotton fabric, hand-sewn. Multi-color. No marks. USA.c.1990s. $18+.

L to R: Figural Candlestick Holders. Pilgrim Man holding Tom Turkey, 9.25"H. Painted resin. Pilgrim Woman holding squash baskets, 8.75"H. Painted resin. Paper label. "Made in China." c.1990s. $25-30 for the set.

Figural Tom Turkey, detailed rear view.

Tom Turkey Whimsical Centerpiece, 10.5"H. Cotton and felt fabric, machine and hand-sewn. Multi-color. Made in China. c.1990s. $12-15.

Bottom view, detail of mould in black script.

Figural Thanksgiving Chalkware (2). L to R: " Pilgrim with Turkey and Musket," 8.5"H x 5.25"W. Chalkware cast from an Eppelsheimer, New York, chocolate mould, catalog item No. 214. Mould number #287. 1995. $200+; "Small Turkey," 4.25"H x 3"L x 2.13"W. Chalkware cast from an attributed Eppelsheimer, New York, chocolate mould, catalog item No. 9662. Mould number #103. Vaillancourt Folk Art, Sutton, Massachusetts. 1999. $100+.

Figurine of Turkey Chasing Boy, "Turkey Dinner," 5"H x 6.25"L. Porcelain and hand-painted. Original box. Scene based on a cover illustration by Norman Rockwell from *The Country Gentleman*, 12/01/17. Limited Edition of 7,500 pieces. Dave Grossman Designs, Inc. Made in Japan. 1982. $70-80 MIB.

Figural Whimsical Jack O'Lantern Figure astride a Tom Turkey, "What a Turkey," 6"H. Paper composition, hand-painted in matte and metallic colors. Circular base with central stem support. Limited edition of 22/2500. Catalog No. 218. Debbee Thibault's American Collectibles, 2000. $225+. Debbee Thibault is a Southern California based artist who made her first papier mâché Santa in 1985. From her original papier mâché designs (now exceeding 200), a rubber mold is made into which liquid paper composition is poured. Each piece is hand-painted by one of the firm's artisans and given a special glaze to effect a vintage look. All her folk art creations, based loosely on early German "veggie" people, are signed and numbered, with an edition limit of 2500. Every spring and fall Debbee issues approximately 25 new whimsical paper composition items. Her website is www.debbeethibault.com.

Figurine of Seated Farmer with a Turkey, "Thanksgiving," 8.25"H x 6.38"W. Ceramic and hand-painted, matte finish. Hang-tag. Designer: M. Nicholl. Item No. HN2446. Royal Doulton & Co., Ltd. Burslem, England (black stamp), 1972-1976, Book value $300+. Auction value $200+.

Figurine of Woman Holding Platter with a Roast Turkey, "Thanksgiving Feast," 6.5"H x 4.25"/3.75" base. Ceramic and hand-painted. Item No. K-509C. Norman Rockwell Collectors Club Figurine. 1977. $30-35.

Figurine of Small Boy Holding Sheaves of Wheat with Small Turkey at his Feet, "November," 5.25"H x 3"W. Ceramic and hand-painted. Black stamp "2300." Red and gold label "Lefton's Exclusives Japan." 1980s. $28-33.

"Kewpie Pilgrim with Turkey Figurine," 4.5"H. Kewpie doll wearing tilted pilgrim hat and holding a roast turkey on a platter. Tan vinyl, No. 602809, The Rose O'Neill Kewpie Collection © Jesco 1994. Made in Indonesia. Licensee: Enesco Corp., Elk Grove Village, Illinois. $75-80 MIB. Rose O'Neill (1874-1944) was a multi-talented illustrator, novelist, and artist. In 1909, she introduced in the pages of *Ladies' Home Journal* an enchanting and charming little chubby and nude elfin creature called the "Kewpie." The smiling, rose-cheeked figure was an instant hit and, since 1913, has graced all types of dolls, novelties, and china decorated items.

Figurine of "Little Girl with Turkey," 10.25"H. Standing peasant girl holding a Tom Turkey. Porcelain with muted pastels of pale blue, gray, brown, and white, painted under glaze. Lladró, Valencia, Spain. Code number #4814. Issued early 1970s. Retired 1981. Impressed blue backstamp "Lladro Hand Made in Spain" and other incised marks. Book value $400+. Auction value $200+.

Figurine of "Pilgrim Bunnykins," 4.25"H x 3.5"W. Bone china and hand-painted. Pilgrim bunny man holding Bible, Pilgrim bunny woman holding basket of food. Stamp "DB212©1999 Royal Doulton. Commissioned by Pascoe & Co, Florida, Limited Edition #26/2500." $50. The Bunnykins line of whimsical rabbits began in 1934 based on the illustrations of a Catholic nun, Sister Mary Barbara (Vernon). For the past seventy years, the Bunnykins images, set in the soft rolling English countryside, have been decorative, entertaining as well as educational. While Bunnykins ware is used primarily by children, many Bunnykins figures have been made for the adult collectible market as well.

Figurine of "Girl with Turkey," 5.75"H x 5.25"L. Seated peasant girl holding a Tom Turkey. Porcelain with muted pastels of pale blue, gray and tan, painted under glaze. Lladró, Valencia, Spain. Code number #4569. Issued 1969. Retired 1981. Sculptor was Fulgenico Garcia. Impressed blue backstamp "Lladro Made in Spain" and other incised marks. Book value $400+. Auction value $250+. Lladró was founded in 1953 by José, Juan, and Vicente Lladró in a small town near Tavernes Blanques, Spain. The first exports to the United States began in 1969. The company is internationally known for their fine porcelain figurines (over 4,000 different items) painted from a palette having over 5,000 different pastel tones. Lladró has produced four other turkey-related porcelains: "Turkeys" (#4525 G) retired 1972; "Girl with Turkeys" (#1038 G) retired 1978; "Little Girl with Turkeys" (#1180 G) retired 1981; and "Turkey Group" (#1196) Edition of 350, retired 1982.

Figurines of Tom Turkey (2). L to R: "Turkey," 6"H (no base), porcelain painted in life-like matte colors. Andrea by Sadek. Made in China. c.1980s. $40-50; "Wild Turkey," 7.75"H (including circular wooden base), porcelain painted in life-like matte colors. Andrea gold and black label. #6349. Andrea by Sadek. Made in Japan. c.1970s. $60-70 MIB. The Charles Sadek Import Company was established in 1936. Under the Andrea trademark the firm is an international manufacturer of high quality, fine porcelain lines of bird and animal figurines as well as tableware and decorative accessories. Andrea was their foremost designer.

Figurine of Tom Turkey, 3.5"H x 4.25"L x 2.88"W. Glazed ceramic (slip-cast in moulds) and hand-painted multi-colors of charcoal, medium brown, tan, teal, yellow, blue, and pinkish rose. Bottom: "Stangl 3275 D.C.F" (artist's initials). c.1940 to 1972 (some reissued until 1978). $400+ book value, $325+ auction value. Rare. The origins of Stangl date to 1814 when Samuel Hill began making utilitarian redware in Flemington, New Jersey. In 1860, Abram Fulper bought the pottery and slowly changed the output to artware. The Fulper Pottery Company was purchased by its principal designer, J. Martin Stangl, in 1930. After closing the artware plant in 1935, Stangl concentrated on the production of hand decorated redware, tableware, and bird figurines at Trenton, New Jersey. In 1940, Stangl started the very popular Birds of America figurine line based on Audubon's bird and fowl prints. When he died in 1972, the pottery was sold to Wheaton Industries, whereupon manufacturing continued until closure in 1978.

Figurine of Tom Turkey, "Fishnet Turkey," 5"H (tail) x 4.75"H (head). Hand-painted porcelain in the "fishnet" motif; green underglaze with black 24K gold, blue, and rose color accents. Studio No. 5077 (Aviary Collection) Blue stamp on base. Herend Porcelain Manufactory, Ltd., Herend Hungary. c.2000s. $332 retail price. $175+ auction price. Herend was established in 1826 by Vinzeny Stingl in the small town of Herend near Lake Balator in southwestern Hungary. In June, 2001, the manufactory celebrated 175 years of producing hand-crafted and painted luxury porcelain goods of the highest quality. The firm now exports porcelain items to over fifty-eight countries worldwide. The now-famous "fishnet" trademark took its original form in 1874 when a company artist designed a fish scale motif based on a feature of an obscure Chinese porcelain plate. The scaly VH (Vieux Herend) pattern, produced in at least eight colors, is extremely popular in the United States.

Turkey Figurines. L to R, Rear row: 3.5"H x 4"L x 3"W. Glazed white ceramic. Bottom stamp "Goebel West Germany." c.1980s, $10-15; 6"H x 4"L x 4"W. Glazed ceramic multi-colors of black, brown, tan, green with a bright red wattle. Bottom green stamp "wreath" design "Japan." c.1980s, $10-15; Front: Hen pecking, 9"L x 4.38"H x 3.5"W. Matte glazed ceramic of brown, tan, beige, and light green. Bottom black stamp "Madeline Originals California Made in U.S.A." c.1970s. $20-25.

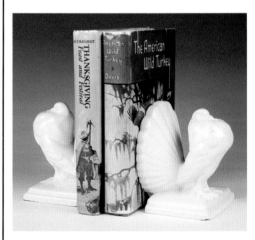

Figural Tom Turkey Bookends (2), 5.75"H x 4.5"L x 5.25"W. Glazed white ceramic. Glazed bottom: Erphila. Incised 13256 Czechoslovakia. c.1918 to 1938. $60+ for the pair.

Figural Turkey Match holders/Multi-use Small Containers (7). L to R, Rear row: 5.25"H x 5.5"L. Glazed ceramic multi-colors of black, white, green, and blue. Unglazed bottom. No marks (Japan?). c.1980s. $10-15; 5.25"H x 4.25"L. Glazed white ceramic. Black stamp under glaze "Made in Japan." c.1980s, $10-15; 6.13"H x 4"L. Glazed ceramic multi-colors of charcoal, green, orange, lavender, and green. Black base "Made in California"; Front row: 5"H x 4.5"L. Glazed ceramic hand-painted multi-colors of cream, royal blue, medium to dark green, orange, and dark rose. Black stamp under glaze "Made in Japan." c.1980s, $10-15; 5.5"H x 5"L. Glazed ceramic colors of tan, blue, and rose. Glazed bottom: impressed 562 USA, (Shawnee) c.1950s. $20-25. The Shawnee Pottery Company, Zanesville, Ohio, ceased operations in 1961 due to its inability to compete with the cost of foreign imported pottery; 5"H x 5.25"L. Glazed ceramic colors of brown, ivory, green, and dark rose. Glazed bottom: impressed Z,34,46; Under glaze: black stamp "Germany," blue stamp Full Bee in a V and ® symbols. Early mark. W. Goebel Porcelain Factory, Rodenthal, Germany. c.1940-1959. $100+; 4.75"H x 5.5"L. Flashed glaze colors of orange and lavender. Unglazed bottom: brown stamp 35 and circular "dime" mark "Made in Czechoslovakia." c.1918 to 1938. $125+.

Limoges-style hinged boxes or cases were used to store perfume and snuff. But the true value of these objects was the artistic designs covering all subject matter. Originally, Haviland and other factories produced a fine quality of porcelain tableware called Limoges porcelain after the town by the same name in France. However, since the seventeenth century, Limoges has produced small expertly crafted hinge boxes for the aristocratic trade. While they still produce such items today, competition from low-cost areas such as China has rushed to fill the void of attractive but inexpensive boxes.

Limoges-style Hinged Boxes (7). L to R: "Pilgrim Boy Kneeling with Pumpkin," 2.88"H x 1.75"L x 1.13"W. Resin, reddish brown box. No marks. c.1990s. $8-13; "Pilgrim Turkey," 6.25"H x 4.5"W. Porcelain brown roly-poly figure. Black stamp "Made in China." c.2000s, $10-15; Roast Turkey on a Platter, 2.75"L x 2"W. Porcelain. The bottom of the box has a scalloped border and the clasp is a carving knife. An orange pumpkin is painted inside the box. Glazed bottom: black script "Arloria Peint Main Limoges France RDn29." c.1990s. $60+; "Tom Turkey Standing on Base," 2.25"H x 1.75"W. Resin, reddish orange pumpkins decorate the bottom box. No marks. c.2000s. $8-13; "Pilgrim Bear with Musket," 3.25"H x 1.5"D. Resin, top of box decorated with fruit. Inside box: blue stamp "November," No marks.c.1990s. $8-13; "Pilgrim Couple," 3"H x 1.38"D. Ceramic, green base; hinge opening is a bow. Inside box: small roast turkey. No marks. c.1999. $15-20; "Standing Tom Turkey," 2.75"H x 1.63"W. Porcelain, turkey mounted on a pedestal stem. Midwest of Cannon Falls. Made in China, c.1990s. $20-25 MIB.

Ornaments

The demand for specialized "old world" **ornaments** for most holidays including Christmas has expanded exponentially since the late 1980s. The honor for this rather recent phenomenon belongs to Christopher Radko. While on a trip to visit relatives in Poland in 1985, he was able to convince some former Polish glass blowers to revive their art of blowing decorative glass ornaments. Since that year, Christopher Radko has been designing and producing holiday decorations of the highest quality. While he has concentrated his efforts on traditional Christmas ornaments, Christopher Radko has also produced specific themed ornaments for every major American holiday. During his eighteen years of exporting ornaments to America from Poland, the Czech Republic, Germany, and Italy, he has sold more than fifteen million ornaments comprising more than six thousand designs. The firm's website is www.christopherradko.com. Success breeds healthy competition and, today, many other boutique firms are designing and exporting ornaments for resale into an increasingly surfeit marketplace. For certain limited/special edition ornaments there exists a rather healthy secondary market. One would hope that the "holiday ornament" market does not suffer the same overproduction fate that caused the "limited edition" plate market to collapse during the late 1970s and into the 1980s.

Ornaments, blown glass. L to R: "Pilgrim Pride," Pilgrim man holding a musket and a turkey, 6.5"H; Pilgrim Woman with pumpkin and fruit basket at her side, 6"H. Made in Poland by Christopher Radko, 1996. $100+ MIB with tags as a set.

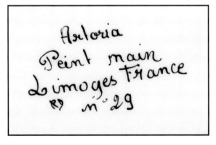

Detail from bottom of Limoges box.

Ornaments, blown glass. L to R: "Thanksgiving – Pilgrim Man and Woman Praying," 6"H; "Pilgrim's Bounty – Pilgrim holding turkey and a pumpkin," 6"H. Made in Poland by Slavic Treasures, 1997/8. $35+ each with tags.

Miscellaneous Decorative Items

Lastly, there are a wide variety of **miscellaneous decorative** items that represent the Thanksgiving holiday but do not comfortably fit into any one particular category. However, they are all emblematic of the artistic representation of Thanksgiving.

Decorative Sign, wood and resin. "Happy Thanksgiving" spelled out in dark green wooden blocks centered by Pilgrim man and woman, 12.25"L. Made in China for Kurt S. Alder. c. mid 1990s. $25-30; Decorative trees (5), 8" to 12"H. Made in China for Department 56. c. mid 1990s. $10 each.

Ornament, blown glass. "Turkey Trot," Pilgrim boy astride Tom Turkey, 5"H. Made in Poland by Christopher Radko. 2000. $40 MIB.

Ornament, blown glass. "Tom Turkey," 6.25"H. Made in Europe by Christopher Radko. c. late 1990s. $45+.

Decorative Large Scale Postcard Die-cut Replica, "A Happy Thanksgiving," 15.5"L x 10"W. Moonlight and roses, USA, Marta Peters. c. late 1990s. $15-20. "Pilgrim Man Holding Turkey," 9.13"H. Hand-carved wood by James Hadoon, Sebastapool, California. c. late 1990s. $50+.

Ornaments, blown glass. L to R: "Turkey," 4.5"H. No. GP326 retired. Polonaise Collection for Kurt S. Adler. 2000. $40+ with tag; "Tom Turkey," 6.25"H. Made in Europe by Christopher Radko. c. late 1990s. $45+; "Corn Cobbler." Tom Turkey perched on corncob, 5.75"H. Made in Germany by Christopher Radko. 1999. $50+; "Thanksgiving Cottage," 3"H. Old World Christmas, Spokane, Washington. 1999 retired. $20+; "Pilgrim Tom Turkey," 6"H. Made in Europe by Christopher Radko. c. late 1990s. $50+; "Tom Turkey," 3.5"H. Made in Germany for Old World Christmas, Spokane, Washington. 2000. $30+MIB.

"Turkey Lights," indoor/outdoor use, ten light set. Made in Taiwan. Silvestri Corporation, Chicago, Illinois. c.2000s. $18 MIB.

Thanksgiving Figures. "Pilgrim Man Holding Corn and Pumpkins," 15.75"H; "Indian Holding Fish and Corn," 20.5"H; and "Pilgrim Woman Holding Basket," 15.75"H. Raffia and white pine. Background: natural wheat sheaf, 24"H. Made in Philippines. Midwest Importers of Cannon Falls. c.1990s. $10-15 each.

"Thanksgiving Light Covers," heavy glass, six covers range from 2.25"H to 3.13"H. Images of Indian, Ear of Corn, Pilgrim Man and Woman, Cornucopia, and Tom Turkey. Made in Taiwan. Old World Christmas, Spokane, Washington. c. late 1990s. $150 MIB.

Doorstops. L to R: "Tom Turkey with Full Tail," 12.25"H x 8"W x 3"L. Painted cast iron mold. Seven pounds. No marks. c.1980s, $30-35; "Tom Turkey," 7.75"H x 7.75"L. Painted cast iron mold. Five pounds. No marks. c.1990s. $18-23.

Thanksgiving Oval Plaque, 14.75"L x 9"W. Painted chalkware "Give Thanks Unto the Lord" in raised gilt letters. Cornucopia design. No marks. c.1970s. $12-15.

Stylized Metal Tom Turkey Candleholder, rust patina welded tinplate, 15.5"H x 11"L x 27"W. Made in Mexico. c. mid 1990s. $25-30.

Nesting Dolls, painted wood (shown closed and open). L to R: "Pilgrim Family," five dolls 7.25"H to 2"H (Pilgrim Man, Woman, Boy, Girl, and Turkey); "Pilgrim Family," three dolls 6.5"H to 1.75"H. (Pilgrim Man, Woman, and Turkey); "Pilgrims, Indians, and Turkey," five dolls 5.5"H to 1.63"H (Pilgrim Boy, Girl, Indian Boy, Girl, and Turkey). Labels "Made in China." c. late 1990s. $12-15 each set.

Tom Turkey Mood Lamp on Base, 8"H x 6.25"W with base, 6.75"H without base. Glossy shades of green and brown with fifteen jewels inset on body. Terracotta oval base with single 7-watt light bulb. Mark: "EK" on base. c.1990s. $100+.

Tom Turkey Mood Lamp, front view.

Metal Candleholders, dark brown painted tin. Cutouts: Tom Turkey, 5.25"H x 6"L, left and right sided. Tom Turkey, 9" x 11"L, square box holder. Label "Made in Haiti." c. mid 1990s. $10 each smaller holders, $13 larger holders.

Stained Glass Tiffany (style) Lamp, "Tom Turkey," 12"H. Uses two 25-watt bulbs. Made in China. Cracker Barrel Old Country Store, Lebanon, Tennessee. 2002. $50.

Outside Decorative Banner/Flag, "Tom Turkey in Field of Pumpkins," 36"L x 24"W. Two-sided image depicts a licensed painting by K. Tice-Phillips. 100% perma-color polyester, print is permanently dyed in the fabric. Made in Mandeville, Louisiana. Toland Enterprises. c. late 1990s. $25-30.

Flashlight with mounted Tom Turkey, 8.75"H. Celluloid/plastic. Turkey body is light source in colors of slate and reddish-brown; white holder. Made in Japan. Pyramid. c.1950s. $30-35.

L to R: Feather Turkey Ornaments (2). 5"H x 4.5"W at tail. Original and dyed turkey feathers, red felt head and wattle, glass eyes, orange fabric wrapped wire legs. Made in Germany c.1930s, $30 for pair; Place Card Holder, "Tom Turkey," 2.5"H. Celluloid body, metal spring legs, place card holder at base. Made in Germany. c. early 1920s. $230+. Rare.

Outside Decorator Banner/Flag, "Pilgrim Couple with Roast Turkey," 52"L x 32"W. Two-sided image. 220 Denier 100% nylon fabric. Made In Canada. Windsport by Ganz. 2000. $50-55.

L to R: Decorative Wooden Puzzles, interlocking hand-cut, stained, and painted, hardwood pieces. "Totem," 9.5"H x 4.5"L x 1.5"W. Fifteen pieces. Top to bottom: sun, ship, Pilgrim, turkey, Indian, pumpkin. "First Thanksgiving," 7"H x 13"L x 1.5"W. Thirty pieces. Stosich Woodlock, Inc. Idaho Falls, Idaho. 1996. $30-50 each.

Serving Tray, two handles, 15.75"L x 10.25"W. Metal body with glass surface. Decal images of Tom and Hen Turkeys on inside glass, tan painted background. No marks. c.1950s. $50+.

Tin Container, 6.75"H x 6" square. Lithographic image. "Fenceline Crossing," Jim Kasper, Wildlife Artist. Limited Edition Tin, 1996. Red Man Chewing Tobacco. Made in USA. $25.

Decorative Plaque, "November," 8" square with metal turkey feather topper. Lithography on wood bound by metal border. Original Children's Theme Calendar, November – Turkey. Artist Nancy Thomas (Nancy Thomas – Art for Living). Yorktown, Virginia. 2002 $90.

Ice Art Sculpture Mold, "Tom Turkey," 8.5"H x 5"L x 6"W. Blue rubber mold for making an ice sculpture centerpiece, directions included. 1978 © CBL. $25-30.

Hand-Hooked Rug, "Tom Turkey," 31"L x 26"W, 8-sided. 100% wool, design R 272. Tan background, black border with garland of leaves. Hand hooked in China. Artist design: Claire Murray, New England. 1995. $275+.

Hand-Hooked Rug, "First Thanksgiving," 54"L x 32"W. Vintage wool on burlap. Primitive scene of Pilgrims and Indians at the first Thanksgiving dinner. Ivory background with alternating ivory and black strip border. Artist signed: "NGS" for N. Gertrude Scott, Maine. Late 1990s. $375+.

Computer Mouse Pad, 9.25"L x 7.25"W. Lithographed polyester pad. Image: Collage of 1900s-era Thanksgiving postcards. USA. Yowzers.com Internet Shoppe. 1999. $15.

Hermés Silk Scarf, "Texas Wildlife," 35" square. 100% vividly multi color printed silk. Central image: Tom Turkey, surrounded by a garland of prickly pear cactus on which various birds are perched. Outer border: encircled by a garland of native flowers with various forms of wildlife. Each of the four corners is encased with wildlife and fowl. Blue ribbon banner: "Faune & Flore In Texas," and "Texas Wildlife." Purple background and black border. 2000; special order. Hermés, Paris, France. $350+.

Decorative Tile, "Tom Turkey," 4.25" square. Ceramic. Colors: sky blue, green background, gray stump and white turkey. No marks. USA. c. 2000. $10.

Chapter 8
PRINTED EPHEMERA AND OTHER PAPER ITEMS

The word *ephemera* first came into use in America in 1751. It is used as a plural noun (of Latin/Greek derivation) to describe items (usually printed items) having no lasting significance or lasting value. The Ephemera Society of America (formed in 1980) has identified 126 different categories of ephemera subject matter. Included under this vast panoply of printed material are broadsides, trade cards, die-cuts, postcards, tickets, letterheads, menus, posters, advertising materials, labels, and programs. If one extends this category to emphasize pictorial content and graphic design of some lasting remedial value, then prints, paintings, photographs, stamps, postal history, manuscripts, illustrated newspapers, pamphlets, magazines, cookbooks, sheet music and records, and even modern day videos could be comfortably included.

Every major holiday has its own vast and fascinating diversity of printed ephemera. Thanksgiving has a wonderful range of imagery, usually focused on the turkey as the icon of this unique American celebration. In this chapter, which could be book length in itself, the focus will be on postcards, printed illustrations, magazine and magazine covers, advertisements, fruit and produce crate labels, stamps, postal covers and history, sheet music and records, and comic strip characters (books and videos).

Illustrated Newspapers

Coincident with a rising tide of literacy in America, a new form of publication was initiated…**the illustrated newspaper**. Actually, the antecedent to America's tabloid newspapers, *The Illustrated London News*, had its beginning in Great Britain in 1842. By the middle of the nineteenth century, America had spawned its own form of illustrated journals. The format of these weekly newspapers, usually sixteen pages in size and measuring 11"L x 16"W, was a series of "woodblock" engravings based on the news of the day, explanatory text, and broadside type advertising.

Many illustrated newspapers, which were highly popular during the latter half of the nineteenth century, published numerous finely drawn wood engravings by prominent American artists. Winslow Homer, Thomas Nast, and Frederick Remington were among those who rendered artistic skill to the pages of these highly attractive newspapers. Today, wood engraving prints from these original pages by the "Big Three" artists are actively sought after.

The first of many American "illustrated" type tabloids was *Gleason's Pictorial Drawing Room Companion* (1851-1854), published by Frederick Gleason of Boston, Massachusetts. This newspaper subsequently became *Ballou's Pictorial Drawing Room Companion* (1854-1859). The second illustrated newspaper was

Frank Leslie's Illustrated Newspaper (12/15/1855-6/1894), published in New York. It became *Leslie's Illustrated* (7/18/1894-6/24/1922) until its merging into *The Judge* on 6/31/1922. During a period spanning over forty years, the Frank Leslie's publishing empire produced over seventeen different journals and gazettes under its masthead name. Lastly, the best-known illustrated journal of them all, as well as the longest running, was *Harper's Weekly* (1/1857-5/13/1916), published in New York. This particular journal set the standard for American illustrated journalism for over sixty years, with at least five publications showing the Harper's masthead. In 1916, *Harper's Weekly* merged into the *Independent*, which was published until October, 1928.

Original wood engravings published by the "Big Three" artists in these aforementioned journals are considered "original art" and command prices ranging from $15 to $150 per print. Illustrations by Maxfield Parrish command much higher prices.

Throughout this book, as observed especially in Chapters 1 and 3, we have used illustrated newspaper prints to amplify a story. In many cases, "one print" is worth "ten thousand words," more or less.

"A New England Thanksgiving Dinner." Artist: J.H. Manning. *Gleason's Pictorial Drawing Room Companion.* Boston. c.1851. 11" x 8" (cut out). $15-20.

Left:
"Preparing For the Harvest Thanksgiving." Artist: M. Walker. *The Illustrated London News,* London, Great Britain. October 3, 1891. 11" x 15.5". Depicting a different type of Thanksgiving. $25-30.

Below:
Prints: L to R: "Thanksgiving Festivities at Fort Pulaski, Georgia." Artist: W. T. Crane. *Harper's Weekly.* New York. November 27, 1862. 11.5" x 16.5". Shows many festive scenes such as "Burlesque Dress Parade" and "Thanksgiving Ball – Interior of a (Battery) Casemate." $25-30; "Thanksgiving in Camp." Artist: Winslow Homer. *Harper's Weekly.* New York. November 29, 1862. 16" x 11". Shows Union soldiers at rest enjoying provisions purchased from the camp's sutler (a non-official commissary agent selling supplies to the troops). $50+.

"Thanksgiving Day in the Army – After Dinner: The Wish-bone." Artist: Winslow Homer. *Harper's Weekly*. New York. December 3, 1864. 16" x 11" Who will get the "lucky break?" $50+.

Two-page Print. "Thanksgiving On the Other Side- No 1 and No. 2" Artist: Thomas Nast. *Harper's Weekly*. New York. December 8, 1877. 11.5" x 16.5" each. A political engraving showing the crown heads of the European countries attempting to carve up Turkey (the country) while her nemesis, Greece, is waiting on the sidelines. $75+.

Left:
Prints: Top to Bottom: "Thanksgiving – A Thanksgiving Dinner Among the Puritans." Artist: J. W. Ehninger. *Harper's Weekly*. New York. November 30, 1867. 16" x 11". Color tint. $30-35; "Thanksgiving – A Thanksgiving Dinner Among Their Descendants." Artist: W.S.L. Jewett. *Harper's Weekly*. New York. November 30, 1867. 16" x 11". $25-30.

"Pride Goeth Before Destruction." Artist: C.S. Reinhart. *Harper's Weekly*. New York. November 24, 1888. 11" x 16". $25-30.

Left:
Prints: Top to Bottom: "Uncle Sam's Thanksgiving Dinner." Artist: Thomas Nast. *Harper's Weekly*. New York. November 20, 1869. 15.5" x 10.5". A political engraving espousing universal suffrage among all the peoples of the world. $50+; "Thanksgiving-Day Among the Puritan Fathers in New England." *Harper's Weekly*. New York. December 3, 1870. 16" x 11" Color tint. An indoors thanks to God with Indian spectators. $30-35.

Magazines

While one may think that the illustrated newspaper was the forerunner of magazines, the first **magazines** – *General Magazine* (Ben Franklin) and *American Magazine* (Andrew Bradford) – were actually first published within days of one another in February 1741. The rest of the eighteenth century saw the issuance of many political tracts, broadsides, and pamphlets, but no magazines of lasting nature.

In the early nineteenth century, a famous magazine that still exists in one format or another, *The Saturday Evening Post*, was established as an illustrated weekly newspaper. The magazine's predecessor had been founded in 1728 and was edited and published by Benjamin Franklin. The journal was then known as *The Pennsylvania Gazette*. In 1821, the name of that weekly was changed to the current *The Saturday Evening Post*. In 1969, its weekly run was terminated in favor of a publishing cycle of somewhat random issuances. The magazine is now published bi-monthly.

While literally hundreds of magazines have come and gone since prior to the American Civil War, *Scientific American* (1845) and *Harper's* (1850) are still published today. After the Civil War, the tabloid sized illustrated weekly newspapers with their politicalized contents began a slow demise in readership. New advances in printing technology and chromolithography heralded the introduction of a new style of magazine in terms of size, scope, style, bold graphics, and color. The appeal of color was very important to a barely literate audience whose buying power was important to the inherent longevity of proliferating and competing monthly magazines. As a cultural phenomenon, many magazines sought to shape opinion and foster change. Others were published strictly for enjoyment purposes. But as content was becoming important, some of America's greatest literary figures and graphic illustrators formed allegiances with various magazines. Today, on the magazine secondary market, a magazine's resale value may be determined only by the cover illustrator – such as N.C. Wyeth, Norman Rockwell, J.C. Leyendecker, Charles Dana Gibson, Maxfield Parrish, James Montgomery Flagg (the creator of "Uncle Sam"), and Harrison Fisher – whereas much of the written content, except for the vintage advertisements, is dated.

The major holidays celebrated in America, especially during the late nineteenth century to the mid-twentieth century, allowed illustrators, by virtue of their intriguing and skillful graphics, to shape their audience's opinion and understanding of the meaning of these events. This was especially true during the huge emigrant wave that hit American shores from 1890 to 1920. Thomas Nast, for instance, was one of the first of many illustrators to formulate the way we expect Santa Claus to look – as a rotund, jolly-faced elfin figure dressed in red and white. As Thanksgiving grew in prominence, cover illustrators did their best to bring home the idea of the giving "thanks for mercies rendered." The illustrations shown here should impress the reader with their diversity, ranging from the serious to the comic in nature.

Foremost among general interest magazines in terms of annual covers devoted to

Thanksgiving were *The Saturday Evening Post* (1821-1830, 1839-present) *Life* (old, 1883-1936), *The Youth's Companion* (1827-1929), *Collier's* (1905-1957), *The New Yorker* (1925-present), and *Puck* (1877-1918). All of these magazines were published weekly. Since there was much competition among magazines for the small but expanding literate market, a magazine could not forego colorful attention-grabbing covers, satirical comment, and a weekly publishing schedule that promised one would not be forgotten in the plethora of magazine offerings. Both *Life* and *Puck* started and ended their publishing lifespan as humor and political satire magazines. Hence, especially in *Puck's* case, the covers and mid-sections were rife with biting commentary on the political condition of the times. *Puck's* chromolithographic illustrations are highly collectible even through the artists (including one of the publishers) were not particularly well-known.

Many other magazines over the years, both of general and special interest nature, used Thanksgiving cover graphics as a way to draw readership. Many of the special interest magazines that were comfortable with a holiday

image included women's, youth or boys, rural Americana, and Christian themed categories. Today, only *The New Yorker* still publishes on a weekly schedule, and its covers are both humorous and attractive. In fact, except for *The New Yorker*, no other magazine today publishes holiday covers of any consequence. Only the newer special-interest cooking and life-style magazines publish a Thanksgiving-oriented cover, and those are mainly photographs of cooked turkeys. While the covers of many defunct and extant magazines still exist, the contents have been trashed. Dealers in magazine covers and advertisements, unfortunately, take a "slaughterhouse" approach to magazines, to wit: a magazine is synergistically worth more than a sum of its parts. Therefore, magazines are gutted for their saleable contents (covers and ads) and, in most cases, the meat is discarded leaving only blood and bones behind. In our opinion, we would hope that ephemera dealers would not break apart such magazines, as each comprises a tiny "time capsule" of their contemporary history. The following images represent a small sample of said covers.

The Saturday Evening Post, November 23, 1901. "The Thanksgiving Number." Unknown artist. 11" x 14". The Curtis Publishing Company, Philadelphia, Pennsylvania. $20-25.

Left:
The Saturday Evening Post. L to R, Top: November 21, 1908. "Thanksgiving Number." Artist: J.C. Leyendecker. Cover only. $30-40; November 13, 1909. "Thanksgiving." $40-50; November 12, 1910. "Thanksgiving." Artist: J. C. Leyendecker. $40-50; Bottom: November 18, 1911. Artist: J.C. Leyendecker. $40-50; November 16, 1912. "Thanksgiving." Artist: J.C. Leyendecker. Cover only. $30-40; November 28, 1914. "Thanksgiving." Artist: J. C. Leyendecker. Cover only. $30-40.

Right:
The Saturday Evening Post. L to R: November 29, 1913. Artist: J.C. Leyendecker. Cover only. $30-40; November 25, 1922. Artist: J.C. Leyendecker. $45-50.

The Saturday Evening Post. L to R, Top: November 25, 1899. "Thanksgiving Number." Artist: T.L. Tithian. Cover only, Color tint. $10-15; November 22, 1902. "Thanksgiving 1902." Artist: J.J. Gould. $20-25; November 21, 1903. "Thanksgiving Number." Artist: Guernsey Moore. $20-25; Bottom: November 18, 1905. "Thanksgiving." Artist: Guernsey Moore. Cover only. $10-15; November 17, 1906. "Thanksgiving Number." Artist: unknown. $20-25; November 23, 1907. "Thanksgiving Number." Artist: J. C. Leyendecker. Cover only. $30-40.

The Saturday Evening Post. L to R, Top: November 13, 1915. Artist: Tony Sarg. Cover only. $15-20; November 20, 1915. "Thanksgiving." Artist: J.C. Leyendecker. $45-50; November 24, 1917. Artist: J. C. Leyendecker. Cover only. $30-40; Bottom: November 30, 1918. Artist: J.C. Leyendecker. Cover only, severely trimmed. $20-25; November 29, 1919. "Thanksgiving." Artist: J.C. Leyendecker. Cover only. $30-40; November 27, 1920. Artist: J.C. Leyendecker. Cover only. $30-40.

The Saturday Evening Post. L to R, Top: November 23, 1929. "Thanksgiving." Artist: J. C. Leyendecker. $50-55; November 26, 1932. "E Pluribus Unum." Artist: J. C. Leyendecker. $50-55; December 2, 1933. "Thanksgiving." Artist: J.C. Leyendecker. $50-55; Bottom: December 1, 1934. Artist: J. C. Leyendecker. Cover only. $30-40; November 23, 1935. "Thanksgiving." Artist: J.C. Leyendecker. $50-55; November 28, 1936. Artist: J.C. Leyendecker. $50-55. Interesting contrast of subject matter among the 1934, 1935, and 1936 covers.

The Saturday Evening Post. L to R, Top: December 1, 1923. Artist: J.C. Leyendecker. Cover only. $30-40; November 29, 1924. "Thanksgiving." Artist: J.C. Leyendecker. Cover only. $30-40; November 28, 1925. "Thanksgiving." Artist: J.C. Leyendecker. Cover only. $30-40; Bottom: November 27, 1926. Artist: J. C. Leyendecker. Cover only. First instance of a color (green) used on a Thanksgiving cover other than black, white, and orange combinations. $35-40; November 26, 1927. "Thanksgiving." Artist: J. C. Leyendecker. $50-55; November 24, 1928. "Thanksgiving 1628-1928." Artist: J. C. Leyendecker. This is one of Leyendecker's most famous covers. $65-75.

The Saturday Evening Post. L to R, Top: November 26, 1938. Artist: J. C. Leyendecker. $50-55; November 25, 1939. Artist: J. C. Leyendecker. $65-70; November 28, 1942. "Woes of an Army Cook." Artist: Norman Rockwell. This was Rockwell's first Thanksgiving cover. Reproduction cover. $10-15; Bottom: November 27, 1943. "Thanksgiving." Artist: Norman Rockwell. Reproduction cover. $10-15; November 24, 1945. "Thanksgiving." Artist: Norman Rockwell. $15-20. November 30, 1946. "Recital after Thanksgiving Dinner." Artist: John Falter. $15-20.

The Saturday Evening Post. L to R: November 27, 1948. Artist: Constantin Alajalov. $15-20; November 24, 1951. "Saying Grace." Artist: Norman Rockwell. One of Rockwell's most poignant covers. $30-35; November 24, 1962. Artist: Jan Balet. Similar theme to the 1948 cover. $10-15.

Life (Magazine). L to R, Top: November 7, 1912. "Thanksgiving Number – The Shrine." Artist: Paul Stahr. Cover only. $20-25; November 5, 1914. "Thanksgiving Number – The Pilgrim's Progress." Artist: Paul Stahr. Cover only. $20-25; November 4, 1915. "Thanksgiving Number – The Vegetarian's Son." Artist: Paul Stahr. $25-30; Bottom: November 14, 1920. "Thanksgiving – The Pessimist." Artist: unknown. $25-30; November 25, 1920. "The Profiteer." Artist: Stetson Crawford. Cover only. $20-25; November 17, 1921. "Thanksgiving – A Pilgrim's Progress." Artist: Norman Rockwell. Cover only. $25-30; November 22, 1923. "Thanksgiving – Ye Glutton." Artist: Norman Rockwell. Cover only. $25-30.

Life (Magazine-old), New York City, New York. L to R, Top: November 29, 1900. "Thanksgiving 1900." Artist: Albert D. Blashfield. Cover only. $20-25; November 27 1902. "Thanksgiving Number." Artist: Albert D. Blashfield. Cover only. $20-25; November 5, 1903. "Thanksgiving." Artist: unknown. Cover only. $20-25; November 3, 1904. "Thanksgiving." Artist: C. Allan Gilbert. Cover only. $20-25; Bottom: November 24, 1904. "Thanksgiving." Artist: W. M. Balfour-ker. Cover only. $20-25; November 2, 1905. "Thanksgiving." Artist: Henry Hutt. Cover only. $20-25; November 7, 1907. "Thanksgiving Number." Artist: T. K. Hanna. Cover only. $20-25; November 3, 1910. "Thanksgiving Number – Unbidden Guests." Artist: P. O'Malley. Cover only. $20-25.

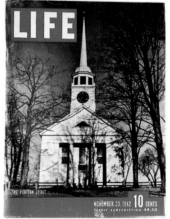

Life (Magazine), Chicago, Illinois. L to R: November 23, 1942. "The Puritan Spirit." Photographed church, built in 1755, was situated in Groton, Massachusetts. $10-15; November 20, 1944. "Thanksgiving." Photographed church, built in 1825, was situated in Tallmadge, Ohio. $10-15.

Life (Magazine). L to R, Top: November 28, 1895. "Thanksgiving Number." Artist: F.G. Attwood. $30-35; November 6, 1913. "Thanksgiving Number." Artist: Power O'Malley. $30-35; Bottom: November 2, 1922. "Thanksgiving Number." Artist: unknown. $20-25; November 18, 1926. "Thanksgiving Number." Artist: unknown. $25-30.

The Youth's Companion, Boston, Massachusetts. 11" x 16". L to R: November 18, 1886. "Thanksgiving Number." Artist: Russell B. Richarson. $15-20; November 29, 1888. "Thanksgiving Number." Artist: Russell B. Richarson. Cover only. $5-10; November 27, 1890. "Thanksgiving Number." Artist: unknown. Cover only. $5-10.

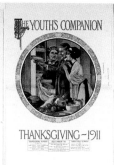

The Youth's Companion. L to R: November 23, 1893. "Thanksgiving Number."
Artist: W. L. Taylor. Cover only. $5-10; November 29, 1894. "Thanksgiving
Number." Artist: H. Burgess. Cover only. $5-10; November 28, 1895. "Thanksgiv-
ing." Artist: Vesper L. George. Cover only. $5-10.

The Youth's Companion. L to R: November 24, 1910. "Thanksgiving Number."
Artist: Arthur Becher. Cover only. $5-10; November 30, 1911. "Thanksgiving."
Artist: William Ballantyne Brown. Cover only. $5-10; November 28, 1912.
"Thanksgiving Number." Artist: Franklin T. Wood. Cover only. $5-10.

The Youth's Companion. L to R: November 26, 1896. "Thanksgiving." Artist: W. L.
Taylor. Cover only. $5-10; November 25, 1897. "Thanksgiving." Artist: W. L. Taylor.
$15-20; November 23, 1899. "Thanksgiving." Artist: unknown. $15-20.

The Youth's Companion. L to R: November 27, 1913. "Thanksgiving Number."
Artist: Arthur Becher. $20-25; November 25, 1915. "Thanksgiving Number." Artist:
J.E. Bird. $20-25; November 22. 1917. "Thanksgiving Number." Artist: unknown.
Cover only. $5-10.

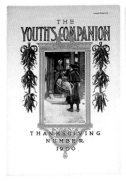

The Youth's Companion. L to R: November 29, 1900. "Thanksgiving Number."
Artist: unknown. $15-20; November 27, 1902. "Thanksgiving Number." Artist: W.
D. Stevens. Cover only. $5-10; November 24, 1904. "Thanksgiving Number." Artist:
unknown. Cover only. $5-10.

The Youth's Companion. L to R: November 25, 1926.
"Thanksgiving 1827-1926." Artist: unknown. Cover only.
$5-10; November 1928. "Thanksgiving." Artist: Charles
Livingston Bull. Cover only. This was the last Thanksgiving
issue before the magazine ceased publication in September
1929. $15-20.

The Youth's Companion. L to R: November 30, 1905. "Thanksgiving Number for
1905." Artist: Arthur E. Becher. Cover only. $5-10; November 28, 1907. "Thanks-
giving Number." Artist: unknown. $15-20; November 25, 1909. "Thanksgiving
Number." Artist: Franklin T. Wood. Cover only. $5-10.

Silent Wings for Training

Collier's The National Weekly. L to R: November 30, 1940. Artist: G. Runge. Cover only. $15-20; November 29, 1947. Artist: Martha Sawyers. $30-40.

Collier's, The National Weekly, New York City, New York. 10.5" x 14". L to R, Top: November 18, 1905. "Thanksgiving Number – The Tramp's Dinner." Artist: Maxfield Parrish. $150-175; November 21, 1908. "Thanksgiving 1908." Artist: Clara Elsene Reck. Cover only. $20-25; November 20, 1909. "Thanksgiving." Artist: Maxfield Parrish. Cover only. $100-125; Bottom: November 19, 1910. Artist: I. Walter Taylor. Cover only. $20-25; November 27, 1926. "Thanksgiving." Artist: Bradshaw Crandel. Cover only. $20-25; November 26 1927. Artist: Twelvetrees. $35-40.

The New Yorker, New York City, New York. 8" x 11". L to R, Top: November 25, 1933. Artist: Rea Irvin. Cover only. $20-25; November 27, 1937. Cover only. $20-25; November 28, 1942. Artist: Constantin Alejalov. Cover only. $15-20; November 25, 1944. Artist: Mary Petty. $25-30. Bottom: November 24, 1945. Artist: Rea Irvin. Cover only. $15-20; November 29, 1947. Artist: Carnott Price. Cover only. $15-20; November 27, 1948. Artist: Peter Arno. Cover only. $15-20; November 26, 1949. Artist: Constantin Alejalov. Cover only. $15-20.

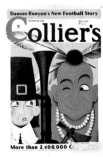  

Collier's, The National Weekly. L to R, Top: November 28, 1931. "Thanksgiving Day." Artist: Everett Watson. Cover only. $25-30; November 26, 1932. Artist: E. de Zayas. Cover only. $20-25; November 25, 1933. Artist: Arthur Crouch. $35-40; Bottom: November 24, 1934. Artist: Antonio Petrucelli. $35-40; November 30, 1935. Artist: unknown. Cover only. $20-25; November 25, 1939. Artist: Jay Irvine. $35-40.

The New Yorker. L to R, Top: November 25, 1950. Artist: Bernelman. Cover only. $10-15; November 24, 1951. Artist: P. Donlou. $25-30; November 26, 1955. Artist: Bernelman. $25-30; November 17, 1956. Artist: Getz. Cover only. $10-15; Bottom: November 30, 1957. Artist: Kraus. $25-30; November 26, 1960. Artist: Bernbaum. $25-30; November 25, 1961. Artist: F. B. Modell. $25-30; November 24, 1962. Artist: Kovarsky. Cover only. $10-15.

The New Yorker. November 25, 1974. "The First Thanksgiving." Artist: James Stevenson. $22-27.

The New Yorker. November 28, 1977. "Turkeys on Parade." Artist: Arnie Lavin. $22-27.

The New Yorker. November 29, 1976. "Guest of Honor." Artist: Saul Steinberg. $25-30.

The New Yorker. L to R: November 29, 1999. "Turkey Day." Artist: Steve Broadner. $5; November 27, 2000. "Thanksgiving.com." Artist: Chris Ware. $5.

The New Yorker. L to R, Top: November 27, 1965. Artist: F.B. Modell. $22-27; November 25, 1967. Artist: Stevenson. Cover only. $10-15; November 30, 1968. Artist: Bernbaum. Cover only. $10-15; November 26, 1984. Artist: Koren. Cover only. $8-10. Bottom: November 28, 1988. Artist: W. Steig. Cover only. $8-10; November 27, 1989. Artist: Koren. Cover only. $8-10; November 26, 1990. Artist: Shanahan. Cover only. $8-10; November 30, 1992. Artist: ST. Cover only. $6-8.

The New Yorker. L to R: December 2, 2002. "Last-Minute Errand." Artist: Michael Sowa. $5; December 1, 2003. "Reverse Play." Artist: Edward Sorel. $5 each.

Puck, 10" x 13.5". L to R, Top: April 22, 1885. "Tough on Turkey – England and Russia, Together, 'Be my Ally, or I'll Give You the Worst Thrashing You Ever Had in your Life.' " Artist: Bernard Gillam. Cover only. That the world powers were trying to bend Turkey to their collective will was a common theme during those times. $75-100; November 24, 1886. "Drop It." Artist: F. Opper. An anarchist is stopped from carrying off "personal liberty." $100-125; Bottom: November 23, 1892. "This is No Crow." Artist: J. Keppler. Cover only. Puck, himself, is ready to carve the Thanksgiving turkey. $75-100; November 25, 1896. "Thanksgiving For What We Are About to Receive, May the Lord Make Us Truly Thankful." Artist: L. Dalrymple. Cover only. $75-100.

Puck (1877-1918), New York City, New York. 13.25" x 10.25". November 28, 1883. "Missed!" Artist: Bernard Gillam. Cover only. $80-100. New York State political satire.

Puck. L to R, Top: November 24 1897. "Waiting For Scraps From the Thanksgiving Table." Artist: L. Dalrymple. Cover only. $75-100; December 6, 1899. (William Jennings) "Bryan's Thanksgiving." Artist: L. Dalrymple. Cover only. Bryan was a candidate in the 1900 Presidential election. $75-100; Bottom: November 22, 1905. "Thanksgiving 1905." Artist: Hassmian. Cover only. $60-80; November 23, 1910. "Thanksgiving 1910." Artist: B. Barer. Cover only. $60-80.

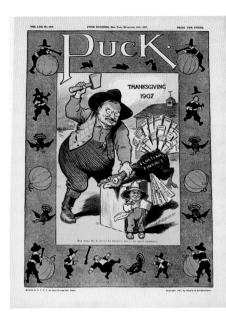

The Judge (1881-1947), New York City, New York. 10" x 14". L to R: November 29, 1902. "Thanksgiving." Artist: unknown. $60-75; November 28, 1903. "Thanksgiving Number 1903." Artist: Florri. Cover only. $30-40; November 21,1908. "Thanksgiving – Come Off the Perch! 'This is My Day,' says the Turk." Artist: Grant E. Hamilton. Cover only. $40-50. *The Judge* was similar to *Puck* in terms of satirical illustrations and content. *Leslie's Illustrated* merged into *Judge* on 6/30/1922.

Puck. 10" x 13.75". November 13, 1907. "Thanksgiving 1907... For What He Is About To Receive, Let Us Be Truly Thankful." Artist: L.M. Glackens. Cover only. Teddy Roosevelt chopping the head off of various swindles hurting the small investor. Déjà vu! $100-125.

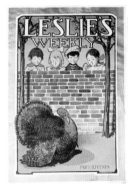

Leslie's Weekly (1894-1922), New York City, New York. 11" x 16". L to R: November 27, 1901. Artist: Ralph Taylor Shultz. Cover only. $30-40; November 1903. "Thanksgiving Number 1903." Artist: unknown. Cover only. $30-40; November 23, 1905. "Thanksgiving Number – Not a Cause For Thanksgiving." Artist: W. Peters. Cover only. $30-40.

Puck. November 18, 1908. "Uneasy Turks." Artist: L.M. Glackens. "Turkey" does not know when the next attempt to do him in will occur. This theme was persistent for over two decades. $100-125.

Leslie's Illustrated Weekly Newspaper. L to R, Top: November 25, 1915. "I Ought To Be Thankful." Artist: Grant E. Hamilton. Cover only. $40-50; November 23, 1916. "Preparedness." Artist: F.X. Leyendecker. $50-60. Bottom: November 23, 1918. Artist: Orson Lowell. $50-60; November 22, 1919. "The Best Table in Today's World." Artist: Sarka. Cover only. $40-50. A satirical and a predictive cover – the German Dachshund is asking for "just a little bone please" from Uncle Sam who is carving up a huge turkey. The very heavy reparations that Germany was forced to pay to the Allies after World War I were a contributing factor to the rise of Nazism under Hitler.

Liberty: A Weekly For Everybody (1924-1951), New York City, New York. 10" x 13" and 8.5" x 11". L to R: December 1, 1934. "Thanksgiving." Artist: Lee Brown. Cover only. $5-10; November 22, 1924. Artist: Frederic Stanley. Cover only. $10-15; November 28, 1936. Artist: Jay McArdle. $20-25.

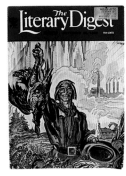

The Literary Digest. L to R, Top: November 22, 1919. Artist: Norman Rockwell. $60-75; November 26, 1921. Artist: Norman Rockwell. Cover only. $50-60; Bottom: November 25, 1933. Artist: Cesare. Cover only. $8-10; November 24, 1934. Photographer: H. Armstrong Roberts. $15-20.

The Literary Digest (1890-1938), New York City, New York. 9" x 12". L to R, Top: November 27, 1926. "The Turkey Drive." Artist: Richard Norris Brooke. Cover only. $8-10; November 25, 1922. "Thanksgiving 300 Years Ago." Artist: E. Jackson. $15-20; Bottom: November 29, 1924. "Fine Weather." Artist: Luigi Chialiva. Cover only. $8-10; November 26, 1927. "Grace Before Meat." Artist: Jan Steen. Cover only. $8-10.

Success Magazine (1897-1911), New York City, New York. 10" x 14". L to R: November 1900. "When the turkey's on the table and the fixin's on the way, I forget I'm over eighty and I bless Thanksgiving Day." Artist: Orson Lowell. Cover only. $10-15; November 1902. "Thanksgiving Number." Artist: Frank X. Leyendecker. Cover only. $20-25; November 1905. Artist: unknown. Cover only. $8-10.

Truth (1886-1914), New York City, New York. 10" x 13.75". November 24, 1894. "Thanksgiving Number." Artist: Johnson. Cover only. $20-30; November 30, 1895. "Thanksgiving 1895." Artist: H.Y. Mayer. Cover only. $20-30; November 1900. "The Thanksgiving Dinner." Artist: J. Wright. Cover only. $20-30.

American Boy (1899-1941), Detroit, Michigan. 11" x 14". L to R, Top: November 1915. "Thanksgiving 1915." Artist: W. W. Clarke. Cover only. $8-10; November 1931. Artist: Albin Henning. Cover only. $8-10; *The Youth's Companion* merged into *American Boy* in 1929. *Boy's Life* (The Boy Scouts' Magazine); (1911 to present), New York City, New York. 10.5" x 13". Bottom: November 1953. "Off to the Village Social." Artist: Harold Eldridge. $12-15; November 1955. "Gotham Avenue School's Annual Thanksgiving Play." Artist: Lowell Hess. $12-15.

Harper's Bazar (1867 to present), New York City, New York. 11.5" x 17". L to R, Top: November 1887. "Thanksgiving Number 1887 – Ye Hymn of Praise." Artist: A. E. Sterner. Front and rear cover only. $15-20; November 1892. "Thanksgiving 1892." Artist: Louis J. Rhead. Brittle front cover only. $5-10. Bottom: *Harper's Weekly*. November 26, 1887. "Thanksgiving 1887." Artist: Rosino Emmett Sherwood. Cover only. $20-25; November 21, 1908. Artist: R. S. $30-40.

Child Life, The Children's Own Magazine (1922 to present), Chicago, Illinois. 9" x 11.5". L to R: November 1922. First Thanksgiving cover. Artist: unknown. Cover only. $5-10; November 1929. Artist: Hazel Frazee. $10-15; November 1923. Artist: Hazel Frazee. Cover only $5-10; November 1939. Artist: Marie Lawson. $10-15. *Children's Play Mate Magazine* (1935 to present), Cleveland, Ohio. 6" x 9". November 1948. Artist: Fern Bisel Peat. $5-10. *Jack and Jill* (1938 to present), Philadelphia, Pennsylvania. 7" x 10". Top: November 1966. "Mary's Thanksgiving Parade in Color." Artist: Jack Weaver. $5-10; Bottom: November 1967. "Wait Till It Cools." Artist: Mildred Zibulka. $5-10; R: November 1961. "Things to Do For Thanksgiving." Artist: Helen Wright. $5-10.

Harper's Bazar. L to R: November 23, 1889. "Thanksgiving 1889." Artist: E. Grasset Gillot. Cover only. $20-25; November 25, 1893. "Thanksgiving Number." Artist: Wm. Martin Johnson. Cover only. $20-25; November 24, 1894. "Thanksgiving 1894." Artist: Louis J. Rhead. Cover only. $20-25. *Harper's Bazar* was a leading women's fashion magazine of that era and stills publishes today with a similar theme.

The Modern Priscilla (1887-1930), Boston, Massachusetts. L to R, Top: November 1908. Artist: O.T. Jackman. $15-20; November 1921. "Thanksgiving Number." Artist: unknown. $18-23; Bottom: November 1926. Artist: Bradshaw Crandel. $18-23; November 1929. Artist: unknown. $18-23. *Modern Priscilla* was a magazine devoted to art needlework, home crafts, and housekeeping.

The Ladies' World (1887-1918), New York City, New York. L to R: November 1901. "Thanksgiving Number." Artist: unknown. $12-15; November 1904. "Thanksgiving Number." Artist: Eliot Keen. Cover only. $8-10.

Woman's Home Companion (1887-1957), Springfield, Ohio. L to R: November 1928. Artist: Rene Clarke. $20-25; November 1936. Artist: Maginel Wright Barney. $20-25; November 1943. Artist: Gustaf Tenggren. $20-25. This magazine was formerly known as *Ladies' Home Companion* from 1886 to 1887.

The People's Home Journal (1885-1929), New York City, New York. 11" x 16". L to R: November 1903. Artist: unknown. Cover only. $15-20; November 1907. Artist: Wm. Lincoln Hudson. Cover only. $15-20.

The Delineator (1873-1937), New York City, New York. 11" x 14". November 1925. Artist: J. Scott Williams. $20-25. *The National News Monthly* (1899- ?), Winnipeg, Canada. 10.5" x 14". October 1933. Artist: Twelvetrees. $15-20. *The Home Circle* (1869 to present), Louisville, Kentucky. 10.5" x 14.5". November 1930. Artist: unknown. $8-10. *Lone Scout* (1915-1924), Chicago, Illinois. 10.5" x 14". November 20, 1920. "The Man in the Moon." Artist: Perry E. Thompson. $15-20. The official magazine of The Lone Scouts of America.

Good Housekeeping (1885 to present), New York City, New York. 8.5" x 11.5". L to R, Top: November 1919. Artist: Jessie Willcox Smith (1863-1935). Cover only. $30-40; November 1927. Artist: Jessie Willcox Smith. Cover only. $30-40. Bottom: November 1933. Artist: B.B.C.B. $20-25; November 1937. Artist: Gaffron. Cover only $15-20.

McCall's Magazine (1897-2001), New York City, New York. 8" x 11". L to R, Top: November 1913. Artist: Deremeaux. $30-40; November 1917. Artist: Julia Daniels. $30-40. *Sunset – The Pacific Monthly* (1898 to present), San Francisco, California. 8.25" x 11". Bottom: November 1926. Artist: Louis Roger. $50-60; November 1933. Artist: Heath Anderson. $30-35.

The Farmer's Wife Magazine (1897-1939), St. Paul, Minnesota. 11" x 14". L to R: November 1930. Artist: Conrad Dickel. $15-20; November 1933. "Thanksgiving." Artist: Revere F. Wistehuff. Cover only. $10-15; November 1936. Artist: C. Twelvetrees. Cover only. $12-15.

The National Farm Journal (1927-1939), Philadelphia, Pennsylvania. 8.5" x 11.75". November 1927. Artist: James Calvert Smith. Cover only. $12-15. *Better Homes and Gardens* (1923 to present), Des Moines, Iowa. 8.5" x 12". November 1924. Artist: N.H. Hinton. Cover only. $10-12. *The Popular Magazine* (1903-1931), New York City, New York. 7" x 10". November 20, 1915. Artist: Leslie Thrasher. Cover only. $12-15. *Good Housekeeping*. L to R: November 1906. "Thanksgiving Morning." Artist: Cushman Parker. $22-25; November 1904. "Thanksgiving Number." Artist: James Preston. $22-25.

Christian Herald (1878 to present), New York City, New York. 10.5" x 14". November 1902. "The Neighbors' Thanksgiving." Artist: W.E. Mears. Cover only. $5-7; November 22, 1911. "The First Thanksgiving Dinner." Artist: unknown. Cover only. $8-10; November 28, 1917. "...the Turkey is the only bird for me!" Photograph. Cover only. $8-10.

The Country Gentleman (1853-1955), Philadelphia, Pennsylvania. 11" x 14". L to R: November 25, 1916. Artist: Paul Branson. $20-25; November 19, 1921. Artist: Norman Rockwell. Cover only. $50-60; November 29, 1924. Artist: Wm Meade Prince. Cover only. $20-25.

The Inland Printer (1883-1958), Chicago, Illinois. 8.5" x 11.75". L to R: November 1899. "Thanksgiving 1899." Artist: R. J. Canfield. Cover only. $50-75; November 1900. Artist: Ralph Seymour. Cover only. $40-60. *The Inland Printer* was the "high tech" publication for the printing/publishing industry.

The Inland Printer. L to R: November 1903. Artist: W. J. Enright. Cover only. $40-60; November 1906. Artist: Warde Thayer. Cover only. $40-60.

Capper's Farmer (1919 to present), Topeka, Kansas. 10.25" x 13.5". L to R: November 1932. Artist: unknown. Cover only. $8-10; November 1935. Artist: C. Twelvetrees. Cover only. $8-10; November 1941. Artist: Dranee Thorne. Cover only. $5-7.

Gourmet Magazine (1950 to present), New York City, New York. 8" x 11". L to R: November 2000. "An American Gathering." Cover photography; November 1999. "A Thanksgiving Primer." Cover photography; November 2001. "Happy Thanksgiving." Cover photography. $5 each.

The American Weekly. 11" x 15". L to R, Top: November 18, 1945. Artist; J.C. Leyendecker. Trimmed. Cover only. $10-15; November 23, 1947. Artist: J. C. Leyendecker. Cover only. $10-15; Bottom: November 21, 1948. "Thanksgiving 1648." Artist: J.C. Leyendecker. Cover only. $10-15; November 20, 1949 "Thanksgiving." Artist: J.C. Leyendecker. Cover only. $10-15. *The American Weekly* was a Sunday magazine supplement to the Sunday newspaper of The Hearst Publishing Company, Inc.

Martha Stewart Living (1990 to present), New York City, New York. 9" x 11". L to R: November 1999. "Celebrating Thanksgiving." Cover photography; November 2000. "Thanksgiving." Cover photography; November 2001. "Thanksgiving." Cover photography. $5 each.

Bon Appétit (1955 to present), New York City, New York. 8" x 10.75". L to R: November 1999."Our Favorite Thanksgiving." Cover photography; November 2000. "Thanksgiving Across America." Cover photography; November 2001. "Thanksgiving – The Ultimate Course-by-Course Guide." Cover photography. $5 each.

Special Interest Food Magazines. L to R: *Bon Appétit*. "A Thanksgiving to Remember." November 2003. Cover photography; *Food & Wine*, "Thanksgiving Guide." November 2003. Cover photography; *Gourmet*. "Thanksgiving Menus." November 2003. Cover photography. $4 each.

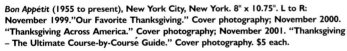

Sunset Magazine (1898 to present), San Francisco, California. 8" x 10.5". L to R: November 2001. "Your Easiest Thanksgiving." Cover photography; November 1999. "Thanksgiving Made Easy." Cover photography; November 2000. "A Western Harvest Thanksgiving." Cover photography. $5 each.

Special Interest Life Style Magazines. L to R: *Country Living*. "Thanksgiving." November 2003. Cover photography; *Martha Stewart Living*. "Giving Thanks." November 2003. Cover photography; *Sunset*. "Thanksgiving Feasts." November 2003. Cover photography. $4 each.

Printed Illustrations, Serigraphs, Posters, Pamphlets, and Other Miscellaneous Ephemera

As we have seen, magazine covers, then and now, emphasized pictorial content and graphic design as a form of "eye candy" to induce the consumer to buy a magazine with a limited shelf life among many competitors. Contemporaneous magazines were produced for a timely practical purpose and, as such, enjoyed an ephemeral existence. However, there were, and are, many items produced by illustrators, graphic artists, and others that have an indeterminate existence. There was the hope that these quasi-ephemeral pieces would have enough appeal to be enjoyed over a certain period of time by a diverse grouping of peoples. To this extent, these items would have some longevity due to either the graphic design or written, but not dated, content.

Of all American illustrators of the late nineteenth century and twentieth century, two names stand out above their equally talented contemporaries: J.C. Leyendecker and Norman Rockwell. **Joseph C. Leyendecker** (March 12, 1874-July 25, 1951) was born in Germany but emigrated to America with his family in 1882. Over the course of his adult life, he was a very prolific illustrator, having painted 322 covers for *The Saturday Evening Post*, 48 for *Collier's*, and over 130 covers for other magazines. He was considered by many to be the unheralded "King of American Illustration." This is because he was responsible for the look of the modern magazine cover, employing elements of his precise draughtmanship to convey a dynamic, elegant, and sophisticated painting style. In the medium of advertising art, he was dominant in rendering a sense of masculinity for a long, success-

ful series of clothing ads for Cluett, Peabody ("Arrow Collar Man") and B. Kuppenheimer. J.C. Leyendecker completed his first cover illustration for *The Saturday Evening Post* for the May 20, 1899 issue and his 322nd and last cover in January 1943. For many years, he painted almost all of the holiday covers for *The Saturday Evening Post*. As seen in the prior section, his Thanksgiving covers are quite memorable throughout issues of not only *The Post* but also *The American Weekly*. J.C.'s cover for *The Post* (November 24, 1928), depicting a vintage Pilgrim in contrast with a "modern" football player, was among his most famous and has been widely reproduced.

Norman Rockwell (February 3, 1894-November 8, 1978) was born in New York City but moved at age seven to upstate New York. In 1910, he sold his first series of painted illustrations. Rockwell's first cover for *The Saturday Evening Post* appeared on May 20, 1916. Interestingly, Rockwell painted 321 covers for *The Post*, just one less than his friend, J.C. Leyendecker. And like Leyendecker, Rockwell produced a similar prodigious output of illustrated covers for 80 magazines, including 47 for *The Literary Digest*, 34 for *The Country Gentleman*, 30 for *Boys' Life*, and 28 for *Life* magazine (old). His last cover, "Celebration," was done for *American Artist* in 1976. In contrast to Leyendecker's polished sophistication, Rockwell was more known for his sentimental rendering of pleasant and humorous subject matter which he termed "countrified realism." Because of that style, he was not that well regarded when ranked among other American illustrators but that mood has somewhat abated today.

The universal humanistic appeal of Norman Rockwell's work, which gathered strength in the 1930s and early 1940s, was the catalyst that inspired him to begin a series of four paintings in 1942. These large format paintings (44" x 48") depicted ordinary American citizens in scenes that portrayed the ideals for which the nation had gone to war. The so-called Four Freedoms paintings (Freedom of Worship, Speech, from Fear, and from Want), completed in 1943 in the depths of World War II, were taken by the U.S. Treasury Department on a 16-city tour to sell war bonds. Approximately $133 million of war bonds were sold to many of the 1,222,000 spectators who turned out for the presentations. Subsequently, *The Saturday Evening Post* reproduced the paintings as inside illustrations in a series of issues. "Freedom from Want," which was number three in the series, was reproduced in *The Post's* March 6, 1943 issue. Not only was the painting reproduced but an accompanying text by Carlos Bulosan was also attached. The painting, depicting a large happy family gathering at Thanksgiving, was the most reproduced painting in other formats, some humorous and others not. Many foreigners resented this painting as illustrative of the overabundance of food on American tables when most of Europe was starving due to the War. An-

other famous Thanksgiving cover illustration, "Saying Grace," was published in the November 24, 1951 issue of *The Saturday Evening Post*; this was considered Rockwell's most famous cover as tabulated in a large reader's poll. The scene portrays an elderly lady and her grandson praying over their meal in busy railroad café.

Both J.C. Leyendecker and Norman Rockwell, illustrators *par excellance*, attempted through their own respective techniques to bring to their audience stories based on a simple humorous or poignant scene; 643 *Post* covers together speak of their success!

Reproduction Print. "Freedom From Want." Original print appeared in *The Saturday Evening Post*, March 6, 1943. Artist: Norman Rockwell. $10-15.

Thanksgiving 1628 ~ 1928
1928

Reproduction Print. Original print appeared on the cover of *The Saturday Evening Post*, November 24, 1928. Artist: J.C. Leyendecker. $5-10.

Accompanying text by Carlos Bulosan, as it appeared in *The Saturday Evening Post*, March 6, 1943. Inclusive.

Reproduction Print. "Saying Grace." Original print appeared in *The Saturday Evening Post*, November 24, 1951. $5-10.

L to R: *The Saturday Evening Post*, November/December 1973. "Meet the Waltons." The cover, a parody of Rockwell's "Freedom From Want" painting, shows the famous 11-member Walton family at Thanksgiving Dinner. *The Waltons* was the first family dramatic television series, airing from 1972 to 1981. $10-15. *National Lampoon* (1970 to present), New York City, New York. "Happy Thanksgiving." *The National Lampoon* is an "in-your-face" humor magazine for adults and the Thanksgiving parody cover says it all. $10-12.

Greeting Card. "Peanuts and The Gang," at their Thanksgiving Table. "From Our House To Yours – Wishes For A Happy Thanksgiving." Charles Schultz. Hallmark Cards. 2002. $3.

Anna Mary Robertson Moses (1860-1961), popularly known as "Grandma Moses," painted her first series of folk art oils when she was seventy-six years old in 1936. After being "discovered" in 1938, she continued to paint landscape scenes, mainly of Vermont, in her own unique primitive "naïve" style. By mid-century, Grandma Moses was considered a truly American cultural icon, best known for her simple, honest, and direct approach to depicting rural countryside venues.

Will Moses is a fourth generation member of the renowned artistic Moses family. Inspired to paint by his grandfather, Forrest K. Moses, another well-known folk painter, Will's style is vividly reminiscent of his famous great-grandmother. Will lives and works out of his Mt. Nebo, New York gallery and home producing serigraphs, prints, etchings, posters, and illustrated children's books and puzzles. Will's graphics are done in specific, one-time limited edition series. His serigraphs are art prints which require a large number of hand-made screens, one for each color. Will's efforts have proven very worthwhile. His scenes are detailed, full of color, yet evocative of former times.

Magazine Ad. "The 90 Thanksgivings of Grandma Moses." General Mills, November 1950. 10" x 13.5". "It's true that the 90th Thanksgiving of Grandma Moses isn't the happiest that America has known..." The Korean War had begun four months prior. This ad shows a copy of the artist's famous painting, "Catching the Thanksgiving Turkey." $15-18.

Serigraph. "Thanksgiving in the Country." 18" x 12" image size. Limited Paper Edition: 117/130 + (35 Artist Proofs). 1999. Artist: Will Moses. Statement: "A simple country scene with the warmth of family and friends coming together to enjoy the great day, each other, and best of all, real farm raised turkeys." $350+.

Serigraph. "Thanksgiving Day." 24" x 18" image size. Limited Paper Edition: 78/350 + (35 Artist Proofs). 2002. Artist: Will Moses. Statement: "...created a painting that reflects the quiet beauty of the small community of Eagle Bridge, New York, where Grandma Moses was born and raised and began her career." $375+.

The following segment explores many other forms of printed materials and ephemera, ranging from prints and posters to simple items such as telegrams and greeting cards.

Puck. "How The Blackberries Missed Their Turkey." "The Turkey: 'So You Children Have Come To Do Me Up, Have You?'" Artist: unknown. c.1890s. $5-10.

Framed Print. "Plimoth Plantation." 20" x 18" image size. Depicts an autumn scene of the early Pilgrim settlement at Plimoth (early spelling). $15 unframed.

Original Poster. "Let's Always Be Thankful in America. Buy Defense Bonds and Stamps." 27" x 9". 1941. Photographed cameo insert of young girl looking at a roast turkey. $40-50.

Broadside. "The Family Dog Presents – Turkey Trot." Thursday, November 23, 1967 at the Avalon Ballroom, San Francisco, California. 5" x 7". Featured band: Big Brother & The Holding Company. The Family Dog was a group of psychedelic artists and rock concert promoters during the 1960s and 1970s. Artist: Rick Griffin (late); he was one of the Big Three artists in the world of Art Psychedelic (1966-1973), producing very colorful and fantastic-style concert posters. $10-15.

Collier's The National Weekly. November 17, 1906. "The Thanksgiving Pumpkin." 20" x 14.5", center section. Artist: Walter Appleton Clark. 1906. $25-30.

Stock Certificate. "Crayoila Oil & Gas Company," Turkey, Texas, 10.5" x 8.5". Good for two shares, dated May 12, 1922. $15-20. Turkey, Texas (population 553) lies 100 miles northeast of Lubbock and 100 miles southeast of Amarillo. It is the hometown of the famous 1930s and 1940s "King of Western Swing," Bob Wills and The Texas Playboys.

Scrap. Embossed, die-cut, heavy cardboard Tom Turkey. 4.5"x 4". Made in Germany. c.1890s. $20-25.

The Palimpsest. "Thanksgiving in Iowa." Special Thanksgiving Edition. Published by The State Historical Society of Iowa. December 1968. 5.5" x 8". This pamphlet reproduces in full color 54 Thanksgiving postcards. $10-15.

The Compleat Turkey. Recycled Paper Press, Chicago, Illinois. Author: Sandra Boynton. 1980. Softcover, 64 pages. An illustrated turkey joke book. "Who Are The Turkeys and What Do They Want?" $8-10.

Left:
101 Turkey Jokes and Riddles. Weekly Reader Books, Middletown, Connecticut. Author: Stephanie Calmenson. 1988. 5.25" x 8". A sample: "What does a turkey do when he's being chased by lions? The Turkey Trot!" or "What kind of a key won't open a door? A turkey!" $5-10.

The Compleat Turkey. An excerpt from page 29: "I Am An Individual!"

"Take a Chance" Gaming Cards, all similar in concept. "Select Your Favorite Girl's Name [by punching her name on the board] and receive a 10 lb. Turkey." 25¢ per chance. Various printers. $10-12 each.

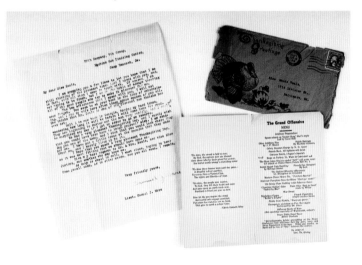

Addressed Envelope, Typewritten Letter, and Thanksgiving Day Menu. Addressed to a Miss Maude Neale, Baltimore, Maryland from a Lieutenant Samuel J. Ware of the 78th Company, 7th Group, Machine Gun Training Center. Camp Hancock, Georgia, dated December 1, 1918. This letter was a thank-you note and best wishes for "a very pleasant Thanksgiving Day." The menu was from his unit's dinner with different military expressions depicting the food served, i.e., "Siege on Turkey, Lt. Ware in Command." $25+

Large Format Advertising Placard. 27.5" x 32.5". Two sided. Soft drink product, 7-Up. $25-30.

was good clean fun. Since all advertising was contained within the pages of a magazine, when the publication was tossed, so were the ad pages. But, as mentioned earlier, magazines are now worth more than the sum of their parts and the collecting of advertisements, by product categories, is a popular hobby.

A fair amount of Thanksgiving advertisements have dealt with various forms of liquid refreshments to be enjoyed with the Thanksgiving meal. Also, certain advertisers utilized the turkey as a convenient prop for promotion of their consumer products. A sampling of such ads is shown below. Note that advertising trade cards are portrayed later in this chapter.

Point of Sale Advertising Cards. Various soft drink products: Coca Cola, 7-Up, and Squirt. $2-5 each.

Postal Telegrams. "Thanksgiving Greetings." Top to Bottom: Postal Telegraph...November 29, 1934. Message: "There will never be another Thanksgiving like this one. May your table be heavy and your hearts light." Western Union...November 1937. Message: "If Wishes Came True, This Thanksgiving would be your Happiest." Western Union envelope and greeting...November 28, 1935. Message: "I am thankful for a friend like you, one that I know to friendship true so here is Thanksgiving joy anew." $5-7 each.

Advertisements

Printed advertisements in magazines or newspapers contribute over 70% of most publications' revenues; special-interest magazines rely even more on advertising cash flow. Over the years, and certainly during times of economic adversity, many publications have seen their stream of advertising revenue virtually disappear – and have found that their circulation base was not substantial enough to cover the overhead necessary to keep in business. As popular as the general interest magazines once were (i.e., *Life*, *Look*, *Leslie's*, *Collier's*, and *The Post*), changing consumer tastes, the advent of television, and certain editorial problems all contributed to those magazines' demise as print advertising declined.

While today's magazine racks are still full of publications reaching out to virtually every taste, many consumers are getting most of their information from television and the Internet. Still, over twenty-five new non-trade magazines start up every year.

During the "Golden Age" of magazine publishing, from the start of the 1920s to the end of the 1960s, magazines were full of colorful advertisements that shaped and formed the way we perceived the acceptability of various products. Advertising premiums, especially for children's products, were a great way to foster loyalty as well – as collecting said items

Magazine Ads. L to R: "It's Maxwell House Coffee Time!" 10.5" x 13.5". c. 1945. "Chase and Sanborn's 'friendly flavor' keeps a Thanksgiving date in the land of the Pilgrims." 10.5" x 13.5". 1940. $5 each.

Magazine Ads. L to R: "Imperial (Blended Whiskey)...it's 'velveted!'"10.5" x 13.5". Message: "This is no time for gobblers. With every distillery in America making war alcohol instead of whiskey, present stocks must last for a longer time..." 1943; "Drink Schenley Royal Reserve (Blended Whiskey), Thanksgiving 1942." 11" x 14". Message: "Americans – this Thanksgiving – welcome the privilege of 'all out' effort." 1942. $5 each. Wartime rationing affected the whiskey industry, requiring the sales of one bottle of spirits per customer.

Magazine Ads. L to R, Top: "Budweiser (Beer)…America's Earliest Thanksgiving…Was For Corn." 10.25" x 14". 1947; Budweiser (Beer)…How The American Turkey Captured France." 10.25" x 14". 1948. Bottom: "Pabst Blue Ribbon…'It's blended…it's splendid!'" 10.5" x 14". 1947; Ballantine Beer…with the flavor that chill can't kill!" 10.5" x 14"; Rendering: "Preparing the Thanksgiving Feast." Artist: Lucile Coros. 1950. \$5 each.

Magazine Ads. L to R: "Call for Calvert – The Whiskey of Good Taste." 10.5" x 13.5" 1938; "Clear Heads Choose Calvert – The Whiskey with the 'Happy Blending!'" 10.5" x 14". 1941. \$5 each.

Magazine Ads. "Cream of Wheat." "Thanksgiving Breakfast would be Cheerless without Cream of Wheat." 11" x 16". 1919. \$10-12; "Give Thanks This Day Goode People for…Cream of Wheat…Thanksgiving." Artist: J.G. Scott. 10.25" x 13". 1923. \$18-20; "Cream of Wheat for Thanksgiving Day and every day." 6.5" x 9.5" 1908. \$10-12; "For Thanksgiving A Fat Young Gobbler, well stuffed!" Artist: James Leslie Wallace. 7.25" x 10.5". 1913. \$10-12.

Magazine Ads. L to R, Top: "Thanksgiving Dinner." Artist: Douglass Crockwell. Number 36 in the series "Home Life in America." 11.5" x 13.5". Message: "Beer belongs…enjoy it." United States Brewers Foundation. 1949; "Thanksgiving Dinner." Artist: Douglass Crockwell. Number 75. 10.5" x 13.5" Message: "In this friendly, freedom-loving land of ours…beer belongs…enjoy it." United States Brewers Foundation. 1952. Bottom: "Thanksgiving Day." Artist: Douglass Crockwell. Number 88. 10.25" x 13.5" 1953; "Thanksgiving Dinner.' Artist: John Gannam. Number 101. 10.5" x 13.5". 1954. \$5 each.

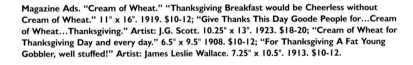

Magazine Ads. L to R: "Campbell's Soups…To Make this Taste the Best…Soup makes the whole meal taste better." 10" x 13". 1923; "McCormick and Schilling…for 'flavor magic' use America's finest spices!" 10.25" x 13.75". 1956. \$10-12 each.

Magazine Ads. L to R: "Turkey Red Cigarettes." Message: "Not until years later did the cigarette-makers dare take the next step – to show a real American girl smoking." 10.25" x 14". c. 1940s. $8-10; "Let's Celebrate. It's Chesterfield." Portraying Marjorie Woodworth – Chesterfield's "Girl of the Month." 10" x 14". 1941. $13-15.

Magazine Ads. L to R: "Texaco Fire Chief Gasoline." "Fast Getaway...you'll get it with 100% Climate-controlled Texaco..." 10.25" x 13.5". 1953; "Thanksgiving deserves full-color snapshots...from Kodak." 10" x 14". c. 1950s. $8-10 each.

Postcards

"At the present day, it is a matter of such frequency that one of the family's descendents is settled in Lowell, one in Illinois, one in New Orleans, one in Charleston, one in Texas, and one, perhaps, in California, we are not to expect that they will all again in company, return to the paternal mansion to participate with their numerous kindred in the festivities of a Thanksgiving dinner. In imagination we may revisit those scenes; but the realities belong mostly to a past generation."

—Reverend John L. Blake, in 1851, in his *Farmer's Every Day Book*

Although written fifty years before the turn of the twentieth century, these words often described a family living at far ends of the country due to the great expansion of the United States. At a time when most people did not have a telephone, when mail was often delivered two or even three times per day, and when it took only a penny or two to post mail, a new means of communication was born: the **postcard.** The picture postcard became the standard means of communication and the automatic choice for a quick hello, a birthday greeting, or a holiday message. Receiving a postcard from a friend or loved one made the day a special one. The phrase, "Drop me a line" was prevalent until telephone service replaced it with "Call me." The number of postcards sent and collected reached amazing proportions during this time. An advertisement in a 1905 *Comfort* magazine proclaimed: "The Postcard craze has spread all over the world, and nearly everyone in the country gets from one to a hundred through the mail each month."

Postcards were a long time in developing due to government postal regulation. The direct ancestor seems to be envelopes with pictures on them. Such envelopes were often printed with pictures of comics, Valentines, and music. Picture postcards in the United States began with the souvenir cards sold at the World's Columbian Exposition in Chicago in 1893. These, however, were not the earliest cards. The first postal card in the United States was copyrighted in 1861 and consisted of a blank front for messages with three lines on the back for the address. It was advertised as half the price of paper and envelopes and ready for instant dispatch. Advertising and souvenir postcards of a visit to a city or popular resort area appeared in 1893. For quick dating purposes, postcards with a divided back – that is, with a printed vertical line down the middle – were permitted in the United States from March 1, 1907 until 1915, as opposed to the undivided back found on cards from 1893-1907. Postcards from 1916-1930 incorporated a white border and appropriately are called "White Border Cards."

View cards quickly led to artist-signed cards, patriotic cards, and greeting cards. Early greeting cards are some of the most beautiful cards ever printed. Publishers competed for sales, printing cards using intricate embossing techniques, high caliber artwork, superior inks, and expensive lithographic processes; they even incorporated additions such as silk, feathers, ribbons, and glitter. Postcards were very popular for all holidays, including Thanksgiving. Various themes appeared over and over again in these Thanksgiving postcards. Obviously, the turkey was the favorite – from being served at family dinners to being chased by a farmer to cartoon quality scenes of turkeys trying to escape the axe for another year.

L to R: Santway series 134, embossed, comical portrayal of a turkey with a top hat and suitcase as he escapes from the farm; San Gabriel Publishing, copyright 1909, signed R. Veenfliet; A turkey is served for dinner; Series 875, embossed postcard with a patriotic influence as flags border the scene, "I'm an Old Bird But I Know You Love me Still!"; Series 499, embossed. As a farmer carries off two turkeys, another turkey makes a comment to his fellow turkey, "That's right, Keep it up, they'll have you next." $10-15 each.

Among the most valuable Thanksgiving postcards are those known as hold-to-light, die cut so that various colors show through when held up to the light. Publisher unknown. $75+.

130

Series T 28. Young child dressed as a clown waves a flag as she rides on a turkey-drawn pumpkin carriage. Publisher unknown, embossed, $10-15.

Some of the most collected Thanksgiving postcards are those with patriotic themes. Although this holiday has not really been considered a patriotic holiday, it should really be considered the first patriotic holiday of all time. Uncle Sam, the American Eagle, and Old Glory are favorite images along with the turkey in a variety of scenes.

Embossed Series 208 by unknown German publisher using a horseshoe trademark presents Miss Liberty draped in an American flag while a second card profiles a young boy waving a flag and riding a turkey. Another card centers on Uncle Sam driving a golden carriage full of food delights pulled by a turkey and in the last one, a young child waves a banner reading "Thanksgiving Greetings" with an ax close by. $20-25 each.

Turkey proudly struts atop a banner with patriotic influence. Publisher unknown, embossed, $7-10.

Four postcards from series 239, copyright 1908, embossed, P. Sanders. In a patriotic setting, each card pictures a Thanksgiving dinner at a flag-draped table. Uncle Sam is serving Miss Liberty; the Army and Navy are served by an Eagle; a typical family enjoys the meal; a pair of elegant young lovers toast each other. $15-20 each.

A firm using the A.S.B. (A.S. Burbank Co.) trademark published series 282 (set of six), which includes a beautiful full-length portrait of Uncle Sam in patriotic colors and a young boy holding onto the golden reins pulling a wagon adorned by the flag. $15-20 each.

L to R: Series published by A & S featuring strong patriotic themes. The embossed set is identified by a banner of "Thanksgiving Greetings" and features red, white, and blue ribbons as a border to Uncle Sam and turkeys; Series 4100 pictures Uncle Sam with two turkeys at his feet, publisher unknown; Uncle Sam glorified with stars carries a turkey, embossed, publisher unknown; Series 429 with Uncle Sam sitting on a pumpkin holding a turkey (notice the Thanksgiving Proclamation at his feet). Embossed, publisher unknown, $15-20 each.

Three postcards from A & S series, "Thanksgiving Greetings," highlighted by a border of gold stars. The series features Uncle Sam and numerous flags and turkeys. $15-20 each.

L to R: Embossed Santway series 100 with portrait of Uncle Sam; Series 350 pictures Uncle Sam letting the turkey out of captivity but tightly holding on with a red ribbon. Embossed, publisher unknown, $15-20 each.

Flags, shields, and banners appear in set 443 by P. Sander. Embossed, $10-15 each.

A.S.B. published set 290 (embossed set of six), a transportation series including beautiful designs of turkeys in a stagecoach, balloon basket, and car, all with appropriate red, white, and blue colors. $15-20.

As with every postcard collection, there are many wonderful postcards that remain unidentified as to publisher or artist but are special in their design. This embossed group, then, is a conglomerate of such cards. All are patriotic in nature and celebrate the American holiday in a special way. $10-15 each.

Many artists used children as the central figure in Thanksgiving cards…mischievous children, sweet demure children, playful children.

Signed HBG (H.B. Griggs) stylized postcard of a young boy dreaming, Series 2263, embossed. The influence of Halloween is pronounced in the scene. $25-30.

Series 252, embossed, Stecher Lith. Co. Young boy sweetly smiles as he looks forward to Thanksgiving. $5-10.

Roses, wheat, and fruit border this card of a young boy with a turkey held with reins and a "wheat" whip; Series 2096, embossed, published by Gottschalk, Dreyfuss & Davis (G.D.D.) $10-15.

Series 252, embossed, publisher unknown. One young child waves his flag as another "rides" a corn-on-the-cob. $10-15 each.

Best Wishes for a Happy Thanksgiving

Young children play a game dressed in their Pilgrim and Indian costumes. Embossed, publisher unknown, $10-15 each.

Series 850, unknown publisher, embossed card. A young child dressed as a cook is pushing a cart with two turkeys as a beautifully dress young girl watches. $10-15.

133

Series 730, unknown publisher, embossed card. Two young girls dressed in their finery frolic with two turkeys. $10-15.

Series 741, unknown publisher, embossed card. A young boy in a sailor suit proudly displays his turkey to two girls both dressed in their long dresses with bows and ruffles. $10-15.

In keeping with the story of the Pilgrims celebrating the first Thanksgiving, many postcards were centered on the landing of the Pilgrims, the relationship of the Pilgrims and Indians, and the celebrations and hardships of their daily lives.

Tuck Series 175, embossed. A Pilgrim returns after the turkey shoot; A Pilgrim serves dinner. Both cards are embellished with a fall-like border. $10-15 each.

L to R: Series B.W. 376, embossed. A border of grapes accents a Pilgrim couple as they sing; Series 256, embossed, publisher unknown. A Pilgrim couple stands with a picture of their homestead in the background; Series 131, embossed, artist A. von Beust features the Pilgrims landing with the boat in the background; Series 800 H.S.V. Litho. Co. (series of six embossed postcards can be recognized by a large horseshoe against a red/white/ and blue background.) $10-15 each.

L to R: A gold border encircles a Pilgrim holding onto a turkey with reins. Embossed, Santway 100 series; Two Pilgrims with a brightly colored patriotic background salute the turkey. Embossed, P. Sanders 325; Two pilgrims cooking outdoors as the turkey peers. Embossed, P. Sanders 502; An Indian and Pilgrim exchange turkey and food items. Embossed, Gold Metal Art 642, $10-15 each.

In addition, postcards featuring blacks are desirable from two standpoints. Images of playful black children or black cooks are some of the most collectible Thanksgiving cards.

Top: A servant brings the turkey out for Thanksgiving dinner, Ullman Manufacturing Co., series 127; Bottom: Published by a company using the horseshoe as a trademark, this exceptional postcard features a black chef enthusiastically holding up his turkey dinner ready to serve to the guests. $20-25 each.

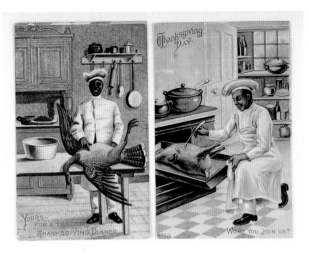

Two embossed postcards, part of series 875, feature black chefs. "Won't You Join Us?" Publisher unknown, $20-25 each.

One of the best Thanksgiving postcard series combines patriotic themes with both black and white children (series 4045). The six cards in this series feature a decorative border of gold stars. Embossed, publisher unknown, $20-25 each.

Two embossed postcards printed in Germany capture the playful antics of black children with a very large turkey. Embossed, publisher unknown, $20-25 each.

L to R: Copyright 1908, M.W. Taggart, N.Y., embossed series T F 607 portrays an old black servant examining the wing of the just-killed turkey. A border of feathers accents the scene; Santway series 226 depicts a black family joyfully greeting the father as he arrives home with a turkey. $20-25 each.

Top: Published by Ullman Manufacturing company, New York, part of series 1988, this card depicts a determined black child riding a turkey; Bottom: "A sudden rise in wool" describes the scene as a young black girl is frightened by the presence of a large turkey. Ullman Manufacturing Co, 1907. $20-25 each.

Messages written on the cards could be only a quick hello or filled with news from loved ones or friends, even gossip in some cases, but in most cases they contained well wishes for the Thanksgiving holiday. For example:

Mrs. E. Smith, Marysville, Ohio, November 26, 1912
"All are in good health and we all join in wishing you lots to be thankful for." M.E.T.

Master Will Webb, Pueblo, Colorado, November 9, 1909
"Dear Little Boy:
Laurent wanted to send a card to you. He said to tell you to eat turkey for him."
With love and kisses, Mrs. G. Harris

Master R. G. Briggs, Johnstown, New York
"Dear Little Sweetheart,
I received your card and how pleased to know that you always think of your auntie. I was homesick for two days. Just wanted to see you all again."
With love, Auntie

Mr. Herbert S. Lane, Dexter, Maine
"Herbert, there is going to be a shooting match at Athens, Nov. 24. Why don't you come over and we will go. The turkeys are awfully thick over here. You come over and we will shoot all we can. I have got a pump gun that will shoot over 25 rods. I will close hoping to see you soon."
Guz E. Downs.

135

A sample of the most common Tuck set (series 123) consisting of embossed Fall scenes and turkey designs, some signed R. J. Wealthy, totalling 24 cards. $7-10 each.

In organizing hundreds of Thanksgiving postcards, the authors have attempted to picture – in addition to themes of children, patriotism, the turkey, Pilgrims, and blacks – examples of postcard series by different artists or publishing houses. Most series were produced in sets of six; some, however, included eight to twelve cards. Some of the series are complete; some, of course, incomplete; and some cards not even identified as to publisher or set they belong to. Whatever the case may be, each postcard is a work of art and certainly should be appreciated.

During the Golden Age of Postcards, from 1907-1915, many publishers produced postcards. Among them were Tuck, Stecker, Winsch, International Art, Whitney, Fred Lounsbury (whose two sets were on sale in 1907 and 1908), Gottschaulk, PFB (Paul Finkenrath of Berlin, a much admired German publisher who exported three sets of six into this country), P. Sander, and E. Nash. Some postcards are signed by the artist; some can be identified by the style of the artist; and some are unknown as to publisher and artist.

The firm of **Raphael Tuck and Sons** had long been established by the time postcard fervor gripped England. Raphael and his sons were quick to grasp the possibilities of pictorial greetings and, in 1880, launched a national contest for talent and original design but also to attract public attention. In 1900, competition for the largest collection of their postally used cards was announced, awarding a prize to a collector with over 20,000 Tuck postcards. Tuck is widely known for its high standards and artistic merits and thereby is the "epitome" of postcard publishers. Tuck postcards are easily identified by a distinctive signature: Art Publishers to Their Majesties the King and Queen. German bombs destroyed the London factory on December 29, 1940. At least seventeen Thanksgiving sets were distributed through Tuck's office in New York. None of these show the red/white/and blue motif that other publishers used. Instead the emphasis was on the Pilgrim and the turkey.

The most common of these is series 123, consisting of twenty-four cards. The major ones in this set are signed by artist R.J. Wealthy and show scenes of turkeys strutting in the barnyard or on a platter ready to be served. Six show Fall scenes with turkeys and six more with a comic nature. The cards appeared in stores throughout the East, South, and Midwest for many years after their first printing in 1910. All have a gold border and are embossed. Series 161 contains twelve cards – six scenes of colonial times and six duplicates of Fall scenes from series 123. Series 162 is a delightful set of twelve embossed cards with gold borders showing comical pictures of turkeys, many dressed as people. Series 175 also contains twelve embossed cards – half dealing with Pilgrims and the other half with turkeys or Fall scenes. Series 186 is a reprint of series 123 with red and white borders, while series 196 deals with children in an outdoor setting. Lastly, series 185 features women and children. It is one of the more scarce series and one of the loveliest.

Tuck set 162, embossed, consists of twelve very colorful turkey designs with comic quotations. "Boys, I feel I'm going to a change of climate." "O. Joy! Buckets of Joy. I gave them the slip!" "These things [the pumpkins] always give mother the blues." $10-15 each.

The most beautiful of all Thanksgiving greetings are those published by **John Winsch**. Winsch postcards can be identified by the five small windows on the left side of the back of the card. Copyright years for Thanksgiving cards by John Winsch are 1910-1915, with the 1912 set featuring Thanksgiving days of the past being favored by most collectors. Although Winsch Publishing was located in Stapleton, New York, the firm used superior German lithography, as Tuck did, and had cards printed in Germany and then imported to the United States for distribution. Winsch postcards sold at two for five cents, when the common price was one cent each. While some Winsch postcards were issued in sets of six, most of the better designs were issued in sets of four. The most collected of the Winsch Thanksgiving postcards are by the American Art Nouveau artist, Samuel L. Schmucker. Schmucker (1879-1921) displayed great passion for art, even as his right arm (dominant) had been crippled from polio as a child. Schmucker's model was his beautiful wife, Katharine, whom he met while enrolled in classes at the Pennsylvania Academy of Fine Arts. Katharine's image was the inspiration for the "Winsch Girl" design that Schmucker is best known for, by the John Winsch Company. He is considered the preeminent artist in the Golden Age of Postcards, reaching its peak in 1911. Winsch continued in business until 1915, a time period in which over three thousand designs were copyrighted.

Winsch 1912 embossed set of six scenes from American history, designed by an unnamed German artist, depicts Thanksgiving Day at an Indian Peace Dinner 1620, seeing a Puritan Relief Ship 1620, First Thanksgiving in Alaska 1868, at Valley Forge 1778, Goldseekers California 1849, and in the South 1913. $25-30 each.

As was true with Tuck and Winsch, publishers as **P. Sander** and **E. Nash** produced greeting cards for all holidays. P. Sander produced seven sets of Thanksgiving cards: series 239 patriotic greetings; series 253; series 325 Puritan man and woman; series 331 cornucopia theme; series 443, and series 502. Nash was the most prolific of all American greeting publishers, being responsible for at least twenty-seven sets.

Winsch 1910 embossed set depicts portraits of Indian and Pilgrim women set against the golden sun, characteristic of work by artist Samuel Schmucker. $30-40 each.

Nash Series 1 portrays different views of children at Thanksgiving. For instance, in one card, a curly-haired child with eyes closed and hands folded prays at a Thanksgiving table protected by an eagle on one side and a turkey on the other; another shows a young boy with a headdress of turkey feathers; still another embossed card pictures three children peering over a fence at a turkey. $7-10 each.

Winsch 1911 embossed set consists of eight cards depicting the beauty of Pilgrim and Indian maidens. Along with the 1910 series, this set is one of the most collectible Thanksgiving series. $30-40 each.

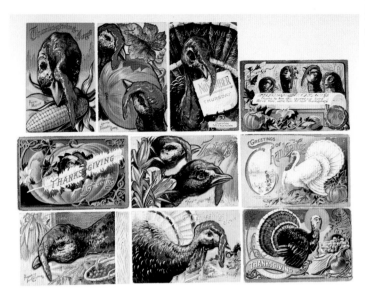

Nash Series 3 and 4 picture a variety of turkeys with comical overtones. One scene depicts s turkey digesting the November calendar, another has a large turkey "after the football game," and a third pronounces "They're coming after us." $7-10 each.

Nash Series 11 includes embossed designs of children with pumpkins, cakes, or pies, all bordered in silver or gold. $7-10 each.

Nash Series 10 features three different groups of children sitting at the Thanksgiving dinner table, to include Pilgrims and Eskimos. $7-10 each.

Right:
Nash Series 19 is a group of beautifully embossed designs of children, each holding up a dessert along with the real menu for Thanksgiving as "Entrée – Health a la Wealth, Prosperity, Garnished with Joys, True Love, Happiness, Long Life. $7-10 each.

Cards representing seven Thanksgiving series by Nash. L: Series 22 with a border of pumpkins encircling a turkey image; Top to Bottom: Series 5, a turkey highlighted by red foliage; Series 26, a head of a young girl transposed onto a turkey; Series 23, featuring Uncle Sam; R: Series 21 on a very bright red background, a young boy carrying a turkey on his shoulder; Series 7, a nature scene with fall leaves and grapes. $10-15 each.

The two most popular signed postcard artists are **Ellen Clapsaddle** and **Frances Brundage**. The children on Clapsaddle cards are described by many as "charming," "delightful," and "the picture of innocence." The faces of these children are repeated on the cards among numerous backgrounds, for which the artist drew upon folklore, traditions, children's games, and nursery rhymes. Ellen Clapsaddle, born the year the Civil War ended, was educated in New York, gave painting lessons as a young lady, and then contracted to work for the International Art Publishing Company of New York – for which she produced over three thousand designs. Wolf Publishing later purchased the International Art Publishing Company. Clapsaddle's cards for International Art were usually embossed; those from Wolf are not embossed and are usually more difficult to find. Of her designs, half are children, the others range from floral to still life in nature. Clapsaddle's children, exhibiting delightful and gentle dispositions, were reflections of the times and are quite popular with collectors. During the height of her career with International Art Publishing Company, she invested her earnings in the postcard industry, only to lose everything with the outbreak of World War I as Wolf closed for business.

International Art Publishing Company manufactured postcards at the facility in Germany as well at a location in Philadelphia. Chester Garre, a partner in International Art Publishing Company, noted, "I can remember watching long lines of girls seated at tables either hand painting or air brushing each card, passing the cards from one to another to place certain colors upon them."

Three postcards signed Ellen Clapsaddle, International Art Pub. Co. L to R: The first two cards, part of Series 1311, picture the sweet and angelic faces of two children with their fruits; A young Pilgrim carrying her basket all highlighted by glitter, Series 4440. $20-25 each.

Artist signed set by Clapsaddle, although an unnumbered set, with red and white backgrounds all center on delightful children with Thanksgiving turkeys. $10-15 each.

Clapsaddle set 51784 includes four portraits of children in white chefs' outfits against dark blue backgrounds, published by International Art Publishing Company. Embossed, $10-15 each.

Frances Brundage was a well-established illustrator of children's books by the turn of the century, illustrating books of Louisa May Alcott and the plays of Shakespeare. She was contracted by Tuck to design cards (1900-1910) and then in 1910 was hired to design for Sam Gabriel in New York City. All together, Brundage designed 24 to 35 sets, approximately one-tenth of the designs by Ellen Clapsaddle. The Sam Gabriel cards are more in the American tradition, with sets designed both for Halloween and Thanksgiving. Some of Brundage's cards, as opposed to the image of "sweet" children from Clapsaddle, depict impish young children and mischievous Puritan youngsters. In contrast, some of the Brundage children were often angelic and serene.

Clapsaddle embossed set 51784 published by International Art Publishing Company features children against a brown background. All children have that angelic innocent look, whether pictured with pumpkins, turkeys, or pumpkin pies. $10-15 each.

A set of eight embossed cards, highlighted by a red border, all capture the merriment and mischievousness of children. Thanksgiving Series 130, copyright 1910, San Gabriel publisher, embossed, artist signed Frances Brundage, $15-20 each.

Series 132 published by San Gabriel with a message of Thanksgiving Day Greetings consists of various pictures of children, some with a demure and sweet look, all cards with a light green border. Embossed, artist signed Frances Brundage. $15-20 each.

Series 2263 published by Leubrie and Elkus Company, embossed, artist HBG (H.B. Griggs). These five cards are part of an exceptional series of twelve, including a Pilgrim couple saluting "Here's to the Day when First the Yankees Acknowledged Pumpkin-Pie with Thankees"; A young girl surrounded by her dolls, both black and white, rolling pie crust, "May your Thanksgiving Pies always turn out well."; Two children being pulled through the air by a turkey, "May you always have a happy combination of Thanksgiving Blessings." $15-20 each.

One postcard artist about whom little is known is **H.B. Griggs**, who designed many signed postcards for Leubrie and Elkus Company, New York. Only two of the approximately three hundred cards designed are signed – one part of Thanksgiving series 2233. Most of her (his) postcards are signed simply "H.B.G." and are considered by many as caricature in nature with a touch of quirky comedy. The cards are very stylistic in nature. Seven sets dealt with Thanksgiving, including series 2212 (four cards), 2213 (four cards), 2233 (twelve cards), 2263 (twelve cards), and 2273 (twelve cards).

Three unusual categories of rare and valuable postcards are (1) mechanical, which often consist of rotating wheels or levers that pull down and thus move a part of the postcard; (2) cards embellished with feathers, ribbons, metallic turkeys, or embroidery designs; and (3) cards that are humorous or comical in nature. W.W. Denslow, an illustrator best known for his work with L. Frank Baum's *Wizard of Oz*, displays his talents as an artist in his Thanksgiving Humor Series 352. R.F. Outcalut, the originator of the Yellow Kid and Buster Brown, was a popular artist whose postcards appeared in Sunday supplements. These postcards could be cut out and saved.

Series 2233 published by Leubrie and Elkus Company, New York (L & E), embossed, artist HBG (H.B. Griggs). The cards portray an old man with a hatchet, "May the Turkey that was dreaming beneath the crescent moon be the treasure of your dinner Thanksgiving afternoon!"; Three young children ready to eat, "May Thanksgiving Day always realize your Fondest Expectations"; A woman chasing a turkey with a knife, "May you catch him in time for dinner." $15-20 each.

Three examples of mechanical postcards. L to R: Pinwheel mechanical card, one of six different designs. The feathers change as the rotating wheel is turned, giving a kaleidoscope effect. ASB trademark, $75; A "projection postcard" that is identical to a 1911 series of Winsch postcards. The maiden, printed on separate stock, projects forward from the underlying card, $100; "Happy Hooligans Tom Turkey" (eyes and mouth move up and down as a lever is pulled). This card was part of a supplement of the Sunday American Journal Examiner. A reader cut out and assembled the card. Very rare. $150.

Series 2233 published by Leubrie and Elkus Company, New York (L & E), embossed, artist H.B. Griggs. These two cards are part of a series of twelve cards that feature for the most part women, one peeling a fruit and one chasing a turkey with a stick. These two cards are the only cards known that have the full signature of H.B. Griggs. $15-20 each.

Four examples of postcards embellished with various materials. L: Real feathers, embossed, unknown publisher; Top to Bottom: Winsch 1912 series enhanced by ribbon and glitter; a barnyard scene with a silver metallic turkey, and a card adorned with silk as in the embossed Barton Spooner card. $15-20 each.

Three comical postcards. Top: two cards from **Thanksgiving Humor Series 352**, artist W.W. Denslow. A couple ready to use an ax on their turkey discovers, "He's too tough for Thanksgiving dinner." The second card depicts a woman crying "Ye Old Fashioned Hasty Pudding" as the Indian runs away with the Thanksgiving chocolate pudding. Bottom: As the gentleman carves the turkey, pieces fly through the air in the direction of the guest. "No More Thank You," copyright 1909 J. Ottmann Lith. Co. N.Y., artist R.F. Outcault. $50-75 each.

At the first sound of the guns in World War I, the era of postcards came to a conclusion; the years 1915 to 1930 saw an end to the postcard craze. Because imports from Germany had ceased, publishers in the United States began printing postcards to try to fill the void. The cards were poor in quality compared to the German-published cards from earlier years. The white border surrounding the pictured area easily distinguishes these later cards. Most are postmarked in the 1920s. With the end of the Golden Age of Postcards, a new way of communication began – the greeting card.

Fruit and Produce Crate Labels

Citrus and vegetable box labels occurred as an outgrowth of the need of growers to differentiate their product to far-flung customers. With the completion of the transcontinental railroad system in the 1880s, citrus growers, primarily, needed a way to identify and advertise a generic product to East Coast buyers dealing in commodity items. The answer was to develop a brightly colored, attractively designed paper label that was attached to the end of a wooden shipping box. Since the many small citrus growers could not effectively market their products beyond their own region, many contiguous growers banded together and affiliated themselves with one of the large co-operative marketing organizations. The growers' co-operatives were responsible for the design and artwork by hiring color lithographers to produce identifying labels for each of their members. From the late 1880s until the mid-1950s, crate labels evolved as an eyewitness to the various trends that transformed America throughout that 70-year reign of paper labels. In the 1950s, cardboard boxes were introduced as a cost saving measure. These cardboard shipping boxes were pre-printed, negating the need for attached labels. The labels, colorful time capsules of fruit and produce marketing, are highly collectible due to their colorful graphic designs.

As seen here, the turkey did not escape the lithographer's brush. Most labels of this sort had brand names identifying the product with notables of the Pilgrim society.

Orange Crate Labels. 11" x 10" L to R, Top: "First American." Randolph Marketing Co., California. c. 1916. $175+; "Gobbler Brand." Cobb & Dofflemyer, Exeter, California. c. 1930s, $100+. Western Lithography, Los Angeles, California was the printer of these two labels. Bottom: "Priscilla." United Citrus Growers, Colton, California. c. 1925. $200+; "John Alden Brand." The Highland Exchange Association, Highland, California. c. 1926. Schmidt Litho Co. of Los Angeles. $200+.

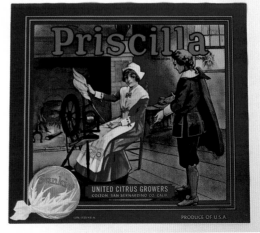

Two early greeting cards that eventually replaced the popular Thanksgiving postcards in the 1920s. $8-10.

Detail of the beautiful artwork and color lithography on the "Priscilla" label.

Produce Crate Label. "Turkey." E. Rosello, Packer. Valencia, Spain. c. 1950s. $45-50.

Miscellaneous Fruit and Vegetable Can Labels. 11" x 4.25". Top to Bottom: "John Alden Brand" Black Cherries, c. 1943; "John Alden Brand" Loganberries, c.1937; "Thanksgiving Brand" Lima Beans, c. 1928; "Thanksgiving Brand" Beets, c. 1927; "Thanksgiving Brand" Sauerkraut, c. 1924. $25-30 each.

Miscellaneous Fruit Can and Crate Labels. 13.5" x 4". L, Top to Bottom: "Colonial" White Cherries; "Pilgrim" Hawaiian Pineapple; "Mayflower" California Fruits; "Pilgrim Brand"; Center: "Governor Winthrop" Apples crate, Yakima, Washington; R, Top to Bottom: "Puritan Brand" Apricots; "Plymouth Maid" Peaches; "Puritan Brand" Whole Apricots in heavy syrup; "Puritan" California Fruits. c.1920s to 1930s. $25-30 each.

Sheet Music and Records

There is no…"I'm Dreaming of a White Christmas" style song for Thanksgiving, but there is an old country style song and even a dance step to commemorate the holiday. "Turkey In The Straw" was one of the oldest minstrel tunes that was finally published with words in 1834 and originally called "Old Zip Coon." This bluegrass style song of four verses was quite popular during Andrew Jackson's presidency from 1829 to1837. It is usually played in G major with a fiddle and banjo or mandolin. Many other verses could be added but the common first verse is as follows:

As I was a-goin'	Turkey in the straw
On down the road	Turkey in the straw
With a tired team	Roll'em up and twist'em up
And a heavy load	A high tuck a-haw
I cracked my whip	And hit'em up a tune called
And the leader sprung	Turkey in the Straw
I says day-day	
To the wagon tongue	

Some of the older sheet music had this melody played on the piano in "rag time" style. The song is a favorite among children and for scout sing-a-longs.

Cranberry Crate Labels. 10" x 7". L, Top to Bottom: "Myles Standish Brand", "Priscilla Brand"; R, Top to Bottom: "Pilgrim Brand," "Turkey Brand." The cited labels are "Cape Cod Cranberries," picked for the American Cranberry Exchange, New York and Chicago. c. 1940s to 1950s. $15-20 each; "Cape Cod Cranberries – Suitsus Brand." Colley Cranberry Co., Plymouth, Massachusetts. c. 1924. $25-30.

Sheet Music. L to R, Top: "The Story of the Country Dance or Turkey in the Straw." By Leasure Porter Lane. Cover and sheet music. Excerpt: "It was about the year 1895 that this title 'Old Zip Coon,' changed to 'Turkey In The Straw'… and they introduced it into the fashionable balls where it became the delight of fashionable dancers and also with dance orchestras and brass bands." c. 1910, $40-50. Bottom: "Turkey In the Straw," concert transcription for piano by David W. Guion. Publisher: G. Schirmer, Inc., New York. c. 1919. $25-30.

While "Turkey In The Straw" was meant to be played and sung, the "Turkey Trot" was a rather famous dance style. Evidence indicates that the "Turkey Trot" was first performed in San Francisco, California in the early 1900s. Since the dance involved a face-to-face movement, it was banned in some venues up to World War I. The name was given to the dance because as the dancers would sway to and fro, going in a straight line around the floor, they would "flap" or "pump" their arms, resembling the wings of a turkey.

Sheet Music. L, Top to Bottom: "Turkey In the Straw – A Rag-Time Fantasie." By Otto Bonnell. Publisher: Leo Feist, New York. c. 1904, $60+; "Turkey In the Straw – A Rag-Time Fantasy." Words by Leo Wood, Music by Otto Bonnell. Publisher: Leo Feist. c. 1920, $50-60. R, Top to Bottom: "Turkey In the Straw," guitar arrangement. Words by Jed Harkins. Publisher: Calumet Music Co., Chicago, Illinois. c. 1941. $30-40; "Turkey In the Straw." violin and piano arrangement. Characteristic dance novelty. Publisher: Century Music Publishing Co., New York. c. 1927. $40-50.

Postcards. L to R: "The Turkey Trot for us." Message: "You want to be very careful that you do not get that new society disease the Turkey Leg. It affects both men and ladies according to the doctor." Publisher: B. Comics. Photograph c. 1910s, $8-10; "Turkey Trot." Artist signed. Unused. German. c. 1910s, $8-10.

Vinyl Records with Slip Covers. L to R: "Turkey in de Straw." By Billy Golden with Orchestra. Negro specialty. Victor Record, Victor Talking Machine Co., Camden, New Jersey. 78 rpm. 10" record one-sided, original price 60¢. c. 1907. $20-25; "Turkey In the Straw." By Fiddlin' Doc Roberts Trio. Instrumental. Romeo Record. c. 1930s. $15-20.

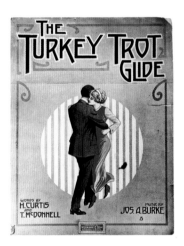

Sheet Music. "The Turkey Trot Glide." Words by H. Curtis and T. McDonnell. Music by Joseph A. Burke. Publisher: Weyman & Son, Philadelphia, Pennsylvania. c. 1910. $15-20.

So, Thanksgiving has had a small share of music devoted to the holiday, some fun and some solemn. During the "heyday" of radio broadcast, many of the popular radio shows produced Thanksgiving shows for their listeners who, perhaps, were not interested in transcriptions of football games.

Vinyl Record. "Turkey In the Straw." By The Merry Singers. Picture Cone Records, Inc., New York. 45 rpm. Yellow vinyl, 6.5" two-sided record. Folk Dances D451. c. 1950s. $10-15.

Postcard. Tuck Thanksgiving Day Post Cards Series No. 40. $15-18.

Record Publisher Booklet. "Thanksgiving in the Camps." Cressey & Allen, Portland, Maine. This booklet lists record selections by Victrola for Thanksgiving listening. c. 1918. $10-15.

It is appropriate, however, to include at least one favorite Thanksgiving hymn that captures the original true meaning of our holiday. In the early 1600s, Dutch settlers brought the "Prayer of Thanksgiving" to the "New World." Music based on a Netherlands folk hymn was later added and it became a favorite in the New England colonies. Today "We Gather Together" is a traditional Thanksgiving hymn sung or spoken by many.

We gather together to ask the Lord's blessing;
He chastens and hastens his will to make known;
The wicked oppressing now cease from distressing,
Sing praises to his name: He forgets not his own.

Beside us to guide us, our God with us joining,
Ordaining, maintaining his kingdom devine;
So from the beginning the fight we were winning;
Thou, Lord, wast at our side, All glory be thine!

We all do extol thee, thou leader triumphant,
And pray that thou still our defender wilt be.
Let thy congregation escape tribulation;
Thy name be ever praised! O Lord, make us free! Amen.

Comic Strip Characters

While the "comic strips" do not now hold the same attraction for youths as they once did, lovable characters such as the *Disney* menagerie, the *Peanuts* gang, and others still are fondly followed by adults and children alike. During the holidays, whether Thanksgiving or Christmas, the "strips" usually have their characters involved in the spirit of the occasion. From comic books, to greeting cards, to videos, our favorite "friends" do their part to put a smile on our faces at holiday time.

Vinyl Cassette Holder. "Radio Revisited Presents" original radio programs – "Thanksgiving." Six cassettes, each having two radio shows taped, dating from 1941 to 1950. $25-30.

Comic Book. *Looney Tunes & Merrie Melodies.* No. 38, December 1944. Published monthly by Dell Publishing Company, Inc., Cover Artist: Leon Schlesinger. $30-35.

Comic Books. L to R: *Walt Disney's Comics.* Vol. 12, No. 3, December 1951. Published monthly by Walt Disney Productions. $35-40; *Marge's Little Lulu.* Vol. 1, No. 29, November 1950. Published monthly by Dell Publishing Company, Inc., $25-30.

Comic Strip. "Blondie." Sunday, November 19, 2000. By Dean Young & Denis Le Brun. *San Francisco Examiner and Chronicle.* Strip conveys a message of sharing Thanksgiving dinner with others. $5.

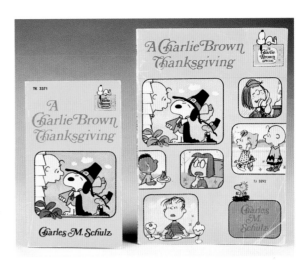

"Peanuts" Memorabilia. L to R, Top: *People Weekly*, February 28, 2000. "You were a good man, Charles Schulz!" Special commemorative tribute on his passing, 1922-2000. Charles Schulz wrote and created the "Peanuts" gang over a nearly fifty-year span until 2000. $20-25; *A Charlie Brown Thanksgiving*. Videocassette, color, 25 minutes. Kartes Video Communications. c. 1986, $20+; *A Charlie Brown Thanksgiving*. Videocassette, color, 24 minutes. Paramount (Viacom). c.1973, $25+. Bottom: Porcelain Table Figurines. Charlie Brown (Pilgrim) 4" H; Lucy (Pilgrim) 4" H; Snoopy (Indian) 3.5" H. All MIB. Peanuts collections. © Kurt S. Adler, Inc., New York. Made in China. c.2000, $10-15 each MIB.

Soft Cover Books. L to R: *A Charlie Brown Thanksgiving*. Charles M. Schulz. Scholastic Book Services, New York. 4" x 7". 90 full color pages. c. 1974, $5-10; *A Charlie Brown Thanksgiving*. Charles M. Schulz, Scholastic Book Services, New York. 6.5" x 9.25", 40 full color pages. 1st printing October 1975. $8-10.

"Peanuts Gallery Collection – Happy Harvest Time" 5.25" H. Figurine. Edition 1E, Piece #9635. Charlie Brown, Snoopy, and Woodstock are counting each other as their biggest blessing of all. Hallmark Keepsake Collections Limited Time Edition. 2002. $20 MIB.

Color Still. *A Charlie Brown Thanksgiving*. Saturday, November 22, 1975. A CBS Television Network Program. 9" x 7". $12-15.

Greeting Card. "Peanuts Collection," Hallmark Cards, Inc., Kansas City, Missouri. All the "Peanuts" characters in a reenactment of the First Thanksgiving Banquet. "Just think of all the great things to be thankful for today, that didn't even exist in 1621...You, for instance!" 16.5" x 8". c. 2000. $3-5.

Laser Disc. *Peanuts Classic – A Charlie Brown Thanksgiving*. Multicolor graphics dust jacket. Color, animated, 24 minutes (1973). Paramount (Viacom). Distributed by Pioneer. Added bonus: "You're Not Elected, Charlie Brown." Color, animated, 25 minutes (1972). 1995, $20-25 MIJ.

Greeting Card. "Peanuts Collection," Hallmark Cards, Inc., Kansas City, Missouri. Snoopy and Woodstock with inflatable balloons. "It's a great day for a HUG...Thanksgiving's not all parades and pumpkin pie, you know!" 16.5" x 8". c. 2003. $3-4.

145

Soft Cover Book. *Garfield's Thanksgiving.* Jim Davis. Ballantine Books, New York. 8.25" x 5.25". 62 full color pages. First edition: November 1988. $8-10.

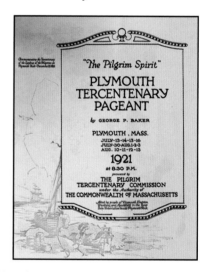

Garfield Memorabilia. L to R: Garfield Figurine. Garfield is dressed as a turkey…"Who Planned This Turkey Party?" 3.5"H x 3.25"D base. Enesco Gift Gallery, Elk Grove Village, Illinois. Made in China. © 1978, $15-18 MIB; Videocassette. *Garfield's Thanksgiving.* Color, animated, 30 minutes. CBS Video/Fox Video. 1992, $25+.

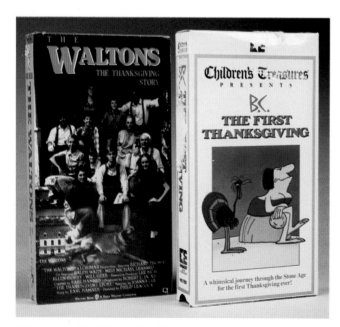

Videocassettes. The Waltons – The Thanksgiving Story. Color, 100 minutes. Warner Home Video. 1991, $25+; B.C. – The First Thanksgiving. By Johnny Hart. Color, animated, 25 minutes. A whimsical journey through the Stone Age for the first Thanksgiving ever. Embassy Home Entertainment. 1984, $20+.

Stamps, Cancellations, and Postal History

The United States Post Office has issued at least five **stamps** celebrating the Pilgrims landing at Plymouth, the Wild Turkey, and Thanksgiving. In addition, since July 1847, when the United States began issuing prepaid postage adhesive stamps, there have been over one million post offices throughout the country in operation at one time or another. Several of these post offices represented cities, towns, and villages with **cancellations** bearing names with foods associated with Thanksgiving. Many of these envelopes also have attractively **embossed or printed cachets** representing various Thanksgiving themes. In the 1930s, America's naval forces had pre-printed Thanksgiving cachets on greeting envelopes for the use of military personnel who were generally stationed at sea and far from home. Speaking of cachets, when a new stamp is issued by the United States Post Office, typically there is a "First Day of Issue Ceremonies," usually held at a post office which bears some relationship to the occasion. There are either firms who employ artists or independent artists who specialize in **hand painting limited edition cachets** on envelopes. The cacheted envelopes with the new stamps attached are then cancelled at the respective post office with the date of issue. These artistically rendered envelopes, called **First Day Covers** (FDC), are very collectible as each envelope is a miniature work of art. Both the United States and other countries have issued stamps honoring James J. Audubon and his works of realistic avian art.

Victorian era **trade cards** and pre-printed salesmen's **calling cards** were used to advertise American goods and services during the late 1890s. Many salesmen of that time would send a card in advance of their trip to buyers, to announce their imminent arrival. With the invention of the telephone in 1876, the use of such cards was made obsolete over the ensuing decade. However, pre-printed turkey images were used to amplify product and service offerings for many years into the early twentieth century.

The Pilgrim Spirit. Plymouth Tercentenary Pageant, Plymouth, Massachusetts. Pamphlet. July/August 1921. In December 1920, The United States Postal Service issued the Pilgrim Tercentenary Issue, a 3-piece set of postage stamps celebrating the 300th Anniversary of the landing of the Pilgrims at Plymouth, Massachusetts in December 1620. $40-50.

Pilgrim Tercentenary Issue 3-piece postage stamp set. L to R: 1¢ *The Mayflower,* from a watercolor by Harrison Eastman, Smithsonian Institution, Washington, D.C. Scott Catalog No. 548. Green. Stamps issued: 137,978,207. FDC 12/21/1920; 2¢ *Landing of the Pilgrims,* from an 1846 engraving by Burt based on a sketch by White. Scott Catalog No. 549. Carmine rose. Stamps issued: 196,037,327. FDC 12/20/1920; 5¢ *Signing of the Compact,* from a painting by Edwin White. Scott Catalog No. 550. Deep blue. Stamps issued: 11,321,607. FDC 12/21/1920. Mint, never hinged set, $75+.

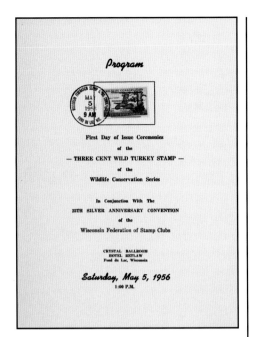

Program – First Day of Issue Ceremonies of the Three Cent Wild Turkey Stamp of The Wildlife Conservation Series. FDC May 5, 1956 at Fond du Lac, Wisconsin. The Wildlife Conservation Series of postage stamps highlighted the importance of protecting wildlife. Other stamps in the series were the Pronghorn Antelope issue in June 1956 and the King Salmon issue in November 1956. $25-30.

First Day Covers – Printed Cachets. Scott Catalog No. 1077, 3¢ Wild Turkey Stamp. Cachet Makers: L to R, Top: House of Farnam, $8-10; Sanders, $13-15; C. George, $20-25. Center: C. George Junior III, $20-25; Texture-craft (cachet design is flocked-raised with a velvet-like texture), $18-20; Velvatone (cachet design is flocked), $18-20. Bottom: Von Ohlen, $20-25; Mile High, $13-15; Unknown, ("Conservation Pledge"), $18-20.

First Day Covers – Mixed Cachets. Scott Catalog No. 1077, 3¢ Wild Turkey Stamp. Cachet Makers: L to R, Top: H. Riemann, $20-25; Boy Scout Troop 41 (Minneapolis, Minnesota), $20-25; Wild Turkey Maximum Photo Card (rose), William Saloman, $18-20. Bottom: Wild Turkey Maximum Card (image based on original Audubon watercolor), printed by Arthur Jaffe Heliochrome Co., New York City, $18-20; A.O. King (embossed), $18-20; Hand painted by Norbert Waldau, $15-18.

Sheet of fifty stamps, mint, never hinged. 3¢ *Wildlife Conservation – Wild Turkey* issue. May 5, 1956. Scott Catalog No. 1077. Brown purple. Stamps issued: 123,159,400. $20+.

First Day Covers – Hand Painted Cachets. Scott Catalog No. 1077, 3¢ Wild Turkey Stamp. Cachet Artists: L to R, Top: Fluegel, $18-20; Knoble (hand drawn and painted), color variety No. 2, $45-50; Knoble, color variety No. 1, $20-25. Center: Powell (block of four), $20-25; Wright, $40-50; Lucinda Strauss, $18-20. Bottom: A.O. Henry, $40-50; A.O. King, "Bugs Bunny" and "Elmer Fudd," $40-50; FDC with scanned "Far Side" contemporary comic by Gary Larson attached to envelope, 1/1, A.O. King, $5-8.

First Day Covers – Printed Cachets. Scott Catalog No. 1017, 3¢ Wild Turkey Stamp. Cachet Makers: L to R, Top: Art Craft (authorized by Wisconsin Federation of Stamp Clubs) $3-5; Art Master $3-5; The Aristocrats – Artist: Dan Lowry – Block of Four, $13-15. Center: C. Stephen Anderson (blue, black and maroon cachets were printed), $20-25; Unknown, $3-5; Unknown (shows a Wild Hen Turkey with Young), $18-20. Bottom: Sanders, $20-25; Cachet Craft – Artist: Ken Boll, $13-15; Kolor Kover, $20-25.

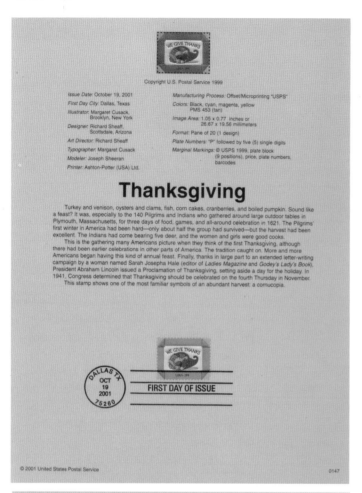

Copyright U.S. Postal Service 1999

Issue Date: October 19, 2001
First Day City: Dallas, Texas
Illustrator: Margaret Cusack, Brooklyn, New York
Designer: Richard Sheaff, Scottsdale, Arizona
Art Director: Richard Sheaff
Typographer: Margaret Cusack
Modeler: Joseph Sheeran
Printer: Ashton-Potter (USA) Ltd.

Manufacturing Process: Offset/Microprinting "USPS"
Colors: Black, cyan, magenta, yellow
    PMS 453 (tan)
Image Area: 1.05 x 0.77 Inches or
    26.67 x 19.56 millimeters
Format: Pane of 20 (1 design)
Plate Numbers: "P" followed by five (5) single digits
Marginal Markings: © USPS 1999, plate block
    (9 positions), price, plate numbers,
    barcodes

Thanksgiving

Turkey and venison, oysters and clams, fish, corn cakes, cranberries, and boiled pumpkin. Sound like a feast? It was, especially to the 140 Pilgrims and Indians who gathered around large outdoor tables in Plymouth, Massachusetts, for three days of food, games, and all-around celebration in 1621. The Pilgrims' first winter in America had been hard—only about half the group had survived—but the harvest had been excellent. The Indians had come bearing five deer, and the women and girls were good cooks.
    This is the gathering many Americans picture when they think of the first Thanksgiving, although there had been earlier celebrations in other parts of America. The tradition caught on. More and more Americans began having this kind of annual feast. Finally, thanks in large part to an extended letter-writing campaign by a woman named Sarah Josepha Hale (editor of *Ladies Magazine* and *Godey's Lady's Book*), President Abraham Lincoln issued a Proclamation of Thanksgiving, setting aside a day for the holiday. In 1941, Congress determined that Thanksgiving should be celebrated on the fourth Thursday in November.
    This stamp shows one of the most familiar symbols of an abundant harvest: a cornucopia.

0147

Left two:
Program First Day of Issue Ceremonies of the *Thirty Four Cent Thanksgiving* Stamp. FDC October 19, 2001 at Dallas, Texas. The self-adhesive stamp shows one of the most familiar symbols of an abundant harvest...a cornucopia of fruits and vegetables. The symbol lies on a surface of partially quilted needlework. "We Give Thanks" appears above the cornucopia and "USA34" appears below it. A small "2001" year date appears in the quilt fold at the stamp's bottom left. The "We Give Thanks" issue was part of the United States Postal Service's *Holiday Celebration Series*. $20-25.

First Day Covers. Scott Catalog No. 3546; 34¢ We Give Thanks Stamp. Top to Bottom: Cachet maker: Hobby Link #6/25, showing a cameo image of Norman Rockwell's "Freedom From Want." Yellow. 6.5" x 3.5" envelope, $15-20; Author's FDCs, plate blocks of four, cancelled October 19, 2001 at Dallas, Texas. $2.50 each.

First Day Cover. Scott Catalog No. 3546; 34¢ We Give Thanks Stamp. Cancelled October 19, 2001 at Dallas, Texas. Cachet Maker: Colorano "Silk." 6.5" x 3.5" envelope. $3-5.

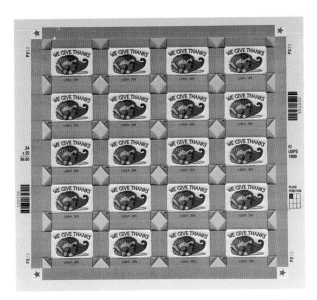

Military Pre-printed Illustrated Cachet. USS Arizona BB-39 Battleship. Thanksgiving Day brown cachet, cancelled November 28, 1935. "In The Great Northwest Bremerton Navy Yard. This famous battleship was sunk at Pearl Harbor, Hawaii during the Japanese sneak attack on December 7, 1941. $200 +.

34¢ We Give Thanks Mint Plate Pane of twenty stamps – upper left plate position. $15+.

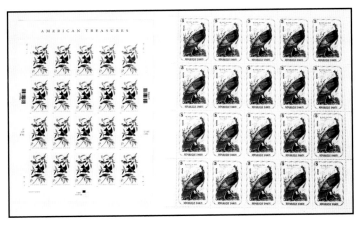

Mint Plate Panes of twenty stamps. L to R: 37¢ John J. Audubon self-adhesive stamps, Scott Catalog No. 3650. This first class-rate stamp pictures Audubon's "Louisiana Tanager, Scarlet Tanager," plate No. 354, from his *Birds of America*. This is the second stamp issue in the United States Postal Service's American Treasures Series. The John J. Audubon stamp was issued June 27, 2002 at Santa Clara, California. Five previous United States stamps feature either Audubon or his artwork. $7.50; Five Goures Meleagris Galloparo (Wild Turkey) stamps issued by the Republic of Haiti. This stamp pictures Audubon's plate No. 1 from his *Birds of America*. $3-5.

Postal Size Card. Franked with a 22¢ Uncle Sam red, white, and blue stamp, Scott Catalog No. 3259 on November 23, 2000. Upper left-hand corner is printed with a multi-color autumnal farm scene. The card is postmarked with a pictorial cancel that features a Pilgrim and Indian woman standing before a banquet table. Cancel is from the We Give Thanks Station at Pilgrim, Kentucky 41250. The foreground is a printed cartoon featuring the year 2000 Presidential candidates, Al Gore and George W. Bush, each holding an axe ready to chop the neck of a turkey with the word "Election" on its back. $8-10.

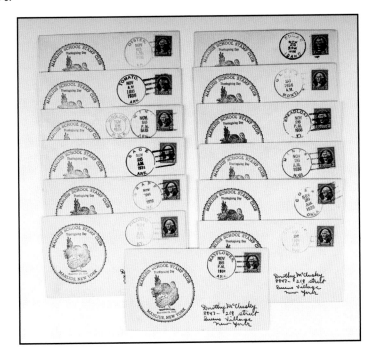

Cacheted Covers, with town names related to Thanksgiving and associated foods. All the covers are printed with the Manlius School Stamp Club, Manlius, New York purple cachet and are cancelled November 26, 1936 (Thanksgiving Day). Each cover is franked with a 3¢ deep violet Washington stamp. Scott No. 720. The following thirteen town names make up the cancels on these covers. L, Top to Bottom: Oyster, Virginia; Tomato, Arkansas; Wing, Arkansas; Sage, Arkansas; Grape, Kentucky; Pilgrim, Kentucky. R, Top to Bottom: Sugar, Idaho; Olive, Montana; Breadloaf, Vermont; Mints, North Carolina; Corn, Oklahoma; Cranberry, Pennsylvania; and Mayflower, Arkansas. Rare set, as many of the post offices do not exist now. $40-50.

Military Pre-printed Cachets with Unit Designations on Covers. L to R, Top: USS Pennsylvania BB-38 Battleship. Thanksgiving Day maroon cachet, cancel November 24, 1932. Survived bombing at Pearl Harbor, Hawaii, received eight battle stars for WWII, ended as target ship for atomic bomb tests at Bikini Atoll, Marshall Islands in July 1946; USS Lexington CV-2 Aircraft Carrier. Thanksgiving Day purple cachet, cancel November 30, 1933. Lost in action at Battle of Coral Sea on 8 May, 1942; USS Relief AM-1 Hospital Ship. Thanksgiving Day, orange cachet, cancel November 29, 1934. Received five battle stars for WWII. Middle: USS Texas BB-35 Battleship. Thanksgiving Day green cachet, cancel November 29, 1934. Received five battle stars for WWII. Now a permanent memorial at Galveston, Texas; Moffett Field, California, home of the USS Macon 2RS-5 Dirigible. Thanksgiving Day green cachet, cancel November 29, 1934; USS Nautilus SS-168 Cruiser Submarine. Thanksgiving Day purple cachet, cancel November 29, 1934. Bottom: U.S. Recovery Ship. Thanksgiving Day brown cachet, cancel Brooklyn, New York November 29, 1934; USS Preston DD-379 Destroyer. Thanksgiving Day olive green cachet, cancel November 26, 1936. Lost in action at the Battle of Guadalcanal 14 November 1942, 116 crew loss out of 251 total; USS Portland CA-33 Cruiser. Thanksgiving Day brown cachet, cancel November 26, 1936. Received sixteen battle stars for WWII. $10-15 each. For major line of battleships add $10.

Civilian Pre-printed Color Cachets. L to R, Top: November 6, 1931 at Turkey, Texas; November 24, 1932 at Boston, Massachusetts (cachet commemorates 301st anniversary of the first Thanksgiving directed by the Massachusetts Bay Government, 1631); November 30, 1933 at Turkey City, Pennsylvania. Middle: November 30, 1933 at Buffalo, New York; November 30, 1933 at Plymouth, Massachusetts; November 26, 1936 at Turkey City, Pennsylvania; Bottom: November 26, 1936 at Cranberry, Pennsylvania; November 26, 1936 at Turkey, North Carolina; November 26, 1936 at Turkey, North Carolina. $8-10 each.

Military Pre-printed Cachets with Unit Designations on covers. L to R, Top: USS New Orleans CA-32 Heavy Cruiser. Thanksgiving Day green and brown cachet, cancel November 26, 1936. Saw major Pacific WWII action; USS Cassin (Young) DD-753 Destroyer. Thanksgiving Day brown cachet, cancel November 25, 1937. Severely damaged at Pearl Harbor, Hawaii; USS Herbert DD-160 Destroyer converted to a High-speed Transport in 1943. Thanksgiving Day brown cachet, cancel November 25, 1937. Middle: USS Turkey AM-13 Minesweeper converted to an Ocean Tug. Red and blue cachet, cancel October 1, 1938; USS Nevada BB-36 Battleship. Thanksgiving Day brown with brown and gold foil sticker cachet, cancel November 23, 1939. At Pearl Harbor, Hawaii, the USS Nevada was the only ship to get underway after the attack, thirty years service; USS Flusser DD-368 Destroyer. Thanksgiving Day brown cachet with mounted 1.5"L photo, cancel November 4, 1939 at Honolulu, Hawaii. Received eight battle stars, fought in every major battle in the Pacific War; Bottom: USS Alabama BB-60 Battleship. Thanksgiving Day black cachet, cancel November 22, 1945. Now a permanent memorial at Mobile, Alabama; USS Tripoli CVE-64 Escort Carrier carrying 28 planes. Thanksgiving Day brownish-orange cachet with mounted 1.5"L photo, cancel February 3, 1948. Reactivated for the Korean War theatre; USS Hector AR7 Navy Repair Ship. Thanksgiving Day brown cachet, cancel November 25, 1948. Spent 43 productive years on active duty serving in the WWII, Korean, and Vietnam conflicts. One of the very first ships to have an on-board female naval officer beginning in 1980. $10-15 each. For major line of battle ships add $10.

Hand-Painted and Unique Cachets/Cancels. L to R, Top: Hand-painted Gladys Adler cachet, cancel November 30, 1934 at Turkey, Texas, $30-35; Hand-painted Glen Osborn cachet, cancel November 30, 1936 at Pensacola, Florida, $40-45; Printed red cachet by Lewis A. Barnard, cancel November 23, 1939 at Fernwood, New York. $25-30. Middle: Printed brown cachet by George Austed, cancel USS Lexington November 30, 1939. Cachet deals with controversy over President Roosevelt's decision to change the "official" celebration of Thanksgiving back one week to November 23 in order to add an extra week of shopping for Christmas. $20-25; Printed black and orange cachet by G. H. Hamilton, cancel November 22, 1941 at Cranberry Isles, Maine. Cachet approved by the Original Order of the Zunks (The Collector's Society), $8-10; Printed red and blue cachet by G. H. Hamilton, cancel November 27, 1942 at Turkey, Arkansas. Cachet sponsored by the Zunks, $8-10. Bottom: Printed black and orange cachet, "Thanksgiving," cancel November 23, 1944 at Plymouth, Massachusetts. Franked with (3) Scott Catalog No. 548, 1¢ Tercentenary Issue, "The Mayflower," stamps which were issued in 1920. $15-18; Printed black cachet, cancel June 13, 1957 at Plymouth, Massachusetts. The boxed cancellation states... "Arrival of Mayflower II, Plymouth, Massachusetts." The cancellation represents the arrival from England of a full-scale reproduction of the original Mayflower. The Mayflower II is now berthed at Plymouth Harbor and is open for tours, $8-10.

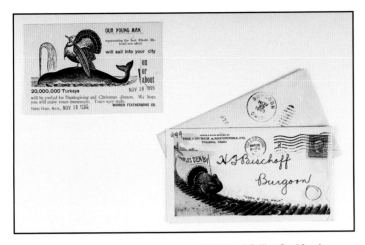

Advertising Card and Cover. Top: Manufacturer's Printed Calling Card for the Warren Featherbone Co. sent to a retailer in Milwaukee, Wisconsin. United States Postal Card 1¢, cancel November 13, 1895 at Three Oaks, Michigan. $15-18. Bottom: Printed Multicolor Advertising Cover for The Church & McConnell Co., Wholesale Grocers, Toledo, Ohio, sent to H.F. Bishchoff, Burgoon, Ohio, cancel March 25, 1908 at Toledo, Ohio. American Lithographer printed the very attractive envelope. Charles Denby was a cigar manufacturer and H.F. Bischoff was a client buying at least 500 cigars each time. On the back of each cover was an accounting as to when and what amount was paid. $25-30 each.

Advertising Trade/Postcard. Calendar card, November 1910. Buster Brown (with axe) and his dog, Tige, advancing towards a gobbler. Artist: R. F. Outcault. First National Bank, Connellsville, Pennsylvania. November 5, 1910, $100+.

Pre-stamped Envelope. Thanksgiving Church Services color photograph cachet. First Day of Issue, 17 November 1981, pre-franked 24¢ Norfolk Island. Norfolk Island is a thirteen-square mile island in the South Pacific Ocean, midway between New Caledonia and New Zealand. It is administratively attached to Australia. On the last Wednesday in November, Thanksgiving Day is celebrated as a public religious holiday on Norfolk Island. This is one of the very few places outside of the United States where Thanksgiving is celebrated by non-U.S. citizens. The Thanksgiving celebration was introduced during the nineteenth century by visiting American whaler men from New Bedford and Nantucket. $8-10.

Advertising Silk. "Wild Turkey." Zira Cigarettes. Factory No. 7 5th District, New Jersey. 1.25" x 2.75". c. 1920s, $40+.

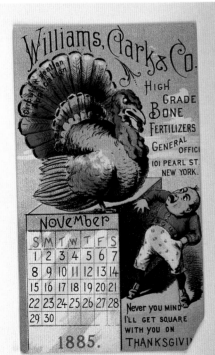

Left:
Advertising postcard. Williams, Clark & Co., advertising high grade Bone Fertilizers with the November 1885 calendar portrayed. "Never you mind. I'll get square with you on Thanksgiving." Very old and rare. $75.

Right:
Framed Walt Disney print of the Thanksgiving meal, with Scott Catalog No. 1355. 6¢ 1996 multicolor Walt Disney stamp, both double-matted. The print features many of the Disney characters as a take-off on Norman Rockwell's "Freedom From Want" painting. 10" x 13", dark cherry stained oak frame. $30-40.

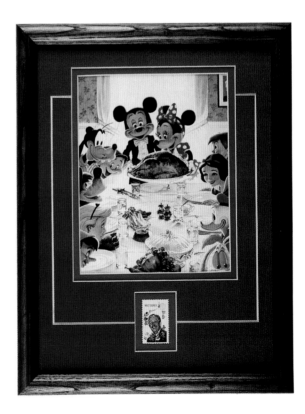

Chapter 9
WHISKEY AND BEER COLLECTIBLES

In a previous chapter on Glass Turkeys, we documented at least ten domestic and foreign manufacturers of figural turkeys in all shapes and sizes. However, when it comes to the manufacturing of ceramic figural turkeys, the famous bourbon whiskey producer, Austin, Nichols Distilling Company, is by far the most important. Due to the dominance of this firm in the production of ceramic figural turkeys over many years, this chapter will be heavily devoted to their wide-ranging output.

Austin, Nichols & Company was founded in New York City in 1855 as a wholesale grocer specializing in distribution of imported teas, coffees, and spirits. Thereafter, for many years, whiskey spirits were purchased from many distilleries for distribution primarily in the Northeast section of the country. In 1933, after the Repeal of Prohibition through the 21st Amendment to the United States Constitution, the company energetically re-entered the spirits market by packaging purchased American bourbon whiskies under the Austin Nichols nameplate. The firm's most recognized brand was and is today ... *Wild Turkey*. This marketing trademark was initiated in the early 1940s as a result of a successful turkey shoot by a then corporate officer and his friends.

In 1971, Austin Nichols, after many years of purchasing bourbon whiskies from other private distilleries, finally purchased a prominent distillery owned by the well regarded Ripy family. The multi-generational Ripy family came from Ireland in the 1860s and settled in the Lawrenceburg, Kentucky area. They started to buy and trade shares in the local distilleries until the family purchased one of their own. Members of the Ripy family were employed in local distilleries as Master Distillers and managers until the late 1970s.

The state of Kentucky is home to twelve operating distilleries that produce from 90% to 95% of the world's supply of bourbon. Federal regulations dictate that no whiskey can call itself "straight bourbon" unless three requirements are met: (1) it must be manufactured in the United States; (2) the grain formula must contain at least 51% corn; and (3) the distillate must be stored at not more than 125 proof (62.5% alcohol) in new, charred, white oak barrels for a minimum of two years. In the case of *Wild Turkey*, the Austin Nichols firm crafts its bourbons out of 75% sweet corn (grown locally), 13% rye (North Dakota), and 12% barley malt (Montana). No other substance may be added to bourbon except distilled filtered water to adjust the proof. Austin, Nichols Wild Turkey (Boulevard) Distillery, located on Wild Turkey Hill in Lawrenceburg (Anderson County), Kentucky, employs about 140 people in their distilling, aging, storage, bottling, shipping, and maintenance divisions. They have a combined warehouse bourbon reserve of some 440,000 barrels (one standard barrel = 31.5

gallons or 119.2 liters) and sell approximately 10% to 12% of their holdings annually.

Five types of bourbon whiskey, ranging from 80 to 101 proof and aged from four to twelve years, are marketed under the *Wild Turkey* trademark today. According to Jimmy Russell, Wild Turkey Master Distiller and long-term employee since 1954, the firm's flagship whiskey is *Wild Turkey*, 101 Proof, Kentucky Straight Bourbon. A limited bottling of Straight 101 Proof Rye Whiskey is also produced. For two interesting articles on the *Wild Turkey* production process as well as the background of Jimmy Russell, Master Distiller, I refer readers to the April/May 2000 and December 2001 issues of *Whisky Magazine* (British spelling). *Whisky Magazine* is devoted to articles on whiskey spirits production and tastings from all over the world.

Whisky Magazine, Norwich, Norfolk, England and Landisburg, Pennsylvania. L to R: Issue #9 (April/May 2000); Issue #19 (October/November 2001) Cover photograph of Jimmy Russell, Master Distiller for *Wild Turkey* Bourbon. $6-8 each.

Arguably, the *Wild Turkey* name is the most well known among competing premium straight bourbon whiskey producers, not only for its quality and taste characteristics, but also for the extensive amount of advertising and promotional muscle backing the trademark. Over the years, Austin Nichols has extensively advertised the *Wild Turkey* brand, especially in high quality print media by the use of full color insertions. These entertaining advertisements have typically appeared during the holiday period and as well as around Father's Day. Not only did these ads promote *Wild Turkey* 8 year 101 Proof Bourbon, they also did "double-duty" by illustrating special and limited edition decanters and associated premiums.

Wild Turkey magazine advertisements. L to R: *Holiday Magazine*, December 1963. "The Responsibility of Being the Best" $5–$7; *Playboy Magazine*, June 1984. "Wild Gifts For Dad," Father's Day. Introduced for sale the "Flying Wild Turkey" ceramic pourer. $6-8.

Below:
Wild Turkey magazine advertisement. *Look Magazine*, December 1979. "Wild Gifts for Christmas," two-page ad highlighting two bourbon proofs, Liqueur, Baccarat crystal decanter and the Series II No. 1 Wild Turkey Lore decanter. $8-10.

One not so obvious fact to collectors of *Wild Turkey* memorabilia concerns the ownership of the distillery and other associated facilities. In 1980, Austin, Nichols & Company was purchased by **Group Pernod Ricard** of France. Then, in December 2001, the Austin Nichols name was dropped in favor of **Pernod Ricard USA**, along with a change in corporate headquarters to White Plains, New York. Pernod Ricard USA now produces both Wild Turkey Bourbon and Seagram's Extra Dry Gin, as well as importing other premium brands, among them Chivas Regal Scotch Whisky, Jameson and Bushmills Irish Whiskeys, and Martell Cognac. The parent company, headquartered in Paris, France, is currently the world's third largest spirits and wine company. For items of interest and facts concerning all aspects of the history and production of *Wild Turkey* brands, a company website is available at www.pernod-ricardusa.com.

Since 1955, Austin Nichols has had produced for them by a variety of manufacturers a prolific amount of wild turkey figural decanters, both glass and ceramic, as well as literally hundreds of "go-with" items. A "go-with" collectible is an advertising specialty item which instills recognition that complements the marketing of a brand. Certain whiskey and beer producers form collector clubs for the sole purpose of insuring brand loyalty and camaraderie by selling special-edition "go-withs" that run the gamut from ashtrays to Zippo-type lighters. On an Internet based auction site such as eBay, the generic **Wild Turkey** category will have approximately 375 items listed at any one time, of which about 75% are attributable to the *Wild Turkey* brand itself.

Wild Turkey Figural Decanters

Austin Nichols, beginning in 1971 and ending in 1989, issued twenty-six Turkey-shaped ceramic whiskey decanters, along with twenty-two matching miniatures. This was accomplished through the production of *four distinct series* of differing themes and formats. The following is a concise listing of *every* decanter and its introduction date by series. Note: All names and descriptions are the official Austin Nichols nomenclature.

Series I (Original Wild Turkey Ceramic Series)

Volume capacity 750 ml. (four-fifths); 101 Proof; miniatures 50 ml; Size: ranging from 9.25" to 13.5" high; miniatures ranging from 4.25" to 5.75" high; glazed finish. All came with gift boxes.

No. 1	The Standing Turkey	1971
No. 1a	The Standing Turkey miniature	1981
No. 2	Turkey on a Log	1972
No. 2a	Turkey on a Log miniature	1981
No. 3	The Flying Turkey	1973
No. 3a	The Flying Turkey miniature	1982
No. 4	Turkey and Poult	1974
No. 4a	Turkey and Poult miniature	1982

No. 5	Spirit of '76 Bicentennial	1975
No. 5a	Spirit of '76 Bicentennial miniature	1983
No. 6	The Striding Turkey	1976
No. 6a	The Striding Turkey miniature	1983
No. 7	Turkey Taking Off	1977
No. 7a	Turkey Taking Off miniature	1983
No. 8	The Strutting Turkey	1978
No. 8a	The Strutting Turkey miniature	1983

The last four miniatures were sold as a set in one gift package. Miniatures are somewhat more rare than their larger counterparts, due to the fact that the 50 ml. bottles could only be legally sold in twenty-seven states and Washington D.C. Full content bottles do not add significantly to the value and the alcohol could cause damage due to leakage or corrosion. Originally, the 750 ml. bottle sold for between $20 and $25. Each of these bottles came with a "hang tag" which was a small information piece concerning the name of the respective decanter. Most of these have not survived over the years and thus are rare. Also, a broken or missing tax stamp does not lessen a decanter's value, but the absence of all other labels will. A gift box in good or better condition will add approximately 25% to the decanter value. Valuations of Series I 750 ml. decanters in excellent condition with boxes range from $30 to $175 individually. Miniature singles range from $15 to $100. A complete set of miniatures has sold from $150 to $300.

Wild Turkey Figural Decanters – Series I. L to R: No. 3 The Flying Turkey, 1973. 11"H $60-75 MIB; No. 4 Turkey and Poult, 1974. 12"H $45-60 MIB.

Wild Turkey Figural Decanters – Series I. L to R: No. 5 Spirit of '76 Bicentennial, 1975. 12"H. $30-45 MIB; No. 6 The Striding Turkey, 1976. 11.5"H. $25-40 MIB.

Wild Turkey Figural Decanters – Series I Original. L to R: No. 1 The Standing Turkey, 1971. 13.5"H. $160-185 MIB; No. 2 Turkey on a Log, 1972. 13.25"H. $100-125 MIB.

Wild Turkey Figural Decanters – Series I. L to R: No. 7 Turkey Taking Off, 1977. 9.25"H. $25-40 MIB; No. 8 The Strutting Turkey, 1978. 10.63"H. $45-60 MIB.

Wild Turkey Figural Decanters – Series I Miniatures. L to R: No. 3a, 1982. 5"H. $15-20 MIB; No. 1a, 1981. 5.5"H. $30-35 MIB; No. 2a, 1981. 5.75"H. $20-25 MIB; No. 4a, 1982. 5.63"H. $15-20 MIB.

Wild Turkey Figural Decanters – Series I Miniatures. L to R: No. 5a, 1983. 5.63"H; No. 6a, 1983. 5.63"H; No. 7a, 1983. 4.25"H; No. 8a, 1983. 5"H. Gift Set $115-130 MIB.

Series II (Wild Turkey Lore Series)

Volume capacity 750 ml.; 101 Proof; no miniatures; Size: ranging from 9.5" to 11.5" high; Bisque (matte) porcelain finish.

No. 1	First of the Lore	1979
No. 2	Wild Turkey of the Winter Forest	1980
No. 3	Keenness of Sight	1981
No. 4	Ready To Fight	1982

The design for each bottle took approximately two years, employing the talents and skills of wild turkey naturalists, wildlife artists, and sculptors. Part of each decanter portrays an open "picture book," highlighting a small facet of Wild Turkey "Lore," according to the theme of each bottle design. While beautiful in construction, this series, for some reason, is not as popular as Series I or III. Valuations of Series II 750 ml. decanters in excellent condition with boxes range from $30 to $80, the higher prices being for No. 3 and No. 4.

Wild Turkey Figural Decanter – Series II Lore. No. 3 Keenness of Sight, 1981. 10.75"H. $50-55 MIB.

Wild Turkey Figural Decanter – Series II Lore. No. 4 Ready to Fight, 1982. 11.25"H. $70-80 MIB.

Wild Turkey Figural Decanter – Series II Lore. No. 1 First of the Lore, 1979. 11.5"H. $30-40 MIB.

Wild Turkey Figural Decanter – Series II Lore. No. 2 Wild Turkey of the Winter Forest, 1980. 9.5"H. $35-45 MIB.

Series III (Wild Turkey Action Series)

Volume capacity 750 ml.; 101 Proof; miniatures 50 ml.; Size: ranging from 6.63" to 13.5" high; miniatures ranging from 3.5" to 6" high. Bisque (matte) porcelain finish.

No. 1	Wild Turkey in Flight	1983
No. 1a	Wild Turkey in Flight miniature	October 1984
No. 2	Wild Turkey and Bobcat	1983
No. 2a	Wild Turkey and Bobcat miniature	October 1985
No. 3	Two Fighting Wild Turkeys	1983
No. 3a	Two Fighting Wild Turkeys miniature	November 1986
No. 4	Wild Turkey and Eagle	1984
No. 4a	Wild Turkey and Eagle miniature	1984
No. 5	Wild Turkey and Raccoon	1984
No. 5a	Wild Turkey and Raccoon miniature	1984
No. 6	Wild Turkey with Poults	1984
No. 6a	Wild Turkey with Poults miniature	1984
No. 7	Wild Turkey and Red Fox	1985
No. 7a	Wild Turkey and Red Fox miniature	1985
No. 8	Wild Turkey and Owl	1985
No. 8a	Wild Turkey and Owl miniature	1985
No. 9	Wild Turkey and Bear Cubs	1985
No. 9a	Wild Turkey and Bear Cubs miniature	1985
No. 10	Wild Turkey and Coyote	1986
No. 10a	Wild Turkey and Coyote miniature	1986
No. 11	Wild Turkey and Falcon	1986
No. 11a	Wild Turkey and Falcon miniature	1986
No. 12	Wild Turkey and Skunks	1986
No. 12a	Wild Turkey and Skunks miniature	1986

With this series, unlike with the first two, Austin Nichols issued not one but three bisque porcelain decanters a year, beginning in 1983 and ending in 1986. The miniatures of the first three decanters in the series were issued one, two, and three years after the original 1983 introduction of the 750 ml. bottles. According to prices paid on Internet auction sites such as eBay, Series III has been the most popular, due to, in most cases, matching a wild turkey with one of its many natural predators in a woodland setting. Many, if not all, of these Series III decanters were made in Taiwan. Original prices for the 750 ml. bottles were from $33 to $40. Valuations of Series III 750 ml. decanters in excellent condition with boxes range from $75 to $175. Miniatures range from $25 to $75 each. Several complete sets of miniatures with boxes have sold in the $800 range while eliciting many bids. In September 2002, a complete set of Series III decanters with boxes (twenty-four in all) was offered for sale on eBay but failed to meet the reserve of $1200.

Wild Turkey Figural Decanter Series III Action. No. 2 Wild Turkey and Bobcat, 1983. 9"H. $125-150 MIB.

Wild Turkey Figural Decanter Series III Action. No. 4 Wild Turkey and Eagle, 1984. 9"H. $100-125 MIB.

Wild Turkey Figural Decanter Series III Action. No. 9 Wild Turkey and Bear Cubs, 1985. 12"H. $80-100 MIB.

Series IV (Habitat Series)

Volume capacity 750 ml.; miniature 50 ml.; Size: approximately 12" high; Bisque (matte) porcelain finish.

No. 1	Habitat I A	1988
No. 1a	Habitat I A miniature	1988
No. 2	Habitat I B	1989
No. 2a	Habitat I B miniature	1989

Since any distillery is legally prohibited from selling *full* decanters directly to the public, the Habitat Series was sold *empty* and, therefore, was available only from Austin Nichols. These special editions were priced at $80 for the 750 ml. size and $35 for the 50 ml. size. The Habitat forest scenes were in development for three years and took eighteen separate models to achieve two matching decanters. According to a news release by Austin Nichols, "each Habitat decanter is finely detailed, superbly colored bisque porcelain sculpture by itself. When placed together, they make a panoramic, living scene. At left, a female wild turkey stops to drink at a pool that is fed by a cascading waterfall. At right, an alert male wild turkey pauses in mid-stride and glances over the activity at the pool…" These decanters are rarely seen at Internet auction sites but would command in the range of $150 to $200 each with the original box. As a complete set, valuations should be in the $275 to $350 range. Since Austin Nichols was winding down its boxed decanter offerings by 1989, the Habitat IB is probably more rare than Habitat IA as fewer were issued. Miniatures have ranged from $100 to $150 each, whereas a full set would command prices in the $175 to $250 range.

Austin Nichols also randomly issued special "commemorative" decanters over the years to mark certain special occasions or anniversaries. These decanters (both glass and ceramic) are all highly collectible, as opposed to limited edition glass decanters whose purpose was to highlight and promote small batches of specially distilled and aged bourbon spirits.

The Special Decanters, their issue dates, and other relevant information, are as follows:

No. 1 **Wild Turkey Crystal Anniversary Decanter** 1955. Size: 9" high, 4.75" wide, 2.5" deep. Image: Clear glass bottle with two hand-painted Tom Turkeys in a forest scene. The decanter came with a box, glass stopper, and a purple neck ribbon with a circular gold foil label. The occasion for the issuance of this bottle was the 100th anniversary of the founding of Austin, Nichols & Company in 1855. This very rare special edition decanter has sold in the $1,500 to $2,500 range.

No. 2 **Liggett & Myers** 1972. Size: 13" high. Image: Standing Tom Turkey, glazed 750 ml. ceramic decanter. The base has a flag-type crest under which are two golf clubs. This decanter was based on the Series I, No. 1 The Standing Turkey mold with appropriate changes. The bottle was made for the Liggett & Myers Tobacco Company, who was the golf tournament sponsor for the United States Professional Golf Association's Open Match Play Championship held at the Pinehurst Country Club (Village of Pinehurst) in North Carolina. The tournament was held from August 21-27, 1972. The winner was Jack Nicklaus, who also won the U.S. Open Championship that year. This rare decanter has sold in the $125 to $175 range.

No. 3 **Charleston Centennial** 1974. Size: 10.25" high, ovoid shape. Image: Obverse – standing Tom Turkey in relief on a glazed 4/5 quart ceramic bottle; Reverse – four colonial attired men throwing bales of tea overboard to the water. This bottle was made for the Charleston (South Carolina) Tea Party Festival, held from November 2-9, 1974. A decal indicated that this bottle was also to commemorate the 200-year history of Charleston from 1776 to 1976, as part of the Bicentennial celebration. The decanter is valued in the $60 to $75 range.

No. 4 **Mack Truck** 1975. Size: 10.5" high. Image: Gold painted Bulldog stopper; white glazed round body with decals of three early Mack trucks; wording, "Built Like a Mack Truck…" This ceramic bottle was issued in 1975 to commemorate the 75th Anniversary of the opening of John Mack's truck manufacturing plant in 1900. During World War I, the famous A.C. Mack truck was introduced, earning an unparalleled reputation for reliability and durability. The AC truck is credited with giving Mack its famous Bulldog identity, and this characterization grew to encompass all Mack products as its corporate symbol by 1932. This is not a particularly popular decanter as there is no obvious identification with Wild Turkey except its contents. The bottle is valued at $10 to $25.

No. 5 **Baccarat Crystal Decanter** 1979. Size: Decanter is 10.5" high with glass stopper inserted and the base measures 7.25" across. The accompanying wooden "Captain's Chest" measures 11" high, 14.5" long, and 10.5" wide, with sisal rope handles on each end for carrying. The *Compagnie des Cristalleries de Baccarat* of France (founded 1764) made these decanters for Austin Nichols. Image: The full lead crystal decanter with a *fleur de lis* type motif and a raised relief "wild turkey in flight" was specially designed as a replica of the Classic Early American Commodore's decanter that was used on the large full masted ocean-going ships of the early 1800s. In addition to the heavy wooden chest that protects the decanter and its contents, along with an orange velvet cover, there is a "certificate of authenticity" card with a registration number indicating the fill date of the decanter. These Baccarat decanter units were sold into the mid-1980s with a retail price of about $250. Valuations for a complete sealed decanter chest unit range from $300 to $500 while the unsealed unit or those missing documentation would sell at a 25% to 50% discount. The crystal decanter should continue to increase in value over the years due to the prestigious nature of its maker.

No. 6 **Wedgwood Crystal Decanter** 1984. Size: 13.5" high. Volume capacity: one liter of Wild Turkey 101 Proof. Image: The front of the full lead crystal decanter has an etched wreath with an etched "wild turkey in flight" inside the wreath. The sealed unit is corked but has a corkscrew and a silver-plated ring stopper. The calabash shaped bottle is encased in a brown velvet hinged box with documentation, and the box is protected by an attractive colorful cardboard sleeve with the wording, "The Wild Turkey Wedgwood Crystal Decanter." *Wedgwood* (founded 1769) in Staffordshire, England, made these decanters for Austin Nichols. When introduced during the 1984 Holiday season, the full decanter set retailed for $200. Valuations for a complete sealed decanter/box unit range from $200 to $250, while unsealed units or those missing documentation or the cardboard sleeve would sell at a 20% to 30% discount.

In honor of America's Bicentennial in 1976, Austin Nichols issued a Limited Special Edition Print rather than a ceramic item.

Framed Print. "Wild Turkey Bourbon Bicentennial Commemorative Print." 22" x 17". Artist: Allen Saalburg 1976. Limited Edition 149/400. $100+.

Whiskey Pitchers (Pub Jugs)

In the nineteenth century, brown spirits distilleries in the British Isles began issuing "whiskey pitchers" to leading pubs or drinking houses. These whiskey pitchers were, in reality, water pitchers for use by the pub's patrons to mix water with their whiskey. In actuality, such pitchers are more correctly termed "*pub jugs*." These pub jugs were given by distillers to pub owners for display items as a promotional tool. From the common early earthenware jugs of a utilitarian nature, prominent distilleries competed with one another to make their jugs the most attractive to paying patrons. By the late 1960s to early 1970s, the collecting of whiskey (pub jug) pitchers in many countries, especially the United States, was becoming very popular. American distilleries were also caught up in this craze and began to issue attractively made jugs only for promotional distribution purposes.

From the early 1970s to the early 1980s, Austin Nichols had both domestic and foreign producers create a series of five whiskey water pitchers for them. Except in one instance, these pitchers were not dated. However, in four out of five cases the pitchers were marked as to manufacturer or locale. No boxes are known to accompany these pitchers. The following is a listing of the Wild Turkey jugs:

No. 1 **Pitcher with Ear Handle and Scoop Lip**. Size: 6.5" high. White glazed body with top rim edged in gold. On one side only, top to bottom, decals of a "Tom Turkey in Flight" and the words "Wild Turkey." On the base bottom is a black stamp with the wording, "101 Proof/8 year old Austin, Nichols Distilling Co. Lawrenceburg, Ky © 1978." Impressed McCoy USA 365. This is the rarest of the Wild Turkey jugs. Valuations are in the $70 to $90 range in excellent condition.

No. 2 **Pitcher with Angle Handle and Ice Lip**. Size: 5.5" high to the spout and 4" across the base. White glazed body with top rim edged in gold and gold line down the handle top. On both sides, top to bottom, decals of a "Standing Tom Turkey" and the words "Wild Turkey," "Bourbon," "101 Proof 8 Years Old." On the base bottom is a black stamp with the wording "Fine Staffordshire Pottery Made in England 101 Proof Bourbon 8 Years Old Austin, Nichols Distilling Co. Lawrenceburg, Kentucky." There also exists a variant of this pitcher without the wording "Bourbon, 101 Proof 8 Years Old." Also, the gold trim is missing on the variant. Valuations are in the $25 to $50 range depending on the amount of ceramic crazing.

Whiskey Pitchers (Pub Jugs). L to R: No. 2 Pitchers with Angle Handle and Ice Lip (two variants), 5.5"H. White glaze, decals $40-50 (no crazing).

No. 3 **Pitcher with Angle Handle and Ice Lip**. Size: 5" high. White squat body with top rim edged in gold. On both sides, top to bottom, decals of "Standing Tom Turkey" and the words "Wild Turkey," "Kentucky Bourbon," "101 Proof 8 Years Old." On the base bottom is a black stamp with the wording "101 Proof/8 Years Old Austin, Nichols Distilling Co. Lawrenceburg, Kentucky ™ *Ceramarte* (in script) Made in Brasil (Brazil)." This pug jug is not often seen. Valuations are in the $25 to $50 range, according to condition.

No. 4 **Pitcher with Ear Handle and Spout Lip**. Size: 6.75" high, 3.25" diameter opening. Brown matte glazed body. On both sides of the pitcher is a high relief of a standing Tom Turkey with the pour spout coming out of his beak. Also in relief on both sides are the words "Wild Turkey." Impressed in the base bottom are the words "Austin Nichols & Co. Lawrenceburg, Ky. Bourbon Whiskey 101." This unique jug is quite impressive in the manner that the wild turkey theme is presented. Valuations are in the $30 to $60 range.

No. 5 **Pitcher with Ear Handle and Ice Lip**. Size: 5.75" high, 3" diameter opening. Mustard yellow glazed body with top rim edged in gold. On both sides, top to bottom, decals of a "Tom Turkey in Flight" and the words "Wild Turkey." On the base bottom is a black stamp with the wording "Fine Staffordshire Pottery Made in England 101 Proof Bourbon 8 Years Old Austin Nichols & Co. Inc. N.Y., N.Y." Introduction was in the late 1960s. This attractive jug holds 1-1/2 pints. Valuations are in the $25 to $50 range according to condition.

Whiskey Pitchers (Pub Jugs). L to R: No. 4 Pitcher with Ear Handle and Spout Lip. 6.75"H, 3.25" diameter opening. Brown matte. Tom Turkey high relief. $30-60; No. 5 Pitcher with Ear Handle and Ice Lip. 5.75"H, 3" diameter opening. Mustard glaze, decals. $25-50.

As noted earlier in this chapter, "go-withs" (which are non-bottle/decanter advertising specialties) can be in themselves very valuable collectibles. While most distillers, wineries, and brewers have issued go-withs to endorse their product lines, Austin Nichols has made a fine art of this business. Over the past three decades and continuing today, Austin Nichols has introduced literally hundreds of go-with items to promote the *Wild Turkey* brand. Among the most highly sought after and, therefore, valuable promotional specialties issued by Austin Nichols are **liquor pourers**. For approximately a six-year period of time starting in 1980, Austin Nichols issued six Wild Turkey pourers. The design of these pourers was based on various decanters from each of their first three series. Austin Nichols termed these as items "porcelain pourers." The pourers were all made of a bisque ceramic material mounted on a green plastic or ceramic base (one item) with the words "Wild Turkey" in white lettering embossed on the front. A cork and stem were attached under the base. Valuations assume a complete cork. The whiskey pourers were introduced in the following order:

No. 1 "**The Striding Turkey**" based on the Series I, No. 6 (1976) decanter of the same name. Size: 3" high (base excluded). This piece is all bisque ceramic including the base. This pourer was not for public sale but was instead used as a "giveaway" promotional item, given by the Wild Turkey liquor representatives to commercial vendors such as nightclubs, taverns, and liquor stores. As such, this pourer is the second rarest of the six. Valuations are in the $50 to $60 range.

No. 2 "**Keenness of Sight**" based on the Series II, No. 3 (1981) decanter of the same name. Size: 3.13" high (base excluded). This pourer also was not for public sale, and was used as a promotional item by the Wild Turkey liquor representatives. Valuations are in the $35 to $45 range.

No. 3 "**First of the Lore**" based on the Series II, No.1 (1979) decanter of the same name. Size: 3.5" high (base excluded). This pourer was introduced through the "Wild Turkey Collectors Society" in 1983. This pourer is the fourth rarest of the six. Valuations are in the $45 to $55 range.

No. 4 "**Ready to Fight**" based on the Series II, No. 4 (1982) decanter of the same name. Size: 3.75" high (base excluded). This pourer was introduced through the "Wild Turkey Collectors Society" in 1984. It is the third rarest of the six, according to Internet auction observation. Valuations are in the $50 to $60 range.

No. 5 "**Wild Turkey in Flight**" based on the Series III, No. 1 (1983) decanter of the same name. Size: 3.5" high (base excluded). This was the only public introduction of a pourer issued in 1984. It was part of a Wild Turkey Pourer Gift Set that included a 750 ml. bottle of Wild Turkey 101 Proof bourbon, housed in an attractive gift box. Valuations, without the box, are in the $15 to $25 range.

No. 6 "**Wild Turkey and Bobcat**" based on the Series III, No. 2 (1983) decanter of the same name. Size: 5.25" high (base excluded). This very attractive pourer was introduced through the "Wild Turkey Collectors Society" in 1985. At that time, the members' price was $15.50. This pourer is the rarest of all six and resale prices reflect that fact. Valuations are in the $160 to $210 range.

Liquor Pourers (Bisque Ceramic). L to R: Wild Turkey in Flight, 1984. $15-25; Wild Turkey in Flight, 1984 (reverse). $15-$25; Ready to Fight, 1984. $50-60; Keenness of Sight, 1982. $35-45; The Striding Turkey, 1981. $50-60.

After liquor pourers, **whiskey flasks** seem to be the items most generally offered for sale on Internet auction sites. Three flasks were issued during the 1980s and 1990s.

No. 1 **Sports Flask**. Silvertoned plastic cover with glass lined interior. Size: 6.5" high, 4.25" in length. The Flying Wild Turkey logo is embossed on the flask front. The paper label on the rear reads "Wild Turkey Kentucky Straight Bourbon Whiskey 86.2 Proof 200 ml. Bottled by the Austin, Nichols Distilling Co. Lawrenceburg, KY." This flask was introduced to the retail trade in September 1984 and was priced at $6.00. Many sellers erroneously assume that the flask cover is either chrome or stainless steel. Valuations are modest, in the $10 to $20 range.

No. 2 **Hip Flask**. Two-tone brown leather cover over a stainless steel pocket flask. Size: 4.38" high, 3.88" wide, 0.88" deep. The words "Wild Turkey" and the standing Tom Turkey logo are imprinted on the stitched leather wrap. The flask holds 5 ounces. Introduced for Christmas 1998, it was originally sold as part of a holiday gift pack with 750 ml. of *Wild Turkey*. Valuations are in the $15 to $20 range.

No. 3 **Hip Flask**. Stainless steel. Size: 4.63" high, 3.63" wide, 0.63" deep. The words "Wild Turkey" and the "Standing Tom Turkey" logo as well as the words "America's Finest Bourbon" are embossed on the flask front. On the base bottom are engraved the words "Stainless Steel 145 ml." Made in China. Introduction date was 1999. These were made for foreign distribution only. Valuations are in the $15 to $20 range.

"Go-Withs". L to R: Wooden Advertising Plaque with rawhide hanger, coated natural pinewood. 7.5"L, 4"W. $15-20; Plastic swizzle sticks (drink stirrers) (Top: Wild Turkey in Flight), 1977. 6.5"L $1; Sports Flask, silvertone plastic cover, 1984. 6.5"H, 4.25"L. $10-20.

Wild Turkey Billboard Reefer/Box Car. Lionel Electric Trains #9837. 027 gauge. 1983-84. 11.5"L, 3.25"H, 2.5"W. $70-90 MIB.

Whisky Flasks. L to R: No. 3 Hip Flask, stainless steel with box, 1999. 4.63"H. $15-20; No. 2 Hip Flask, Two-toned brown leather cover, 1998. 4.38"H $15-20.

There are a plethora of other Wild Turkey "go-with" items, some of which stretch the imagination regarding the degree to which the *Wild Turkey* trademark was applied to certain items. Lionel Trains, for instance, as part of their "Favorite Spirit Series," issued billboard reefer toy train cars with the logos of several liquor distillers. The "Wild Turkey" reefer car is quite popular. Other items, such as plaques, scarves, jigsaw puzzles, and swizzle sticks all were emblazoned with a *Wild Turkey* logo. Some are shown in the following pictures.

Wild Turkey Puzzle Box, 500 pieces, 1984. Format size: 16"W x 20"L. $25-40 MIB.

Wild Turkey Puzzle completed.

Wild Turkey Scarf. Grey cotton with maroon printing, repeat design of encircled Wild Turkey in Flight. 21"W x 22"L. $10-15.

The Wild Turkey Ceramic Society/Wild Turkey Fliers Club

In order to meet collector demand for concise information on *Wild Turkey* decanters and other offerings, Austin Nichols originally began publishing a semi-annual newsletter. The first issue of *The Wild Turkey Ceramic Society Newsletter* was introduced for Summer 1984. The mission statement issued by Austin Nichols indicated that the newsletter was to be filled "with news, information and special features of interest to you" (the collector). However well the intent, the newsletter was published only annually (with one name change, to *The Wild Turkey Collectors Newsletter*) and the last issue was published as the fifth issue for Summer 1988. Extant copies of these very informative newsletters are now rare.

An outgrowth of *Wild Turkey* collector interest generated by the newsletters was the formation of the **Wild Turkey Fliers Club** by Austin Nichols in January 1985. The purported reason for the Fliers Club existence, according to Austin Nichols, was that so many collectors "asked for moderately priced, short run *Wild Turkey* collectibles they could buy by mail." Therefore, beginning in 1985, the Wild Turkey Fliers Club began issuing "for members only" porcelain collectibles that were very limited editions and not sold to the general public. Membership in the club ($8 and $10 for one year for individuals and families respectively) allowed individuals to purchase *one* of each collectible offered; families would be eligible to purchase *two* of each collectible offered. Colorful brochures accompanied the various Fliers Club offerings. Coincident with declining collector interest in ceramic decanters as well as other ceramic "collectibles" and "go-withs," the Fliers Club disbanded in early 1989. This was not unique to Austin Nichols, as collector ennui was felt across the board by all distillers due to the glut in the marketplace by nearly twenty years of offerings endemic to the industry.

A complete list of Wild Turkey Fliers Club offerings and introduction dates follows:

No. 1 **Paperweight Figurine** (bisque) "Wild Turkey and Bobcat." Size: 6.63" high. April 1985. Original member's cost $32.95. Not often offered for sale. Valuations in the $75 to $100 range.

No.2 **Porcelain Collector's Plate #1** "Proud Wild Turkey." Size: 8.5" diameter. Gold banded. Artist: Ken Davies. July 1985. This was the first plate of five originally planned editions. Original member's cost $31.95. Valuations are in the $100 to $125 range with box.

No. 3 **Porcelain Wall Plaque #1** (bisque) "Wild Turkey in Flight." Size: 12.25" high. May 1986. Original member's cost $33.95. Valuations in the $75 to $125 range.

No. 4 **Porcelain Collector's Plate #2** "Wild Turkey on a Log." Size: 8.5" diameter. Gold banded. Artist: Ken Davies. August 1986. Original member's cost $31.95. Valuations in the $40 to $60 range with box.

No. 5 **Porcelain Decanter** (bisque) "The King of America's Forest Birds." 1.75 liters. Size: 12.5" high, 12.5" length. Approximately 1650 made. June 1987. Original member's cost $200. This very limited edition is rarely offered. Valuations can range upwards of $700.

No. 6 **Porcelain Water Pitcher** "Wild Turkey Pug Jug." Size: 7.5" high. White glazed body with multicolored Tom Turkey hand-painted bisque relief as part of the design with upswept wings forming a scalloped rim. July 1987. Seldom seen on the auction market. Valuations vary widely, but sales have been recorded in the $150 to $190 range.

No. 7 **Three Christmas Ornaments** "Wild Turkey" in three scenes: (1) perched on Gift Boxes, (2) perched on Santa's Hat, and (3) perched within a Christmas Wreath. Fall 1987. Made in Mexico. Rarely seen at auction but sales have been recorded in the $125 to $150 range.

No. 8 **Porcelain Wall Plaque #2** "Proud Turkey." Size: 11" high. Bisque hand-painted body. Based on a Ken Davies painting. Made in Mexico. May 1988. Original member's cost $39.95. Valuations in the $60 to $80 range.

No. 9 **Porcelain Collectors Plate #3** "The Flying Wild Turkey." Size: 8.5" diameter. Gold banded. Artist: Ken Davies. June 1988. Original member's cost $31.50 (but the retail price was $35 to non-members). Valuations in the $80 to $100 range with box.

No. 10 **Wild Turkey Snowdome.** A porcelain Tom Turkey with full tail enclosed in a snowdome set on a hand-stained wooden teak base. Size: 5.25" high. July 1988. Made in Taiwan. Original member's cost $29.95. Valuations for this seldom offered snowdome are in the $150 to $200 range with box.

The Wild Turkey Collectors (Society) Newsletters. First Issue 1984 through Fifth (last) Issue 1988. 8.5"W x 11"L format. Two-sided, tan paper. Published by Austin, Nichols for "Collectors Everywhere." $25-75 per issue.

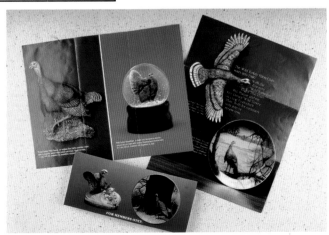

Three select Fliers Club Brochures for purchasing limited edition collectibles. 8.5"W x 11"L format. Full color. Published by The Wild Turkey Fliers Club. $10-15 each.

No. 11 **Three Christmas Ornaments.** "Wild Turkey" in three scenes: (1) perched on Twin Gold Bells, (2) in flight with Christmas Tree, and (3) perched on Snowman. Fall 1989. Valuations are in the $150 to $175 range, but these ornaments are rarely offered for sale.

Left:
Wall Plaque #2 "Proud Turkey." Porcelain bisque. 11"H x 8"W, 1988. $60-80.

Below:
Three Christmas Ornaments. "Wild Turkey" in three holiday motifs, 1987. $125-150 MIB.

In 1988, as demand for these Fliers Club items abated, restrictions on members' purchases loosened. For instance, members, "by popular demand," could buy as many Fliers Club collectibles as they wished while supplies lasted. Members would also be able to receive a 10% discount on the 1988 Habitat decanter as well as on the 1988 Porcelain Collectors Plate #3, which was not a true exclusive club offering.

The introduction of the Series IV No. 2 Habitat B decanter in 1989 brought to an end a remarkable era of eighteen years of *Wild Turkey* ceramic and glass collectibles offerings by Austin Nichols. Over that time frame, Austin Nichols issued seventy-six collectible items including pourers (excluding flasks and "go-withs") through their retail distribution channels and/or to the Fliers Club membership. However, Austin Nichols was not alone in offering novelty decanters and other items. During the "Golden Age" of the special/limited edition production of ceramic decanters in the 1970s and early 1980s, over one hundred distillers, brewers, and wineries were issuing "collectibles," with the subtle inference of possible future investment value. Remember that during the 1970s the compounded annual rate of inflation in the United States was 7.4% and in the 1980s, a still robust 5.1% annually. Thus, the collectibles market boomed for all sorts of items, especially plates and figurines. All these so-called valuable collectibles were vying for the collector's dollars that were being steadily eroded by inflation. Eventually, massive amounts of material saturated the market with the result that most hyped offerings never appreciated in value and, in fact, many today languish below their issue prices twenty or thirty years later. However, *Wild Turkey* offerings, averaging about four collectibles per year, have maintained their value and, in several cases, have brought five to ten times their original prices.

Other Turkey Figural Decanters/Steins

Most other distillers during the "Golden Age" did not bother to issue turkey-styled figural decanters, figuring rightly that Austin Nichols had that market gobbled up. Even the most prolific bottle issuer, Jim Beam Distillery, while supplying over five hundred bottles to collectors, did not produce a turkey figural decanter. To our knowledge, only three other distilleries offered turkey figural decanters to collectors. They are described below.

Ezra Brooks Distilling Company

In addition to the Jim Beam Distillery, Ezra Brooks was one of the earliest distillers to issue decanters, first making them in 1964. By the time Ezra Brooks discontinued making decanters in 1985, the firm had introduced more than three hundred different figural bottles to the collectors' market. Since 1988, Ezra Brooks has had three owners. The rights to the brand name are now owned by the David Sherman Corporation (DSC), headquartered in St. Louis, Missouri. Founded in 1958, DSC is a leading marketer, bottler, importer, and exporter of beverage alcohol products. While Ezra Brooks Kentucky Straight Bourbon Whiskey 90 Proof is still distilled in Kentucky, it is bottled in St. Louis.

In 1971, Ezra Brooks issued a *White Turkey* figural decanter with box based on a mold formed by Ronald Hughes of Chicago, a noted sculptor in the United States and Europe. This decanter (in reality of a domesticated turkey) was a limited edition of 5,496 pieces.

Tom Turkey Figural Decanter, "White Turkey." White glazed body with red head and neck. 1971. 8.75"H, 7.5"L, 7"W at tail. Ezra Brooks "Collector Series" Heritage China R.H.-15. $35-45 MIB.

Ski Country Ltd.

This company was also a very prolific issuer of special edition decanters for national distribution. The decanters were first made in 1972 and were issued by The Foss Company of Golden, Colorado. The first Ski Country decanter, of skiers, was originally intended to commemorate the 1972 Winter Olympics. Over subsequent years, Ski Country has produced over 150 decanters representing 15 separate categories. They have tended to specialize primarily in birds and some animals. Their typical production run for the 4/5 (750 ml.) bottle size has been in the 2,400 to 3,600 decanters range, with minis about 30% to 60% fewer. Ski Country has also made 1/2 gallon, 1.75 liter and even a one-gallon size. The one-gallon size was issued as Ski Country's salute to the United States 1976 Bicentennial and was represented by the famous *Birth of Freedom* decanter, depicting two well-designed golden eagles. That monster decanter is valued in the $2,100 to $2,300 range. The *Widgeon*, in the Banded Waterfowl series, represented the largest decanter run, with 12,000 750 ml. and 4,800 minis produced when released in 1979.

Ski Country, as part of its Game Birds category, also produced a beautiful *(Wild) Turkey*. Contrary to normal releases, the 1,200 minis were released first, in 1975, and featured an "upside-down" bottom fill. In 1976, 2,130 4/5s size decanters were released. Due to the intricate detail on the mini, it is valued higher than its larger counterpart. Valuations for the minis range from $110 to $150 while the 4/5s size range from $100 to $140.

Today, Ski Country is owned by Frank and Jacque Willburn from Amarillo, Texas. Their club website (www.skicountrydecanters.com) is quite informative with pictures, quantities produced and current prices of all output. To my knowledge, Ski Country has not produced any decanters since 1995.

Wild Turkey Figural Decanter, "Wild Turkey." Multicolor porcelain matte body. 1976. 10.25"H, 4.13" diameter base. Made in Japan. Four/fifths quart capacity. Ski Country, Golden Colorado. $100-140.

Hoffman Distilling Company

In 1983, Julian Van Winkle III, a scion of an old bourbon producing family, purchased the very small Commonwealth Distillery near Lawrenceburg, Kentucky. At the same time, the Hoffman Distilling Company, owned by the Wertheimer family, was sold to Commonwealth. Up to that point, Hoffman had made over fifteen individual series of decanters, the best known being their Mr. Lucky series of leprechaun-shaped decanters. Decanter production, which started in 1971, was generally terminated in 1987 some years after the sale to Commonwealth, a company still in existence operating under the *Old Rip Van Winkle* label.

In 1980, Hoffman made a natural looking *Tom Turkey and Hen* vignette scene in a 250 ml. decanter mounted on a wooden base. Valuations (with base) are in the $75 to $100 range. In 1987, as a special order, Commonwealth made a limited edition miniature ceramic decanter of a *Standing Tom Turkey*. This 5.25" high decanter is the miniature version of the decanter designed by W. D. Gaither for the National Wild Turkey Federation in 1980. Valuations are in the $35 to $50 range. The Gaither *Turkey Gobbler* decanter is quite rare, with only 1500 made. Due to its exquisite beauty, this decanter is the most highly sought after of any of the ceramic bottles and is expensive. It was never filled with whiskey.

Anheuser-Busch Brewing Co. (Budweiser)

In 1998, this St. Louis, Missouri based brewery issued four pewter lidded ceramic beer steins in their *Upland Game Birds* series. The third edition of this series was entitled *Wild Turkey* and depicts three turkeys – one Tom and two Hens – in their natural environment. The artwork by artist Pat Ford is encircled by other upland game birds in deep ceramic relief. The base has a continuous border of acorns in relief. An acorn and oak leaf design decorates the hinged lid. The limited edition size of 5,000 steins with a decorated box was produced with the original retail price of $75. The stein item number is CS327 and they were made in Brazil by *Ceramarte*. Other birds in the series are the Ruffled Grouse, CS316; Prairie Chicken, CS337; and Pheasant, CS319. Over the years Anheuser-Busch has produced more than sixty series of beer steins with no end in sight. Due to a rather continuous offering of this stein on Internet auction sites, valuations have settled in the $55 to $65 range with the box. It is not too surprising that Budweiser issued this particular series. Over the years after World War II, Budweiser heavily advertised the complementary use of beer as the drink of choice at Thanksgiving dinner.

Underside of stein base. Numbered 2709.

Wild Tom Turkey and Hen Figural Decanter. Porcelain matte body. Multicolor turkeys standing on hay colored foliage. Unglazed white base, mounted on black painted wooden base. 1980. 7.5"H, 5.75" diameter base. Wooden base: 1"H, 7" diameter. 200 ml. capacity. Hoffman Distilling Company. $75-100 with base.

Wild Turkey Beer Stein with Ear Handle, "Wild Turkey." Cream colored glazed body with deep ceramic relief. Insert cameo of wild turkeys. Pewter hinged lid. 1998. 8.5"H, 4.88"D. Item number CS327. 5000 made in Brazil by *Ceramarte*™. Anheuser-Busch Brewing Company. $55-65.

Originally distillers' use of special limited ceramic decanters was an obvious ploy to distinguish themselves from one another due to the rather commodity nature of their products. Besides the implied investment value attributed to the "scarcity" of the novelty decanters, another reason that distillers used this marketing method was the fact that the domestic consumption of "brown spirits" was on the decline. Therefore, the incessant introductions of decanters over a two decade period ending in the late 1980s absorbed not only excess capacity but also allowed the distillers to maintain some sales parity with the up and coming "white spirits" revolution in consumer taste habits. However, as foreigners found "brown spirits" to be more affordable as their economies strengthened, domestic distillers did not need expensive advertising programs to further their sales efforts. Now leading "brown spirits" producers, such as *Wild Turkey*, find themselves as part of a global liquor sales consortium serving the tastes of consumers worldwide. The collecting public of decanters today only have Jim Beam and, perhaps, Ski Country as the only quasi-active issuers of figural bottles. Therefore, valuations of the older select items of limited production should continue to rise.

Right:
Wild Turkey Figural Miniature Decanter, "Standing Tom Turkey." Multicolor porcelain matte body in woodland setting. 1987. 5.25"H, 4.25"L. Made in Taiwan. Hoffman Original. $35-50.

Left:
Wild Turkey Figural Decanter, "Turkey Gobbler." Multicolor porcelain matte body in woodland setting. 1980. 11.25"H, 9.5"L, 6.75"W. 1500 made, only for members of the National Wild Turkey Federation. Made in Taiwan. Decanter was hand sculpted, signed and numbered by W.D. Gaither, Erlanger, Kentucky. $250-300.

Underside of decanter base with description.

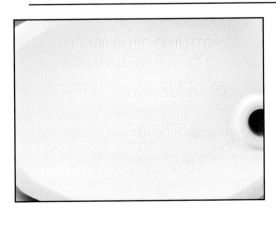

The archaeological record going back at least 50,000 years indicates that several species of prehistoric turkeys occupied a large portion of contiguous United States and the Mexican portions of North America. There is also substantial empirical evidence that these indigenous turkeys were extensively domesticated, not necessarily for food, but for their handsome feathers and bones which were used in the manufacturing of various household implements. Southward in Mexico, evidence indicates that the wild turkey was domesticated by the Aztec Indians prior to the discovery of North America by Columbus in 1492. In 1498, the turkey was taken to Spain on a return voyage as part of the "treasure" of the New World. From Spain, the turkey was distributed to other parts of Europe, arriving in England in 1541. Thus the turkey preceded the exodus of the Pilgrims to America by nearly eighty years.

When Hernando Cortes arrived on the shores of central Mexico (Sierra Madre Oriental) in April, 1519, he found a highly developed empire of native American people called Aztecs/Mexica who reigned from 1300 A.D. Religion was extremely important in Aztec life, and they worshipped hundreds of gods and goddesses. The Aztecs had many agricultural gods because their culture was based heavily on farming. Therefore, when the Spaniards arrived in Mexico, they observed immense numbers of domesticated turkeys. These ancient Mexicans regarded the turkey as a bird of good omen, using the feathers for clothing as well as for personal and religious ornamentation. Likewise, when the Spaniards, under Coronado, began the early exploration of Northern Mexico and southwestern United States from 1554 to 1595, they found large flocks of domesticated turkeys kept only for their feathers. As such, turkey images adorn early southwestern Indian pottery. Modern descendants of not only the ancient pueblo dwellers but also Indians of various Mexican states have utilized the turkey as an important image of folk art and in their customs. In the state of Chihuahua, Mexico, there is a small village called Juan Mata Ortiz. Inspired by the found ceramic shards of an ancient Indian civilization called "Casas Grandes," a local inhabitant, Juan Quezada, in 1974, began making thin walled earthenware *ollas*, covered with intricate designs based on both the Casas Grandes and Mimbres Indian cultures. Some thirty years later, Juan's international recognition as a master potter helped turn Mata Ortiz into a village of potters numbering over four hundred artists.

Mata Ortiz pottery, based on unusual shapes bearing innovative animal motifs or abstract use of prehistoric designs, is in the midst of an expanding artistic movement featuring talented Mexican potters.

"Turkey Dance – Pueblo of Jemez, New Mexico." Reproduction of original lithograph. 11.5" x 8.75" (image size 9"x 6.5"). Artist: P. Moran. Julius Bien & Co. Lith, N.Y., produced for the Eleventh Census of the United States – 1891. $125-130.

Postcard. "A Hopi Thanksgiving." c. 1920s. Publisher: Detroit Publishing Co. "Phostint" card #11248. $12-15.

Acoma Pottery

One of the most fabled places in New Mexico in terms of antiquity is Acoma. It is called the "sky city" because of its remote location 357 feet high on a flat mesa top. The Keres Pueblo of Acoma dating from 1300 is one of the oldest continuously inhabited communities in the United States, with an estimated all year population of 1,300 persons. It was first visited by the Spaniards in Coronado's Expedition of 1540, but the Acomas did not formally submit to Spanish rule until 1699. Today, Acoma can be visited by those interested in an Indian pueblo virtually untouched by outside influences. One of the mainstays of their economy is the making and selling of

Cooking and Storage Pot, fired clay. 9.5"H x 11"D x 34" circumference. Stylized design of turkeys done in colors of terra cotta and black. Artist: Jesus Tena, Mestizo Indian; Mata Ortiz, Casa Grandes, Mexico. $130-150.

Decorative Olla (Pot), fired clay. 4.5"H x 5.25"D x 16.75" circumference. Stylized design of four flying turkeys done in colors of brown and gray over an intricate geometric design utilizing black and terra cotta paints on a white base. Artist: Efren Ledezma, Mata Ortiz, Casa Grandes, Mexico. $100-120.

polychrome pottery to those intrepid tourists who take the time to visit. And Acoma potters are justifiably famous for their decorative artistry with stylized depictions of nature. The signing of pottery, initiated during the 1960s, adds more value when a piece is signed by one of the capable descendants of the Histia, Lewis, or Chino families.

Signature of Eva Histia, family member of Mary Histia (1881-1973), one of Acoma's most celebrated potters.

Acoma Effigy Pottery. L to R: Turkey figurine, fired clay and polychrome paints on white slip. 6.75"H x 5.5"L x 5.5"W. Two-legged Tom Turkey with "seed " disk design, c. 1980s. Artist: Eva Histia. $100-120. Turkey figurine, fired clay and polychrome paints on light tan slip. 4.25"H x 5.5"L x 5.25"W. Sitting turkey design with circular disks on bases, c.1970s. Artist: Jessie Garcia (deceased). $130-150. Turkey figurine, fired clay and polychrome paints on terra cotta slip. 6"H x 6.25"L x 6.5"W. Sitting turkey, wings extended with "seed " disk design, c.1970s to 1980s. Artist: S.L. Stevens. $120-140.

L to R: Basket, coiled handle, fired clay and polychrome paints on white slip. 4.75"H x 3.75"D. Two-headed turkey design with flowers, c. 1990s. Artist: D. Patrick – Acoma. $50-60. Turkey figurine, fired clay and polychrome paints on light brown slip, matte finish. 5.5"H x 5.25"L x 4.5"W. Repeated series of "u" and "v" marks to indicate feathers, c. early 1940s. Artist: Maria Vigil – Jemez Pueblo, New Mexico. $250-275; Turkey figurine pot, fired clay and polychrome paints on white slip. 4.25"H x 3.5"L x 3.75"W. Stylized design with raised tail and a 2.25" diameter opening, c.1970s. Artist: Rita Malie – Acoma. $50-60.

Zuni Fetishes

A *fetish* is an animal carving from such diverse materials as polished stone, shell, amber, deer antler, and wood. The carved fetish is said to house the spirit or supernatural qualities of that animal. These animal fetishes traditionally have been used as talismans and amulets for success in hunting and fishing. Today, the tribal uses of fetishes have broadened to include the power of a "good luck" charm. Among all of the American Indians of the Southwest, the Zuni Indians are acknowledged as the fetish carvers of the highest quality. Because of the aesthetic considerations of a finely rendered fetish, tourist interest in such art objects has increased significantly. It is estimated that there are between two hundred and four hundred part-time and full-time fetish carvers at Zuni to support the demand. The Turkey fetish represents both an important food source as well as the many realistic uses of its feathers.

Turkey Fetish, spring green Serpentine stone. 1"H x 1.38"L x 0.75"W. Seated turkey with inlaid turquoise eyes, c. 2000. Artist: Saville Hattie – Zuni Pueblo. $35-50.

L to R: Turkey Fetish. Picasso Marble. 1.25"H x 1.13"L x 1"W. Seated turkey, fantail with inlaid turquoise eyes, c.1999. Artist: Todd Lowsayater – Zuni Pueblo. $45-50. Turkey figurine, fired clay and polished blackware. 2.5"H x 2"L x 2.25"W. Standing Tom Turkey, no decoration, c. late 1990s. Artists: Dorothy and Paul Gutierrez – Santa Clara Pueblo. $30-35.

Navajo Carvings

Each of the American Southwest tribes and pueblos are well known for their respective signature art forms. The Navajos traditionally are well known for their intricately designed rugs, pottery, jewelry, and sand paintings. However, Navajo folk art in the form of contemporary figurative wood carvings is becoming very important and popular.

L to R: Turkey Figurine, carved, painted and decorated cottonwood. 11.5"H x 6.75"W. Tom Turkey with leather cowboy boots, c. late 1990s. Artist: Reed Herbert – Northeastern Arizona Navajo. $60-70. Turkey figurine, carved, painted, and decorated cottonwood. 10.75"H x 6.13"W. Tom Turkey with rawhide and felt leggings, c. late 1990s. Artist: Reed Herbert – Northeastern Arizona Navajo. $60-70.

L to R: Turkey figurine, carved, painted and decorated cottonwood. 12"H x 6.38"W. Stylized Tom Turkey on base, c. late 1990s. Artist: Ruby Herbert and Family – Northeastern Arizona Navajos. $55-65. Turkey figurine, carved, painted and decorated cottonwood. 8.75"H x 6.5"W. Tom Turkey on base, c. late 1990s. Artist: Leslie Herbert – Northeastern Arizona Navajo $55-65.

L to R: Turkey figurine, carved, painted and decorated cottonwood. 4.5"H x 3"L x 4.63"W. Tom Turkey on base, c. late 1990s. Artist: Fredrick Eskeets – Navajo. $35-40. Turkey figurine, carved, painted and decorated cottonwood, also using felt and pipe cleaners. 5.5"H x 5.75"L x 4.38"W. Tom Turkey with split wood tail, c. late 1990s. Artist: Leslie Herbert – Northeastern Arizona Navajo. $50-60. Turkey figurine, carved, air-brushed painted and decorated cottonwood. 8.75"H x 6.13"W. Tom Turkey with black suede boots, c. late 1990s. Artist: Leo Herbert – Navajo, Fruitland, New Mexico. $75-85.

Hopi Kachinas

Another Southwest Indian art form is the *Kachina Doll*. These are authentic representations of ceremonial Kachinas, who are elaborately costumed masked religious male members of the Hopi and Zuni Pueblo tribes. The Kachinas, an integral part of pueblo Indian life, are greatly revered. One of their main functions is to bring rain for the spring crops. Accurate Kachina carvings or dolls are always formed from the root of the cottonwood tree. While tribal carvings were originally used to instruct children about the hundreds of Kachina spirits, today, these same religious icons are carved as art objects.

Turkey Kachina Doll, carved, painted and decorated cottonwood root. 6.5"H, 8" wingspan, 2.75" diameter base. Turkey Kachina known as "Koyona." The turkey is a "racer," and when it arrives at the Hopi mesas it brings gifts, which are fruits and vegetables strung on yucca. The Turkey Kachina then races young men in the plaza for the gifts he brings. c. 2000. Artist: Lee Chapella – Hopi Indian from the 1st Mesa (Polaca, Arizona). $250-300.

L to R: Turkey Kachina Doll, carved, painted and decorated with turkey down feathers and suede outfit. 8"H, 6" arm span. This Kachina is agile and moves throughout the trees with the greatest of ease. The trees are its playground. c. late 1990s. Origin: probably Oaxacan. $40-50. Day of the Dead Turkey Offering, painted plaster with cloth poncho. 6.25"H x 3"L x 2" deep. Skeleton figurine holding turkey offering. c.1999. From Oaxacan Day of Dead market. $15-20.

Oaxacan Carvings

As the turkey is also native to Mexico with two species represented, one of which is not seen in the United States, it is only natural that wood carvings and other materials are also used in representing this bird. In Mexico, turkeys are called *guajolotes*. In the Oaxacan state, one of Mexico's largest and poorest states, the Zopotec Indians have carved toys and masks for hundreds of years as part of their rich folk art tradition. The tools of the carver are quite simple – machetes for the forming and kitchen or pocket knives for the finishing. The wood comes from the *copalitto* tree, a small-leafed hardwood that is soft and workable when fresh. Over ninety percent of these carvers today, representing two hundred families, come from one of three small villages outside the city of Oaxaca. Inspiration for their carvings comes from many sources, ranging from the immediate world of village life to the spiritual world of dreams. But in all cases, the menagerie of objects is always brilliantly painted with an imaginative fantasy design of great originality. The most surrealistic of carvings are called *alebriges* (or *alebrijes*), an undefined word meaning objects that are derived from the artist's ceremonial visions, perhaps induced from mind-expanding drugs. Alebrige figures are among the most original and highly sought of all Oaxacan carvings.

L to R: Turkey Nodders (3), carved, painted and decorated dried tropical fruit pit with a copal wood head. 1.7" to 2.13"H. These "loose-neck" turkeys are individually carved from a dried pit and the head is made from native wood. A needle and thread ties the head to the pit, which creates a "bobble" in a slight breeze. c.2000 – The Mexican state of Oaxaca. $5 each. Turkey Alebrige Figurine, carved, painted and decorated copal wood. 3"H, 3.5"L, 2.25"W. Seated Tom Turkey carving. c.2000. Artist: Joaquin Hernandez Vasquez – Zapotec Indian, village of Tilcahelte, Oaxaca, Mexico. $25-30. Turkey Figurine, carved painted and decorated copal wood. 6.25"H, 3.25"W. Standing Tom Turkey with beads accents on unpainted wood. c. early 1990s. Artist: Erasto Ramirez – Zapotec Indian, Oaxaca, Mexico. $40-50.

Turkey Alebrige figurine, carved, painted and decorated copal wood. 5.5"H x 6"L x 6"W. Tom Turkey one-of-a-kind hand carved from a single piece of wood, c. late 1990s. Artist: Carlos Morales, a famous carver from the village of Arrazola (site of an old sugar hacienda and plantation), one of the three small villages in Oaxaca carrying on the alebrige carving tradition. $100-125.

Mexican Tourist Pottery

After the Mexican Revolution ended in 1921, the collecting world viewed "serious" Mexican art through the eyes of social realism and libertarian muralists such as Diego Rivera, Jose Clemente Orozco, and David Alfaro Siqueiros. The so-called Mexican mural movement was openly sponsored by leftist elements in the Mexican government to promote the elevation of indigenous local cultures.

It was only after World War II that the tourist base expanded from visiting historic archeological sites to visiting some of the more rural districts, as Mexico's infrastructure improved to accommodate tourists interested in bringing home something unusual. Therefore, throughout the more traveled areas of Mexico there arose a large "cottage industry" devoted to producing "folk art," specifically for tourists as popular souvenir items. The State of Jalisco, with Guadalajara as its capital, is well known for ceramics ranging in quality from the highly decorated, glazed items to the more utilitarian terracotta pottery pieces. Specifically, decorative items such as casseroles and banks were part of the figural pottery movement called "tourist ware" from the area of Tlaquepaque.

Figural pottery is both handmade and/or mould made, and the pieces are fired at very low temperatures from 300-400 degrees Fahrenheit for a short period of time. The items are then painted with either natural water-based pigments or artificial aniline dyes mixed with a setting agent such as egg whites. Over the years, depending upon the skill of the application of paint as well as the degree to which the object is handled, the paints on these items are subject to flaking.

Turkey Covered Casserole, glazed with rare black painted head. Lid 10.5"L, basket-weave design nest with handles 10.75"L. Tlaquepaque, c.1940-1970s, marked: Mexico. $250-275.

L to R: Turkey Covered Casserole, glazed with blue neck. Lid 7"L, basket-weave design nest with handles 7.25"L. Tlaquepaque, c.1940-70s, marked: Mexico, also with rubber stamp. $125-150; Turkey Covered Casserole, glazed with bluish purple neck. Lid 5"L, basket-weave design nest with handles 5"L. Tlaquepaque, c.1940-70s, marked: Mexico. $75-100; Turkey Covered Casserole, glazed with multicolor nest. Lid 6"L, basket-weave design nest with handles 6.25"L. Tlaquepaque, c.1940-70s, marked: Mexico. $100-125.

Turkey Covered Casserole, glazed with pinkish tan neck. Lid 10.25"L, basket-weave design nest with handles 10.25"L. Tlaquepaque, c.1940-70s, marked: Mexico. $200-225.

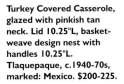

Turkey Covered Casserole, glazed with medium to light green neck. Lid 10.25"L, basket-weave design nest with handles 10.25"L. Tlaquepaque, c.1940-70s, marked: Mexico. $200-225.

L to R: Turkey Figurine Coin Bank, fired clay and aniline paints. 8.5"H x 5"L x 5.75"W. Three-legged figural turkey bank with coin slot on body. Tlaquepaque, c.1940-70s, no mark. $75-100; Turkey Figurine Coin Bank, fired clay and natural terracotta paint. 7.75"H x 5"L x 5.13"W. Three-legged figural turkey bank with coin slot on body. Tlaquepaque, c.1940-70s, no mark. $50-75.

Turkey Covered Casserole, glazed in the terracotta brown neck. Lid 10.25"L, basket-weave design oval nest with handles 9" x 10.25". Tlaquepaque, c.1940-70s, not marked. $150-175.

Turkey Figurine, light green aniline glaze with "pebbly" neck, decorated in colors of black and brown. 7.75"H x 5.5"L x 6"W, label: Pilar Gift Shop, Mazatlan, Sinaloa State, Mexico, c.1980s. $60-75.

Turkey Covered Casserole, glazed with glue and green "pebbly" surface on neck. Lid 10"L, basket-weave design nest with handles 9.5"L. Tlaquepaque, c.1940-70s, marked: Mexico. $175-200.

Turkey Figural. Plaster of Paris, 3.5"H. Polychrome painted, wire legs. Made in State of Sonora, Mexico. $20-25.

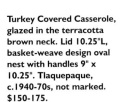

Chapter 11
TOYS AND RELATED ITEMS

Depending upon where one was raised geographically and during what particular era of time, Thanksgiving was mainly an event-related holiday having to do with family get-togethers, turkey shoots, parades, and football games. In comparison, other major holidays represented by Easter, July 4th, and Halloween had wide appeal for children, due to the related gifts and favors associated with the holiday. Christmas, obviously, was exceptional with regard to the depth, quality and quantity of gifts both given and received, covering virtually every possible toy category.

Although Thanksgiving is not a traditional gift and novelty giving holiday, the Thanksgiving week alone typically represents 5% to 7% of annual U.S. traditional toy sales. The Friday after Thanksgiving is reputed to be the heaviest sales day of the year, because shoppers are taking advantage of pre-Christmas sales to begin the month-long process of purchasing Christmas gifts.

According to The NPD Group (National Purchaser Daily), an international consumer marketing company specializing in tracking consumer purchasing and behavior, the toy and video game industry has recorded total retail sales in the U.S. in excess of $30 billion annually for the five years ended 2003. Of this impressive volume, traditional toys represent two-thirds, whereas growing quite rapidly are video game systems.

Of the fifteen toy categories tracked by NPD Funworld®, specifically related Thanksgiving toys fall into one of the following four groupings: Dolls, Plush Toys, Games/Puzzles, and All Other Toys (i.e. tin-plate windups and banks). One example of how Thanksgiving has ranked in terms of sales of major holidays' offerings of Toys, Favors, and Novelties can be found in the *Wholesale Trade List No. 26 for 1924-1925* (Favors and Novelties), produced by Dennison, a major manufacturer. This list provides an insightful look at buying demand for major retail outlets during the early 1920s. It devotes eighteen pages to Halloween, sixteen pages to Christmas, nine pages to New Year's and only five pages to Thanksgiving. The toys mentioned here were minor in nature and are more novelty-like. Some eighty years later, there is one holiday gift trend that has become persistent: the strength of Halloween celebrations to have both child and adult appeal. In fact, Halloween has become the second largest commercial holiday in the U.S., with $7 billion spent on it annually.

Dolls

One of the largest traditional toy categories in terms of unit value is that of **Dolls**. As opposed to action figures and accessories, which appeal almost exclusively to males, dolls hold a strong attraction for females. While dolls have been popular from the beginning of American history, each generation has had its favorites – inspiring fads and crazes yielding to a varied range of collectible dolls. Cabbage Patch dolls are a recent example of this craze, with little interest in them today. Dolls, typically, were either made to be played with as childhood favorites or, in many instances, displayed with many outfits and accessories.

Thanksgiving dolls were represented by either a Pilgrim or its counterpart Indian figure. Such dolls were static display items more in keeping with the historic perspective of the holiday. Some of America's most loved and best-known doll manufacturers, such as **Mattel, Annalee Mobilitee Dolls**, and the **(Madame) Alexander Doll Company**, have had offerings for Thanksgiving. While Mattel's "Barbie" dolls and Madame Alexander's "Wendy" dolls are feverishly collected, it is the Annalee Mobilitee Doll Company that has distinguished itself with the range and depth of Thanksgiving doll offerings.

Barbara Annalee Thorndike, nee Davis (1915-2002) started a small, home-based craft industry making cotton cloth dolls and puppets in 1934 in Concord, New Hampshire. Over the next thirty years, Annalee and her husband perfected the manufacturing of wool-based felt dolls. Annalee wanted her dolls to tell a story through expression, detailed clothing, and proper positioning, unlike other crude cloth dolls of the early twentieth century. Her dolls were famous for their creatively painted felt faces portraying sunny dispositions. Wire frames designed by Annalee's husband provided the internal support to allow the finished dolls to be positioned into poseable or "mobilitee" figures according to the desired motif. When the doll company incorporated in 1955, it was called Annalee Mobilitee Dolls in recognition of this very unusual feature. By the mid-1960s, Annalee's dolls were being marketed on a nationwide basis. With the expected expansion in volume, a "Factory in the Woods" in Meredith, New Hampshire was built and is still in use today, providing employment for over 350 locals. The firm has an extensive catalog of felt dolls. A series of dolls tend to be reissued each year for at least a three-year period but with only minor changes in clothing or accessories. Approximately one-third of the full line is discontinued each year. In terms of Thanksgiving offerings, from 1960 through 1997, the Annalee Doll Company has issued over twenty-two styles and sizes of turkeys; six Pilgrim Man and Woman dolls; nine Indian Man and Woman dolls; and at least fifty-five different Pilgrims and Indian Mouse dolls and sets. Between 1,500 and 3,000 Thanksgiving oriented dolls are produced each year for each item description, in prices ranging from $25 to $50 depending on size and sets.

While more "doll-like" than dolls, the ouput of **Byers' Choice Ltd.** offers an enchanting departure from the norm through their line of "Carolers" figures outfitted in the appropriate holiday garb.

L to R: Pilgrim Woman, 13"H; Pilgrim Man, 13"H; both hand sewn dyed cotton and linen. Byers' Choice Ltd. Chalfont, Pennsylvania. Created for Plimoth Plantation, Plymouth, Massachusetts, 1999. $75-85 each.

Pilgrim Man Holding a Turkey, 9.5"H. Hand sewn dyed felt, turkey made of feathers. Byers' Choice Ltd. 2003. $70. Byers' Choice was established in 1981 as a family business handcrafting a line of "Carolers" figures. Today, approximately 180 artisans work for company and their cumulative output is sold in over 3,000 specialty stores.

L to R: Pilgrim Woman Mouse, 13.5"H; Pilgrim Man Mouse, 14.5"H; both hand sewn dyed felt and linen. Annalee Mobilitee Dolls, Meredith, New Hampshire, 1965. $25-30 each.

Pilgrim Man and Woman, 8"H x 10" across. Couple is standing on two brown felt circular platforms. Dolls dressed in Pilgrim-Harvest hand-sewn clothing in felt and linen; hand painted faces. Included is a basket with corn and a pumpkin. Hang tag #4904, Annalee Mobilitee Dolls, Meredith, New Hampshire, 1990. $50-55.

Thanksgiving "Wendy" doll, 8"H; blonde hair and movable brown eyes. Dressed in the colors of autumn, yellow plush sweater trimmed with pumpkin appliqués and green rickrack "vines," cotton pumpkin paint pants. Included is a felt, multi-colored 4"H turkey. Style #35680. Blue and pink striped and polka dot box, Made in China, NRFB 2003. The (Madame) Alexander Doll Company, New York, New York. $65-70. The Alexander Doll Company was founded in 1923 by Madame Beatrice Alexander Behrman (1885-1990). The first dolls were constructed of cloth. Over the succeeding years, Madame Alexander's handcrafted dolls were known for their quality, style, and innovations such as plastic, introduced after World War II. Her best known doll, Wendy, an 8" tall hard plastic doll, has continued in production for over fifty years. While Madame Alexander sold her company in 1988, the tradition of her doll line continues today with a full line of baby, play, and collectible dolls.

L to R: Tom Turkey with Indian Girl, 7"H, hang tag #3158, 2000 made, Annalee, 1988. $50-55; Indian Boy with Bow and Arrow, 7"H, hang tag #3090, 2078 made, Annalee, 1987, $45-50; Tom Turkey, 7"H, hang tag #3160, 3,348 made, Annalee, 1989, $45-50. All hand sewn felt. Annalee Mobilitee Dolls, Meredith, New Hampshire.

Plush and Stuffed Animals

The **Plush** or **Stuffed Animal** category is another childhood favorite. This category is more cross-gender due to the everlasting popularity of the American teddy bear. As opposed to dolls, plush animals are much more "user friendly" and can stand up to a fair amount of playful abuse. While stuffed toys probably originated in Germany, American stuffed toys have enjoyed over one hundred years of popularity. This category is also subject to fads, as witnessed by the Beanie Baby phenomenon which reached a crescendo in the late 1990s.

Needless to say, the plush area of collecting is very emotionally charged due to the on-going desirability of stuffed bears, animals, and licensed character dolls. With the use of cheaper synthetic acrylic plush, as opposed to natural mohair, Far Eastern manufacturers have flooded the plush animal market over the past several decades with items that have very little collector value. But to a child, these "warm fuzzies" still can give hours and hours of safe and secure contentment.

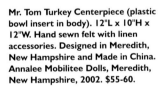

Mr. Tom Turkey Centerpiece (plastic bowl insert in body). 12"L x 10"H x 12"W. Hand sewn felt with linen accessories. Designed in Meredith, New Hampshire and Made in China. Annalee Mobilitee Dolls, Meredith, New Hampshire, 2002. $55-60.

L to R: "Tucky" (Turkey), 6.25"H, Article No. 1314, 1952 to 1957: mohair plush body, dark brown tipped wings and tail of white felt, head and neck of red velvet, wire legs, chest tag Steiff GmbH. $300-375. Quite rare! "Tucky" (Turkey), 4.25"H, Article No. 1310, 1952 to 1958: same material construction, chest tag, Steiff GmbH. $250-300. Rare. "Putty" (Turkey), 6"H, Article No. 3367/14, 1978 to 1983: Dralon plush and felt, dark brown tipped wings and tail of felt, head and neck of Trevira-velvet. Button in ear tag. Steiff GmbH., $125-175. Rare (mainly European distribution). In the *Steiff Price Guide (Dolls, Teddy Bears, Animals)*, 403 Steiff figures are identified, photographed, and valued on 190 pages. Margarete Steiff (1847-1909), a home-bound polio victim, made her first stuffed toy (an elephant) in 1880. By 1903, the first teddy bear was introduced in brown mohair and quickly exported to America. Steiff, for the past 125 years, has produced a wonderfully varied line of plush and felt toys for children of all ages.

American Stories Collection: Pilgrim Barbie Doll (special edition), 11.5"H. "Be there as Pilgrim Barbie comes to America on the Mayflower." Barbie is dressed in the costume of the New World. She comes with a printed booklet about her trip and is carrying a faux basket of corn. The American Stories featured historically themed dolls with a small storybook detailing the relative adventure of each doll. Barbie was portrayed as a Pilgrim, Patriot, Pioneer, Colonial Girl, Civil War Nurse, and an American Indian, each introduced from 1995 to 1997. Serial number 12577. Pictorial box. 1995. The original Barbie "teenage fashion model" doll was first introduced in 1959 at the New York Toy Fair. Mattel, Inc., El Segundo, California. MIB $25-30.

L to R: Plush Turkeys (Beanie Babies). "Gobbles," 7"H, tag style #4034, polyester, plush/plastic beans, machine sewn (Korea). Birthday 11/27/96, Retired 03/31/99. MWMT (Mint with Mint Tag) $4-6; "Lurkey," 7"H, tag style #4039, polyester plush/plastic beans, machine sewn (China). Birthday 06/13/2000, Retired 03/14/01. MWMT $5-7. Ty, Inc., Oakbrook, Illinois. H. Ty Warner introduced his first Beanie Baby on January 3, 1993. Prior to mid-1997, the Beanie Baby became America's newest craze for the popular and inexpensive plush toy. By 2003, the tenth anniversary of the plush phenomenon, over 816 Beanie Babies and variants had been introduced, with a retail value in excess of $6 billion.

Plush Turkey. "Ivan (Sergezevich Turkeynyev)," Tom Turkey, 18"H, acrylic plush and cotton, machine sewn, pinback badge: "Don't let the turkeys get you down." Shell made in Korea. Sandra Boynton's signature turkey and other plush animals of her own design are called "zoominaries." Sandra is a well-known designer of whimsical greeting cards and other accessories. Recycled Paper Products, Chicago, Illinois. $45-50 with badge.

Plush Turkey. "Puffkins! Strut the Turkey Puffkin," 5"H, acrylic plush, machine sewn, protected ear tag, style #6666, Puffkins Collection. Birthday 05/07/98. Made in China. Swibco, Lisle, Illinois. $7-10 MWMT.

Plush Turkey (Beanie Babies). "Tommy," 5.5" H with tag. Polyester fiber/polyester pellets. Handmade in China. Ty, Inc., Oakbrook, Illinois. Birthday 11/21/02. MWMT $10.

L to R: Plush Turkeys. "People Pals," Tom Turkey, 13"H, tag, polyester plush, machine sewn, dressed in Pilgrim attire with plastic boots; "People Pals, "Hen Turkey," 13"H, tag, acrylic plush, machine sewn dressed in Pilgrim attire with plastic boots. Made in China. A & A Plush, Inc., Compton, California. $30-35 set.

L to R: Plush Turkeys. "Playful Plush," Tom Turkey, 12"H, multicolor acrylic plush and velveteen, machine sewn. 1988. Made in China. Chrisha Creations, Ltd., Greenville, Rhode Island. $10-15; "Terence the Butterball Turkey," Tom Turkey, 10"H, acrylic plush and multicolor felt tail, machine sewn, "squeaker" button in breast. Introduced as an advertising premium from Butterball Brand Turkey, 1987. "Squeezem's" Company, Huntingdon, Pennsylvania. $10-15.

Games and Puzzles

Probably the largest toy category in terms of unit volume is that of **Games and Puzzles**. Due to the category's specification, virtually every game from preschool to adults is included as well as card games and puzzles of every size and complexity. However, there are very few games representing Thanksgiving or even the greater Pilgrim experience. Boxed board games today reflect themes licensed by leading television programs. Unfortunately, video games are replacing board games as the premier at-home form of entertainment. Jigsaw puzzles have had a greater amount of variety in their offerings, considering there were two separate "booms" for the jigsaw puzzle craze. The older wood-based puzzles peaked in 1908-1909 whereas the golden age of die-cut, cardboard jigsaw puzzles occurred during the Depression era of the early 1930s. All that was needed was a single technological change to bring the industry to where it is today. Prior to the 1890s, puzzles were laboriously made using a jigsaw to cut out individual pieces of painted or lithographed wood. The replacement for the jigsaw was the die press, which was able to stamp out literally hundreds of lithographed cardboard pieces in very little time. This single technological event dramatically lowered the price of production, so that puzzles in many ornate and complex pieces were available to the general market. Therefore, inexpensive puzzles were an entertainment standby during hard times of the 1930s. These puzzles today continue to enjoy a steady pace of popularity.

Vintage Wooden Jigsaw Puzzle, 8"L x 6"W. The puzzle is titled "Thanksgiving Party" and depicts four children feasting at the dinner table. Over 75 lithographed wooden, intricately cut pieces. Copyright 1905. J.I. Austen Co., Chicago, Illinois. This firm was a divided backs postcard publisher in the early twentieth century. $75+.

Jigsaw Puzzle Box, "Pastime Puzzle." Parker Brothers, 5.5"L x 9.25"W. Original cardboard box.

Pastime Picture Puzzle, "First Thanksgiving." 14"L x 10.5"W. Puzzle consists of over 250 laminated wooden pieces, some artistically cut in the shapes of animals, geometric figures and alphabetical initials. The theme of this puzzle was based on a famous painting by Clyde O. DeLand of Philadelphia. U.S. Patent No. 1236378. Designs of shaped pieces copyrighted 1932 by Parker Brothers, Inc. U.S.A. $150-175.

Jigsaw Puzzle Box, "Hobby Jig Saws." Jaymar Specialty Co. 10"L x 7"W. Original multicolor cardboard box.

Hobby Jigsaws, "Wild Turkey." 14"L x 22"W. Puzzle consists of over 300 die-cut cardboard pieces showing a Tom Turkey perched on a tree branch. Copyright 1943. Jaymar Specialty Co, New York, NY. $15-20.

Action Board Game. "Cold Turkey," The Game with the Motorized Cube Kicking Bir-r-rd! "Freezin' Freddy the turkey is trotting on thin ice…" Battery operated. Milton Bradley (purchased by Hasbro in 1984), Springfield, Massachusetts. 1995. $20-25.

Action Board Game. "Snuffy Smith's Hootin Holler Turkey Shoot." Comes with metal gun, cork ammunition, and automatic self-scoring target. Lithographic gameboard measures 17"L x 11"W.

Target board for "Snuffy Smith's Hootin Holler Turkey Shoot." 17"L x 11"W. Licensed by King Features Syndicate. Copyright 1947. Jaymar Specialty Company, New York, NY. $50+.

169

Motion Activated Wall Plaque. "Lucky Tom, The Talkin' Turkey (and singing)." A Turkey Gobbler head (rubberized) is hoisted on a plaque. 11.75"L x 15.5"W x 10" deep. Activated by a 12V AC adaptor or batteries. Synchromotion animated. Head turns side-to-side while speaking twelve phrases and two songs. c. 2000. Gemmy Industries. Made in China. $20-25.

Other Toys

The last toy category for which Thanksgiving has some relevance is that of **All Other Toys**, a "catch-all" segment for any number of disparate groupings. Chief among them as pertains to Thanksgiving are cast-iron banks and tin plate windup toys. Both cast-iron and tin plate materials enjoyed over one hundred years of usage before being superceded in some regard by technological process advances related to more durable and/or less costly materials. After wood and paper materials, cast-iron items enjoyed superior durability from the 1840s to the early 1940s. Unfortunately cast-iron is subject to rusting, which has caused surface pitting and loss of original paint. In addition, reproductions of various cast-iron objects have been flooding the collectible market at an alarming rate. It is estimated that some 10,000 still banks and 250 mechanical (animated) banks, all different, (and mainly cast-iron) were produced from the late 1860s to the late 1930s. Similarly, tin plate (a thin veneer of tin bonded to iron or steel) also enjoyed a certain superiority due to the new lithography process, which added a variety of colors and designs directly to the surface of the object. Tin plate has been in existence from the 1850s to the early 1940s. This material experienced a renaissance after World War II due to the presence of Japanese toy makers in the popular grouping of wind-up toys, especially space-age items. Compared to older cast-iron toys, tin plate items were produced in tens of millions over many years and near mint toys exist today in good numbers.

L to R: Pottery Still Toy Banks. Turkey, 4.25"H x 4.38"L x 2.5"W. Shades of dark to light blue glaze. Coin slot on right side of body. Black stamp "Made in Czechoslovakia," c.1918 to 1938. $60-75; Turkey, 4"H x 3.38"L x 3.13"W. Shades of brown with red head and wattle. Coin slot on back of tail. No marks. $15-20. Pottery banks were produced in glazed as well as unglazed finishes and were difficult to identify since most of them were not marked. There are relatively few older banks left because one had to break the bank in order to retrieve the banked coins.

Tin Plate Wind Up Mechanical Turkey, 5"H x 5.5"L x 4.75"W. Multi-color lithographed tin plate body. When wound, the turkey walks forward as his tail feathers raise and lower on his back. As the tail raises upward, the colorful tail feathers fan out and extend to double the tail's original size. Key operated. Cardboard box with Turkey and Peacock graphics. Blomer & Schuler (Jumbo elephant mark). Made in U.S. Zone Germany, c.1947 to 1953. $225-275.

Wind Up Mechanical Turkey, 5.75"H x 6.25"L x 5.25"W. Multi color lithographed metal tail and wing tips. Mohair-type plush feathers cover the body while a red chenille-type material completes the head and wattle. Yellow plastic feet. Key operated. No marks. $75-100. Alps Shoji Ltd., Tokyo, Japan, c.1950. Alps, founded in 1948, proceeded to produce both the Tin Plate Turkey and Peacock toys as production was moved from Germany to Japan due to a cost saving measure. Since the early 1970s, Alps has become a manufacturer of industrial and consumer electronics.

L to R: Cast-Iron Still Toy Banks (Barnyard Animals). Turkey, 3.5"H x 3.25"L x 2.63"W. Aluminum bronze color; Turkey, 3.5"H x 3.25"L x 2.63"W. Dark metallic brown with remnants of red paint on head and wattle. Cast-iron banks were produced in a foundry and were cast in two sections joined with one long bolt. Coin slot opening is between two rows of tail feathers. No marks. Made by A.C. Williams Company, c.1905 to 1935. $250-350. A.C. Williams Co. was established in Chagrin Falls, Ohio in 1844 where it produced Empire stoves, flat irons, and pruning tools. After a company move to Ravenna, Ohio in the late 1890s, A.C. Williams began making still banks, especially those dealing with comic strip characters, animals, and buildings. They were one of two leading producers of still banks until the start of World War II. Today, A. C. Williams, through two wholly owned companies, produces and markets magnesium, aluminum, and iron alloy castings.

Chapter 12
SPECIAL THANKSGIVING DAY EVENTS

For 350 years after the First Thanksgiving meal, religious activities remained at the core of the holiday celebration. After the Civil War ended in 1865, traditional religious fervency and enthusiasm ebbed due to a population dispersion westward and the influx of immigrants from many countries. In spite of widening secularism, the extended family became the home base and the center of holiday activities, especially prior to the traditional meal itself. Depending upon the region of the country, Thanksgiving festivities took on a more lively tone, a far cry from the original Puritan institution of a holy day of solemn prayer. And, while the Thanksgiving meal was the time to share with family and friends, this indulgence extended into providing holiday dinners and food baskets to the inmates of public institutions. For many well-to-do Americans, this "feel good" philanthropy fulfilled the need for some semblance of religious overtones to a holiday that was in the process of losing its original meaning.

Right:
"Thanksgiving," *Gleason's Pictorial Drawing Room Companion.* c.1851-1854. 11" x 15.5". Artist: Kilburn Del. Color Tint. $30-35.

"Thanksgiving Sketches." *Harper's Weekly,* December 6, 1866. 21.5" x 15.5". The Preparation, Arrival Home, The Rich Man's Turkey, The Poor Man's Turkey, Frolic with Children, After Dinner. Artist: C.G. Bush. $70-75.

L to R: "A Real Thanksgiving." *Harper's Weekly,* November 28, 1896. 11" x 15.5". Artist: F.C. Yohn. $25-30. **"Over-Indulgence – A Spoiled Thanksgiving."** *Harper's Weekly,* November 28, 1896. Artist: Alice Barber Stephens. $25-30. Showing the contrast between the "haves" and the "have-nots."

L to R: "Preparing For Thanksgiving." *Harper's Weekly,* November 28, 1868. 11" x 15.5". Artist: J. W. Ehninger. $25-30. **"The First Thanksgiving Dinner"** (for a poor little immigrant girl). *Harper's Weekly,* November 28, 1868. 11" x 15.5". Artist: W. S. L. Jewett. $25-30.

"Thanksgiving Day in New York City – Divine Service In the City Prison or the Tombs." *Frank Leslie's Illustrated Newspaper,* December 12, 1874. 16.5" x 11". Artist: Hyde. $25-30. The accompanying article indicated that the "poor prisoners confined in the tombs" received 320 pounds of turkey, 114 pounds chicken, 150 pounds corned pork, 1 bushel onions, 150 mince pies, and 1 barrel of apples for their Thanksgiving dinner.

Over time, extending from the late nineteenth century, Thanksgiving activities that held interest for many Americans have included turkey "shoots," sporting events such as football games, parades, turkey "trots," and human footraces.

Turkey Shoots

It was apparent to many wildlife officials and conservation leaders that as the nineteenth century came to a close, the wild turkey was suffering a somber fate. Excessive turkey hunting either for the food markets or for sport eliminated this bird from huge areas of its former range. It is hard to believe that until successful restocking programs were introduced in 1937, the last recorded wild turkey sighting in the state of Connecticut was 1813 … and in Massachusetts the year was 1851! Similarly, eastern and mid-western states did not record an observation until after 1881. By 1900, the only significant remaining self-sustaining wild turkey populations were located in inaccessible areas such as large southern swamps and remote western mountain ranges. In fact, throughout much of the Montana, Wyoming, and Arizona Territories, hunting wild game for the holiday table was established as a western Thanksgiving custom especially among ranchers and U.S. troops on Indian duty.

"Thanksgiving Dinner For the Ranch." Limited Edition Print. 10.875" x 8.375". Artist: Frederic Remington. Original was from *Harper's Weekly*, November, 1889. $15-20.

Due to the encroachment of civilization upon original wild turkey habitats, sport hunting was restricted to organized turkey shoots in the wild – either on private hunting reserves or in a suitable secured area surrounding a community. Several "hunting" formats prevailed. In the older and less formal situations, captured wild turkeys were randomly released in a contained environment and stalked by selected hunters. In the newer and more controlled format, a live turkey was tied to a block of wood, thus hindering its escape. The hunter marksmen took turns firing at the bird from some distance (i.e., 75-100 yards) in order to provoke some competition. In the more humane twentieth century, live turkeys were replaced with either paper targets (the prize being a live gobbler) or various-sized clay "pigeons." Today, there are various commercial turkey shoots which consist of target shooting

with 12-gauge shotguns at a distance from 20 to 30 yards depending upon the length of the barrel. So-called "shooting houses" around the country organize and set rules for a competitive turkey shoot. A website devoted to competition turkey shooting is www.turkey-shoot.net.

"Sports In America – Shooting Turkeys For Thanksgiving Day." *The Illustrated London News*, November 19, 1859. 16" x 10.5". Artist: Darley – American. Chromolithograph. "…represents a party of American sportsmen out in the snow shooting wild turkeys." $30-35.

"The Turkey Shoot." Reproduction print of original – 1857. 15.75" x 12.25" (image size 10" x 7"). Artist: Tompkins H. Matteson. $12-15.

"The Turkey Shoot." Reproduction print of original – 1879. 15.75" x 12.25" (image size 14" x 7"). Artist: John W. Ehninger. $12-15.

"The Turkey Shoot." *Outdoor Life*, November, 1954. Artist: Robert Doares. Cover portrays camaraderie of an organized countryside turkey shoot. $7-10.

"Turkey Shoot – Chickens, Turkeys, Hams," Saturday, June 24, 1972. East Westmoreland, New Hampshire. Poster, 14" x 22". Also featured were Ernie and Dot Lind, famous exhibitionist shooting duo of that era. $10-15.

Sporting Events – Football Games

Football historians generally attribute November 6, 1869 as the birthdate of inter-collegiate football, when teams from Rutgers and Princeton Universities met. Beginning in the 1880s and for the next twenty-five years, a series of rules and regulations were initiated as important steps in fostering an evolution from rugby-style play to the modern game of American football. These included the dimensions of the playing field, the length of the game, the size of the squads, the type of uniforms and protective gear, the legalization of the forward pass, and the scoring systems. By the mid-1890s, 120,000 athletes from colleges, sports clubs, and high schools participated in over 5,000 Thanksgiving Day football games across the nation.

Top to Bottom: "The Ardor and the Joy of a Game of Foot-Ball." *Harper's Weekly*, November 10, 1888. 15" x 11". Artist: Frederick Barnard. The accompanying article written by the famous football coach, Walter Camp, said: "Ten thousand people, the bulk of them flying college colors, would make a grand sight anywhere, but nowhere could such charmingly picturesque groupings be found as those of the annual Thanksgiving Day game at the Polo Grounds." $100-115; "Thanksgiving Day in New York– As It Is." (Yale and Princeton Game) *Harper's Weekly*, November 28, 1891. 16" x 11". Artist: W. T. Smedley. Hand colored. $100-115.

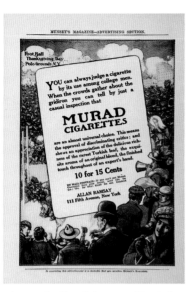

Advertisement for *Murad* cigarettes. "Football Thanksgiving Day Polo Grounds, N.Y." *Munsey's Magazine*, 1905. 6.75" x 10". "You can always judge a cigarette by its use among college men." $10-15.

Football Program, "Detroit Lions vs. Chicago Bears." November 29, 1934 with game ticket stub and signed by Football Hall of Famer and All-American Quarterback Earl "Dutch" Clark. $450+.

Football Program, "Detroit Lions vs. Cleveland Browns." November 23, 1989. Final score: Detroit 13-Cleveland 10. $10-15.

Similarly, college players, disappointed to see their football prowess end as graduation loomed, decided to form teams for pay, representing the better and "name" players of the day. The first professional football game in the United States took place in 1895, made up of former college and club players representing the towns of Latrobe and Jeanette, Pennsylvania. In 1920, the American Professional Football Association was formed, bringing legality and consistency to a hodge-podge group of teams always on the verge of financial failure. In 1922, the league was reorganized into a stronger National Football League, which still exists today in spite of other failed competitive professional leagues. Thereafter, with the expansion of the league into larger eastern and mid-western cities, professional football attracted larger numbers of talented college players, and increased attendance made the league economically viable.

The first professional football Thanksgiving Day game was played in 1934 between the newly renamed Detroit Lions and the Chicago Bears at the University of Detroit Stadium. An estimated sell-out of 26,000 spectators witnessed a Chicago victory (19-16), and the Detroit Lions' traditional Thanksgiving Day game was born, due to its initial success both on the field and at the box office. Except for the six World War II years, Detroit has played every Thanksgiving Day to the present at the existing Pontiac, Michigan Silverdome Stadium. Of the 64 games played (through 2003), Detroit has recorded a 33W – 29L – 2tie mark.

Football Program, "Detroit Lions vs. Green Bay Packers." November 26, 1953. Final score Detroit 34-Green Bay 15. $60-65.

Football Program, "Detroit Lions vs. Chicago Bears." November 25, 1999. Final score: Detroit 21-Chicago 17. $10-12.

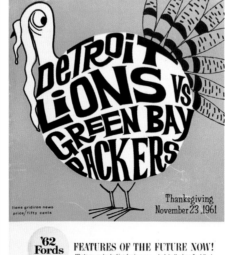

Football Program, "Detroit Lions vs. Green Bay Packers." November 12, 1961. Final score: Green Bay 17-Detroit 9. $50-55.

Football Program, "Detroit Lions vs. New England Patriots." November 23, 2000. Final score: Detroit 34-New England 9. 61st Thanksgiving Day Game, Pontiac Silverdome (Capacity 80,311). $10-12.

At the collegiate and even the high school levels, many of these holiday games were conducted between bitter rivals, and the games were rotated among the stadiums of each school or at a large neutral city stadium. These vintage hotly fought games attracted crowds of over 40,000 spectators, forcing Thanksgiving Day church services to end early in order to accommodate the fans. This led the prominent *New York Herald* newspaper in 1893 to comment: "Thanksgiving Day is no longer a solemn festival to God for mercies given…It is a holiday granted by the State and Nation to see a game of football." The comparisons between the strict Pilgrim man and the collegiate football player were obvious.

Much has changed over the years since this editorial, due to the scheduling of games for conference championships, football bowl bids, as well as lifestyle changes necessitating fewer college and high school games actually played on Thanksgiving Day. Selected regional rivalries highlighted here include Cornell/Pennsylvania, Texas/Texas A&M, two black schools Howard/Lincoln, Pa., and the military schools.

The University of Pennsylvania *Quakers* and the Cornell University *Big Red* have played 110 games together as Division 1-AA schools, and the number of games played ranked #5 in terms of competitive outings. From 1893 through the 2003 season, Pennsylvania holds a 63 to 42 edge with 5 ties. Penn and Cornell have met on Thanksgiving 61 times, most recently in 1989. Most of these games were played at the famous Franklin Field in Philadelphia. Opened in 1895, Franklin Field is the oldest stadium in use in the NCAA.

Below:
Football Programs. L to R: "Cornell *Big Red* vs. Pennsylvania *Quakers*." November 29, 1923. Franklin Field, Philadelphia. Final score: Cornell 14-Pennsylvania 7. $125+. "Cornell vs. Pennsylvania," November 28, 1929. Final score: Penn 17-Cornell 7. $90-100. Older programs from this series, which is among the top five in college football in terms of duration, are quite pricey. A 1915 program sold for $1,520 in 2003, attracting ten bids.

Football Programs. L to R, Top: "Cornell vs. Pennsylvania," November 25, 1926. Final score: Cornell 10-Pennsylvania 10 (tie). $110-125; "Cornell vs. Pennsylvania," November 24, 1945. Final score: Penn 59-Cornell 6. $25-30. **Bottom:** "Cornell vs. Pennsylvania," November 28, 1946. Final score: Penn 26-Cornell 20. $25-30; "Cornell vs. Pennsylvania," November 27, 1947. Final score: Penn 21-Cornell 0. $25-30.

Depiction of a Pilgrim and a Football Player. *The Inland Printer*, November, 1905. Cover 8.25" x 10.5". Artist: N. Guy Chilberg. $20-25.

"Thanksgiving 1628-1928" color print. Original illustration was from *Saturday Evening Post*, November 24, 1928. Artist: J. C. Leyendecker. $10-15.

Football Programs. L to R, Top: "Cornell vs. Pennsylvania," November 25, 1948. Final score: Cornell 23-Penn 14. $25-30; "Cornell vs. Pennsylvania," November 24, 1949. Final score: Cornell 29-Penn 21. $25-30; "Cornell vs. Pennsylvania," November 25, 1950. Final score: Cornell 13-Penn 6. $20-25. **Bottom:** "Cornell vs. Pennsylvania," November 24, 1951. Final score: Penn 7-Cornell 0. $20-25; "Cornell vs. Pennsylvania," November 26, 1953. Final score: Cornell 7-Penn 7 (tie). $20-25; "Cornell vs. Pennsylvania," November 25, 1954. Final score: Cornell 20-Penn 6. $20-25.

Football Programs. L to R: "Cornell vs. Pennsylvania," November 24, 1955. Final score: Cornell 37-Penn 7. $20-25; "Cornell vs. Pennsylvania," November 22, 1956. Final score: Cornell 20-Penn 7. $10-25; "Cornell vs. Pennsylvania" November 28, 1957. Final score: Penn 14-Cornell 6. $20-25.

Another outstanding rivalry is the meeting between the University of Texas *Longhorns* and the Texas A&M *Aggies*. An informal poll organized by *USA Today* ranked this showdown as the second most interesting rivalry in the country after the Michigan/Ohio State series. For many years, this intra-state rivalry was held on Thanksgiving Day, trading off between Austin, Texas, (Memorial Stadium) and College Station, Texas, (Kyle Field).

Football Programs. L to R: "Texas *Longhorns* vs. Texas A&M *Aggies*," November 29, 1934. Final score: Texas 13-Texas A&M 0. $150-175; "Texas vs. Texas A&M," November 24, 1960. Final score: Texas 21-Texas A&M 14. $40-50; "Texas vs. Texas A&M," November 26, 1964. Final score: Texas 26-Texas A&M 7. $40-50.

"Air view – A&M College Game on Thanksgiving Day, College Station, Texas," postally unused, c.1930s. Kyle Field, as it is now known, has been expanded to a seating capacity of 80,200. The 2001 Thanksgiving Day game attendance set an all time record of 87,555 fans. $10-15.

Since 1894, there have been 109 meetings between these two schools, with Texas holding a decided edge of 70 to 34 with 5 ties. One Aggie tradition that has always prevailed took place on the night before this game. A giant football rally was held around an immense bonfire made up of timbered and cut-up logs reaching fifty-five feet tall. This campus bonfire had been held (except for 1963) every November since 1909, with the aim to generate school spirit for the Aggies to beat their archrival, Texas, in football. Unfortunately, tragedy struck on November 18, 1999, as the logs, which were being placed on a three-tiered stack reaching fifty-nine feet, collapsed due to containment failure. Twelve A&M students were killed and over thirty injured. While much controversy ensued after this accident, it appears that the bonfire tradition will eventually resume with much greater safety standards and professional involvement. This football rivalry is now played on the Saturday after Thanksgiving.

Football Program. "Texas vs. Texas A&M," November 27, 1958. Final score: Texas 20-Texas A&M 0. $45-50. Note the "cartoonish" image of the program. Most programs of the 1950s and 1960s were playful in their graphic description of the rivalries. By the 1970s and continuing today, cover "art" was either generic stock or photographs of players. On this program, "Bevo," Texas' longhorn mascot, is attempting to roast his Aggie nemesis in a large dish.

Football Programs. L to R, Top: "Texas vs. Texas A&M," November 25, 1965. Final score: Texas 21-Texas A&M 17. $40-50; "Texas vs. Texas A&M," November 24, 1966. Final score: Texas 22-Texas A&M 14. $40-50. Bottom: "Texas vs. Texas A&M," November 29, 1974. Final score: Texas 32-Texas A&M 3. $30-35; "Texas vs. Texas A&M," November 26, 1999. Final score: Texas A&M 20-Texas 16. $15-20.

The traditional Thanksgiving football rivalries have also existed among the nation's black schools; among the keenest was that of the Howard University (Washington D.C.) *Bisons* and the Lincoln University (Pennsylvania) *Lions.*

It should be remembered that for over a seventy year period (1892-1964) prior to the Supreme Court mandated integration of schools, there were, at one time or another, over ninety football playing colleges which had only black students and which, with very rare exceptions, played only other teams comprised of black players. In the Middle Atlantic Region, Howard played Lincoln in a series of fifty-five games starting in 1894 and stretching until 1960 when Lincoln dropped the sport. Howard held a very slight advantage of 24-23 with 8 ties. This series was, up to that time, America's oldest gridiron classic between predominantly black institutions.

"Virginia Polytechnic Institute (VPI) *Gobblers* vs. United States Military Academy (Army) *Cadets,*" October 18, 1947. "Turkey Shoot...Grand Prize...a V.P.I. Gobbler..." Final score: Army 40-VPI 0. $35-40.

"Thanksgiving Football" Second Brigade *United States Marine Corps.* Fourth Regiment vs. Sixth Regiment. November 25, 1937. Shanghai, China. $100-125.

In some countries, notably Canada and Mexico, major universities played American football in seasons that evolved around games played on dates very close to our Thanksgiving. Closer to home, who does not remember high school football championships played on Thanksgiving Day?

Football Programs. L to R, Top: "Howard *Bisons* vs. Lincoln, PA. *Lions,*" November 25, 1926. Final score: Howard 32-Lincoln 0. $65-75; "Howard vs. Lincoln," November 29, 1934. Final score: Howard 13-Lincoln 6. $55-60; "Howard vs. Lincoln," November 27, 1941. Final score: Lincoln 21-Howard 0. $35-40. Bottom: "Howard vs. Lincoln," November 1946. Final score: Howard 7-Lincoln 6. $20-25; "Howard vs. Lincoln," November 26, 1953. Final score: Howard 12-Lincoln 7. $10-15.

Our country's military academies also played some of their games on or around Thanksgiving. The Virginia Polytechnical Institute *Gobblers* played a traditional rival, the Virginia Military Institute *Keydets,* during a time when football programs were shaped like footballs for important games. VPI (or Virginia Tech as they are now known) also played the United States Military Academy (Army) Black Knights, or *Cadets.* The program of this game poses an interesting dilemma! If one served in the peacetime military overseas, there was a good chance that a Thanksgiving Day championship game, somewhere in the world, would be held among rival naval battleship groups or major corps level units.

"Virginia Polytechnic Institute (VPI) *Gobblers* vs. Virginia Military Institute (VMI) *Keydets,*" November 24, 1927. Final score: VMI 12-VPI 9. $175+.

Football Programs. L to R, Top: "Universidad Nacional Autonoma de Mexico *Pumas* vs. Instituto Politechico Nacional *White Burros,*" November 29, 1952. Final score: UNAM 20-IPN 19. $10-12; "Universidad Nacional vs. Instituto Politechico," November 24, 1951. Final score: UNAM 43-IPN 0. $10-12. This series began in 1936. Through 1997, out of sixty games played, UNAM holds a 33 to 23 advantage with 4 ties. Bottom: "Central High School vs. Northeast High School," Philadelphia, Pennsylvania. November 24, 1949. Final score: Northeast 7-Central 0. (53rd Annual Thanksgiving Day Game). $10-12; "1st Annual Thanksgiving Azalea Bowl Championship Game," 1951. Round robin between four junior high school teams of the New Hanover School District, Wilmington, North Carolina. $10-12.

Some of these classics had their start in the late nineteenth century. In San Francisco, California, the high school football championship was almost always played on Thanksgiving at the indomitable Kezar Stadium. Traditional rivals and stalwart opponents such as Lowell, Polytechnic, St. Ignatius, Sacred Heart, Lincoln, Washington, Balboa, Mission, Galileo, and Commerce high schools fought bitter duals for the rights to "own the city by the Bay." Of all the city rivalries, the Lowell/Polytechnic games, held on or around Thanksgiving Day, were the most intense, attracting over 40,000 spectators.

Football Programs. L to R: "Lowell High School *Indians* vs. Polytechnic High School *Parrots*," San Francisco, California. November 29, 1928. Final score: Lowell 8-Poly 6. $40-50; "Lowell vs. Polytechnic," San Francisco, California. November 1, 1930. $40-50.

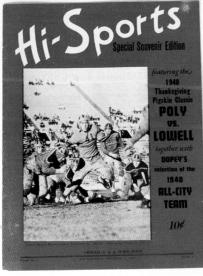

Football Program. "Polytechnic vs. Lowell – 1940 Thanksgiving Pigskin Classic," November 21, 1940. Going into this game, Poly was 5-0 (first) and Lowell was 0-6 (last) in A.A.A. City League Standings. By virtue of Poly's win, this heated series was tied at twelve games each. Over 41,000 fans enjoyed the game. $25-30.

In the new millennium, Thanksgiving still remains for many… "a holiday granted…to see a game of football." Whether one attends or watches a televised version of one of two professional football games now played on Thanksgiving, attends a college or high school event, or merely plays "touch football" with family and friends, this popular American tradition should endure for many eons.

Macy's Thanksgiving Day Parade

Once the Civil War was brought to its conclusion, many discharged veterans found themselves seeking companionship with those who had shared experiences. They joined the many patriotic, social, and veterans' organizations to better assimilate themselves back into a peacetime society. One popular event was the *military Thanksgiving parade*. While many of the military units on parade were composed of Civil War veterans, others were made up of militia units, "target companies" (quasi-military clubs set up for the sole purpose of target shooting for prizes), firemen and police units, and military oriented clubs for younger men. Regardless of their backgrounds, these participants turned out in full dress uniforms to march "military style" and to indulge in large fireworks displays at the culmination of the parades. As the Civil War veterans and the like became aged and World War I intruded into one's collective consciousness, this type of parade was considered *passé*.

However, after World War I had ended and Americans resorted back to peacetime pleasures, Gimbel's Department Store in Philadelphia sponsored the first Thanksgiving Day parade in 1921. This was an attempt by the leading retailer to kick off and promote the holiday buying season. Given the "anything goes" mantra of the "Roaring Twenties," the promotion caught on and, by the end of the decade, Thanks-

"Poly vs. Lowell" Team Roster. Both football coaches pictured here went on to coach at the local college and professional teams level.

giving Day parades with a Christmas flavor were being sponsored by leading department stores in cities across the country. This promotion instigated and was mainly responsible for the traditional Friday after Thanksgiving becoming the busiest shopping day of the year.

On November 27, 1924, R. H. Macy and Company sponsored their first Thanksgiving Day parade. Macy's had just finished an ambitious rebuilding program and could rightly advertise themselves as proprietors of "The World's Largest Store," which was located on 34th Street and Broadway in New York City. Therefore, the reasons for that first parade were obvious: it would publicize Macy's ascendancy as the dominant retailer and would also call attention to the fact that the Christmas shopping season was now officially open and that Macy's was the ideal store to patronize. This reasoning persists even today through many books and publications written about the parade.

The first parade was a big event in New York, as it traveled over a long, five-mile route. It featured over one thousand Macy's employees dressed as clowns, pirates, sheiks, knights-in-armor, cowboys, cowgirls, and even Quakers. There were floats and bands and many zoo animals borrowed from the Central Park Zoo. And, with a nod towards Mardi Gras, there was a so-called "conceit squad" of people wearing grotesquely huge heads. As the parade was such a success, Macy's, without much prodding, decided to turn it into an annual holiday event.

In 1927, the parade featured for the first time the predecessors to the helium-filled balloons that are so evocative of today's parade. The first air-filled balloons represented a dragon, an elephant, a toy soldier, and Felix the Cat. In 1933, Macy's added sound effects to the balloons, and in 1934, in collaboration with Walt Disney, produced the first of many Disney-designed characters such as Mickey Mouse, the Big Bad Wolf, and Pluto the Pup balloons.

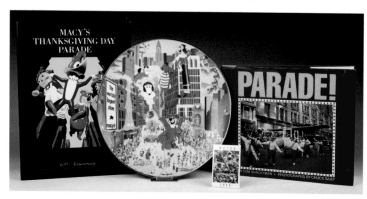

L to R: Book, *Macy's Thanksgiving Day Parade – 60th Anniversary* (1986). $25-30. Plate: "Macy's Thanksgiving Day Parade," 10.25" diameter. Artist: Melanie Taylor Kent, Briggsmore, China U.S.A. Plate No. 265 Limited Edition 12/31/83. $125-130. Pin badge: Macy's Thanksgiving Day Parade, 1990. $18-23. Book: *Parade!* (based on the 1984 Macy's Parade). $20-25.

Macy's Thanksgiving Parade passing the Columbus Monument at 59th Street. Postmarked 8-26-39. *"Dear Lois, Arrived in N.Y. Monday. The Fair is swell – elegant. Have been trying to explore N.Y. – It really is big! If you get a chance to come to the Fair next year, don't miss it...Love Margie."* $30-35.

Life Magazine. October, 2001. "America's Parade – A Celebration of Macy's Thanksgiving Day Parade." $10.

Macy's Thanksgiving Parade passing on Broadway. Modern colorized version of astronaut balloon. Hallmark Cards. 2003. $2.

Life Magazine. "America's Parade," view of Betty Boop balloon.

Due to the onslaught of World War II, the parade was canceled for the years 1942, 1943, and 1944. Its restart in 1945 saw the introduction of nine huge new balloons as well as the first broadcast of the parade on television – albeit carried only locally.

In 1947 and 1948, two events occurred that effectively made the local Macy's parade America's parade, to be shared across the country instead of just by New Yorkers. The first was the release of 20th Century Fox's 1947 movie, *Miracle of 34th Street.* This movie, which featured Maureen O'Hara, John Payne, child star Natalie Wood, and Edmund Gwenn, revolved around a sweet plot concerning the true existence of Santa Claus. It was one of the most popular films of 1947 (and remains a Christmas classic), earning an Academy Award nomination for Best

Movie. The publicity introduced movie-goers everywhere to the floats, balloons and, especially, to the Macy's Santa Claus. The second event was that in 1948 NBC began broadcasting the parade nationally, with host and hostess commentators as well as Grand Marshals. Color television was added in 1960. In the intervening years, the parade has gotten bigger and better in spite of occasional inclement weather and high winds. Balloons today must meet specific maximum size requirements: 70 feet high, 78 feet long, and 40 feet wide.

Advertisement, *The New York Times*, Wednesday, November 23, 1955. 14.68" x 22.5" (full page). In 1955, Danny Kaye was the parade's "Court Jester" and his daughter, Dena, was "Queen of the Parade." Other notables were Hopalong Cassidy, Pinky Lee, Rin-Tin-Tin, and Howdy Doody and his gang. $12-15.

giving Day Parade is as much a part of the Thanksgiving celebration as eating roast turkey with all the trimmings, along with pumpkin and mince pies.

Sheet Music: "March of the Christmas Toys," the official song of the Macy's Thanksgiving Day Parade. Words and music by Ruth Roberts and Bill Katz, 1954. $40-50. Ticket: "Macy's 44th Thanksgiving Day Parade (1970)." Full VIP unused ticket admitting one to the 34th Street Center Grandstand, #1258. $7-10. Pennant: hard red felt pennant, "Macy's Parade 1988." 18" x 8". $35-40. Pennant: hard multi-color felt pennant, "Macy's Thanksgiving Day Parade." 29" x 12". This pennant was printed prior to 9/11/01 and shows the World Trade Center Twin Towers in the skyline of New York City. 2001. $25-30.

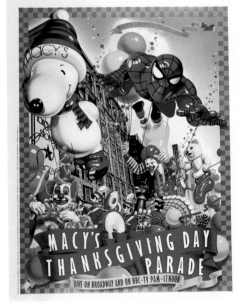

Poster: "Macy's Thanksgiving Day Parade" (1987). 21" x 28". Image content featured the parade balloons: Snoopy, Spiderman, Ronald McDonald, Snuggle, Woody Woodpecker, and the famous annual Tom Turkey. This very limited printed poster was intended for in-store use only. $100-115.

Plate. "Macy's Thanksgiving Day Parade 75th Anniversary." Ceramic, 8.5"D. Tom Turkey in shades of brown with a 1.5" inch navy blue rim decorated with yellow stars. Made in China. 2001, $15-18.

Cuero's Turkey Trot

Cuero, Texas, with a population of 6,800, is located in the south-central part of the state in DeWitt County. From its incorporation in 1875, the town and surrounding areas became well known for their truck farming, cotton, livestock and poultry industries. Agribusiness still dominates the local economy today, though the cotton and turkey businesses have declined in significance.

Texas, around the turn of the nineteenth century, was ideally suited as a habitat for the wild turkey. The high grasses, the many river bottoms, and plenty of mast from pecan, live oak, elm trees, grasses and shrubs provided an abundant food supply for the free range turkey. With the topography so well suited to turkey raising, it was natural that Texas would enter the field of turkey culture.

In the early days of the state, the turkey center for Texas was a small area around the towns of Cuero, Gonzales, Goliad, and Victoria. Due to its favorable environment, this particular area produced most of the turkeys, the majority of them in the wild state. Roads were very

Of all of the whimsical balloons developed over the years, the most popular – with seven separate appearances – has been the Peanuts character, Snoopy. The 2-1/2 mile 2001 parade, which was the 75th anniversary of the event, delighted more than two million local on-lookers and sixty million television viewers with a record fifteen huge helium-filled balloons. In spite of the horrific terrorist attack in New York City on September 11, 2001, Macy's management, with the blessings of the country's President, decided that the show must go on. In 2001, the Macy's Parade had a decidedly patriotic flavor. One of the featured floats was a giant Statue of Liberty, which became a focal point of the parade. The New York Police Department and other emergency workers were also represented, holding two 54-foot flag banners meant to represent the World Trade Center Towers. The Macy's Thanks-

bad in those days, presenting a major handicap in getting the area's turkey growers' produce to market. Farmers would therefore pool their turkeys and "drive" or herd them to the nearest turkey buying center. There was quite a technique to driving turkeys. The efforts of five to ten men were required to properly drive a flock of turkeys numbering in the thousands a distance of about twenty-five miles over a two-day period. Since the big turkey market days were in November for the Thanksgiving market and in December for the Christmas market, drivers often encountered inclement weather, with the area's creeks prone to overflow. However, the seasonal driving of turkeys was considered an outing or a break in the monotony of the usual farm life.

Turkey driving, which began in the early 1900s, ended after 1917 when sellers stopped driving turkeys and instead transported them to market in trucks as the local roads improved. The old marching of turkeys had been so picturesque that visitors in Cuero would marvel at the sight. In 1912, a group of Cuero businessmen, sensing the interest of these visitors and wishing to encourage turkey raising, decided to start a celebration with a turkey drive down the town's main street as the main event. These businessmen operated dressing plants for turkeys so it was good business to advertise South Texas turkeys. Since a popular dance at that time was the "Turkey Trot," this name was adopted for the event.

Book, *Turkeys in Texas – A History of the Turkey Industry in Texas*, by Isabella Kruse Schaffner, 1954, signed. $50-60.

"Turkey Trot Parade at Cuero, Texas. November 26, 1912." First year of the town's Turkey Trot. Publisher: Central Postcard Company, Fort Scott, Kansas, postally unused. $35-40.

The first Cuero Turkey Trot proved an enormous success, with large big-city publications all carrying stories of the celebration. An estimated thirty thousand spectators thronged Cuero, watching dignitaries, bands, floats, and of course, eighteen thousand live strutting turkeys appearing in the line of march. The parades, exhibits, entertainments, and coronation of a Sultan and Sultana (Turkish influence!) became more ambitious at each successive Trot celebration.

From the first event in 1912 to the last one in 1947, there were ten staged Turkey Trots. Then a bumper crop in turkeys, however, caused a drastic reduction in the price per pound. Over the next several years, turkey production in Texas declined, with the state becoming a distant fourth behind California. Economics brought an end to the traditional Cuero Turkey Trot with its floats, bands, and thousands of strutting domestic turkeys.

But only for a while. In 1973, when Cuero was planning its centennial celebration, a certain group of citizens decided to reinvigorate

the Turkey Trot by adding a carnival, parade, live entertainment, arts and crafts, Chili Cook-off, and special booths for turkey-based food recipes. They renamed this three-day event the "Cuero Turkeyfest," which is still in existence today. The climax of this October festival is the "Great Gobbler Gallop." This final event is an annual turkey race between the cities of Worthington, Minnesota and Cuero, Texas. It is a two-heat race – one heat in each town each year – and the best time of the races determines the winner. Two titles are at stake: the "World's Fastest Turkey" and the winning town, calling itself the "Turkey Capital of the World."

Bottles: "Cuero Centennial & Turkey Trot: 1872-1972," October 20-23, 1972. Two soda pop bottles, front and back, decorated and embossed. $7-10 each. Can: "King Turkey Beer," Worthington, Minnesota. Turkey Capital of the World. 12 fl. oz. $10-12.

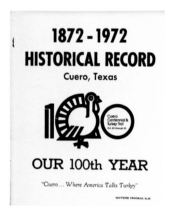

Program: "1872 – 1972 Historical Record Cuero, Texas." Full magazine sized program for Cuero Centennial & Turkey Trot, October 20-23, 1972, 64 pages, photo history of town. "Cuero... Where America Talks Turkey." $35-40.

Left:
L to R, Top: Cover: Postally used one-cent postal card, postmarked Cuero, Texas, September 5, 1922 to Rochester, Minnesota. $10-12; Cover: Postally used envelope franked with 3-cent stamp, postmarked Cuero, Texas, November 11, 1936, to South Milwaukee, Wisconsin. Gray cachet, Texas Centennial Celebration 1836-1936. $15-20; Cover: Postally used envelope franked with 6-cent air-mail stamp, postmarked Cuero, Texas, May 19, 1938 to Belton, Texas. Maroon cachet, First Flight from Cuero, May 19, 1938. $15-20. Bottom: "A Drove of Turkeys near Cuero, Texas," published by Central Postcard Company, Fort Scott, Kansas. #800-2. $17-20; "Turkey Trot, November 26, 1912, Cuero, Texas," published by Central Postcard Company, Fort Scott, Kansas. #99. $17-20; "Cuero Turkey Trot, Cuero, Texas," published by Curteich-Chicago "C.T. Color tone," postally used, postmarked Cuero, Texas, November 22, 1943, to Norristown, Pennsylvania. Text: *"typical western town – very small."* $12-15.

Individual race bibs, authors' race numbers for the 2000 race. No value.

T-shirt, "Cuero Texas Turkey Fest," 2001. $15-18. Postcard. "DeWitt County Courthouse (1896), Cuero, Texas." Westward Photo & Graphics, Masonville, Colorado. $1.

Human Turkey Trot Footraces

Two major events shaped jogging as a means to get fit and stay healthy. The late Jim Fixx wrote a compelling book called *The Complete Book of Running*, and about the same time Frank Shorter – representing the United States in the 1972 Munich, Germany, Olympics – won the gold medal in the men's marathon. This set off a massive upsurge in interest, whereby the low cost and convenience of jogging and running attracted people from all ages and all walks of life. As the running community has grown over the past three decades, there are now over two thousand races annually from which to choose, with most distances ranging from 3.1 miles to 26.2 mile marathons. Competitive running allows opportunities for even the most casual jogger to test his/her ability and to set goals.

Many running races have a particular theme or are held at certain times of the year to celebrate annual events. At Thanksgiving, there are approximately two hundred footraces all across our country called "Turkey Trots." They are usually held either on Thanksgiving Day itself or on the succeeding weekend. Sponsors say that these "trots" attract upwards of 400,000 runners.

The largest Turkey Trot in the far West, and the second largest in the United States in terms of runners, is held in Dana Point (Orange County), California. In 2001, this race – in which the primary sponsor was Ocean Spray cranberry products – enjoyed its 25th anniversary as a premier running event. The race featured a 10K (6.2 miles) race, a 5K (3.1 miles) Masters, and a 5K Open Start. There are also "Hot to Trot" races of shorter distances for children. The authors of this book have regularly attended and competed in this Thanksgiving Day event for many years. It's a great way to lose about 10% of the calories that we ingest later in the day.

"Dana Point Turkey Trot 2001," start banner and participants.

"Dana Point Turkey Trot 2001," finish banner and participants.

"Dana Point Turkey Trot 2001," turkey costumes.

"Turkey Trot" race entry forms for the 1999 and 2000 races at Dana Point, California. $5 for both.

Right and above right: "Dana Point Turkey Trot 2001," 5K race participants. Author on right in second photo.

Other Activities

If "turkey shoots," spectator events, or "turkey trots" did not prove inspirational, there were other events leading up to or on Thanksgiving Day that helped one to enjoy this holiday. Card games, pie-eating events, and even travel seemed to fit the bill.

"Dana Point Turkey Trot 2001," official T-shirt.

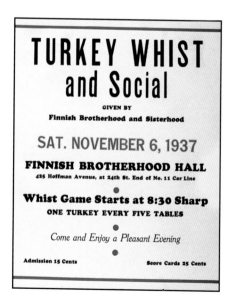

"Dana Point Turkey Trot 2001," authors' photograph.

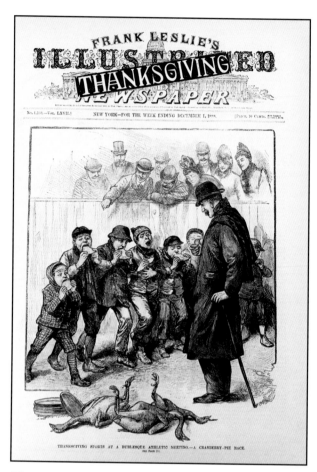

"Thanksgiving Sports at Burlesque Athletic Meeting – A Cranberry-Pie Race," *Frank Leslie's Illustrated Newspaper* (Thanksgiving issue), December 1, 1888. 11" x 18". Color tone. $35-40.

TURKEY WHIST and Social

GIVEN BY

Finnish Brotherhood and Sisterhood

SAT. NOVEMBER 6, 1937

FINNISH BROTHERHOOD HALL

425 Hoffman Avenue, at 24th St. End of No. 11 Car Line

Whist Game Starts at 8:30 Sharp

ONE TURKEY EVERY FIVE TABLES

Come and Enjoy a Pleasant Evening

Admission 15 Cents   Score Cards 25 Cents

Broadside: "Turkey Whist and Social" – Given by Finnish Brotherhood and Sisterhood." November 6, 1937. San Francisco, California. One turkey every five tables was the prize. $15-20.

Travel memorabilia from Turkey Run State Park, Marshall, Indiana. Created in 1916 from a former land holding, the park has 1521 acres of "unspoiled natural beauty." L to R: Pennant, purple felt, "Turkey Run State Park." 26.5"L x 9"W. c.1950s. $15-18; Plate: 10"D, ceramic, multi-color, floral border. Central image shows the "Turkey Run Inn." c. early 1960s. Mark: Jonroth England; made by Adams Potteries, Staffordshire, England. $20-25; Views Folder Card, "Turkey Run State Park, Marshall, Indiana." 18 art-color tone views of the park's natural beauty and the Inn, © 1941 by Curt Teich & Co., Inc. Chicago, Illinois. $10-15.

The title of this chapter is a little deceiving only because our purpose and interest is to discuss and portray those collectibles associated with hunting. Otherwise, one can learn many things about turkeys and hunting by joining the *National Wild Turkey Federation* (in which the authors are members, but not hunters).

The NWTF is a not-for-profit organization dedicated to the conservation of the American Wild Turkey and preservation of the turkey hunting condition. It was originally incorporated in 1973 in Fredericksburg, Virginia, but national headquarters are now located in Edgefield, South Carolina. *Turkey Call* magazine is the official bimonthly publication of the NWTF. The magazine not only has articles on the restoration, conservation, and hunting of the American Wild Turkey, it also carries many advertisements related to outfitting the turkey hunter.

The NWTF also publishes *The Caller*, a quarterly newspaper providing information about NWTF chapter activities and events. The NWTF's comprehensive web site, www.nwtf.org, is very useful for factual information concerning the remarkable history of wild turkey restoration and habitat enhancement, general hunting facts, and characteristics of the five wild turkey subspecies in North America.

The Caller (a quarterly publication of NWTF to report on chapter activities and events). L to R: Winter 2003; Spring 2003; Summer 2003; Fall 2003. Free to NWTF members.

NWTF Member self-adhesive labels. No value.

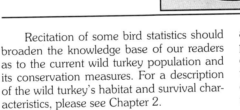

Turkey Call magazines. L to R, Top: June/August 1973 (first issue); July/August 1998 (25th Anniversary Collector's Edition). Bottom: May/June 1998, May/June 2000. $25 (first issue), others $5.

Recitation of some bird statistics should broaden the knowledge base of our readers as to the current wild turkey population and its conservation measures. For a description of the wild turkey's habitat and survival characteristics, please see Chapter 2.

Population and Conservation

Due to the relentless surge of human populations moving ever westward across the American continent from the time of the Civil War to the end of World War I, much habitat important to the survival of many wild animal species was destroyed. Due to its importance as a major source of protein in the food supply chain, wild turkeys were hunted almost to extinction except for pockets where extreme terrain conditions protected them. By the time of the Great Depression, wild turkeys had virtually disappeared from 18 of the 39 states that were part of its historical range. At its low point the population was estimated at 30,000 turkeys. However, help was on its way! In 1937 the Federal Aid in Wildlife Restoration Act was enacted at the request of hunters and sportsmen. This Act imposed an excise tax on hunting equipment with the proceeds earmarked for wildlife conservation projects such as the purchase and protection of wildlife habitats.

Turkey Call magazines, 2003. L to R, Top: January/February; March/April; May/June. Bottom: July/August; September/October; November/December. $5 each.

Right and above right:
"A Thanksgiving Surprise" November 28, 1908, series 1016.6, $7; "Thanksgiving Hunting Was More Exciting Then Than Now," postally unused, Leubrie & Elkus publisher, H.B. Griggs artist, series 2263, $10-15.

"Woman Fair and Turkeys Wild." (In this progressive age in which we are living, a woman brings us our Thanksgiving.) Full color print published by E.R. Herrick & Co., N.Y., 1898, originally published in *Truth Magazine* in 1894. 21"x 14". Artist: W. Granville-Smith, American illustrator and painter, 1870-1938. $100-110.

"Hunting Wild Turkeys – The Attack." *Harper's Weekly*, February 3, 1872. 11" x 16". Artist: A Boyd Naughton. $25-30. The accompanying article noted that "the Indian name for turkeys is 'oocoocoos'. It will probably never supersede the common appellation which was given in consequence of the supposed Turkish origin of the American bird."

When the National Wild Turkey Federation was founded in 1973, it was estimated that 1.3 million turkeys existed on the American continent. Due to the efforts of the NWTF, federal and state game agencies, and other volunteer organizations, the wild turkey has registered a historic comeback: it has been either successfully established or reestablished in forty-nine of fifty states (Alaska excepted), for a current population of 6.4 million turkeys. Today, turkey hunting is one of the largest types of hunting in the United States with over 2.6 million sportsmen considering themselves active or occasional turkey hunters. The NWTF has also experienced growth in membership from its original 1,200 members in 1973. Today, over thirty years later, 506,000 members belong to the NWTF throughout 2,000 chapters in both the United States and Canada as well as in eleven foreign countries. Through the NWTF's efforts, nearly $160 million has been raised and spent on wild turkey conservation projects throughout the United States, Mexico, and Canada.

A major conservation project over the years has included helping the various state wildlife agencies to trap wild turkeys from areas of full population densities and transport them to areas of suitable habitat but with sparse populations. Another important, but expensive, on-going conservation project has been the preservation, development, and restoration of appropriate habitat areas for all five subspecies of the American Wild Turkey.

One successful fund raising venture began in 1976, when the NWTF began issuing the annual *Wild Turkey Stamp* – a private revenue stamp. Similar to their more highly visible philatelic brethren, the federal *Wild Migratory Bird Hunting Permit (Duck) Stamp*, turkey stamps have yet to generate much collecting interest beyond turkey hunters with NWTF membership. Considering that only 20% of turkey hunters belong to the NWTF, much missionary work is needed to educate turkey hunters about the advantages of belonging to the NWTF, especially the very important uses of membership dues and fund raising activities for conservation projects. Each wild turkey stamp image is a reproduction of a commissioned painting by a noted American wildlife artist. In 1976, for instance, artist Russ Smiley painted a trio of Florida Osceola turkeys, entitled "Watch Gobbler." That first stamp and the next three succeeding stamps through 1979 had a face value of $3.00. From 1980 to the present, the face value has been $5.00. The quantity printed annually has been fifty thousand stamps and, in order to increase collectibility, all unsold stamps remaining after a five-year period are shredded.

Right:
Framed and matted cutouts to hold first ten years of National Wild Turkey Stamps, inclusive from 1976 through 1985. $50-55.

Matted cutouts to hold first twenty-one years of National Wild Turkey Stamps, inclusive from 1977 through 1997. Center print artist is A. Anderson. 18.75" x 20". $100-125.

These wild turkey stamps also are released in a First Day Cover format with a reproduction of the artist's print as envelope cachet.

Examples of First Day Cover cachets with Wild Turkey Stamps, description of stamp and featured artist biography. Top: The 1982 Wild Turkey Stamp and cachet, entitled *Autumn Monarch* by Robert Abbett, cancelled at Turkey, North Carolina, November 25, 1982. Bottom: The 1983 Wild Turkey Stamp and cachet, entitled *Sultan Stroll* by Lee LeBlanc, cancelled at Turkey, North Carolina, November 24, 1983. $10-12 each.

The NWTF has released, over time, other revenue stamps in their *Wild Turkey Research Stamp* and *Collector Stamp* series at a higher face value. Lastly, collectors can also purchase a signed and numbered limited edition print by respective turkey stamp artists, matted in conjunction with the stamp or with a stamp and a medallion coin, either in silver, nickel, or bronze.

Framed and matted cutout of the 1980 National Wild Turkey Print, entitled *Explosion in Corn*, #192/600 by artist Walter Walje. Also the 1980 $5 Wild Turkey Stamp, *Silvestris*. $110-125.

Left:
Framed and matted cutout of the 1983 National Wild Turkey Print, entitled *Sultan Stroll* #142/1600 by artist Lee LeBlanc. Also the 1983 $5 Wild Turkey Stamp, *Intermedia* and a silver medallion. $125-140.

Hunting – Turkey Calls

Whether one is hunting Tom Turkeys in the springtime or Toms and Hens in the fall, the equipment and gear are essentially the same – only it is much improved over the past thirty years. While camouflage clothing and choice of weapon (shotgun, muzzleloader, rifle, or bow and arrow) are now required for the hunter, *turkey calls* are very important not only from the practical standpoint of "calling" a bird to the gun but also from a collectible standpoint.

A ***turkey call*** is a homing device; that is, it is an instrument capable of mimicking the extensive vocabulary of the wild turkey in an attempt to draw the bird to within close proximity of the caller-hunters. There are three types of calls depending upon the needs of the hunter: (1) friction calls; (2) air-activated calls; and (3) locator calls. *Friction calls* are reasonably easy to master, the premise being that one part rubs against the other to create a sound. The various sub-categories of the friction calls include: (1) box call; (2) scratch box (for Hen Turkey sounds); (3) push-pull calls; and (4) slate-and-peg calls. Accordingly, there are also several sub-categories of *air-activated* calls: (1) diaphragm calls; (2) tube calls; and (3) wingbone calls (traditionally made from the wing bones of a Hen Turkey). Finally, *locator calls* are designed to "shock" a Tom Turkey into gobbling to reveal its position, typically in the hours before sunrise. A shock gobble from a Tom Turkey means that it was in response to a call that mimics a predator – an owl, coyote, or other birds such as crows that scare or surprise the turkey into revealing its position.

Four postcards showing a variety of hunters – the sportsman, the woman, the Pilgrim, and the young boy. "Thanksgiving Greetings," November 23, 1914; "May you always capture Thanksgiving Blessings," L& E publisher, artist: H.B. Griggs, series 2233; "Thanksgiving Joys," postally unused, series 256F; "Thanksgiving Greetings," November 19, 1910. Guy Downs writes his friend Herbert, "There is going to be a shooting match at Athens, Nov. 24. Why don't you come over and we will go. The deer are awful thick over here. You come over and we will shoot all we can. I have got a pump gun that will shoot over 25 rods every time…" $10-15 each.

"Winchester – Factory Loaded Shotgun Shells – the Cock of the Woods." Color print. 11" x 16". $70-80. The original Winchester Repeating Arms Co. poster was 15" x 25". An original poster in very fine condition sold for $760 at a Past Tyme Pleasures auction (San Ramon, California) in May 2000.

"Shoot Dupont Powders – Wild Turkey." Trade card. $20-25.

Many wild turkey hunters are also serious call collectors, spending time and, in some cases, serious money, for turkey calls. The "collectibility" of a call can be determined by whether it is: (1) a unique, one-of-a-kind non-commercial call or a numbered series of calls handcrafted by a respected turkey hunter; (2) an unusual variety of a call; (3) a call made from exotic woods or other natural materials; and (4) an older, non-gimmicky call from a famous commercial call maker. The scarcity of the call and the pedigree of the maker go a long way in determining the free market valuation, now ranging from $30 to $3000. Various on-line Internet auction services have brought these collectible calls to the attention of a much larger market, which, just a few years ago, was relegated to only the fraternal society of turkey hunters. To encourage the continuing emphasis on elevating callmaking to a fine art form, the NWTF has asked a well respected callmaker to produce a limited edition series of calls for awards at the annual convention and banquet, as well as for sale to participants. Similar activities occur at NWTF-sponsored chapter meetings.

The making of turkey calls is a very individualized form of creativity, rendering it a unique form of American folk art. While some forms of turkey calls were advertised for sale as early as the 1880s, the first *patented* call was a box call. The Gibson Turkey Call, made and sold by Gibson and Broddie of Dardenelle, Arkansas, was patented January 5, 1897. As the wild turkey population declined over the decades, there was probably little need for calls. The majority was produced by larger old-time commercial callmakers such as P.S. Olt, M.L. Lynch, Quaker Boy Calls, and Penn's Woods Products, the latter considered the oldest call-making company in the United States. Cer-

tainly, during the last seventy years there was a fair amount of individual activity by legions of turkey hunters handcrafting their own unusual calls, which were wholly dependent on the availability of natural materials, innate wood crafting ability, and local hunting conditions and surroundings. These calls were functional items used exclusively for hunting. When a hunter developed a local reputation for successful calling, he was persuaded to make extra calls for give-away or for sale to fellow hunters. The emergence of this "cottage industry" contributed to the welfare of many hunters/

Cover and Letter. "Peters Cartridges and Loaded Shells are Superior." Cancel – encased circular stamp "St. L. & Texark, R.P.O. (Railroad Post Office), May 2, 1902." Addressee: "Miss L. Katharine Dependahl, St. Louis, Missouri." Letterhead: "The Peters Cartridge Company, Cincinnati, Ohio." $225+. Rare combination.

Box Call ("Gobble Box"). M.L. Lynch, Liberty, Mississippi. Model 103G. Honduran mahogany. Boat 6.7"L, Paddle 8.63"L. Michael ("M.L.") Lynch is mentioned in Earl Mickel's book, *Mick's Picks*, on page 146. $40-50.

callmakers in between hunting seasons. Some of the more innovative makers have patented their calls, due to their unique qualities or design characteristics.

Technological advances in turkey call production, especially by the larger commercial callmakers, continues. Lately, there is a trend towards the use of synthetic materials that permit calls to operate at a much higher frequency range. A higher pitched call replicating the sound of an excited Hen will help a Tom to respond better and hear from a greater distance.

Cover, reverse: Full-color showing firm's selection of "metallic and shotgun ammunition, paper shells."

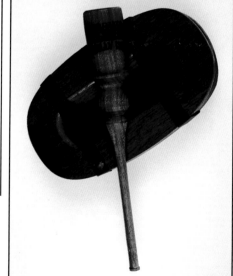

Right:
Slate Call ("Alabama Cackler"). White Hunter Game Calls by Billy White, Abbeville, Alabama. Billy is mentioned in Earl Mickel's book, *Mick's Picks*, on page 237. Mahogany with walnut striker. Bed 7"L, Striker 8.25"L. $100-110.

Slate and Peg Call. Crafted, dated, and signed by Dan West, Macon Missouri #54, March 2000. Wild black cherry wood with slate bottom. 4.5"H x 2.38"D. Dan is mentioned in Earl Mickel's book, *The Best of the Rest*, on page 235. $125-140.

Double Slate over Glass ("Grand National"). H.S. Strut, Cedar Rapids, Iowa, Model 00864. Copyright 1992. Slate bed 4"D, Striker 5.5"L. MIB. $25-35. Double Slate Call. Quaker Boy Call, Orchard Park, N.Y. It is "the Original D.D. Adam's #12736." Quaker Boy had an agreement with D.D. Adams, Jr. of Thompsontown, Pennsylvania from 1981 until his death in 1988 to use the name D.D. Adams Double Slate. Size: 3.5"D with 6.38" Plexiglas striker. D.D. Adams is mentioned in Earl Mickel's book, *Mick's Picks*, on page 2. $60-75.

Slate Call with Two Strikers ("Pocket Purr"). Wild Ones, Auburn, New York, by Randy Russell, c.1998. Maple body 4.75"L, Strikers 7" to 7.25"L. Laser artwork. $40-50.

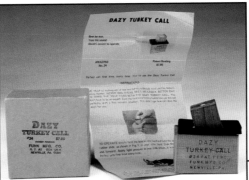

Dazy Peg & Slate Call ("Amazing"). (Eldon) Funk Mfg. Co., Newville, Pennsylvania. #24 Patent Pending, c. late 1960s. Maple. Size: 2.75"L x 1.75"W x 1.75"H. Eldon is mentioned in Earl Mickel's book, *The Rest of the Best*, on page 78. $50-60.

Diaphragm Call ("Single D"). H.S. Strut Model 00800. Patented. Premium flexlatex. Copyright 1992. MIB. $10-15.

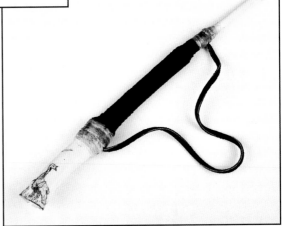

Wingbone Call ("Suction Call"). Have Gun Will Travel, Prattsville, Alabama, by Stephan L. Willingham, c.2000. Three bone call, hand decorated and hand wrapped with leather and sinew and numbered #6. 8.5"L. $40-50.

Top: Box Call. Crafted, painted, dated and signed by Randy Russell, Wild Ones, Auburn, N.Y. #5 of a very limited edition in January 2000. Black walnut with acrylic painted lid of a scene of two Tom Turkeys. Paddle 10"L, call body 7"L. $75-100. Bottom: Box Call. Crafted, painted, dated and signed by Randy Russell, Wild Ones, Auburn, N.Y. #93 of 100 calls made in his very first edition in 1998. Body was made from 200-year-old northeastern cedar salvaged from the demolition of a barn silo. Sides are walnut and poplar. The lid is butternut and has a colored wood burning of four Tom Turkeys and one Hen. Paddle 10"L, call body 7"L. Randy is mentioned in Earl Mickel's book *The Rest of the Best*, page 193. $200-225 each.

Bottom detail of Box Call #5.

Bottom detail of Box Call # 93.

Box Call. Crafted and signed by Dale E. Rohm, Blair, Pennsylvania. Lid decorated and signed by NWTF's Executive Vice President and CEO Rob Keck. #267 of a limited edition series of 1700 in the year 2000. Layers of red cedar and black walnut constitute the lid and call body. For awards and sale at the NWTF Convention and events. Paddle 9"L, call body 6.5"L with velveteen carrying bag. Dale is mentioned in Earl Mickel's book, *Mick's Picks*, on page 194. $275-300.

Box Call ("Fool Proof"). M.L. Lynch, Liberty, Mississippi, Model No. 101, dated 1965. Cedar (?). Paddle 8"L, call body 5.5"L. With original box $60-75.

Box Call. Penn's Woods Products, Delmont, Pennsylvania. Cedar and walnut, painted and decorated. Paddle 9"L, call body 6.75"L. $50-75.

To learn more about turkey callmakers, there are two limited printing books by the renowned hunter, Earl Mickel. In his books, *Turkey CallMakers, Past and Present (Mick's Picks)* and *Turkey CallMakers (The Rest of the Best)*, Earl exhaustively sought out and interviewed more than six hundred contemporary United States callmakers active from the late 1970s to the late 1990s. There are probably several multiples of that number who have also produced functional calls. However, in Earl's two books, he has established a rating system based on, not quality or workmanship, but the collectible potentiality of the call. The reputation of the maker, the age of the call, the quantity made, and whether the call was signed and dated determines the value for collectibility purposes.

Boat Tail Call. Crafted, dated, and signed by Ron L. Clough, Close Calls, Easton, Maryland. Made for Western Kansas Chapter of NWTF 1998 Banquet. Dated 3/31/98. Body made from New York butternut and lid from Maryland curly wild cherry. Paddle 12.25"L, call body 11.5"L. Ron is mentioned in Earl Mickel's book, *Mick's Picks*, on page 50. $100-150.

Below:
Crank Turkey Call. Philip S. Olt Co., Pekin, Illinois, Model CT-220 (U.S. Patent No. 3,793,767). MIB with instructions insert and chalk, c.1963. Walnut, mahogany, and cedar woods. 5"L x 1.75"W x 2.25"H. $150-200.

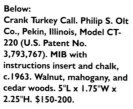

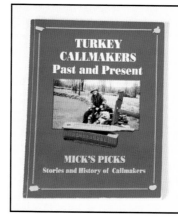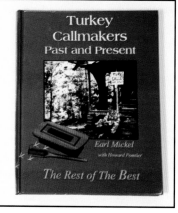

Books by Earl Mickel. L to R: *Turkey Callmakers – Past and Present: Mick's Picks*, Special Edition #75 of 500, signed and inscribed, 1994. $175-225; *Turkey Callmakers – Past and Present: The Rest of the Best*, signed and inscribed, 1999. $70-80.

One callmaker stands out among all others…the late Neil "Gobbler" Cost (1923-2002) of Greenwood, South Carolina. According to Earl Mickel, "…Neil Cost is the finest custom callmaker the country has ever seen. His reputation is unsurpassed in the turkey fraternity, and his calls are among the best obtainable for field work." Neil Cost was so renown for his unstinting emphasis on quality and workmanship that there are three limited edition printing books written specifically on his turkey call construction methodology, selection of appropriate woods and their characteristics, as well as a wealth of turkey hunting stories and anecdotes. The books, *Making Turkey Callers in the Gobbler's Shop*, *Neil Cost Talks Turkey*, and *The Last Hurrah*, explore the mystique behind the man known as the Master of all Masters and the Stradivarius of Caller Crafting. Neil, who started producing several varieties of turkey calls in the late 1950s, is probably most esteemed for his *boat paddle* call. At 13 inches in length, the boat paddle call is significantly longer than his single or double-sided box call. Also, Neil's boat paddle call is primarily made out of a solid block of butternut for tone, with a cedar lid for sound. However, the genius of the man is in the toning of the instrument to achieve the correct acoustical qualities for a greater range of sounds.

In 1989, Neil entered into a five-year contract with Dick Kirby of *Quaker Boy* in Orchard Park, New York, to produce twenty-five boat paddle turkey callers annually through 1993. According to the book, *Neil Cost Talks Turkey*, in 1996 Neil, Dick Kirby, and the NWTF struck a deal for *Quaker Boy* to produce 1,000 Neil Cost signed reproduction callers to sell to collectors as well as for award items at NWTF-sponsored banquets. From 1978 through the contract expiration in 1993, it is estimated that Neil made from 200 to 250 boat paddle calls. On Internet auction sites, collectors will find – in addition to his "match call" boxes, slate and scratch box calls – a range of boat paddle calls for sale. These calls are ones Neil made for one of three purposes: (1) individual use, (2) one of 125 or so Neil made under the auspices of *Quaker Boy* and, (3) one of the 1,000 made as reproductions using Neil's production template. In March 2001, a "Fat Lady" boat paddle caller of butternut (the last ever made) sold on eBay for $11,100 and attracted forty-one bids. Neil's calls made for *Quaker Boy* usually command prices from $2,000 to $2,500. The commemorative reproductions sell in the $250 range. Readers should realize that there is a very wide range of prices for identical calls on Internet auction sites as supply and demand is quite variable and turkey call collecting is still in its early stages of development.

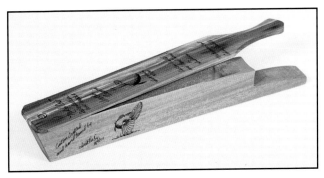

Boat Paddle Call. A Neil D. Cost Reproduction Boat Paddle. Custom crafted, hand tuned, dated, and signed by Dick Kirby 3/3/01. Mahogany boat/red cedar paddle. 12.5"L. Artwork. $225-275.

Detail of Boat Paddle Call.

Detail of Boat Paddle Call, top view.

While turkey calls are a very necessary item to attract the turkey's attention, sometimes a well-positioned turkey decoy is the final stroke to lure a Tom Turkey into a safe shooting range. While there are Tom, jake (juvenile male), and Hen decoy styles, the positioning of two or more Hen decoys with a single jake in open country is a sure attractant to an otherwise suspicious Tom Turkey.

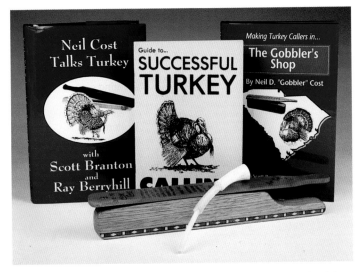

Books. L to R: *Neil Cost Talks Turkey with Scott Branton and Ray Berryhill,* **Special Edition of #962 of 1500. Signed (Neil Cost), 2000. $30-35;** *Guide to Successful Turkey Calling,* **Monroe Burch. $15-20;** *Making Turkey Callers in The Gobbler's Shop with Scott Branton and Ray Berryhill,* **Special Edition #962 of 1500. Signed (Neil Cost), 1999. $30-35. Foreground: Box Call and Wingbone Call.**

Decoys. "Turkey Flock" box contains two hens and one jake. Lightweight flexible foam decoys, 28"L, 12"H. Feather Flex Decoys. $40-45.

Targets. "Turkey Targets," ten life-size Tom Turkey head targets for adjusting shotgun pattern. Image 14.5" x 14". Thompson Target Technologies. $1-1.50 each.

Books. L to R, Top: *Illumination in the Flatwoods – A Season With the Wild Turkey*, 1995. $25-30; *Hunting the American Wild Turkey*, 1975. $20-25; *East of The Slash*, 1996. (signed) $20-25. Bottom: *NRA – Turkey Hunters Guide*, 1979. $40-50; *The Turkey Hunters Guide*, 1962. $40-50; *Wild Turkey Hunting, NRA Hunter Skills Series*, 1991. $10-15; *Tom Foolery 2000*, 1997. Signed and inscribed, $20-25.

There you have it! With the proper equipment and gear, a well-patterned shotgun, trusty turkey calls, and, perhaps, realistic decoys, you are ready for your trophy turkey. But, if you are an armchair hunter, there are several PC-compatible video games offering a fairly realistic interactive hunting experience for that in-between hunting season boredom.

L to R: *Wild Turkey Hunt*, CD-Rom Interactive Hunting Game. Five hunting locations to obtain the "Grand Slam." ValuSoft. $7-10; *Wild Turkey Hunt*, CD-Rom Interactive Hunting Game. Three hunting locations. ValuSoft. $7-9.

Magazines. L to R, Top: *Sports Afield*, article "Wild Turkey Hunting," December 1939; *Field & Stream*, article "Ozark Gobblers," November 1938. Bottom: *Field & Stream*, article "How to Call Turkeys," November 1963; *Field & Stream*, article "Gobbler Setups That Even the Odds," March 1999. $10-15 each.

Also, there are literally hundreds of excellent books, publications, magazines, and videos, all purporting to educate either the beginning or skilled hunter in the complexities and techniques of hunting the wild turkey. One of the best is the *National Rifle Association of America's Hunter Skills Series – Wild Turkey Hunting*. The NRA's guide stresses that along with the recreation of hunting and woodsmanship are the responsibilities: "the safety, ethics, and conservation necessary to perpetuate the sport. Modern turkey hunting is a marvel of game and habitat management..." One can access their extensive website, www.nra.org, for information on all aspects of wild game hunting.

Lastly, there are commercial websites such as www.huntingnet.com which includes a specific site, www.turkeyhunting.com, giving over one hundred pages of content about the wild turkey, hunting techniques, articles, and a very enjoyable turkey hunting game to test your skills.

Books. L to R, Top: *The Complete Hunter – Wild Turkey*, 1996. $30-40; *Wild Turkey Symposium – Proceedings of the Seventh National*, 1995. $15-20. Bottom: *Turkey Hunter Digest*, 1986. $10-12; *The Education of a Turkey Hunter*, 1974. $60-75; *The Wild Turkey and Its Hunting*, copyright 1914, Reproduction 1984. $75-90; *Wild Turkey Country*, 1991. $20-25; *Field Guide to Wild Turkey Hunting*, 1984. $10-15.

Magazines. L to R, Top: *Hunter, Trader, Trapper*, cover artist – Edwin Balenbaugh, December 1935; *Outdoor Life*, article, "A Girl's Version of a Turkey Hunt," November 1905. Bottom: *The American Rifleman (NRA)*, article "Calling Wild Turkeys Calls For Technique," March 1971; *Turkey – Monthly Magazine for Turkey Hunters*, Vol. I, No. 1 (Premiere Issue), March 1984. $25 (first issue), others $10-20 each

BIBLIOGRAPHY

Chapter 1

Agel, Jerome, and Jason Shulman. *The Thanksgiving Book*. A Dell Trade Paperback, 1ˢᵗ Edition, Nov., 1987.

Alcott, Louisa May. *An Old-Fashioned Thanksgiving*. Nashville: Ideals Publishing, 1993.

Anderson, Joan. *The First Thanksgiving Feast*. New York City: Clarion Books, 1984.

Appelbaum, Diana Karter. *Thanksgiving An American Holiday An American History*. Facts on File Publications, 1ˢᵗ Ed., 1984.

Arnosky, Jim. *All About Turkeys*. New York: Scholastic Press, 1998.

Atwood, William Franklin. *The Pilgrim Story*. Plymouth, Massachusetts: Memorial Press Group, 1940.

Bailey, Arthur Scott. *The Tale of Turkey Proudfoot*. New York: Grosset and Dunlap, 1921.

Ballam Anthea and Julia. *Mayflower, The Voyage that Changed the World*. Alresford, Hants, England: O Books, 2003.

Barksdale, Lena. *The First Thanksgiving*. New York: Alfred A. Knopf, 1942.

Barth, Edna. *Turkeys, Pilgrims and Indian Corn – The Story of the Thanksgiving Symbols*. New York: Clarion Books, 1975.

Blanchard, Amy E. *A Dear Little Girl's Thanksgiving Holidays*. Racine, Wisconsin: Whitman Publishing Co., 1924.

Children's Digest. Concord, New Hampshire: *Parent's Magazine*, November, 1952.

Darby, Ada Claire. *Brave Venture*. Philadelphia: John C. Winston Co., 1953.

Devlin, Wende and Harry. *Cranberry Thanksgiving*. New York: Parents' Magazine Press, 1971.

Dickson, Paul. *The Book of Thanksgiving*. A Perigree Book, Nov. 1995.

Drake, Samuel Adams. *On Plymouth Rock*. Boston: Lee and Shepard Publishers, 1897.

Fleming, Thomas J. *One Small Candle The Pilgrims First Year In America*. W.W. Norton & Company, Inc., 1963.

Fritz, Jean. *Who's That Stepping on Plymouth Rock?* New York: Coward-McCann, Inc., 1975.

Garis, Howard R. *Uncle Wiggily and the Turkey Gobbler*. New York: Charles E. Graham & Co., 1929.

Geller, L.D. *The Pilgrims A Brief History*. Plymouth, Massachusetts: Cape Cod Publications, 1992.

George, Jean Craighead. *The First Thanksgiving*. New York: Philomel Books, 1993.

Hays, Wilma Pitchford. *Christmas on the Mayflower*. New York: Coward-McCann, Inc., 1956.

Hays, Wilma Pitchford. *Pilgrim Thanksgiving*. Eau Claire, Wisconsin: E.M. Hale and Co., 1955.

Hetrick, Lenore. *The Giant Thanksgiving Book*. Dayton, Ohio: Paine Publishing Co., 1935.

Holisher Desider. *Pilgrims Path The Story of Plymouth in Words and Photographs*. New York City: Stephen-Paul Publishers, 1947.

Holmes, Knowlton B. *The Mayflower and Her Master's Table*. Plymouth, Massachusetts: The Rogers Print, 1952.

Irish, Marie. *Tip Top Thanksgiving Book*. Syracuse: The Willis N. Bugbee Co., 1930.

Lowitz, Sadyebeth and Anson. *The Pilgrims' Party*. New York: Grosset & Dunlap, 1932.

Luckhardt, Mildred Corell. *Thanksgiving Feast and Festival*. Abingdon Press, 1ˢᵗ Ed., 1984.

Of Plymouth Plantation 1620-1647. Introduction by Francis Murphy. New York City: Modern Library College Editions. 1981.

Patrick, James B. ed. *Mayflower II Plimouth Plantation*. Fort Church Publishers, Inc., 1993.

Preston, Effa E. *The Children's Thanksgiving Book*. Lebanon, Ohio: March Brothers, 1928.

Pumphrey, Margaret B. *Stories of the Pilgrims*. Chicago: Rand McNally & Co., 1910.

Ramsey, Helen. *The Thanksgiving Festival Book*. Chicago: T.S. Denison & Co., 1945.

Russell, Francis. *American Heritage: The Pilgrims and The Rock*. American Heritage Publishing Co. October, 1962 Vol. XIII, No. 6.

San Souci, Robert. *N.C. Wyeth's Pilgrims*. San Francisco: Chronicle Books, 1991.

Schenk, Esther M. *Thanksgiving Time*. Chicago: Lyons & Carnahan, 1932.

Smith, E. Brooks, and Robert Meredith. *The Coming of the Pilgrims*. Boston: Little, Brown and Co., 1964.

Thanksgiving Harvest Festivals. New York: The Metropolitan Museum of Art, 1942.

The First Thanksgiving A Pop-Up Book. Western Publishing, 1994.

The Plymouth Compact of 1949 (A Plan for the Future Development of Plymouth), 1949.

The Story of the Pilgrims. Boston: John Hancock Life Insurance Company, 1923.

The Timechart History of America. New York: Barnes & Noble, 2003.

Travers, Carolyn Freeman ed. *The Thanksgiving Primer*. Plymouth, Massachusetts: Plimoth Plantation Publication, 1987.

Weinstein-Farson, Laurie. *The Wampanoag*. New York City: Chelsea House Publishers, 1989.

Weisgard Leonard. *The Plymouth Thanksgiving*. Garden City, New York: Doubleday & Co., Inc., 1967.

Chapter 2

Audubon's America. Donald Culross Peattie, ed. Boston: Houghton Mifflin Co., 1940.

Audubon's Birds of America. Introduction and Descriptive Captions by Ludlow Griscom. New York: The MacMillan Company, 1950.

Dickson, James G., ed. *Proceedings of the Seventh National Wild Turkey Symposium*. Mechanicsburg, Pennsylvania: Stackpool Books, 1996.

Hewitt, Oliver H., ed. *The Wild Turkey and Its Management*. Washington D.C.: The Wildlife Society, 1967.

Hutto, Joe. *Illumination in the Flatwoods A Season With the Wild Turkey*. New York City: Lyons & Burford, 1995.

Marsden, Stanley J., and J. Holmes Martin. *Turkey Management*. Danville, Illinois: The Interstate, 1939.

Purina Turkey Book. Ralston Purina Company, March, 1938.

Schaffner, Isabella Kruse. *Turkeys in Texas A History of the Turkey Industry in Texas*. San Antonio, Texas: The Naylor Company, 1954.

Smith, Abbie. *King Gobbler*. Boston: The Educational Publishing Company, 1906.

Smith, E.Y. *Growing Turkeys*. Ithaca, New York: Cornell University Extension Bulletin #717, May, 1947.

The Turkey Breeding Flock. Ithaca, New York. Cornell University Extension Bulletin #912, 1950.

The Larro Turkey Book. General Mills, Inc., 1947 Larro Feeds.

Tyler, Ron. *Audubon's Great National Work The Royal Octavo Edition of The Birds of America*. Austin: University of Texas Press.

Williams, Jr., Lovett E. *The Book of the Wild Turkey*. Tulsa, Oklahoma: Winchester Press, 1981.

Wild Turkey Country. Minoka, Minnesota: North Word Press, 1991.

Chapter 3

Atterbury, Paul. *20th Century Ceramics*. London, England: Miller's Octopus Publishing Group Ltd., 1999.

Baker, James W., and Elizabeth Bragg. *Thanksgiving Cookery*. New York: The Brick Tower Press, Nov. 1997.

Berolzheimer, Ruth, ed. *250 Ways to Prepare Poultry and Game Birds*. Chicago: Consolidated Book Publishers, 1954.

Bleier, Edward. *The Thanksgiving Ceremony*. New York: Crown Publishers, 2003.

Blue, Anthony Dias and Kathryn K. *Thanksgiving Table*. New York: Harper Collins, 1990.

Boegehold, Lindley. *The Perfect Thanksgiving Book*. New York: Lorenz Books, 1995.

Burns, Diane L. *Cranberries Fruit of the Bogs*. Minneapolis: Carolroda Books, 1994.

Cameron, Angus, and Judith Jones. *The L.L. Bean Game and Fish Cookbook*. New York: Random House, 1983.

Davern, Melva. *The Collector's Encyclopedia of Salt & Pepper Shakers, Figural and Novelty*. Paducah, Kentucky: Collector's Books, Second Series. 1990.

Dietz, F. Meredith. *Let's Talk Turkey – Adventures and Recipes of the White Turkey Inn*. Richmond: The Dietz Press, 1948.

Divone, Judene. *Chocolate Moulds: A History and Encyclopedia.* Oakton, Virginia: Oakton Hills Publications, 1987.

Dorchy, Henry and Laurie. *The Chocolate Mould.* Editions Ephemera, 1999.

Drachenfels, Suzanne von. *The Art of the Table.* New York: Simon & Schuster, 2000.

Finegan, Mary J. *Johnson Brothers Dinnerware.* Statesville, North Carolina: Signature Press, Inc., 1st Edition, 1993.

Garrison, Holly. *The Thanksgiving Cookbook.* New York: Macmillan, 1991.

Keck, Rob. *Wild About Turkey.* Memphis: The Wimmer Companies, 1996.

Livingston, A.D. *Wild Turkey Cookbook.* Pennsylvania: Stackpole Books, 1995.

Poultry (The Good Cook Techniques and Recipes). New York: Time-Life Books, 1978.

Recht Penner, Lucille. *Eating the Plates A Pilgrim Book of Food and Manners.* New York: Simon and Schuster, 1991.

Rinker, Harry L. *Collector Plates –The Official Price Guide.* New York: House of Collectibles, 1999.

Rinker, Harry L. *Dinnerware of the 20th Century The Top 500 Patterns.* New York: House of Collectibles, 1st Edition, 1997.

Rogers, Rick. *Thanksgiving 101.* New York: Broadway Books, 1998.

Ruffin, Frances and John. *Blue Ridge China Today.* Atglen, Pennsylvania: Schiffer Publishing Ltd, 1997.

Snyder, Jeffrey B. *Flow Blue, A Collector's Guide.* Atglen, Pennsylvania: Schiffer Publishing Ltd, 4th Edition, 2003.

Totally Turkey Thanksgiving Cookbook. Oakland: Artex Housewares, 1996.

Wolfe, Ken. *Chef Wolfe's New America Turkey Cookery.* Los Angeles: Aris Books, 1984.

Wolfman, Peri and Charles Gold. *Forks, Knives & Spoons.* New York: Clarkson Potter/Publishers, 1994.

Chapter 4

Florence, Gene. *Degenhart Glass and Paperweights.* Cambridge, Ohio: Degenhart Paperweight and Glass Museum, Inc., 2nd Edition, 1992.

Chapter 5

Huxford, Sharon and Bob. *McCoy Pottery.* 1st Edition. Paducah, Kentucky: Collector Books, Updated values, 1997.

Wasbotten, Marilyn, and Robert Tardio. *Cookie Time* (With Vintage Cookie Jars from the Andy Warhol Collection). New York: Harry N. Abrams, 1992.

Chapter 7

Buehl, Oliva Bell. *Christopher Radko's Ornaments.* New York: Clarkson Potter/Publishers. 1999.

Whiteneck, Peggy. *Collecting Lladró.* 2nd Edition. Iola, Wisconsin: Krause Publications, 2003.

Chapter 8

Apkarian-Russell, Pamela E. *Postmarked Yesteryear.* Portland, Oregon: Collector's Press, 2001.

Clear, Richard E. *Old Magazines.* Paducah, Kentucky: Collector Books, 2003.

Hennessey, Maureen, and Anne Knutson. *Norman Rockwell, Pictures For The American People.* New York: Harry N. Abrams, Inc. 2nd Printing, 2000.

Janello, Amy, and Brennon Jones. *The American Magazine.* New York: Harry N. Abrams, 1991.

Ketchum, William C. *Grandma Moses, An American Original.* New York: Smithmark Publishers, 1996.

Kovel, Ralph and Terry. *The Label Made Me Buy It.* New York: Crown Publishers, Inc., 1998.

McClelland, Gordon T., and Jay T. Last. *Fruit Box Labels.* Santa Ana, California: Hillcrest Press, Inc., 1995.

Willoughby, Martin. *A History of Postcards.* London: Bracken Books, 1994.

Chapter 9

"Bourbon Hero, Wild Turkey's Jimmy Russell." *Whisky Magazine,* The Whisky Publishing Company, Landisburg, Pennsylvania (bi-monthly). Issue #19, October/November 2001.

"Wild Turkey Behind the Scenes." *Whisky Magazine,* The Whisky Publishing Company, Landisburg, Pennsylvania (bi-monthly). Issue #9. April/May 2000.

Chapter 10

Barbash, Shepard. *Oaxacan Wood Carving.* San Francisco: Chronicle Books, 1993.

Hayes, Allan, and John Blom. *Southwestern Pottery Anasazi to Zuni.* Flagstaff, Arizona: Northland Publishing. 2nd Printing, 1997.

Lowell, Susan, et. al. *The Many Faces of Mata Ortiz.* Tucson, Arizona: Rio Nuevo Publishers, 1999.

Chapter 11

Fendelman, Helaine & Jeri Schwartz. *The Official Price Guide Holiday Collectibles.* 1st Edition. New York: House of Collectibles, 1991.

Goodfellow, Caroline. *A Collector's Guide to Games and Puzzles.* Secaucus, New Jersey; Chartwell Books, 1991.

Luke, Tim. *Miller's American Insider's Guide To Toys & Games.* London, England: Octopus Publishing Group Ltd., 2003.

Koskiner Edith and Johan. *Steiff Price Guide.* Annapolis, Maryland: Gold Horse Publishing, 1999.

Pfeiffer, Gunther, *Steiff Sortiment 1947-1995.* Taunusstein, Germany, 1995.

Rinker, Harry L. *Collector's Guide To Toys, Games & Puzzles.* Radnor, Pennsylvania: Wallace-Homestead, 1991.

Rogers, Carole. *Penny Banks – A History and a Handbook.* New York: E.P. Dutton, 1977.

Sabin, Francene and Louis. *The One, The Only, The Original Jigsaw Puzzle Book.* Chicago, Illinois: Henry Regnery Company, 1977.

Whitehill, Bruce. *Games – American Boxed Games and their Makers 1822-1992.* Radnor, Pennsylvania: Wallace-Homestead, 1992.

Wholesale Trade List No. 26 1924-1925. Toy Favors, Holiday Decoration. Reproduced by L-W Book Sales, Gas City, Indiana. 1985.

Chapter 12

Crager, Meg. *Macy's Thanksgiving Day Parade (60th Anniversary).* New York City: Quarto Marketing, 1986.

Shachtman Tom. *Parade!* New York City: Macmillan Publishing Company, 1985.

Chapter 13

Bland, Dwain, *Turkey Hunter's Digest.* Northbrook, Illinois: DBI Books, Inc., 1986.

Burch, Monte, and Bill Harper. *Guide to Successful Turkey Calling.* Humansville, Missouri: Outdoor World Press, Inc., 1987.

Clancy, Gary. *The Complete Hunter Wild Turkey.* Cowles Creative Publishing, Inc., 1996.

Cost, Neil D. "Gobbler," Scott Branton, and Ray Berryhill. *Making Turkey Callers in the Gobbler's Shop.* Brainerd, Minnesota: Bang Printing, 1st edition, 1999.

Cost, Neil D. "Gobbler" with Scott Branton and Ray Berryhill. *Neil Cost Talks Turkey.* Brainerd, Minnesota: Bang Printing, 2000.

Davis, Henry E. *The American Wild Turkey.* Georgetown, South Carolina: Small Arms Technical Publishing Company, 1949.

Elliot, Charlie. *Field Guide To Wild Turkey Hunting.* Delmont, Pennsylvania: Penn's Woods Products, Inc., 1984.

Groves, Earl. *Tom Foolery 2000.* Wildwoods Outdoor Publications, 1997.

Hanenkraft, William Frank. *The Education of a Turkey Hunter.* New York City: Winchester Press, 1974.

Harbour, Dave. *Hunting the American Wild Turkey.* Harrisburg, Pennsylvania: Stackpole Books, 1975.

Johenning, Leon. *The Turkey Hunter's Guide.* Waynesboro, Virginia: The Humphries Press, Inc., 1962.

McIlhenny, Edward A. *The Wild Turkey and Its Hunting.* New York City: Doubleday, Page & Company, 1914.

Mickel, Earl. *Turkey Callmakers Past and Present (Mick's Picks).* Pennsylvania: Private Printing, 1994.

Mickel, Earl, with Howard Pomtier. *Turkey Callmakers Past and Present: The Rest of The Best.* Honesdale, Pennsylvania: Paragon Press, 1999.

Turkey Hunter's Guide. National Rifle Association of America, 1979.

Wild Turkey Hunting. National Rifle Association of America, 1991.

Wineman, Jr., Wade S. *East of the Slash.* Greenville, Mississippi: OK Publishing Company, 1996.

Marks

Kovel, Ralph and Terry Kovel. *Kovel's New Dictionary of Marks – Pottery and Porcelain 1850 To The Present.* New York City: Crown Publishers, Inc., 1986.

Lehner, Lois. *Lehner's Encyclopedia of U.S. Marks on Pottery, Porcelain and Clay.* Paducah, Kentucky: Collector Books, 1988.